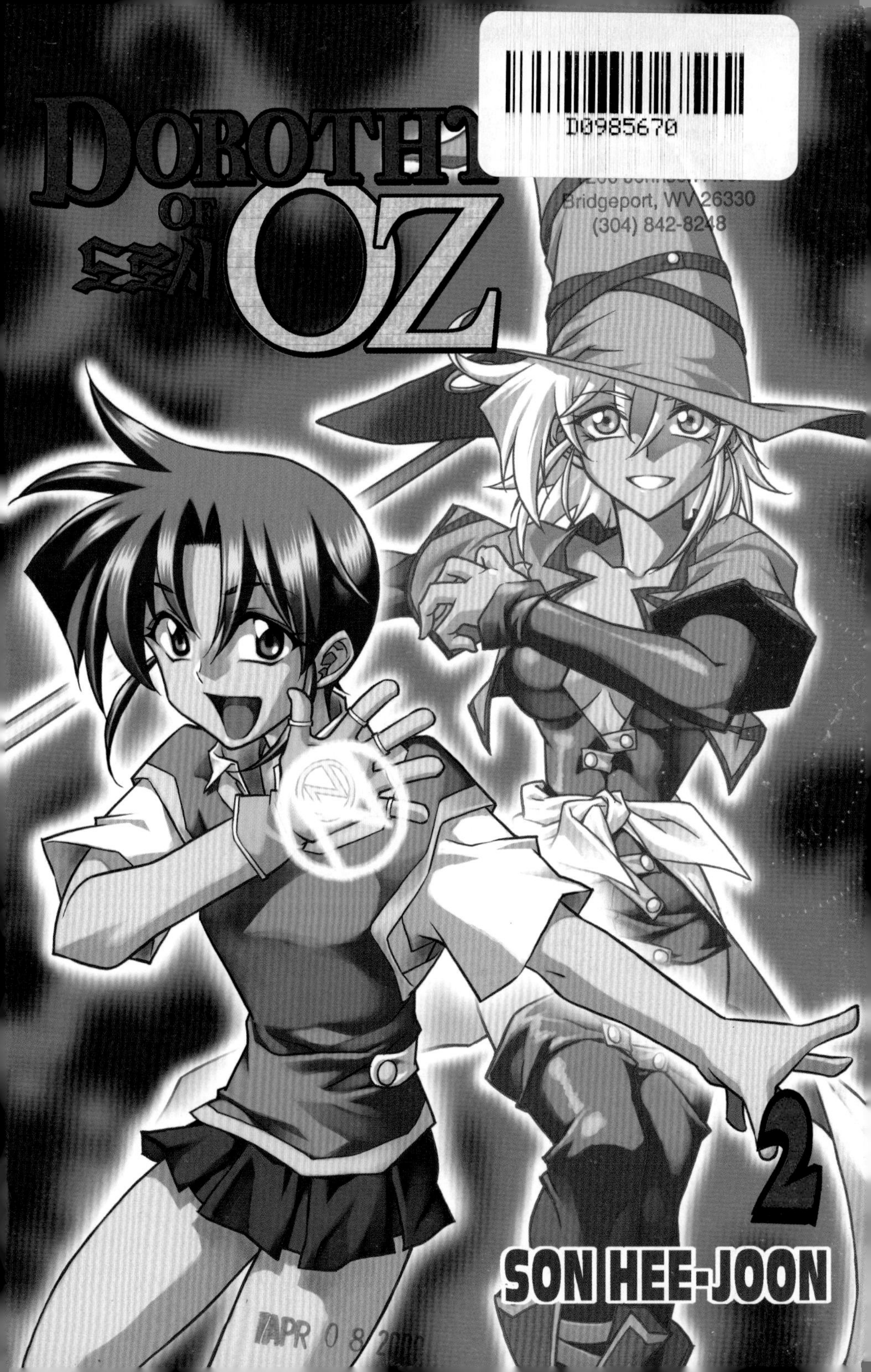
DOROTH
OF
도로시
OZ
2
SON HEE-JOON

DOROTHY OF OZ 2
CONTENTS

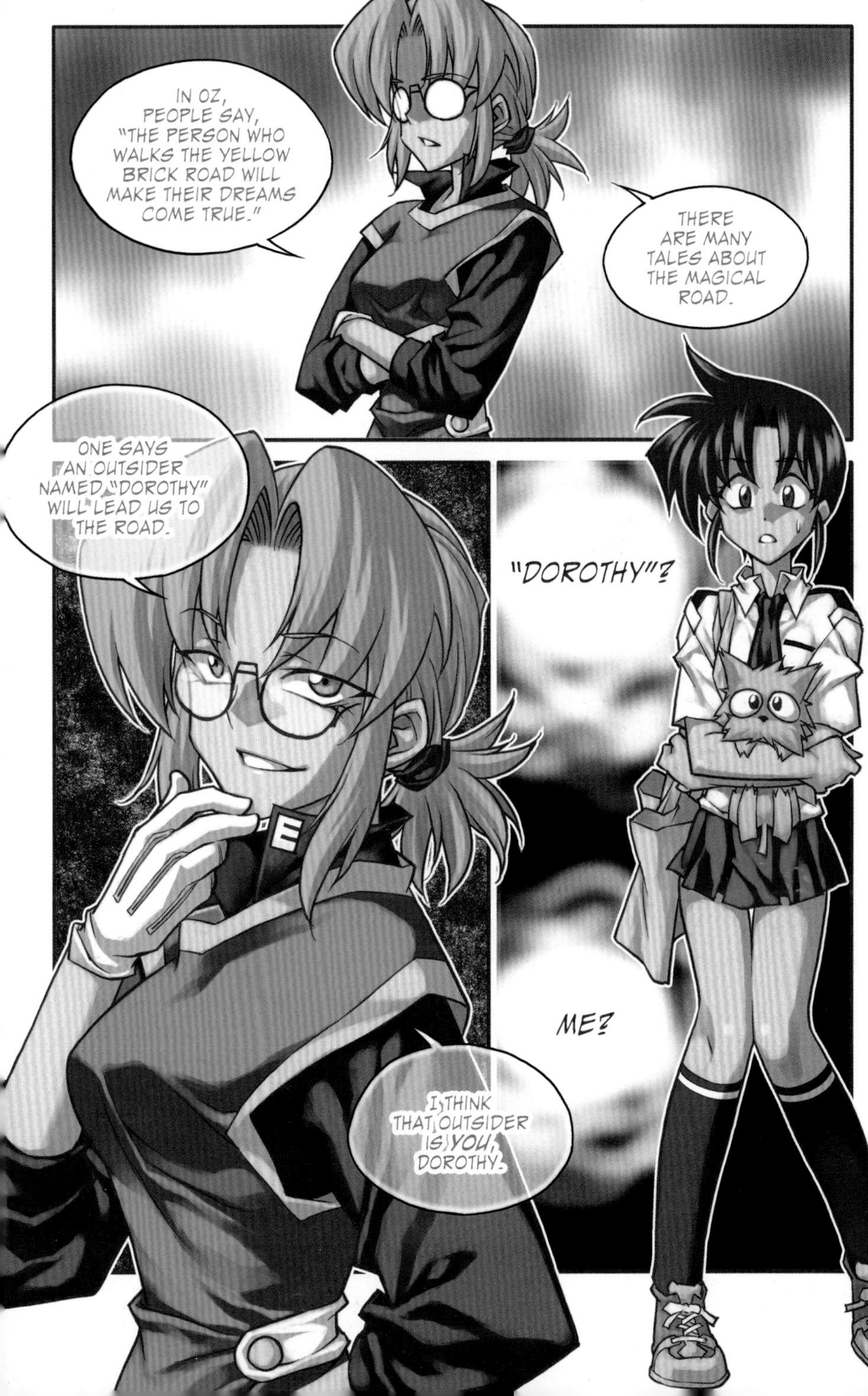

IN OZ, PEOPLE SAY, "THE PERSON WHO WALKS THE YELLOW BRICK ROAD WILL MAKE THEIR DREAMS COME TRUE."
THERE ARE MANY TALES ABOUT THE MAGICAL ROAD.
ONE SAYS AN OUTSIDER NAMED "DOROTHY" WILL LEAD US TO THE ROAD.
"DOROTHY"?
ME?
I THINK THAT OUTSIDER IS YOU, DOROTHY.

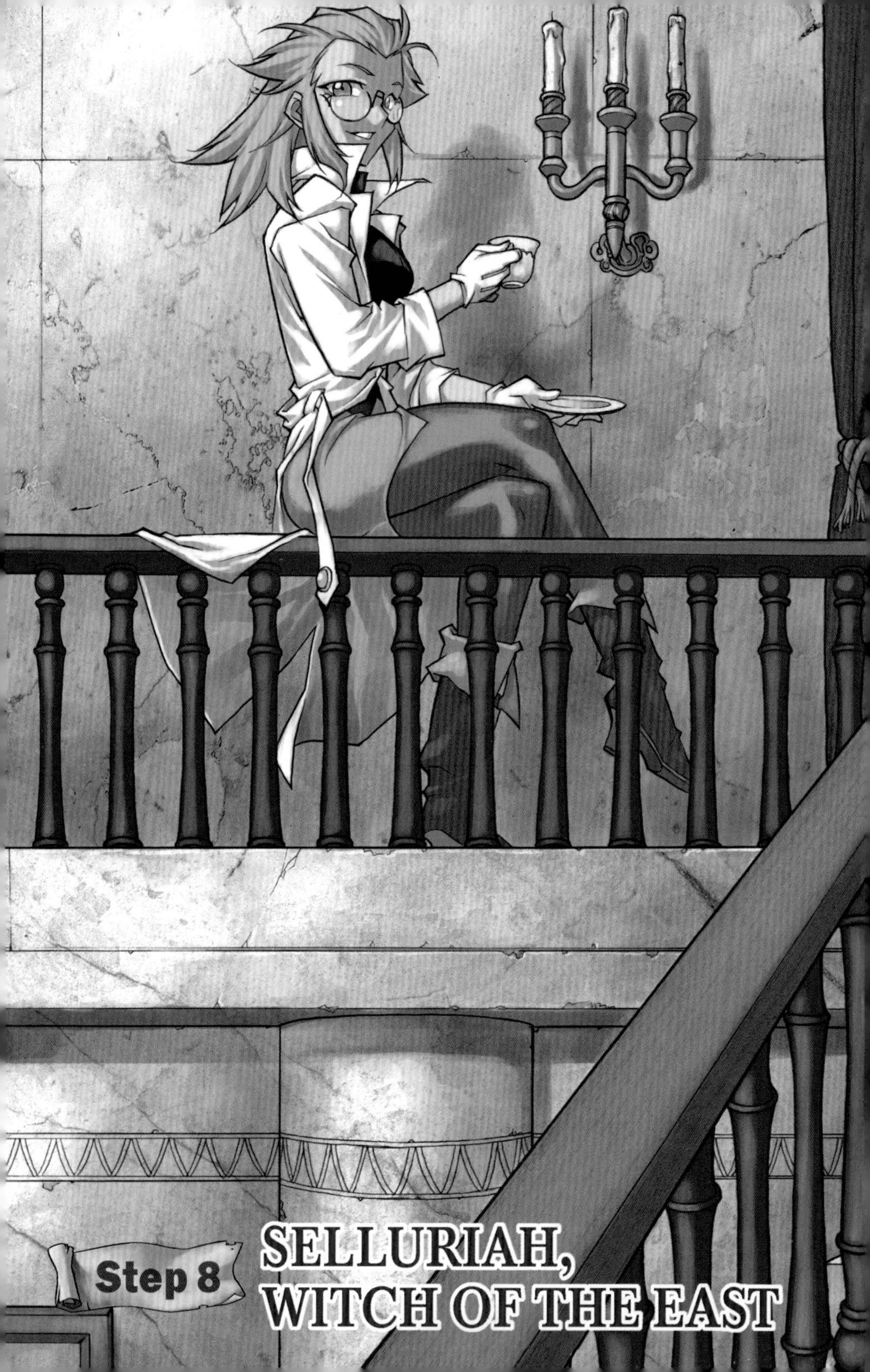
Step 8
SELLURIAH,
WITCH OF THE EAST

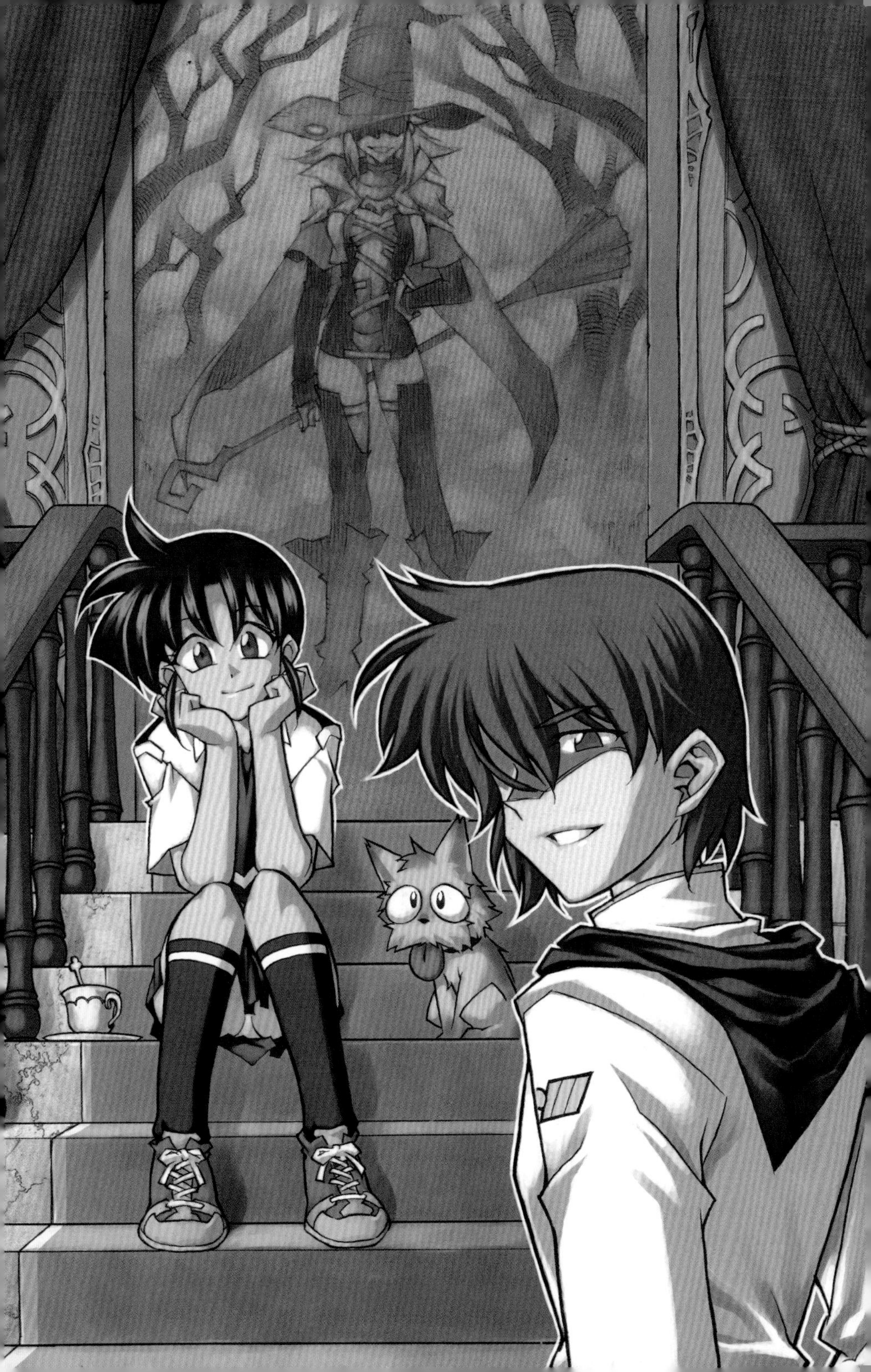

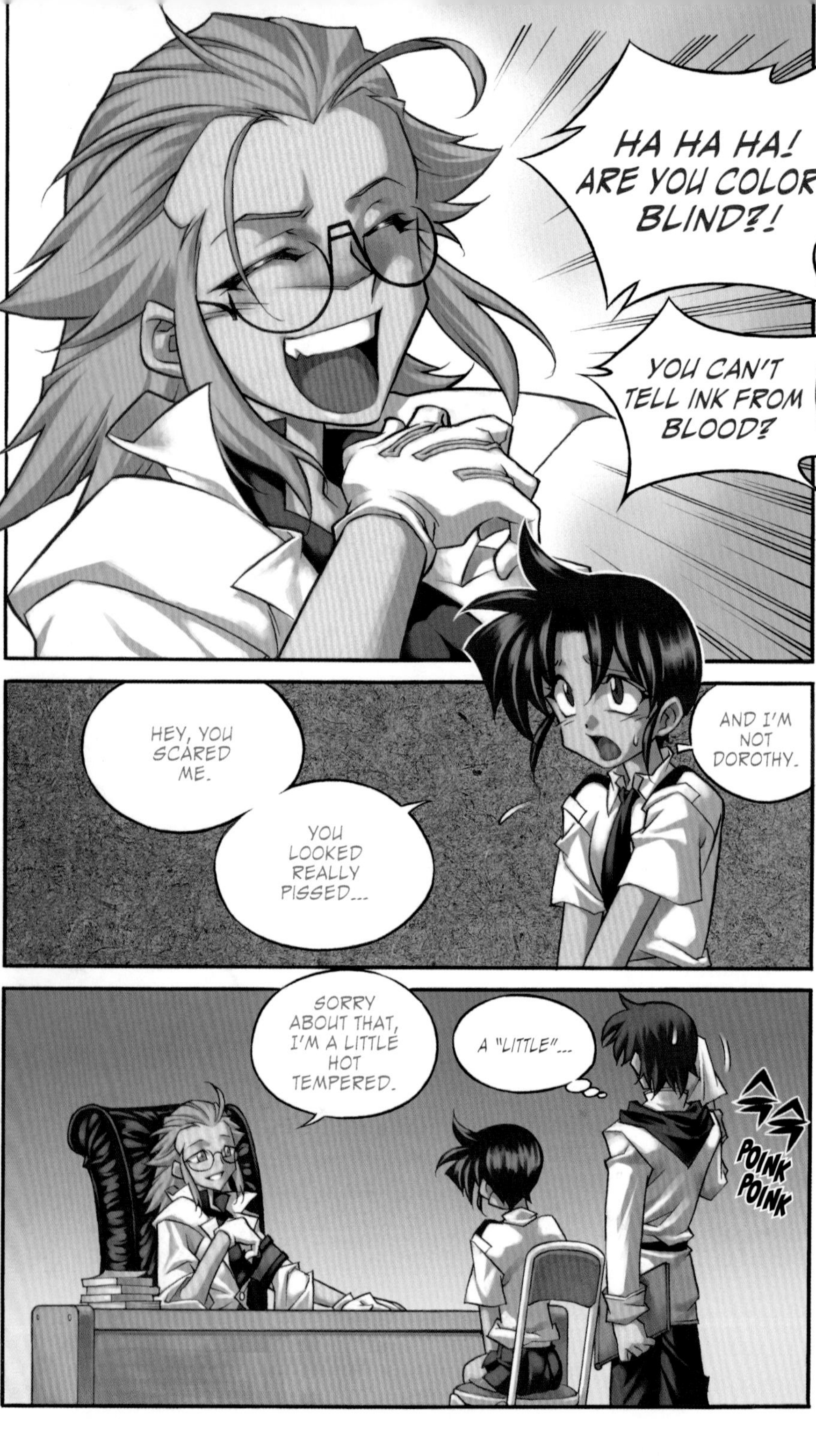
HA HA HA! ARE YOU COLOR BLIND?!
YOU CAN'T TELL INK FROM BLOOD?
HEY, YOU SCARED ME.
YOU LOOKED REALLY PISSED...
AND I'M NOT DOROTHY.
SORRY ABOUT THAT, I'M A LITTLE HOT TEMPERED.
A "LITTLE"...
POINK POINK

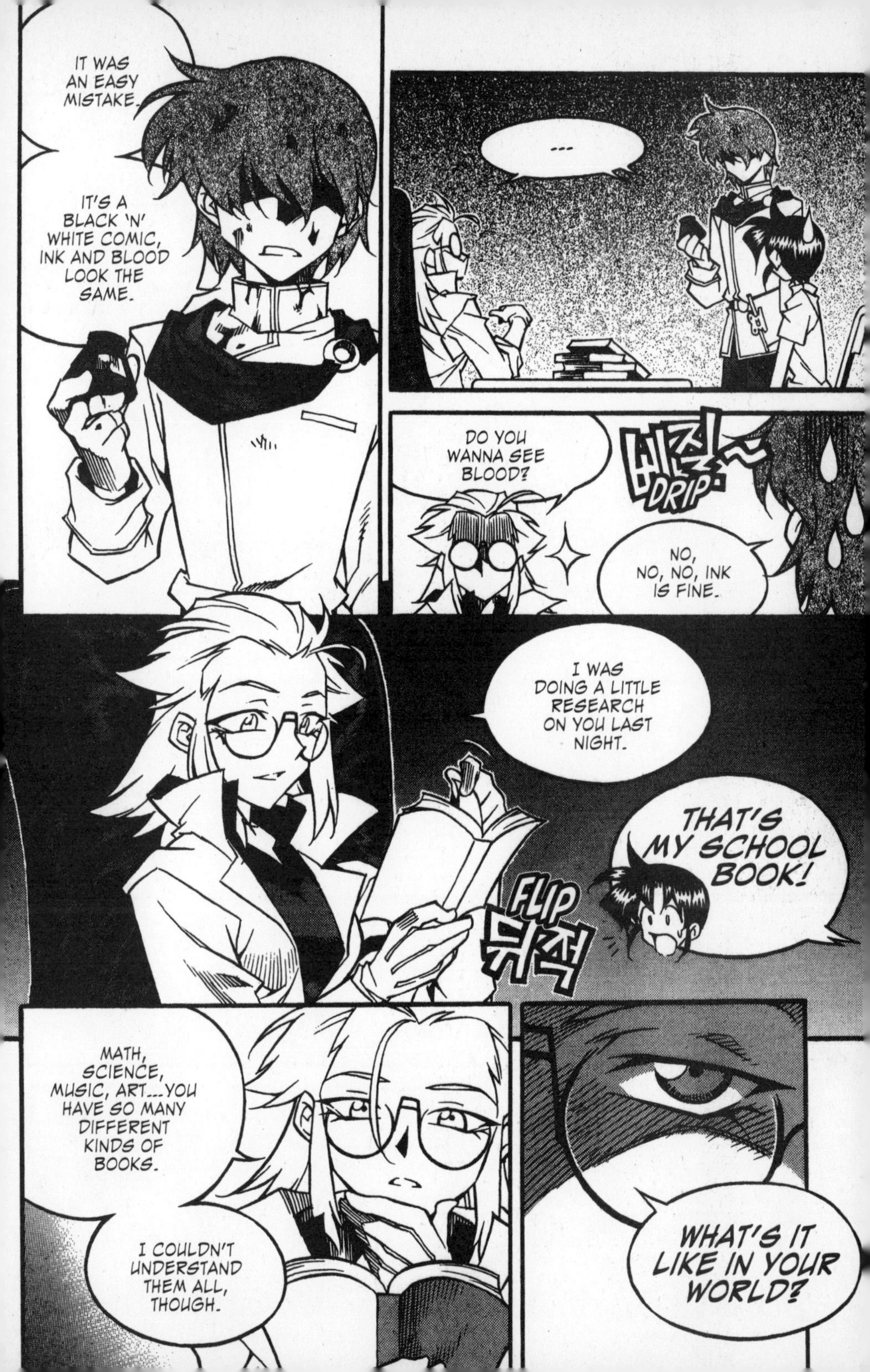
IT WAS AN EASY MISTAKE.
IT'S A BLACK 'N' WHITE COMIC, INK AND BLOOD LOOK THE SAME.
...
DO YOU WANNA SEE BLOOD?
DRIP
NO, NO, NO, INK IS FINE.
I WAS DOING A LITTLE RESEARCH ON YOU LAST NIGHT.
THAT'S MY SCHOOL BOOK!
FLIP
MATH, SCIENCE, MUSIC, ART...YOU HAVE SO MANY DIFFERENT KINDS OF BOOKS.
I COULDN'T UNDERSTAND THEM ALL, THOUGH.
WHAT'S IT LIKE IN YOUR WORLD?

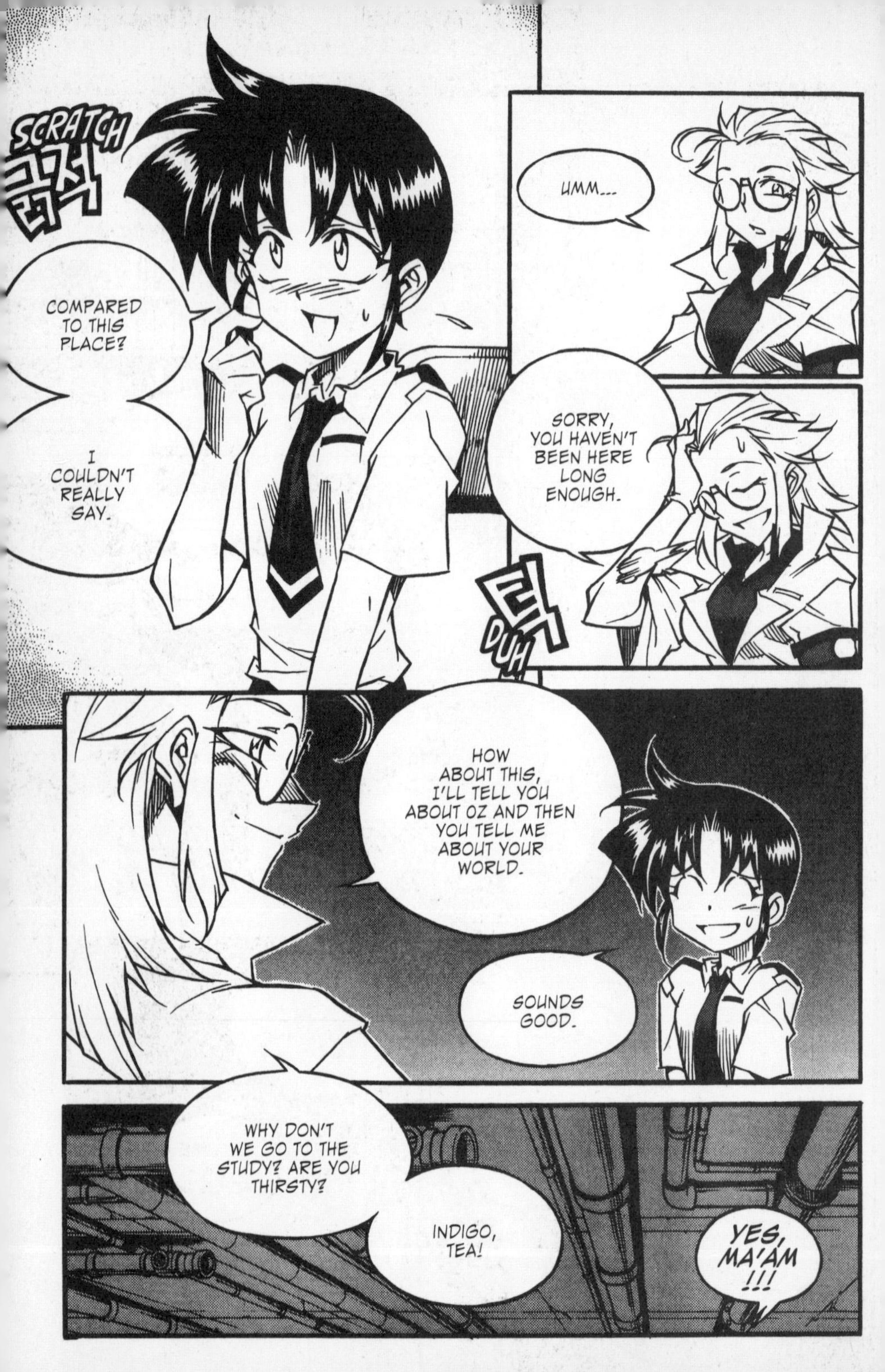
SCRATCH
긁적
COMPARED TO THIS PLACE?
I COULDN'T REALLY SAY.
UMM...
SORRY, YOU HAVEN'T BEEN HERE LONG ENOUGH.
턱
DUH
HOW ABOUT THIS, I'LL TELL YOU ABOUT OZ AND THEN YOU TELL ME ABOUT YOUR WORLD.
SOUNDS GOOD.
WHY DON'T WE GO TO THE STUDY? ARE YOU THIRSTY?
INDIGO, TEA!
YES, MA'AM !!!

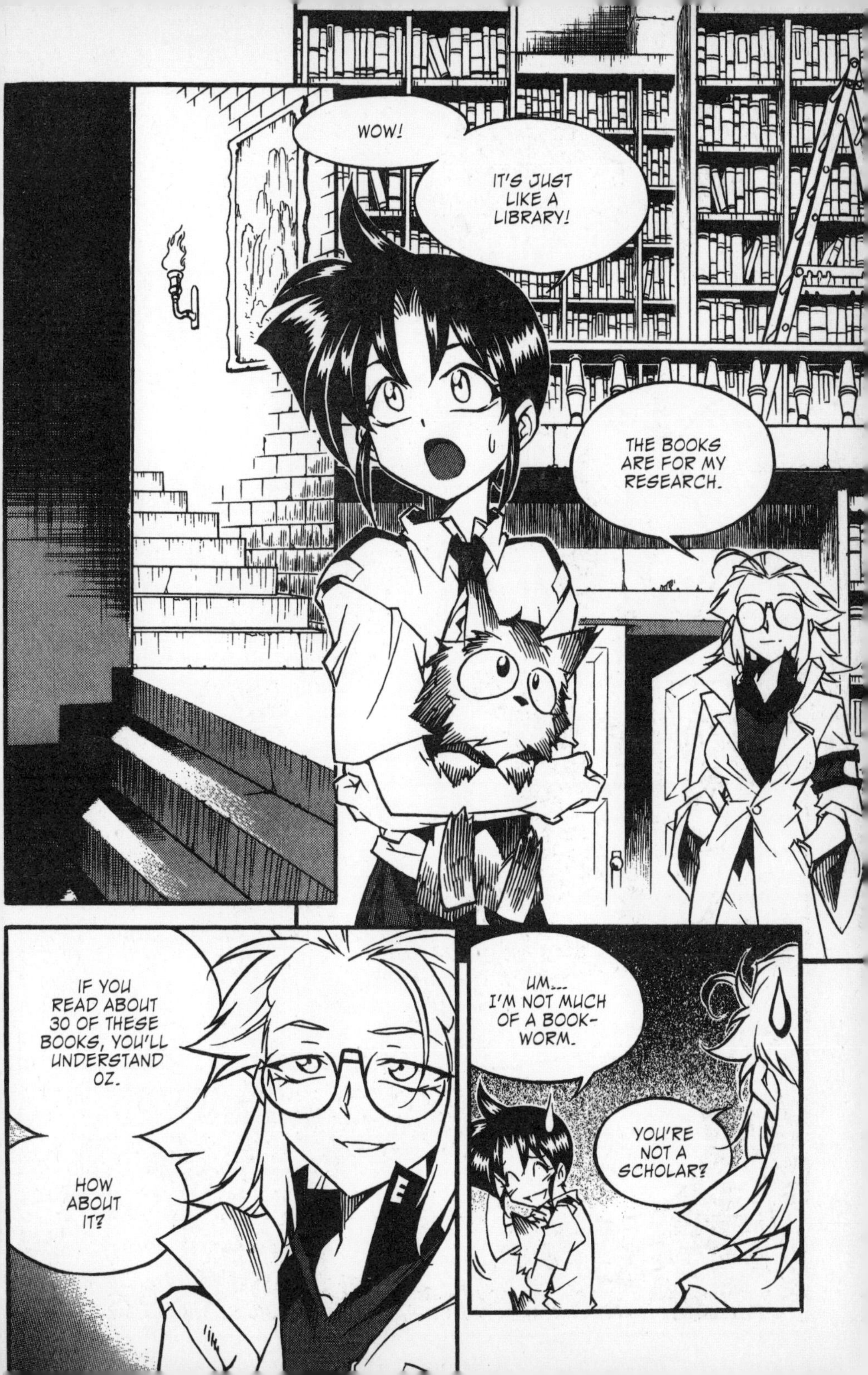
WOW!
IT'S JUST LIKE A LIBRARY!
THE BOOKS ARE FOR MY RESEARCH.
IF YOU READ ABOUT 30 OF THESE BOOKS, YOU'LL UNDERSTAND OZ.
HOW ABOUT IT?
UM... I'M NOT MUCH OF A BOOK-WORM.
YOU'RE NOT A SCHOLAR?

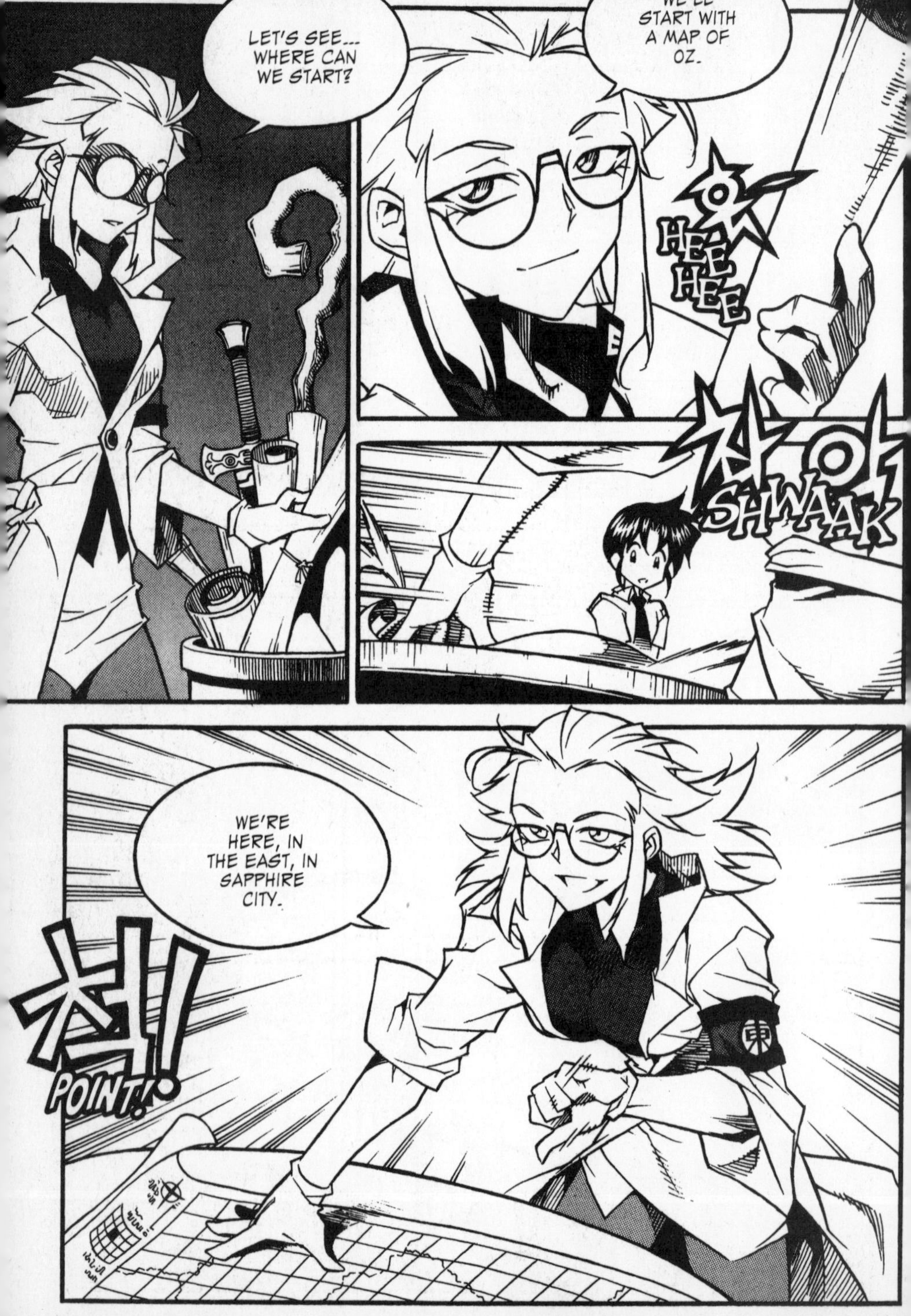
LET'S SEE... WHERE CAN WE START?
WE'LL START WITH A MAP OF OZ.
HEE HEE
SHWAAK
WE'RE HERE, IN THE EAST, IN SAPPHIRE CITY.
POINT!

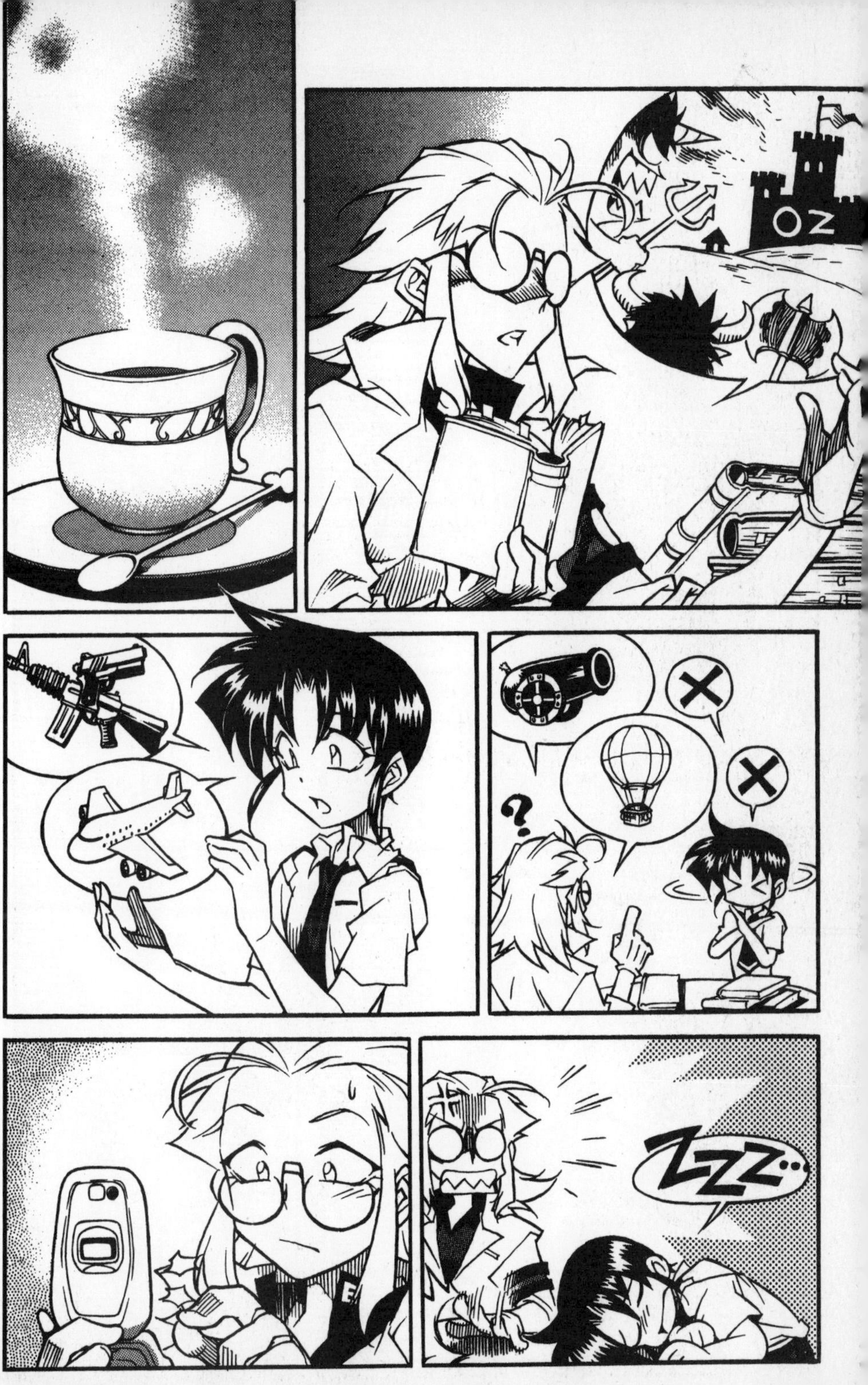
OZ
?
ZZZ...

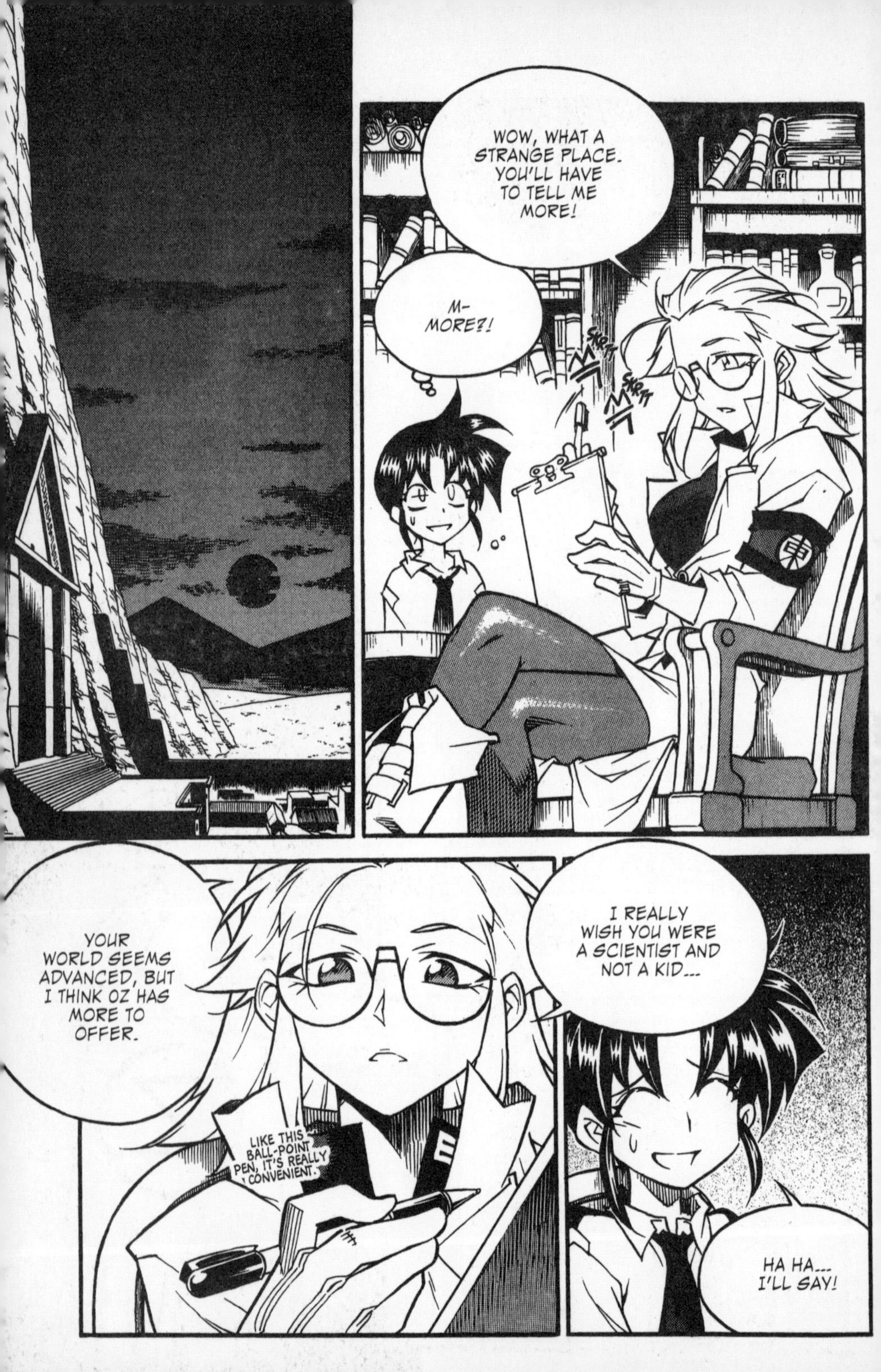
WOW, WHAT A STRANGE PLACE. YOU'LL HAVE TO TELL ME MORE!
M-MORE?!
SKRTT
SKRTT
YOUR WORLD SEEMS ADVANCED, BUT I THINK OZ HAS MORE TO OFFER.
LIKE THIS BALL-POINT PEN, IT'S REALLY CONVENIENT.
I REALLY WISH YOU WERE A SCIENTIST AND NOT A KID...
HA HA... I'LL SAY!

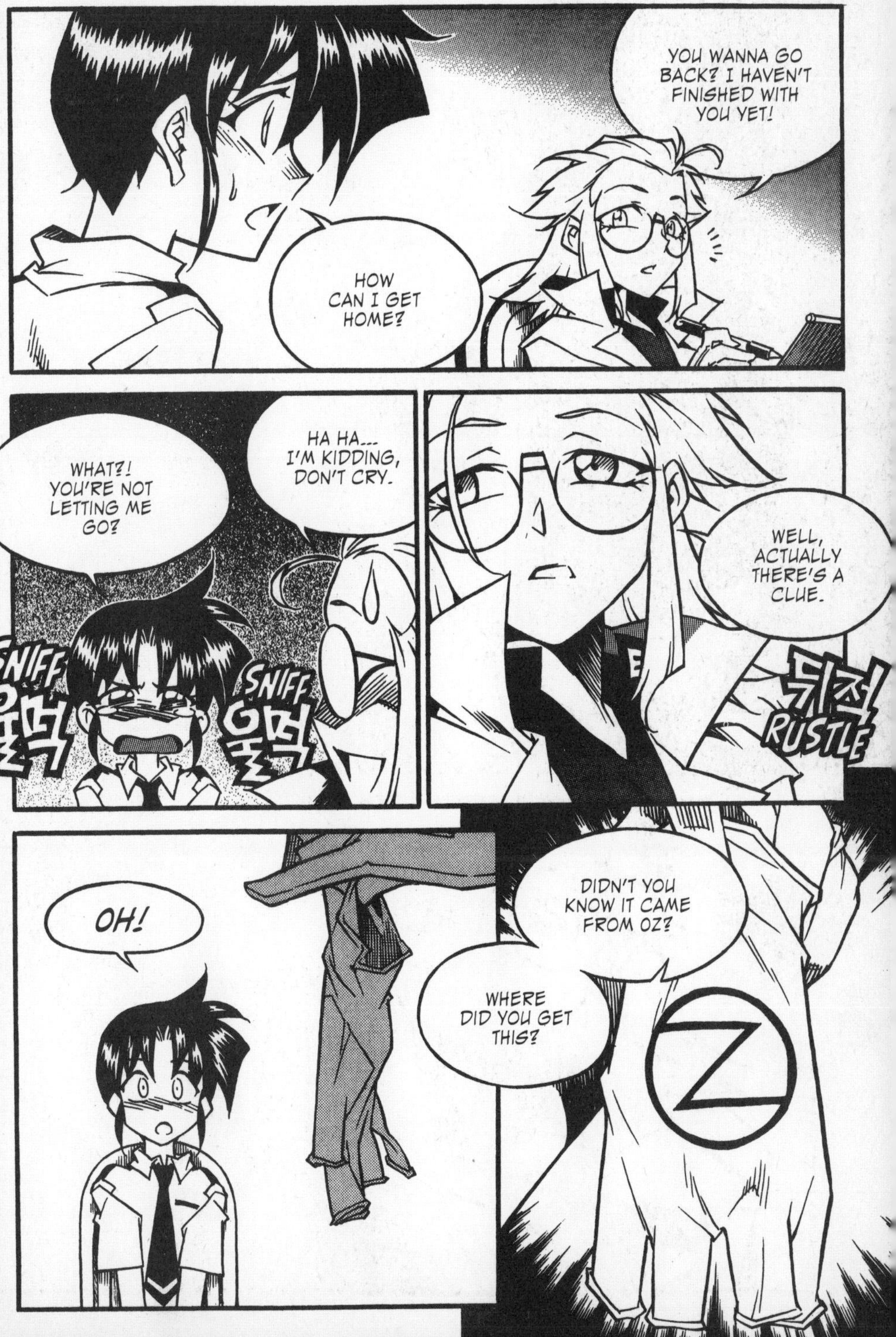
HOW CAN I GET HOME?
YOU WANNA GO BACK? I HAVEN'T FINISHED WITH YOU YET!
WHAT?! YOU'RE NOT LETTING ME GO?
SNIFF
훌쩍
SNIFF
훌쩍
HA HA... I'M KIDDING, DON'T CRY.
WELL, ACTUALLY THERE'S A CLUE.
뒤적
RUSTLE
OH!
DIDN'T YOU KNOW IT CAME FROM OZ?
WHERE DID YOU GET THIS?

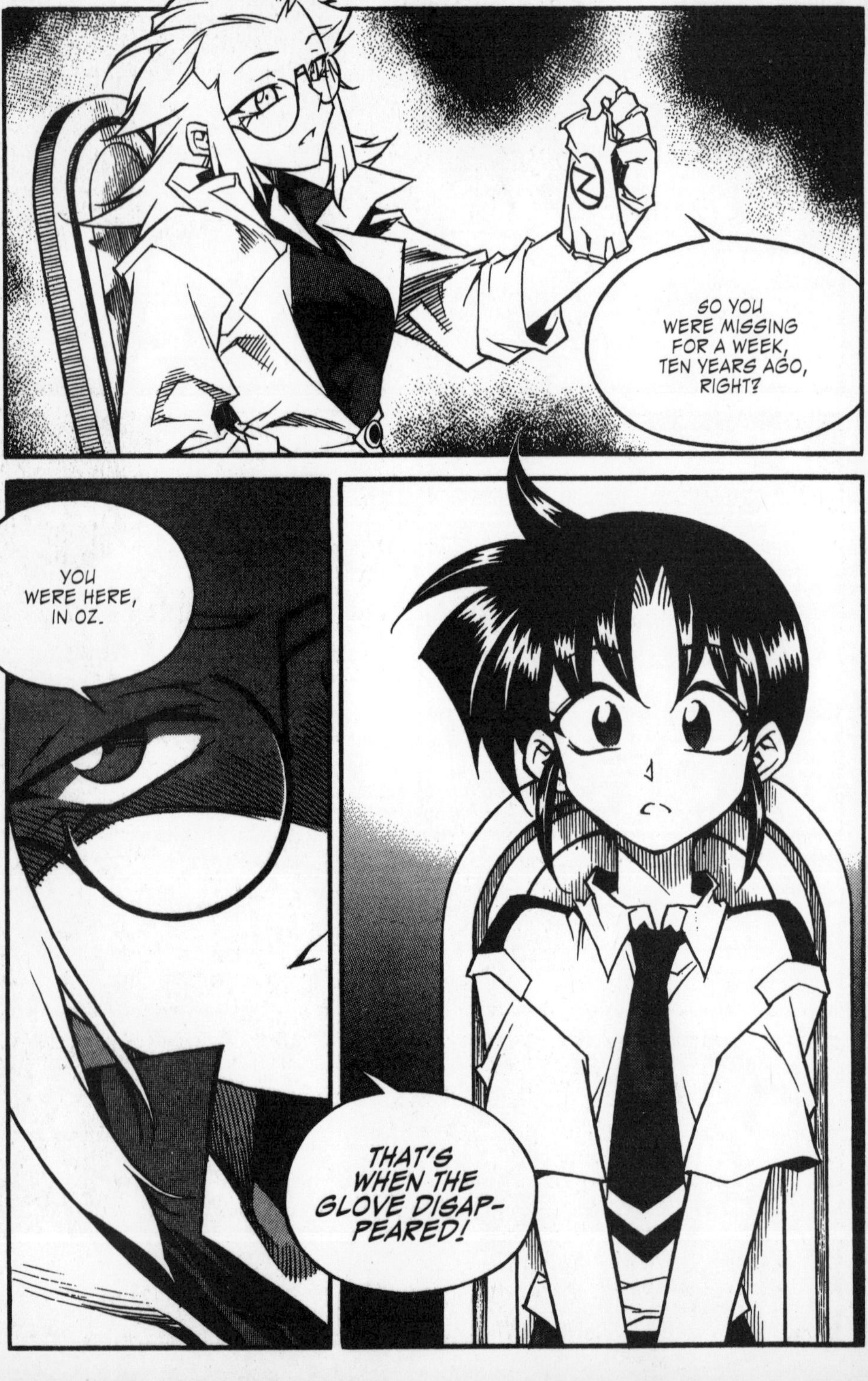
SO YOU WERE MISSING FOR A WEEK, TEN YEARS AGO, RIGHT?
YOU WERE HERE, IN OZ.
THAT'S WHEN THE GLOVE DISAP-PEARED!

DID I COME TO OZ ON THE YELLOW BRICK ROAD?

WHAT WAS I DOING HERE?

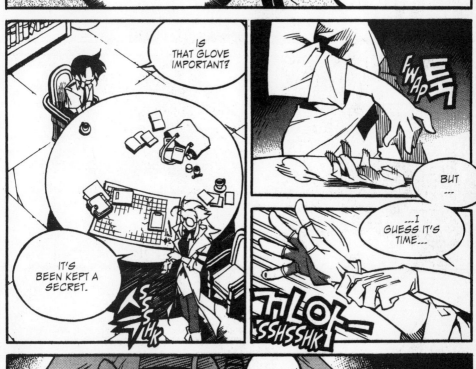

IS THAT GLOVE IMPORTANT?

IT'S BEEN KEPT A SECRET.

BUT ---

---I GUESS IT'S TIME---

---TO SHOW YOU THE GLOVE'S TRUE POWER!

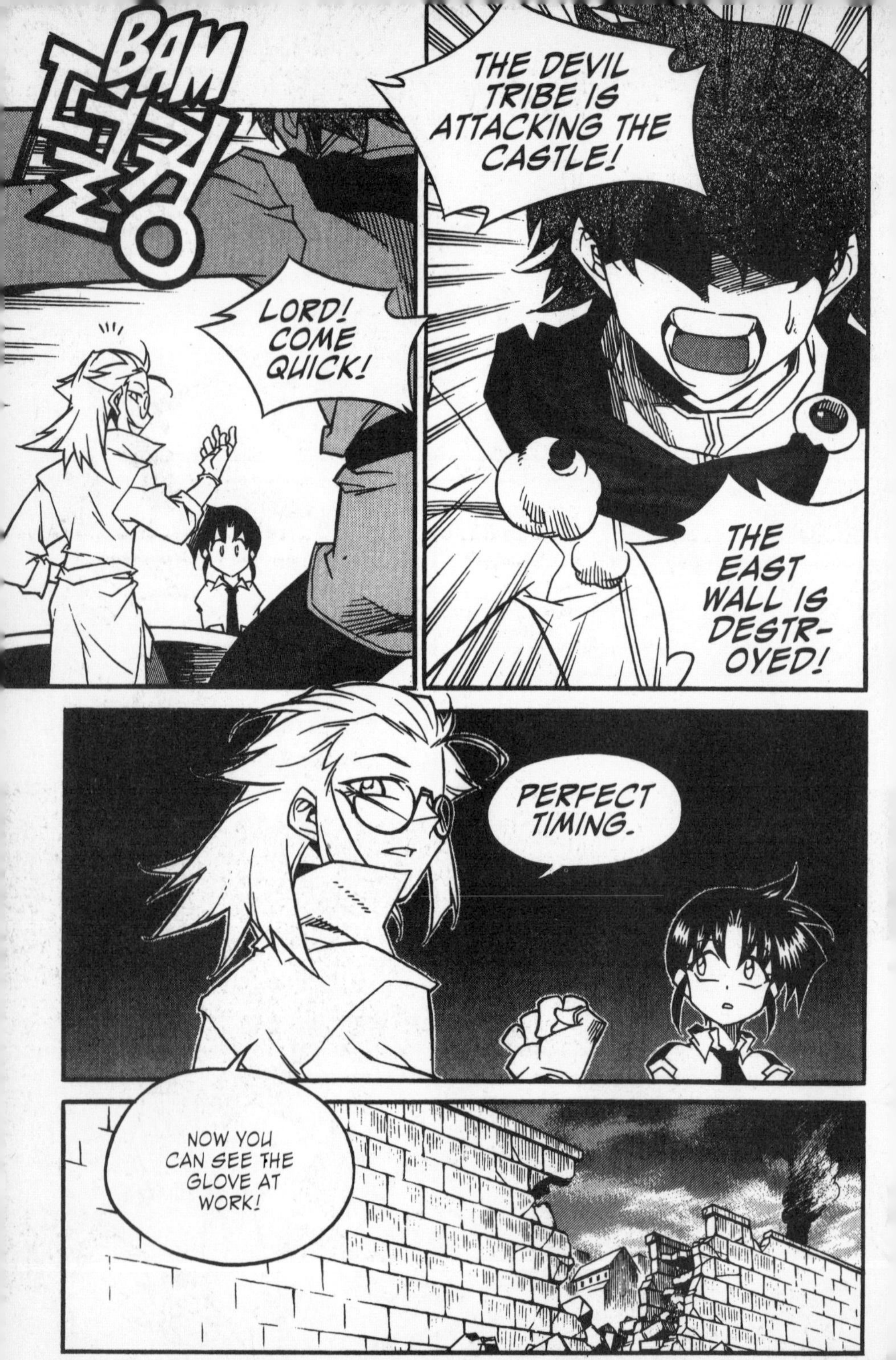
BAM
TSSSH!
THE DEVIL TRIBE IS ATTACKING THE CASTLE!
LORD! COME QUICK!
THE EAST WALL IS DESTR-OYED!
PERFECT TIMING.
NOW YOU CAN SEE THE GLOVE AT WORK!

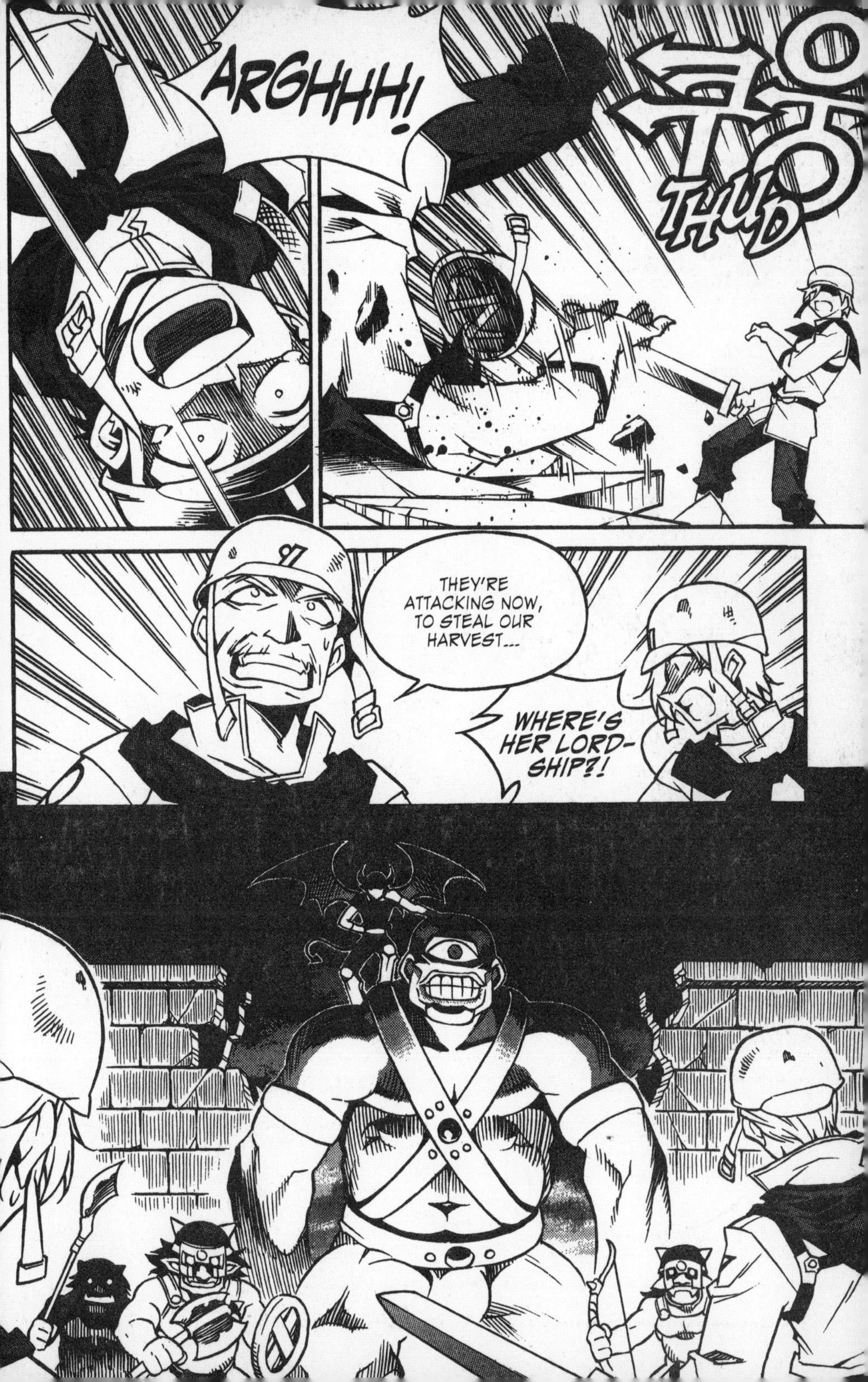
ARGHHH!
THUD
THEY'RE ATTACKING NOW, TO STEAL OUR HARVEST...
WHERE'S HER LORD-SHIP?!

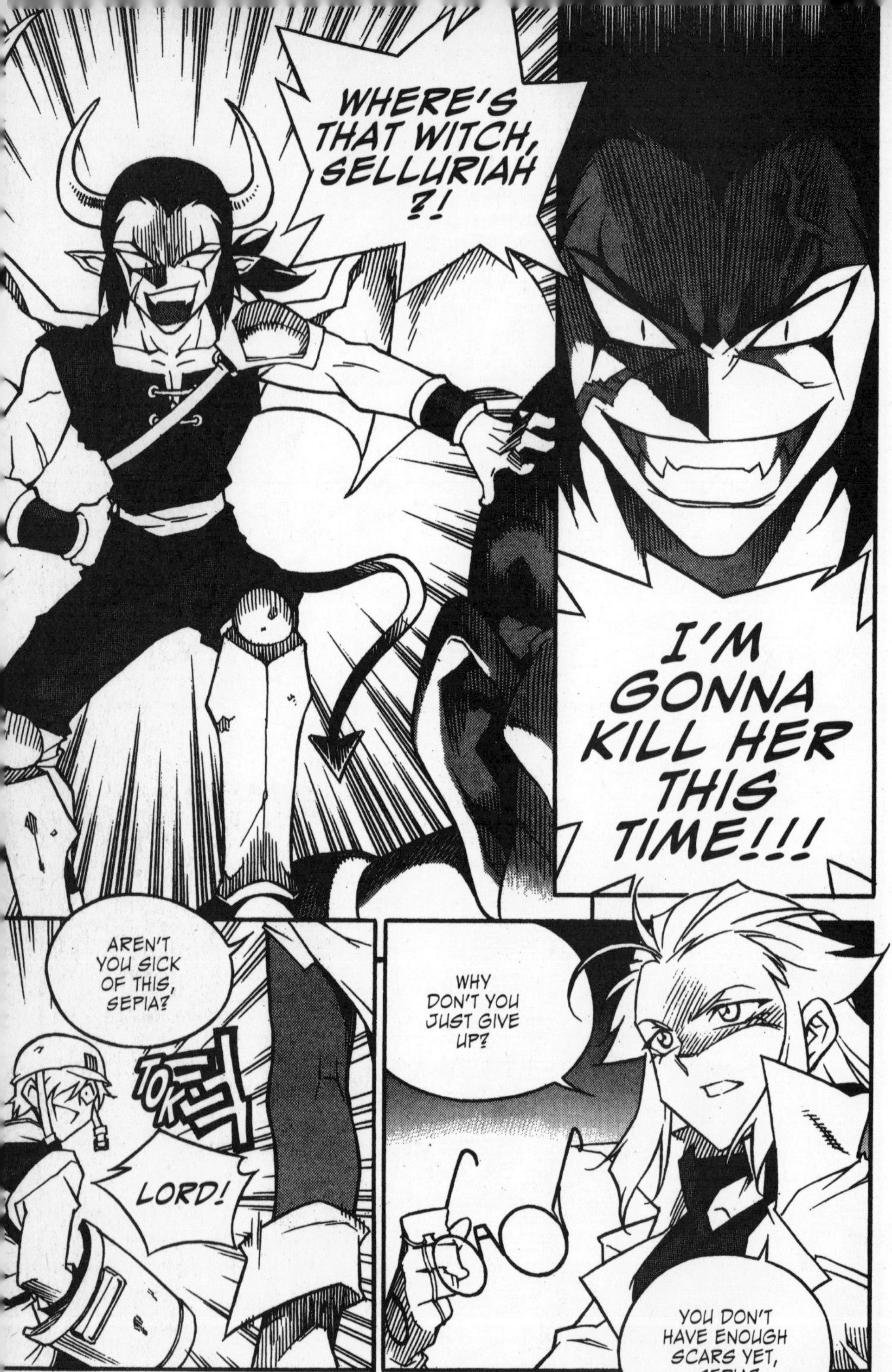
WHERE'S THAT WITCH, SELLURIAH ?!
I'M GONNA KILL HER THIS TIME!!!
AREN'T YOU SICK OF THIS, SEPIA?
TOK
LORD!
WHY DON'T YOU JUST GIVE UP?
YOU DON'T HAVE ENOUGH SCARS YET, SEPIA?

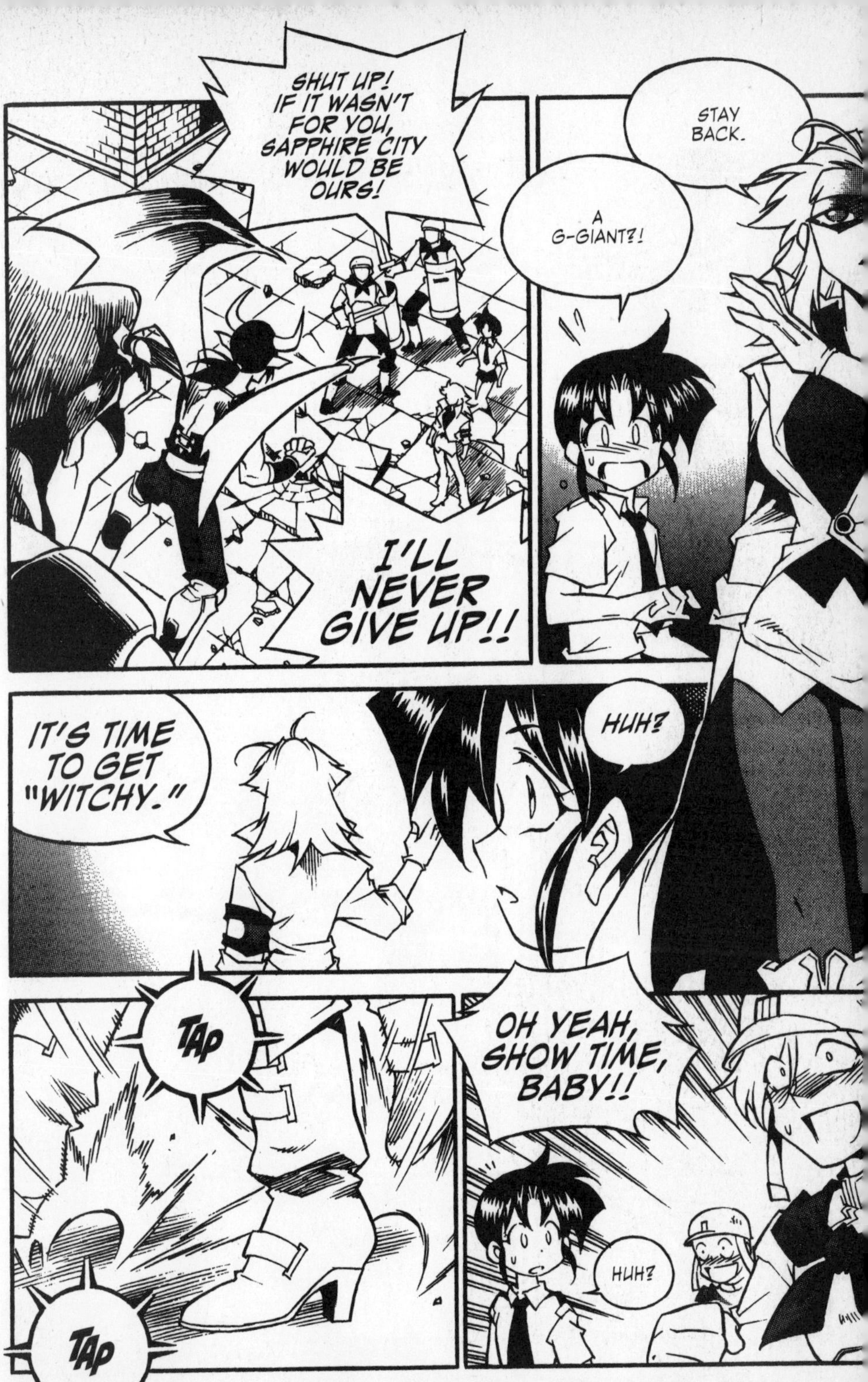
SHUT UP! IF IT WASN'T FOR YOU, SAPPHIRE CITY WOULD BE OURS!
I'LL NEVER GIVE UP!!
STAY BACK.
A G-GIANT?!
HUH?
IT'S TIME TO GET "WITCHY."
TAP
TAP
OH YEAH, SHOW TIME, BABY!!
HUH?

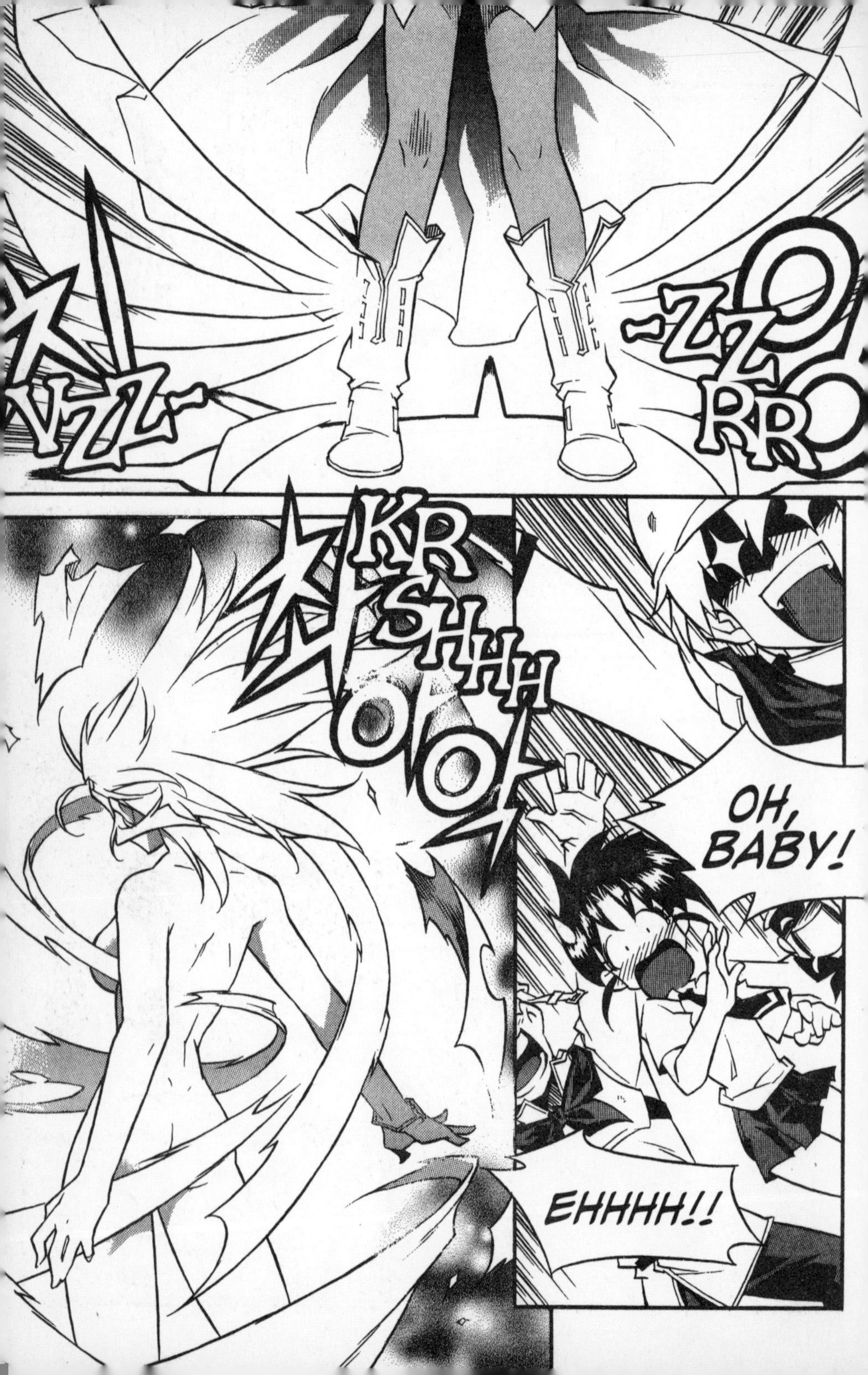
-ZZZRRROO
VZZZ-
KRSHHHOOO
OH, BABY!
EHHHH!!

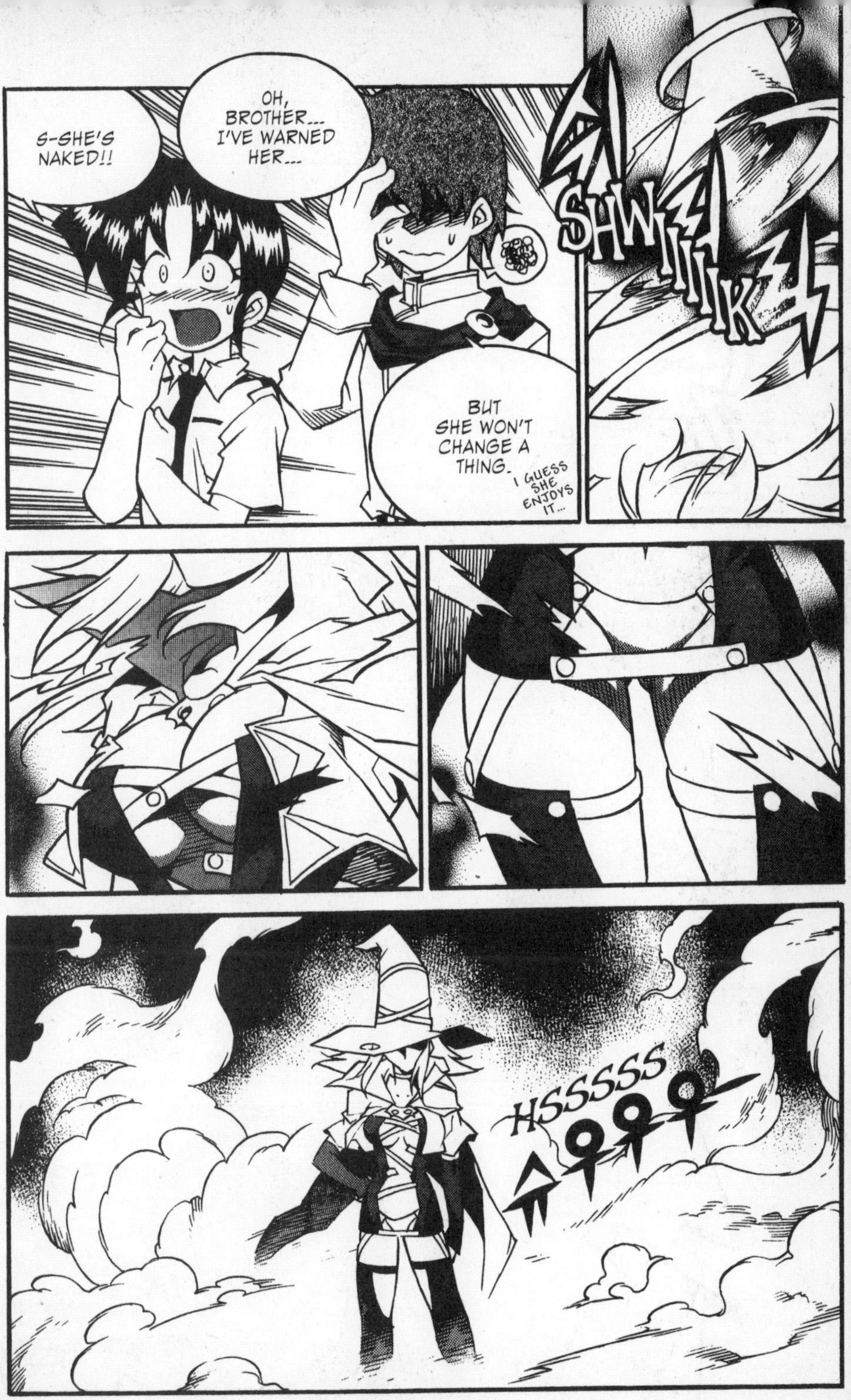
S-SHE'S NAKED!!
OH, BROTHER... I'VE WARNED HER...
BUT SHE WON'T CHANGE A THING.
I GUESS SHE ENJOYS IT...
SHWIIIIIK
HSSSSS

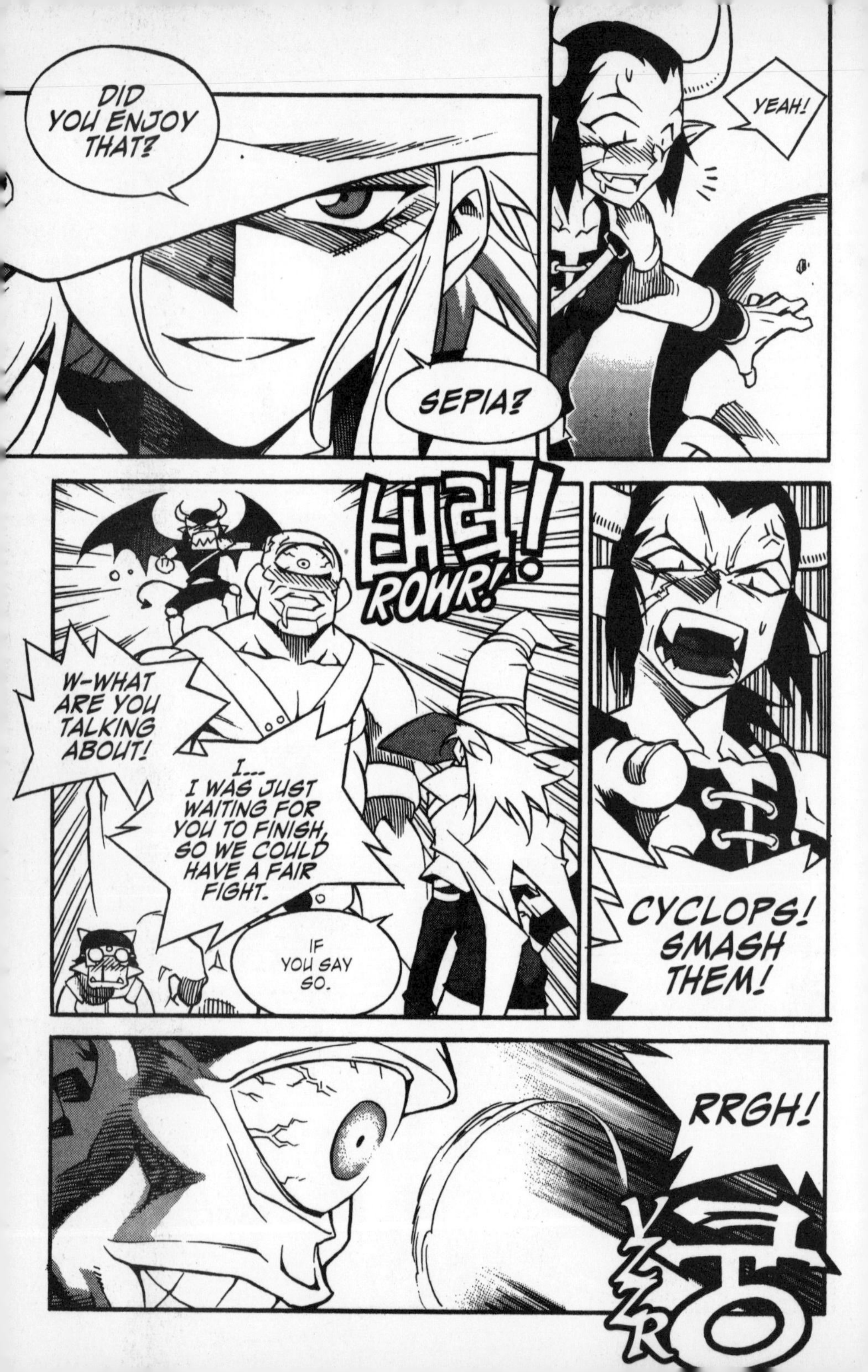
DID YOU ENJOY THAT?
SEPIA?
YEAH!
ROWR!
W-WHAT ARE YOU TALKING ABOUT!
I... I WAS JUST WAITING FOR YOU TO FINISH, SO WE COULD HAVE A FAIR FIGHT.
IF YOU SAY SO.
CYCLOPS! SMASH THEM!
RRGH!
VZZR

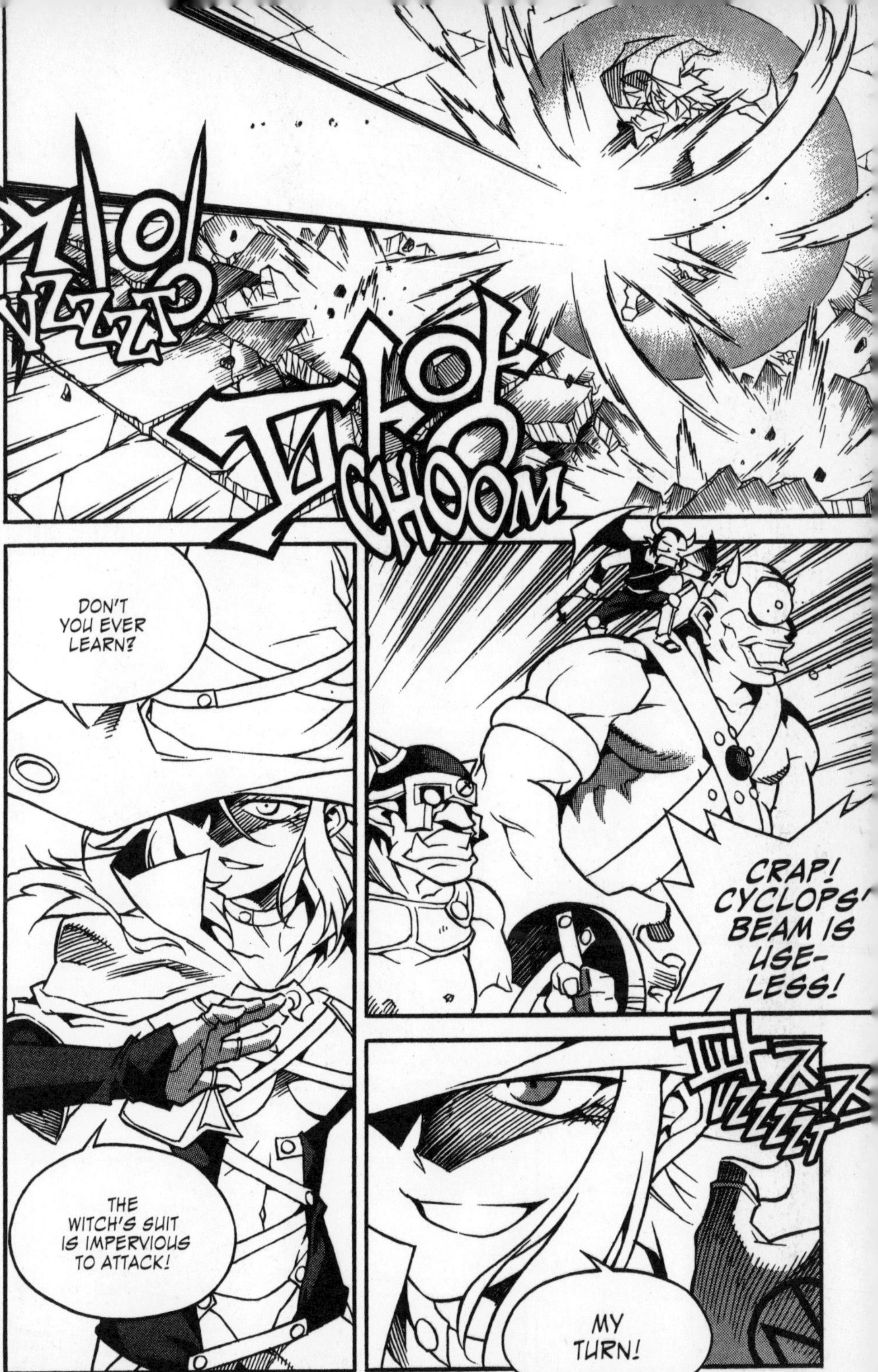
VZZZT
CHOOM
DON'T YOU EVER LEARN?
CRAP! CYCLOPS' BEAM IS USE-LESS!
THE WITCH'S SUIT IS IMPERVIOUS TO ATTACK!
VZZZZT
MY TURN!

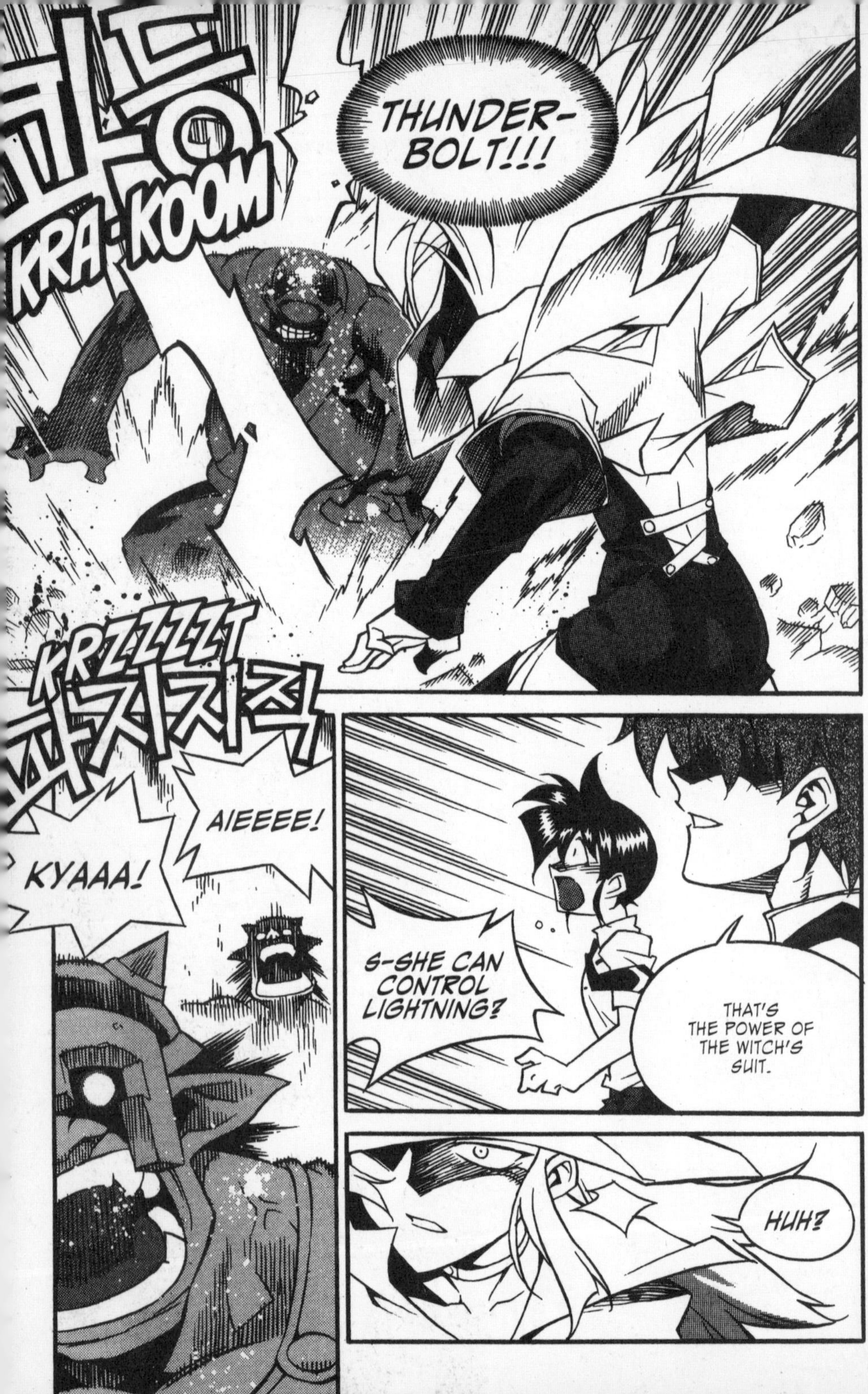
KRA-KOOM
THUNDER-BOLT!!!
KRZZZZT
AIEEEE!
KYAAA!
S-SHE CAN CONTROL LIGHTNING?
THAT'S THE POWER OF THE WITCH'S SUIT.
HUH?

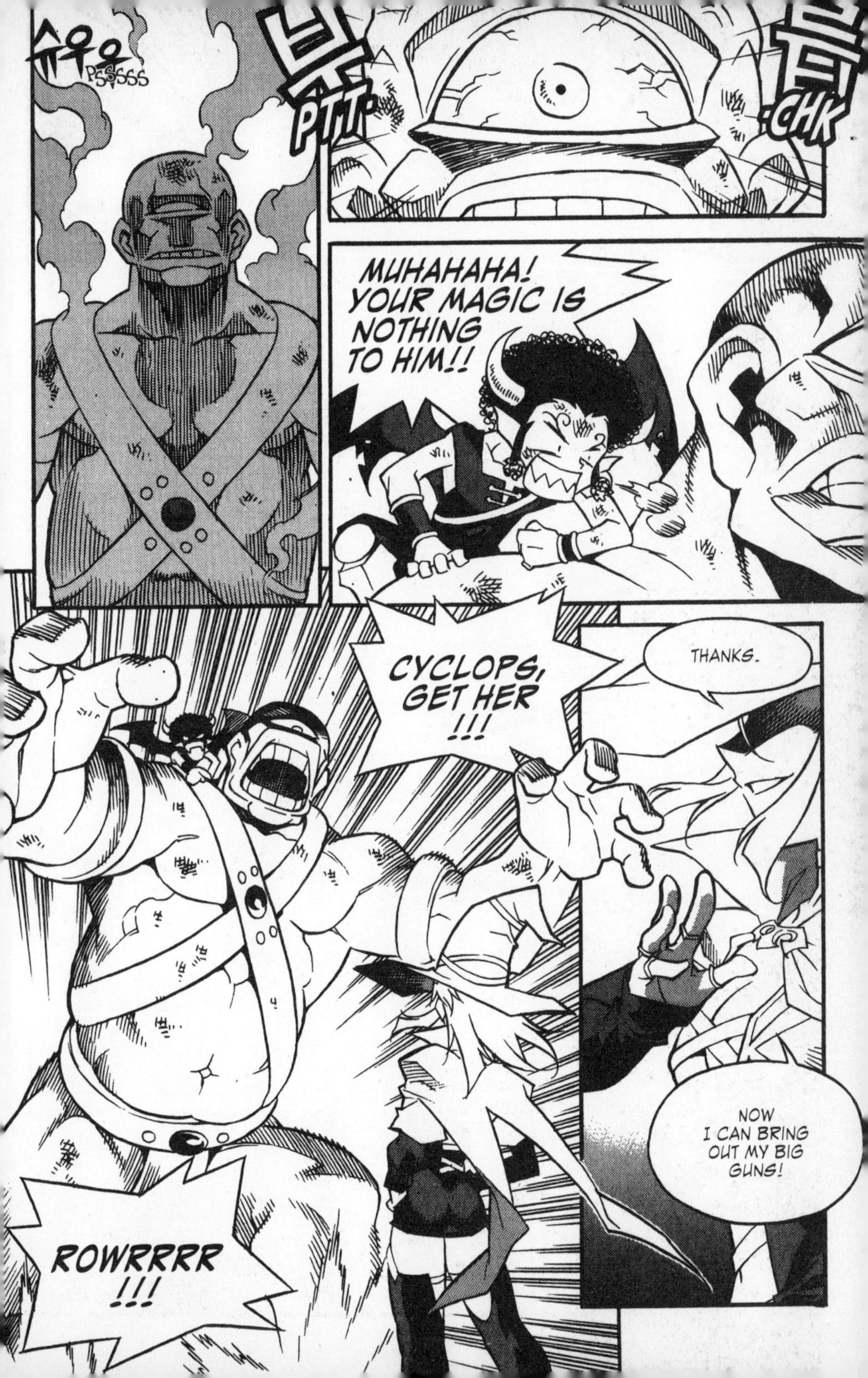
슈우우
PSSSSS
빠
PTTT
칙
-CHK
MUHAHAHA! YOUR MAGIC IS NOTHING TO HIM!!
CYCLOPS, GET HER !!!
THANKS.
ROWRRRR !!!
NOW I CAN BRING OUT MY BIG GUNS!

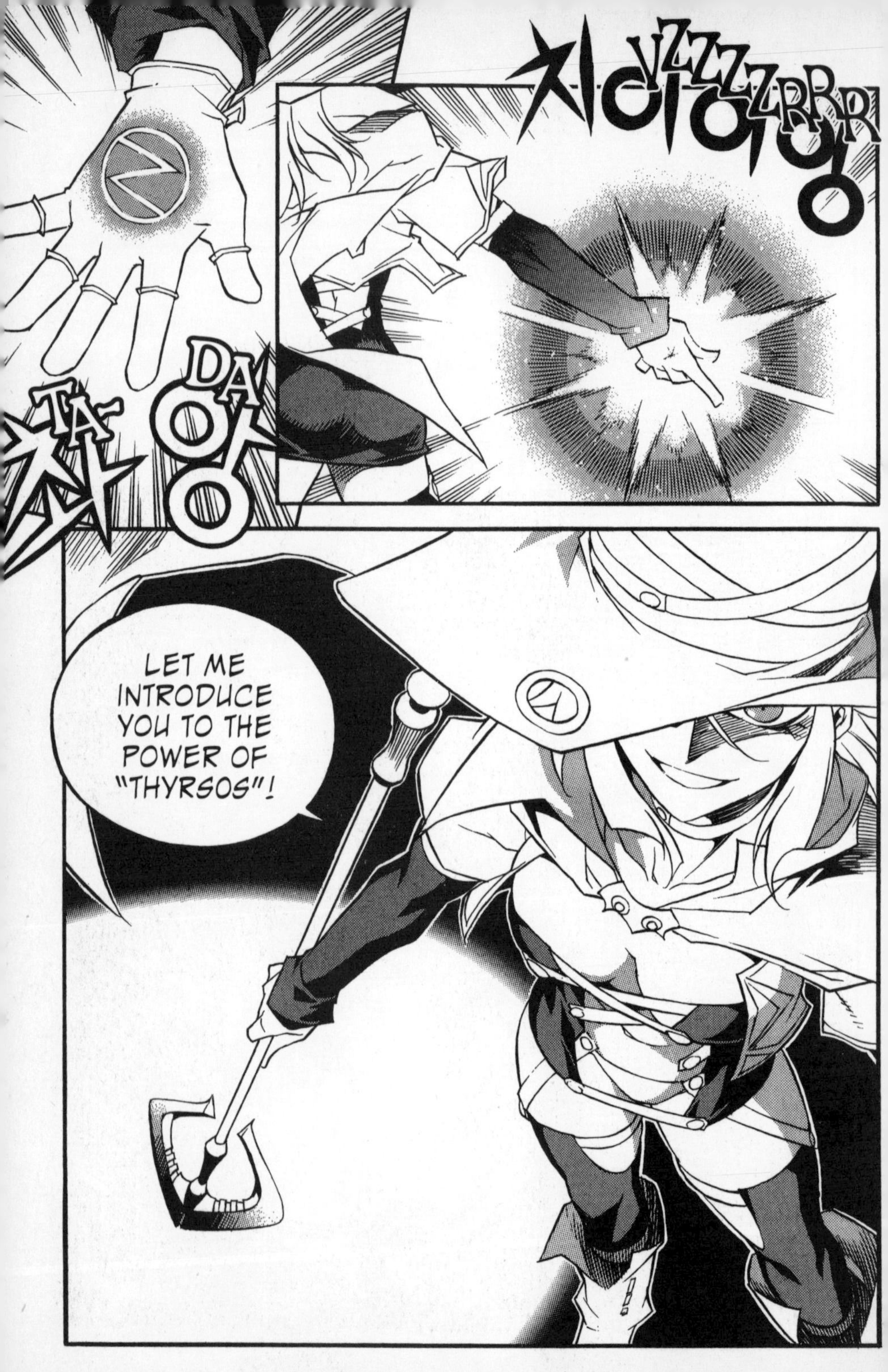

지이이잉 ZZZZZRRR
TA- 잘 DA 앙!
LET ME INTRODUCE YOU TO THE POWER OF "THYRSOS"!

Step 9 THYRSOS

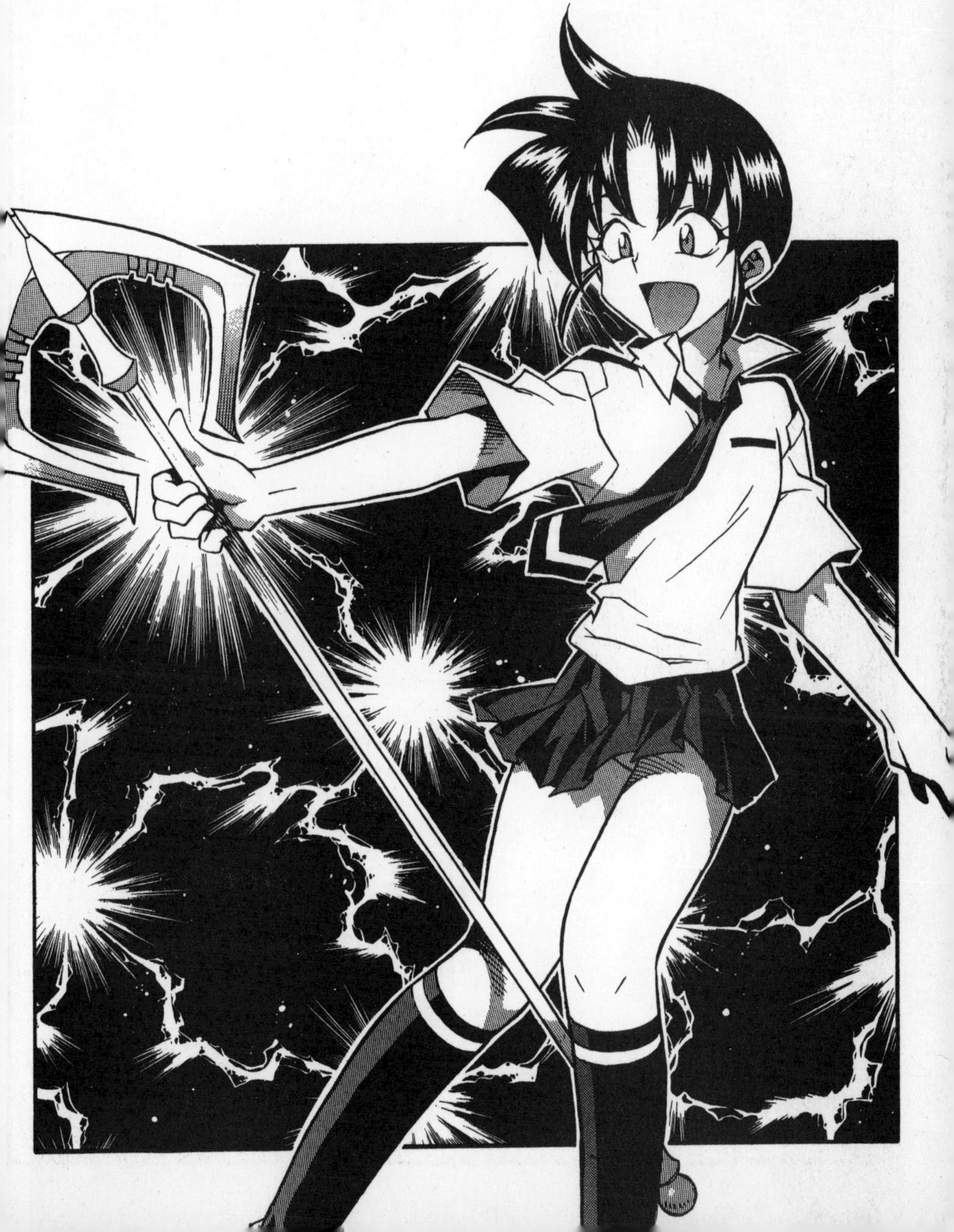

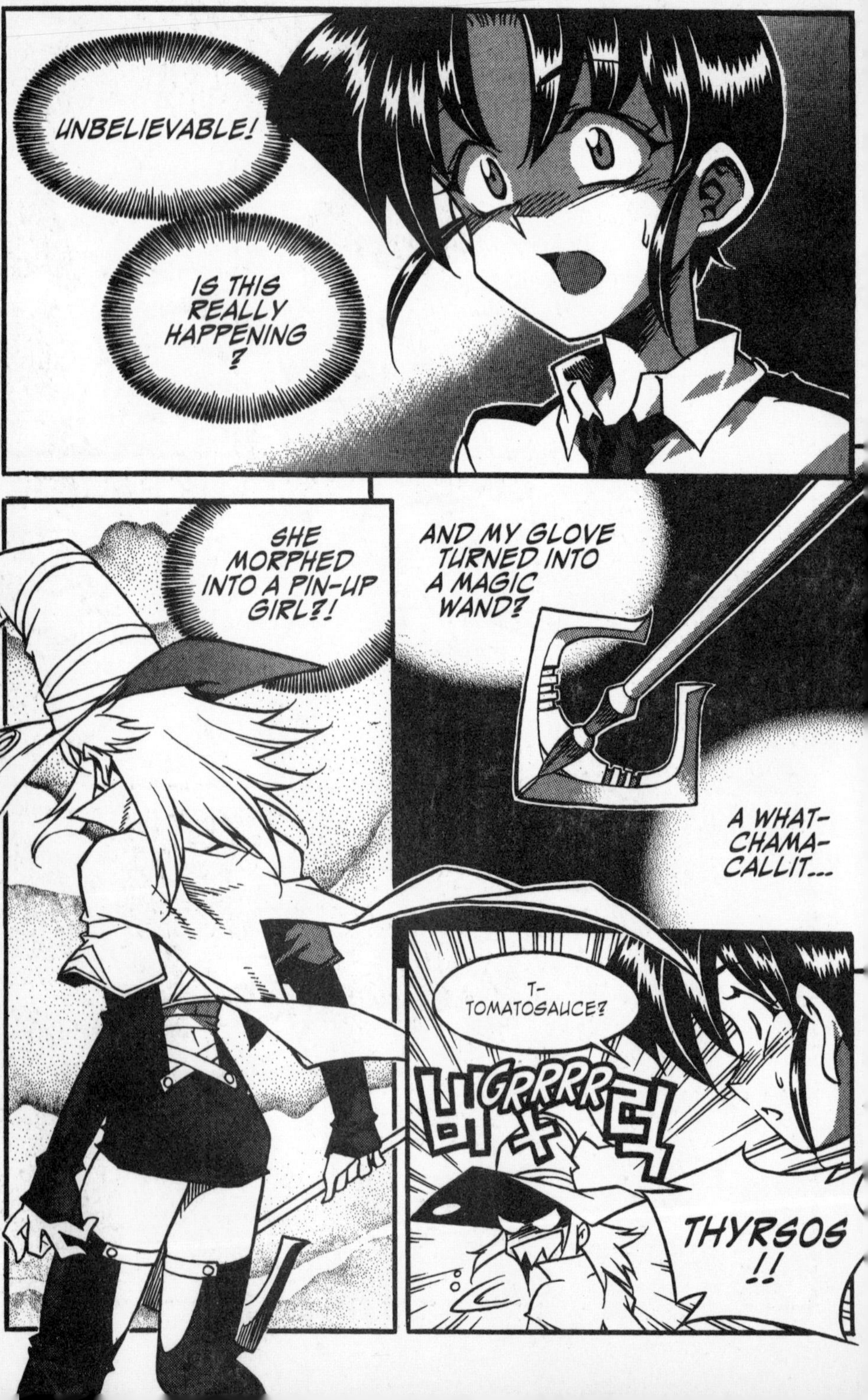
UNBELIEVABLE!
IS THIS REALLY HAPPENING?
AND MY GLOVE TURNED INTO A MAGIC WAND?
SHE MORPHED INTO A PIN-UP GIRL?!
A WHAT-CHAMA-CALLIT...
T-TOMATOSAUCE?
GRRRR
THYRSOS!!

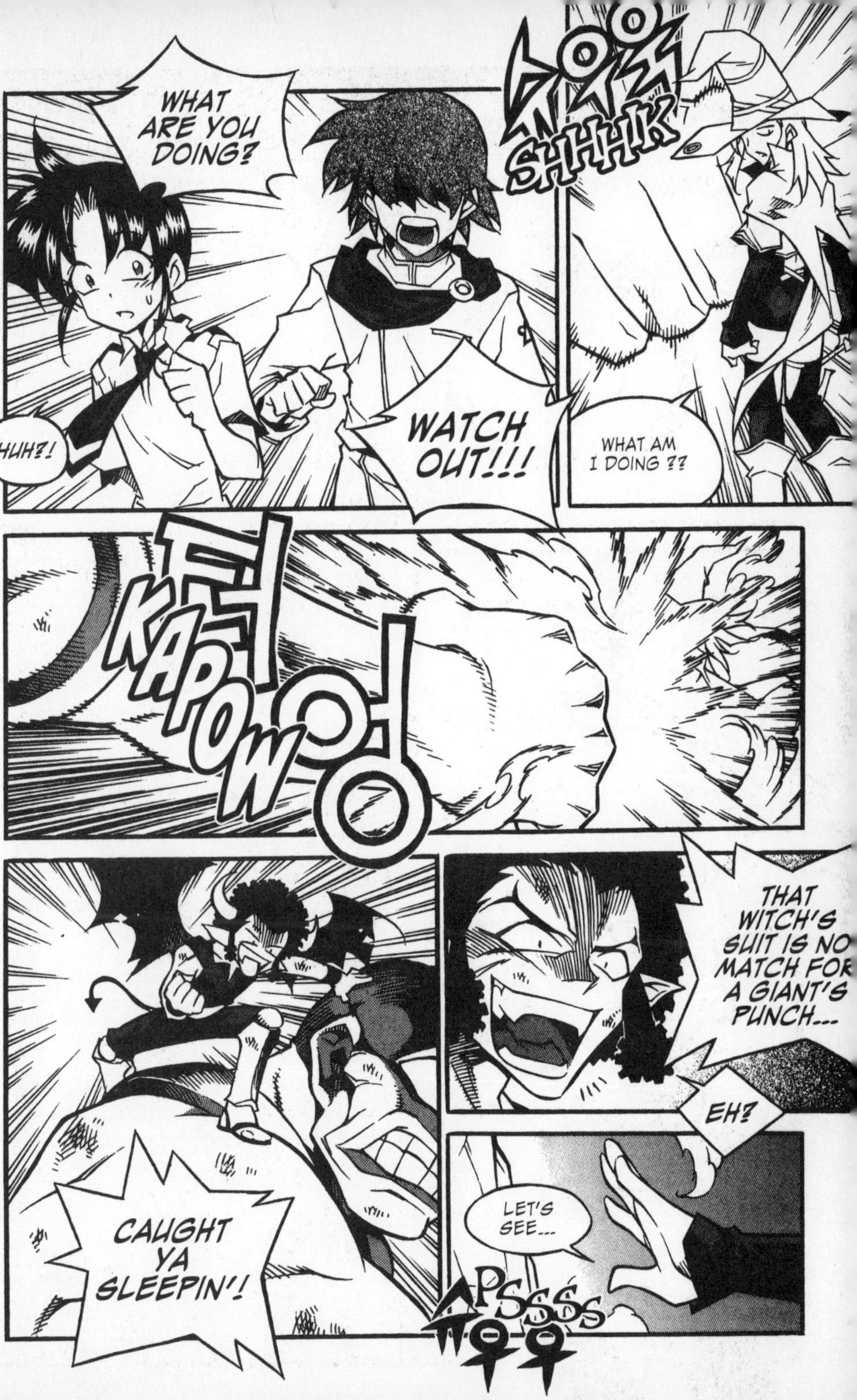
WHAT ARE YOU DOING?
HUH?!
WATCH OUT!!!
SHHHK
WHAT AM I DOING ??
KAPOW
THAT WITCH'S SUIT IS NO MATCH FOR A GIANT'S PUNCH...
CAUGHT YA SLEEPIN'!
EH?
LET'S SEE...
PSSSS

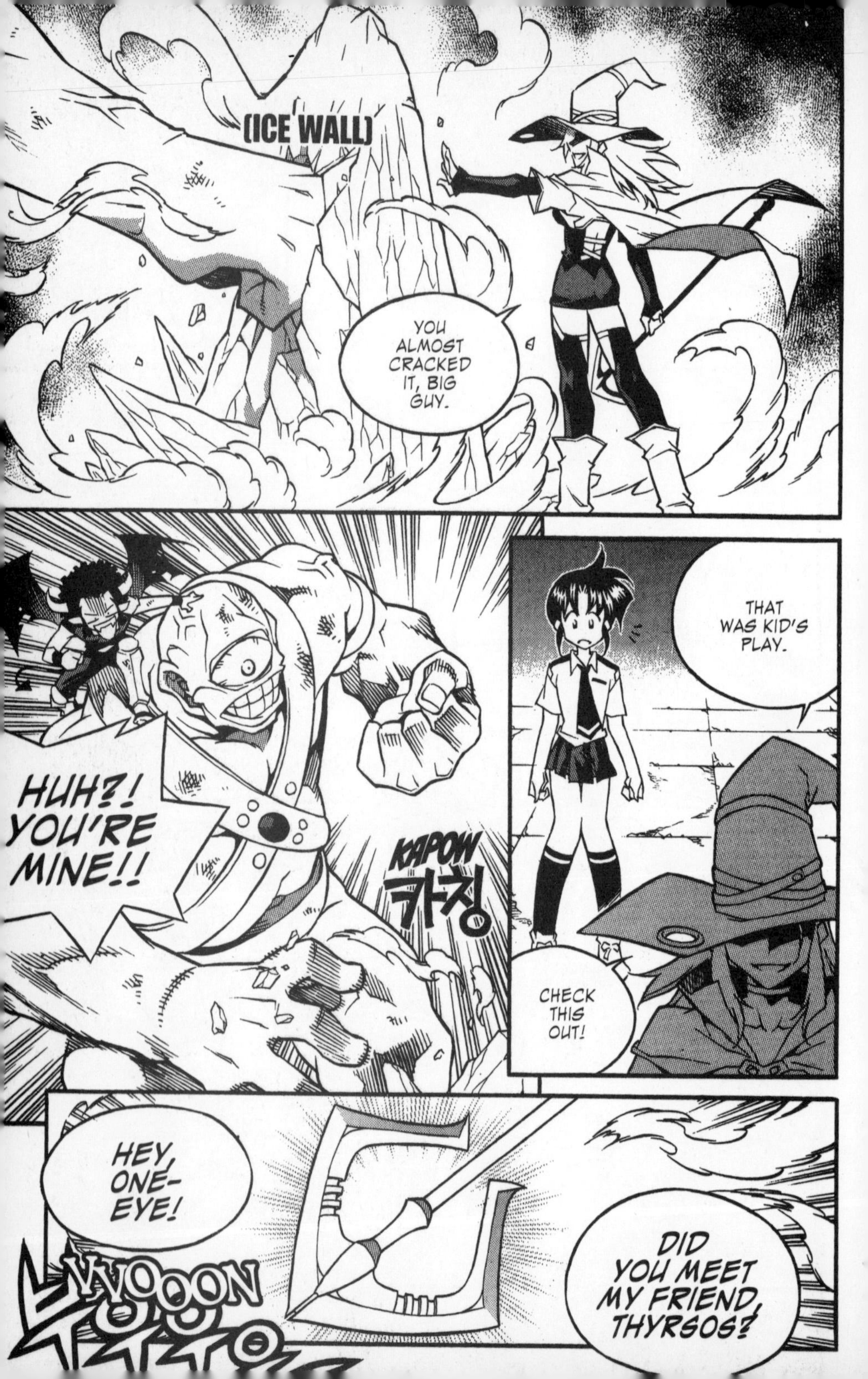
(ICE WALL)
YOU ALMOST CRACKED IT, BIG GUY.
THAT WAS KID'S PLAY.
HUH?! YOU'RE MINE!!
KAPOW
카칭
CHECK THIS OUT!
HEY, ONE-EYE!
VVOOOON
DID YOU MEET MY FRIEND, THYRSOS?

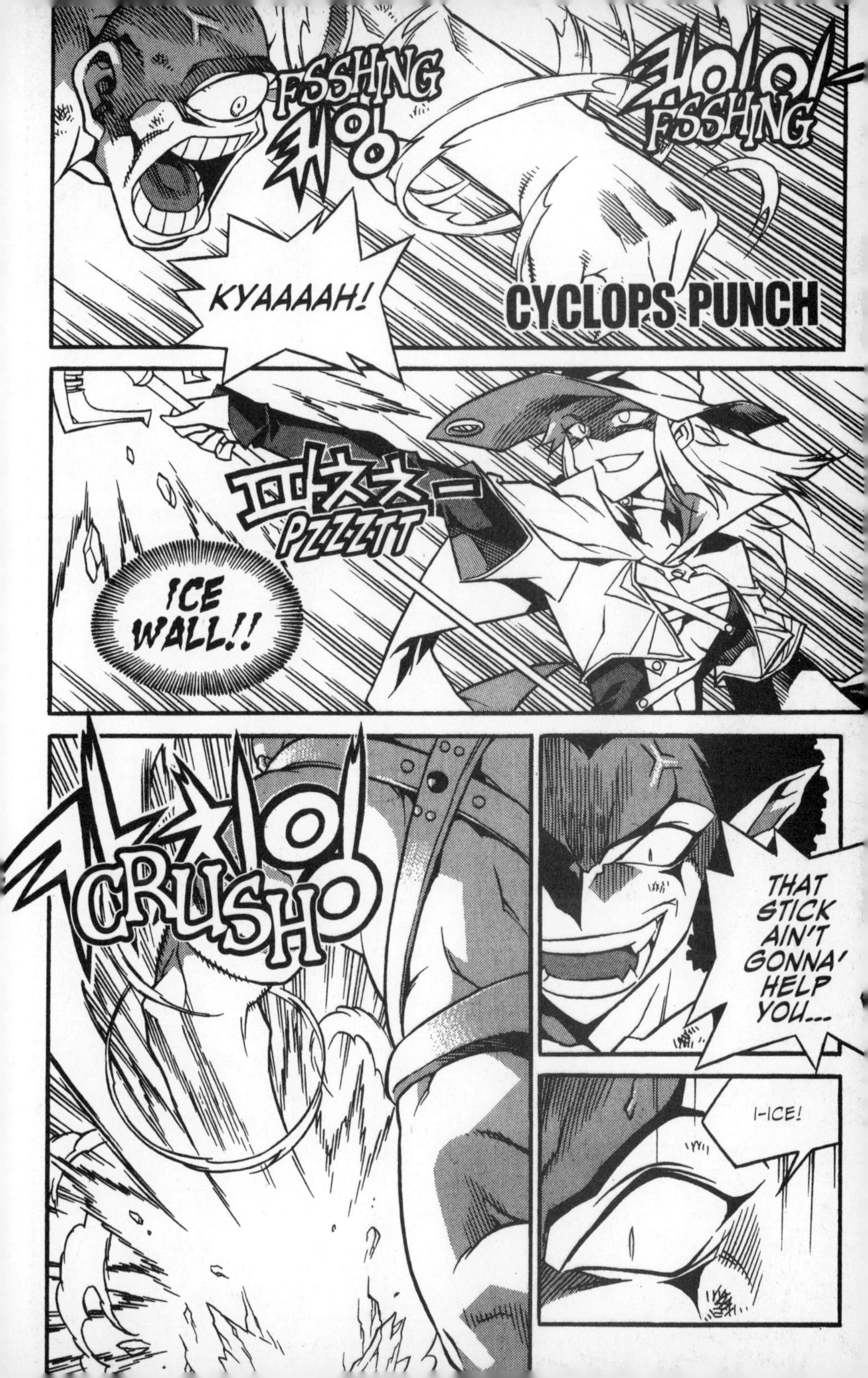
FSSHING
FSSHING
CYCLOPS PUNCH
KYAAAAH!
PZZZTT
ICE WALL!!
CRUSH
THAT STICK AIN'T GONNA' HELP YOU...
I-ICE!

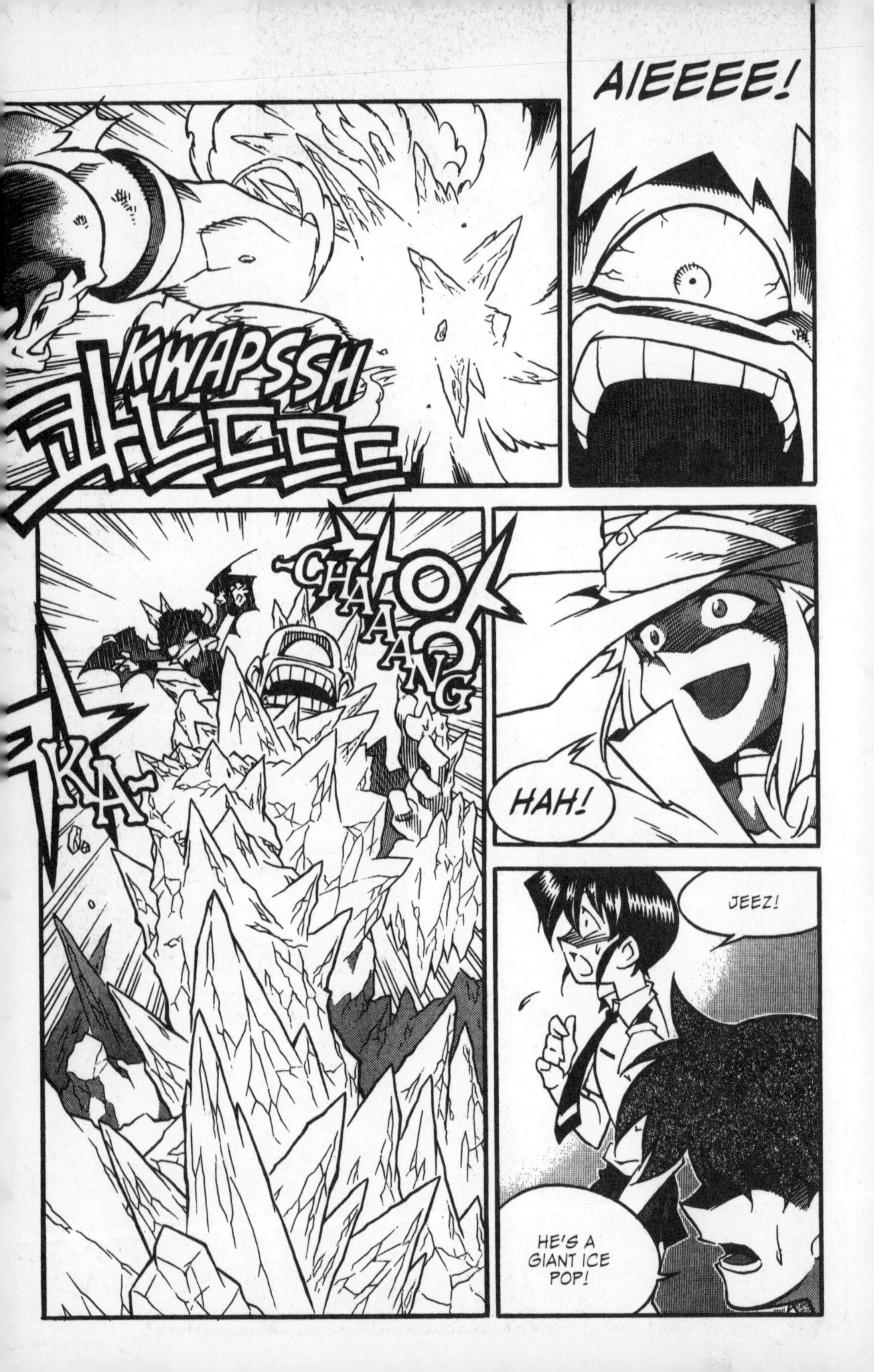

KWAPSSH
AIEEEE!
KA-
CHAAAANG
HAH!
JEEZ!
HE'S A GIANT ICE POP!

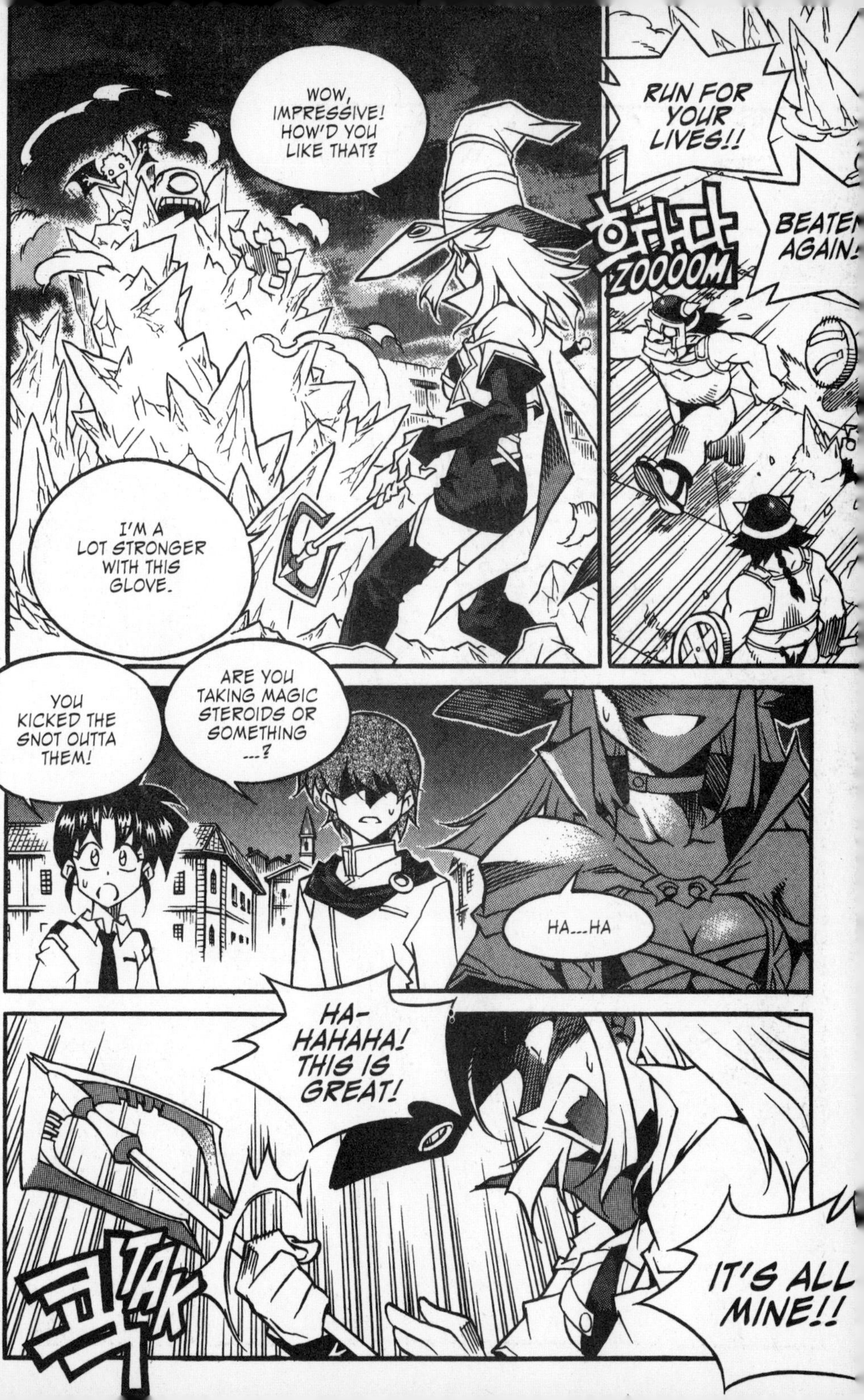
WOW, IMPRESSIVE! HOW'D YOU LIKE THAT?
I'M A LOT STRONGER WITH THIS GLOVE.
RUN FOR YOUR LIVES!!
ZOOOOM
YOU KICKED THE SNOT OUTTA THEM!
ARE YOU TAKING MAGIC STEROIDS OR SOMETHING ...?
HA...HA
HA-HAHAHA! THIS IS GREAT!
TAK
IT'S ALL MINE!!

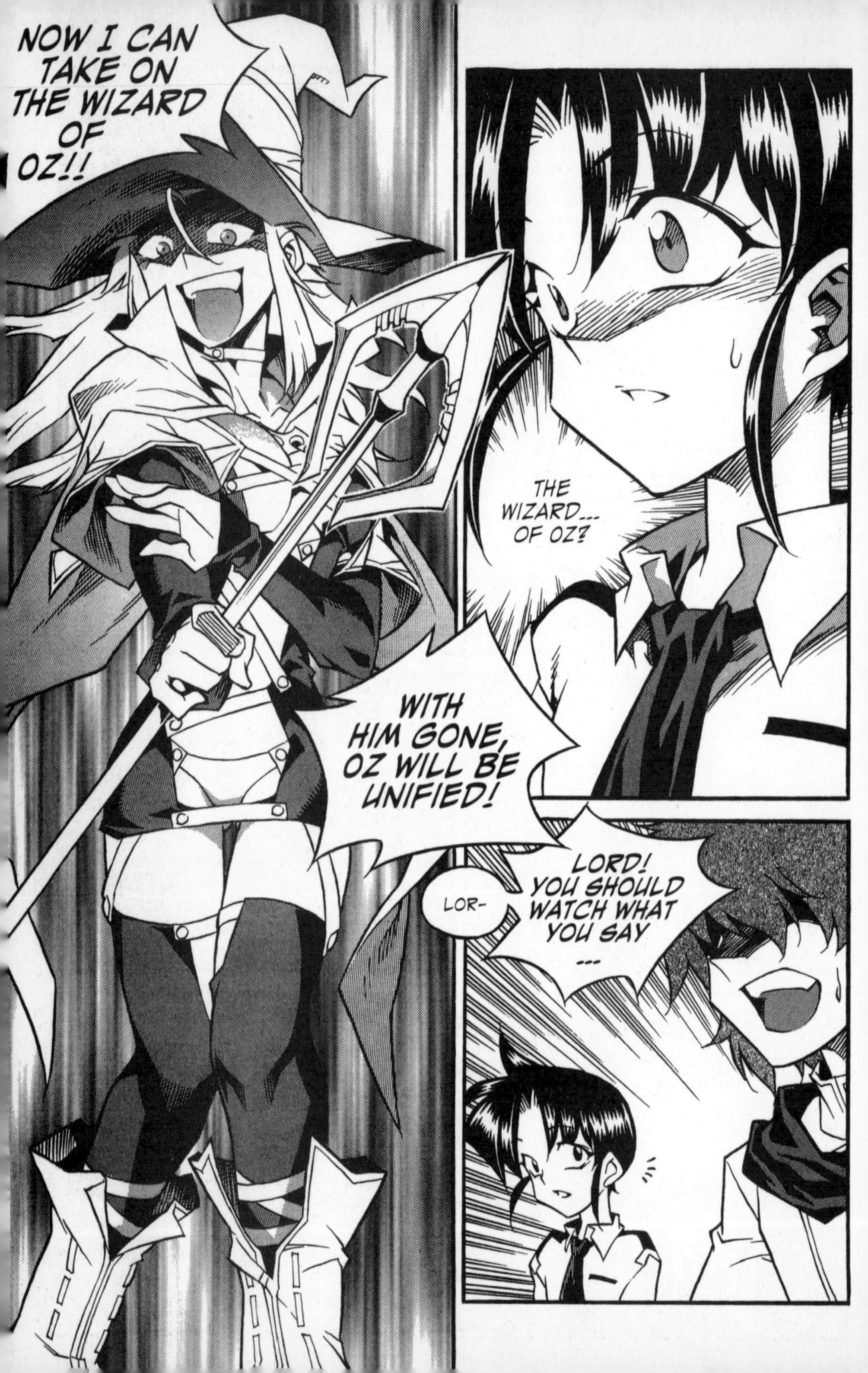
NOW I CAN TAKE ON THE WIZARD OF OZ!!
THE WIZARD... OF OZ?
WITH HIM GONE, OZ WILL BE UNIFIED!
LORD! YOU SHOULD WATCH WHAT YOU SAY ...
LOR-

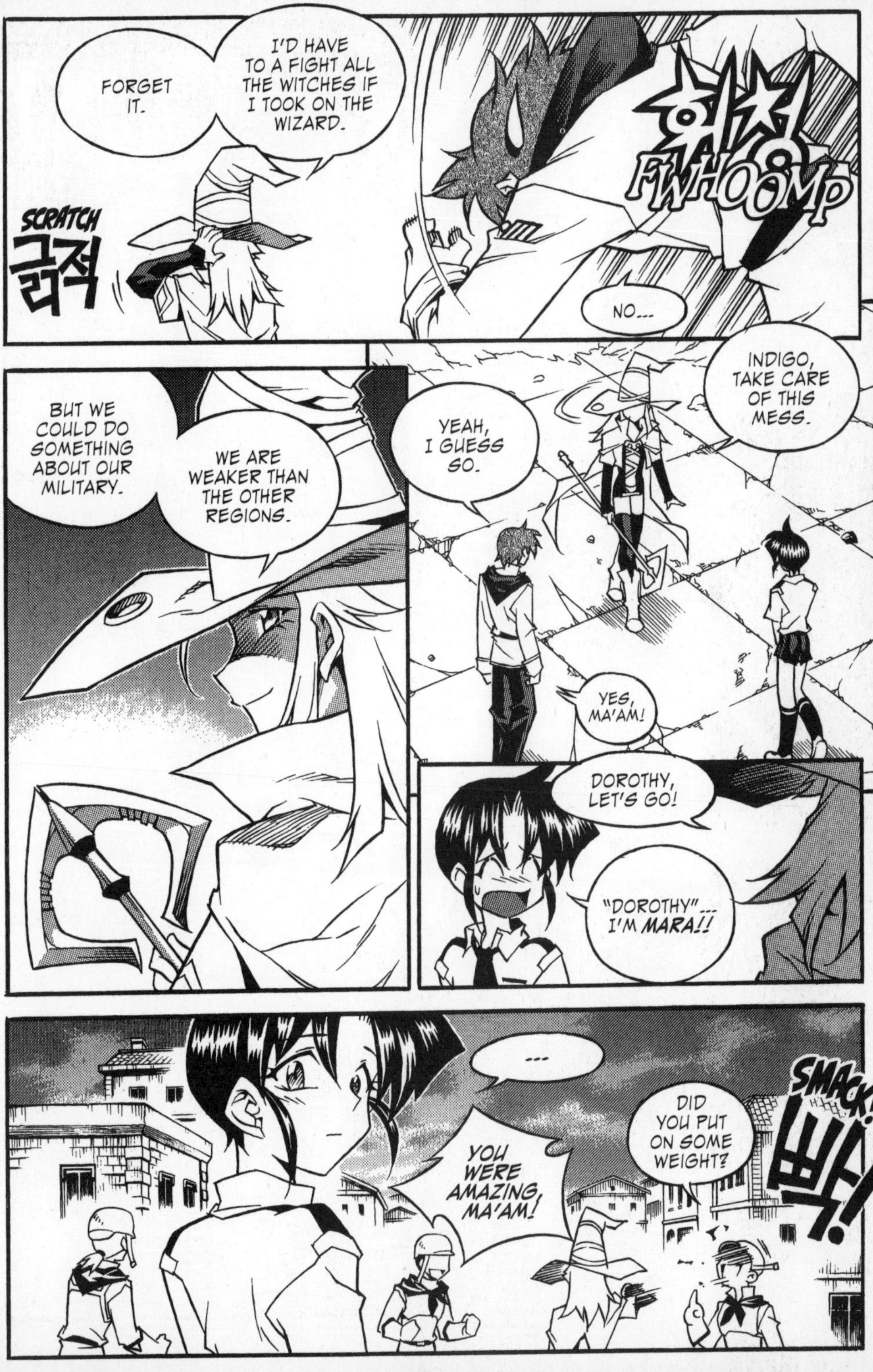
FORGET IT.
I'D HAVE TO A FIGHT ALL THE WITCHES IF I TOOK ON THE WIZARD.
SCRATCH
긁적
화악
FWHOOMP
NO...
INDIGO, TAKE CARE OF THIS MESS.
YEAH, I GUESS SO.
BUT WE COULD DO SOMETHING ABOUT OUR MILITARY.
WE ARE WEAKER THAN THE OTHER REGIONS.
YES, MA'AM!
DOROTHY, LET'S GO!
"DOROTHY"... I'M MARA!!
...
YOU WERE AMAZING, MA'AM!
DID YOU PUT ON SOME WEIGHT?
SMACK!
빡!

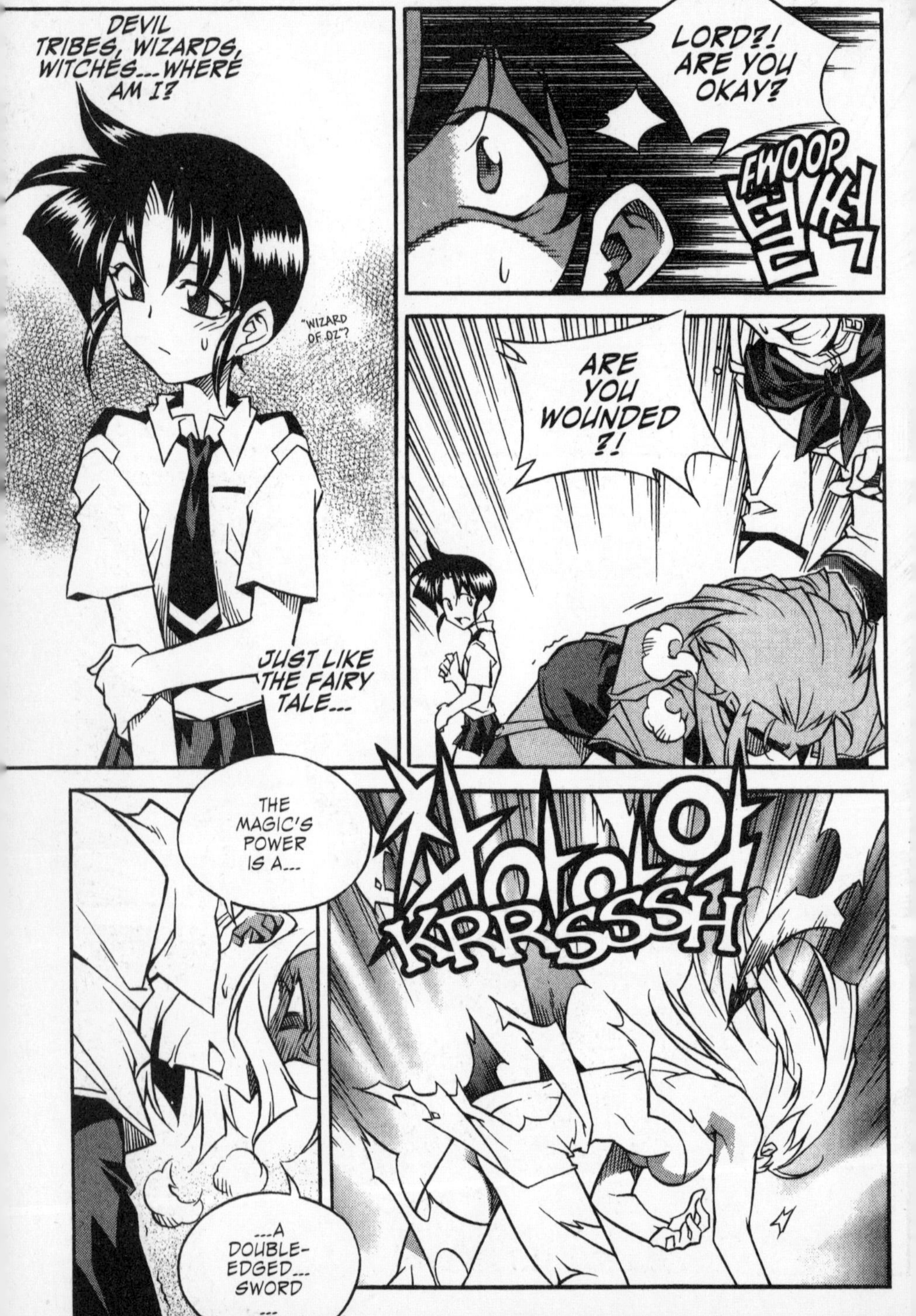
DEVIL TRIBES, WIZARDS, WITCHES... WHERE AM I?
"WIZARD OF OZ"?
JUST LIKE THE FAIRY TALE...
LORD?! ARE YOU OKAY?
FWOOP
ARE YOU WOUNDED ?!
THE MAGIC'S POWER IS A...
KRRSSSH
...A DOUBLE-EDGED... SWORD ...

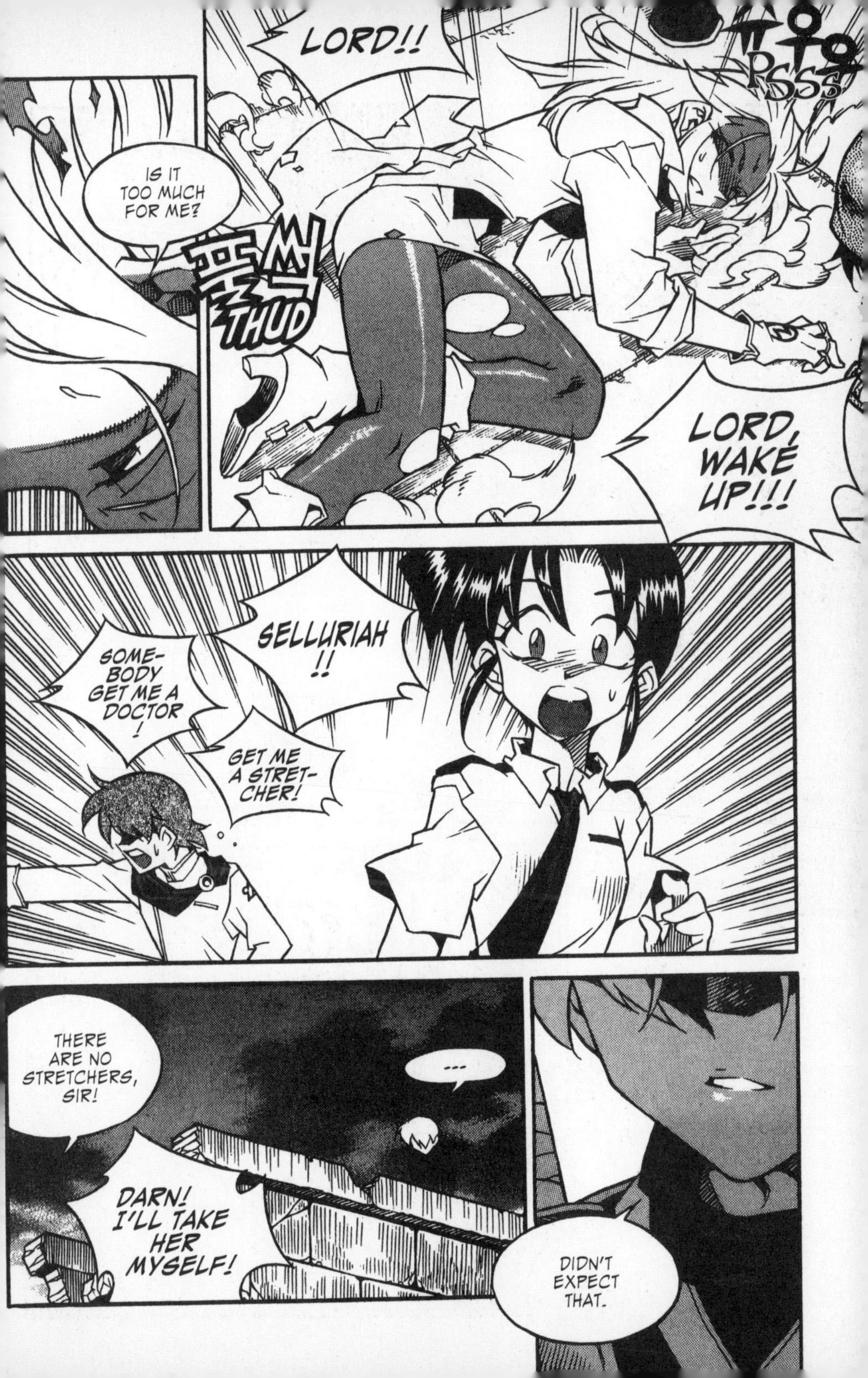
LORD!!
PSSS
IS IT TOO MUCH FOR ME?
THUD
LORD, WAKE UP!!!
SELLURIAH !!
SOMEBODY GET ME A DOCTOR!
GET ME A STRETCHER!
THERE ARE NO STRETCHERS, SIR!
...
DARN! I'LL TAKE HER MYSELF!
DIDN'T EXPECT THAT.

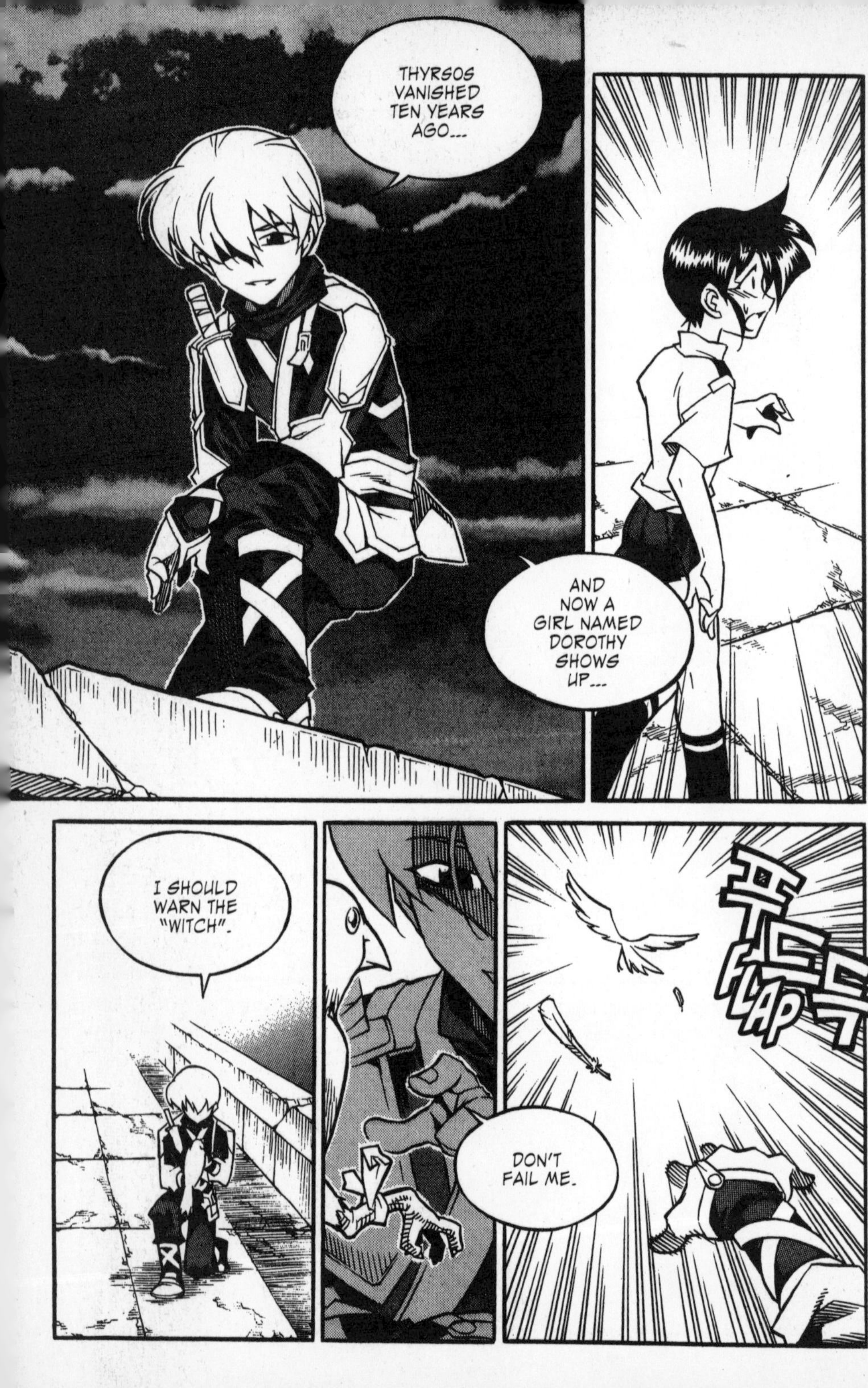
THYRSOS VANISHED TEN YEARS AGO...
AND NOW A GIRL NAMED DOROTHY SHOWS UP...
I SHOULD WARN THE "WITCH".
DON'T FAIL ME.
FLAP

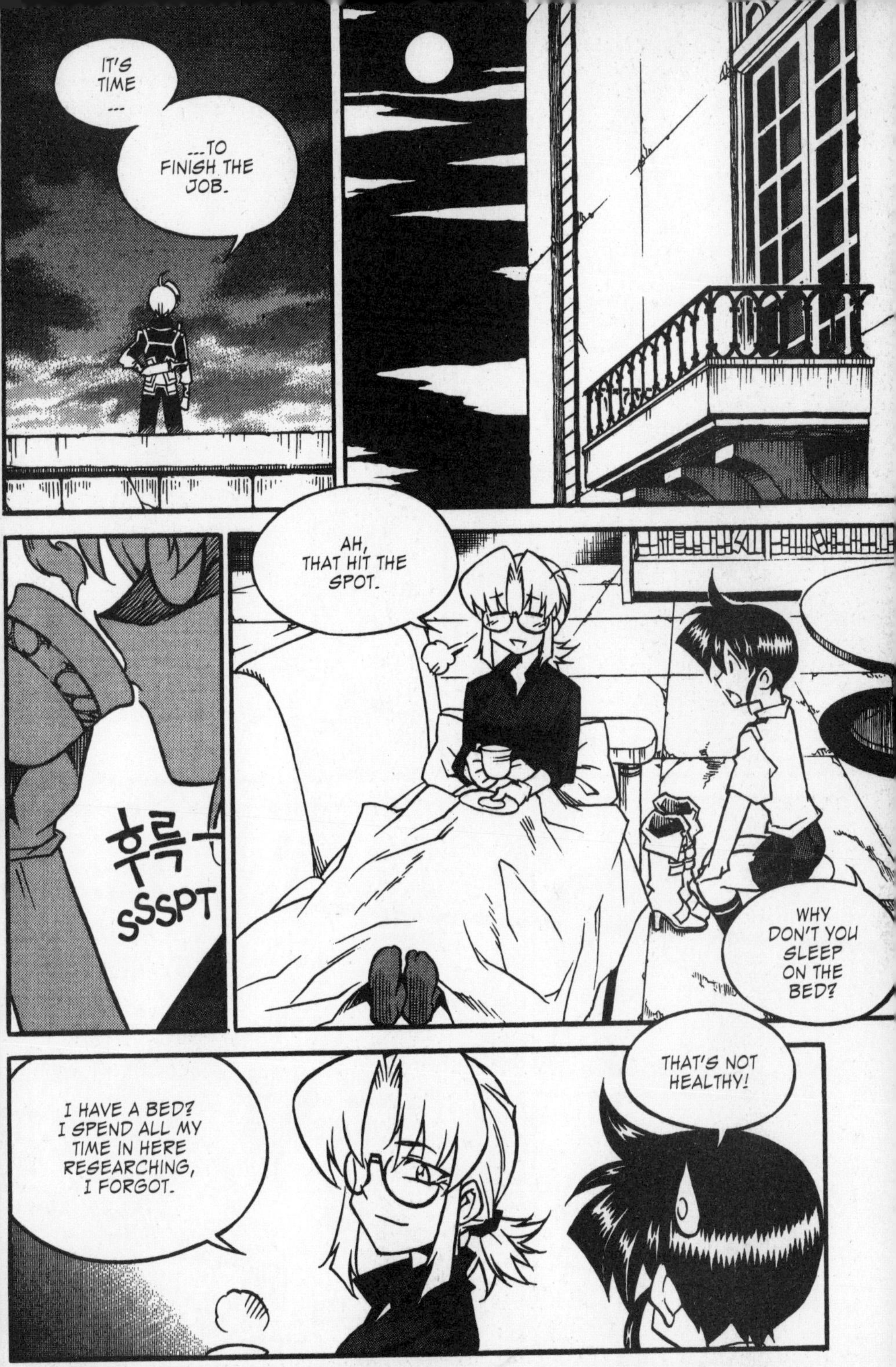

IT'S TIME ---
---TO FINISH THE JOB.
AH, THAT HIT THE SPOT.
후릅-
SSSPT
WHY DON'T YOU SLEEP ON THE BED?
THAT'S NOT HEALTHY!
I HAVE A BED? I SPEND ALL MY TIME IN HERE RESEARCHING, I FORGOT.

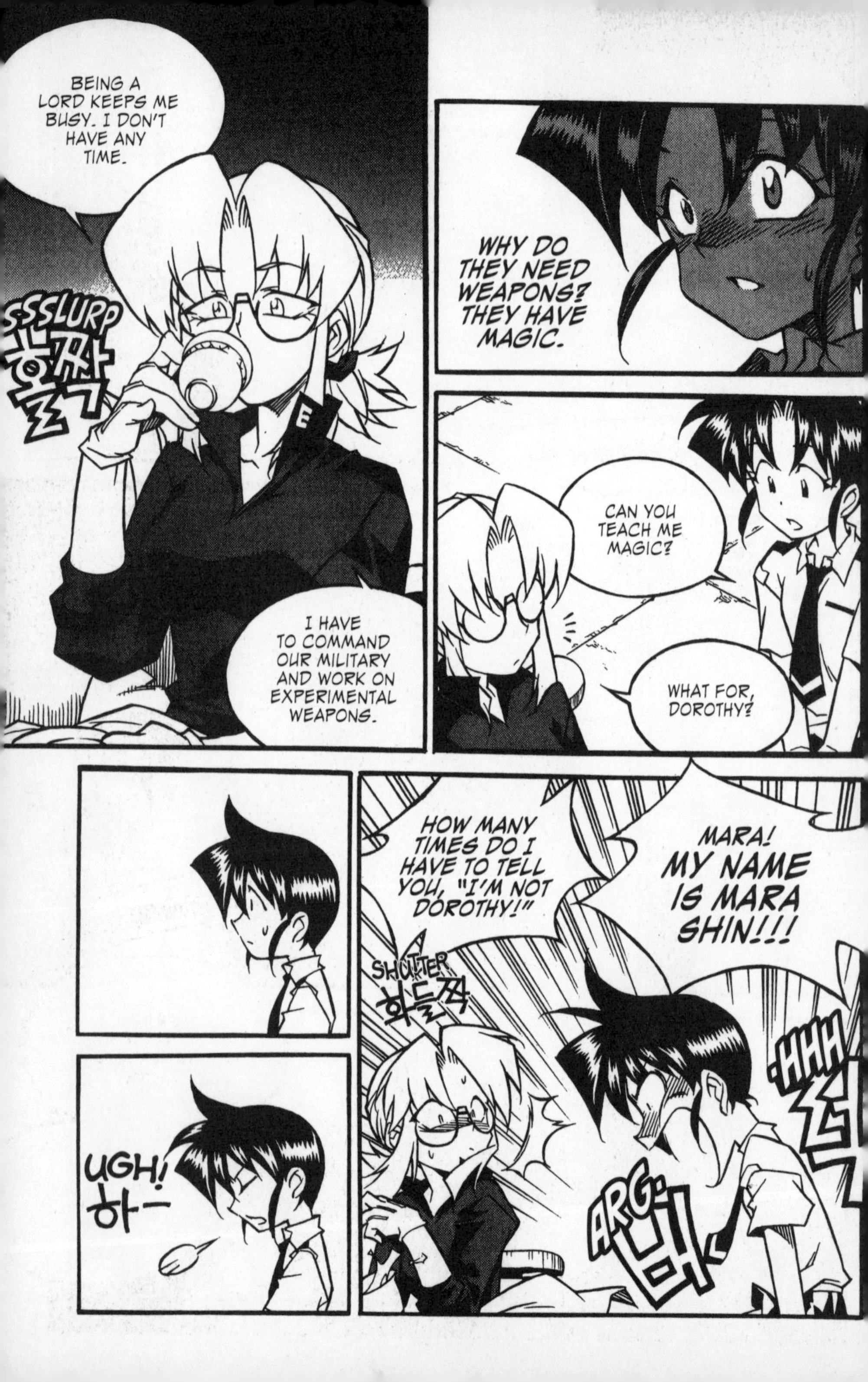

BEING A LORD KEEPS ME BUSY. I DON'T HAVE ANY TIME.
SSSLURP
I HAVE TO COMMAND OUR MILITARY AND WORK ON EXPERIMENTAL WEAPONS.
WHY DO THEY NEED WEAPONS? THEY HAVE MAGIC.
CAN YOU TEACH ME MAGIC?
WHAT FOR, DOROTHY?
UGH!
HOW MANY TIMES DO I HAVE TO TELL YOU, "I'M NOT DOROTHY!"
MARA! MY NAME IS MARA SHIN!!!
SHUTTER
ARG-HHH

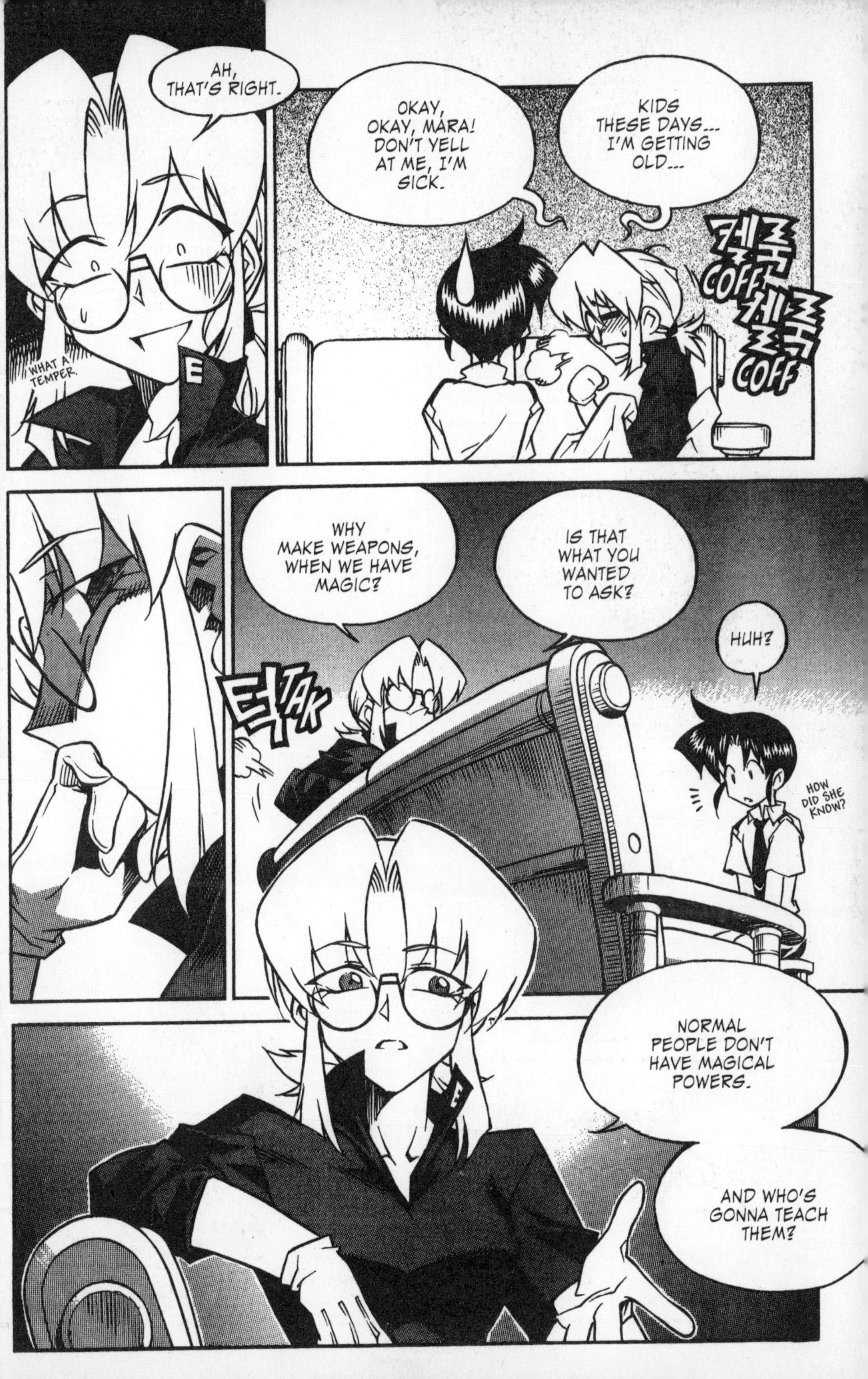

AH, THAT'S RIGHT.
WHAT A TEMPER.
OKAY, OKAY, MARA! DON'T YELL AT ME, I'M SICK.
KIDS THESE DAYS... I'M GETTING OLD...
켁 COFF
켁 COFF
WHY MAKE WEAPONS, WHEN WE HAVE MAGIC?
IS THAT WHAT YOU WANTED TO ASK?
HUH?
TAK
HOW DID SHE KNOW?
NORMAL PEOPLE DON'T HAVE MAGICAL POWERS.
AND WHO'S GONNA TEACH THEM?

B-BUT YOU JUST USED MAGIC.

NO, IT WASN'T REALLY MAGIC.

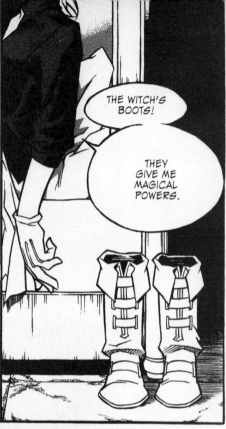

THE WITCH'S BOOTS!

THEY GIVE ME MAGICAL POWERS.

IT'S MORE LIKE THE POWER OF SCIENCE.

THOSE BOOTS?

ARE YOU A SCIENTIST OR A WITCH? OH, I FORGOT. YOU DON'T LIKE TO BE CALLED A WITCH!

TEN YEARS AGO, I WAS CALLED A WITCH.

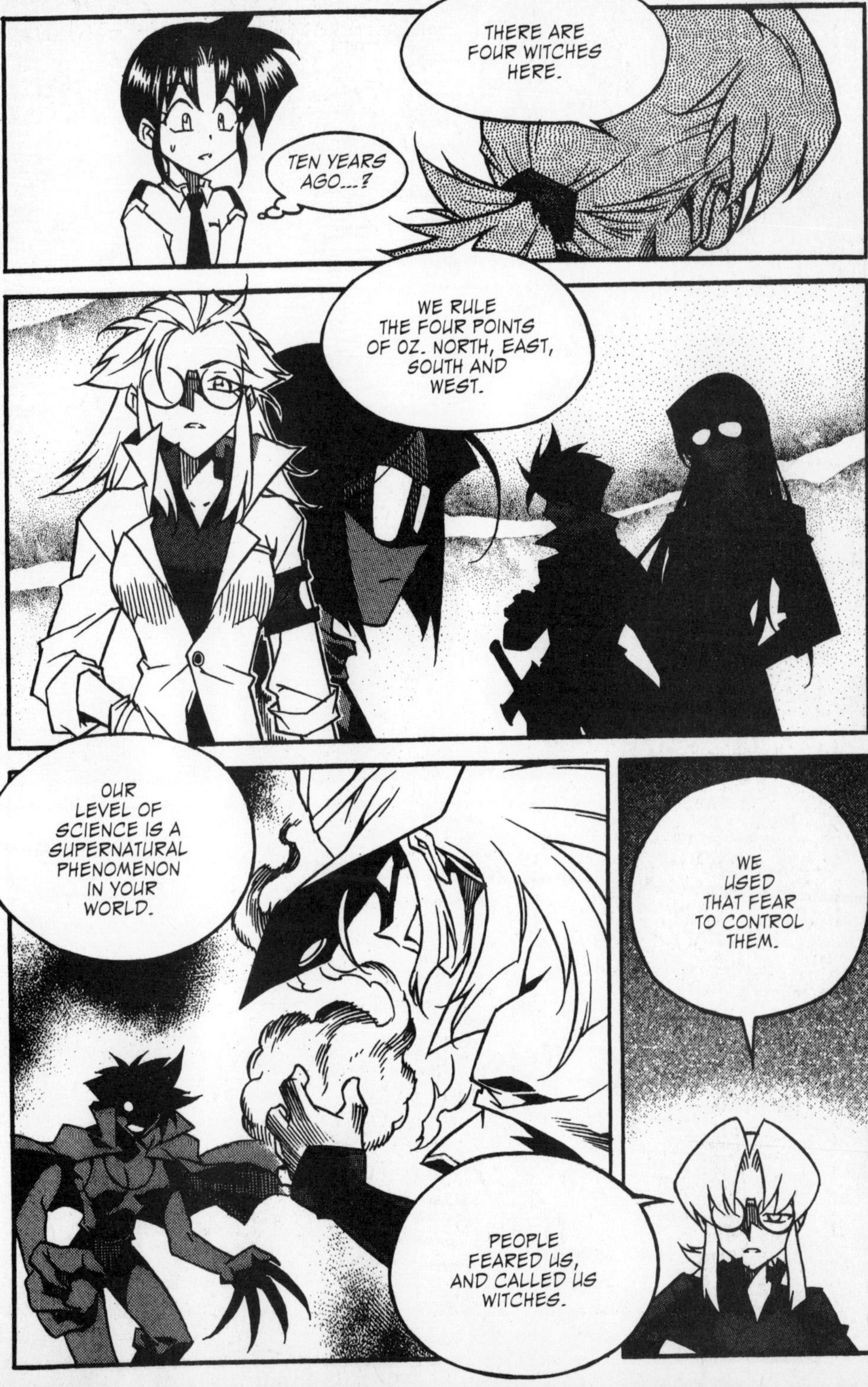

THERE ARE FOUR WITCHES HERE.
TEN YEARS AGO...?
WE RULE THE FOUR POINTS OF OZ. NORTH, EAST, SOUTH AND WEST.
OUR LEVEL OF SCIENCE IS A SUPERNATURAL PHENOMENON IN YOUR WORLD.
PEOPLE FEARED US, AND CALLED US WITCHES.
WE USED THAT FEAR TO CONTROL THEM.

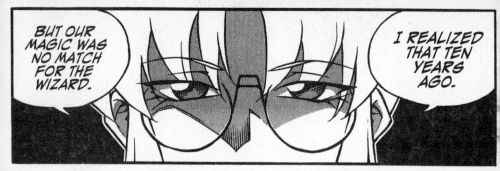

BUT OUR MAGIC WAS NO MATCH FOR THE WIZARD.

I REALIZED THAT TEN YEARS AGO.

THE W-WIZARD?

OZ

THE RULER OF OUR LAND.

PEOPLE CALLED HIM WIZARD, BUT I THOUGHT HE WAS A SCIENTIST LIKE ME.

I WAS FOOLISH TO THINK I COULD DEFEAT HIM!

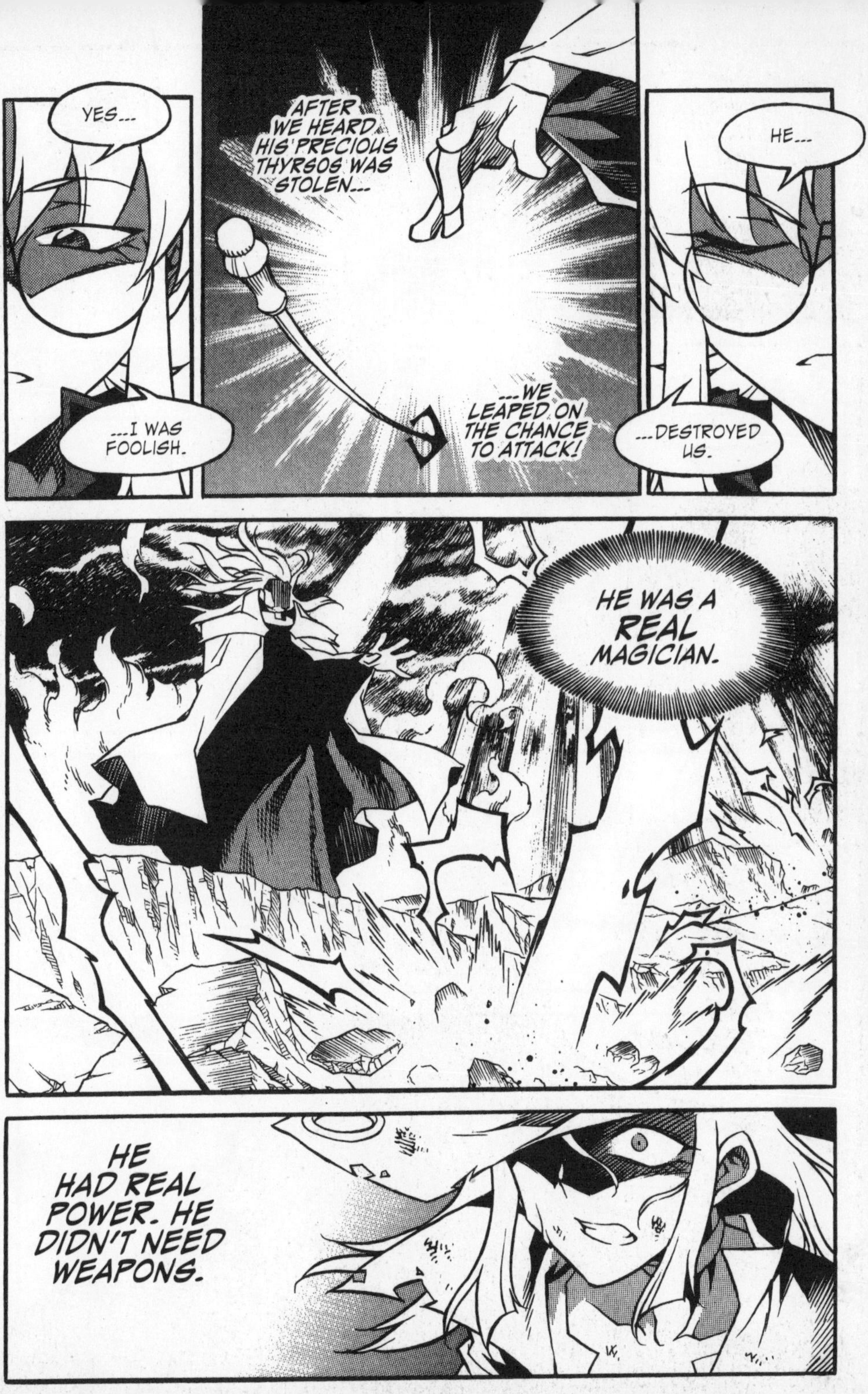
YES...
...I WAS FOOLISH.
AFTER WE HEARD HIS PRECIOUS THYRSOS WAS STOLEN...
...WE LEAPED ON THE CHANCE TO ATTACK!
HE...
...DESTROYED US.
HE WAS A REAL MAGICIAN.
HE HAD REAL POWER. HE DIDN'T NEED WEAPONS.

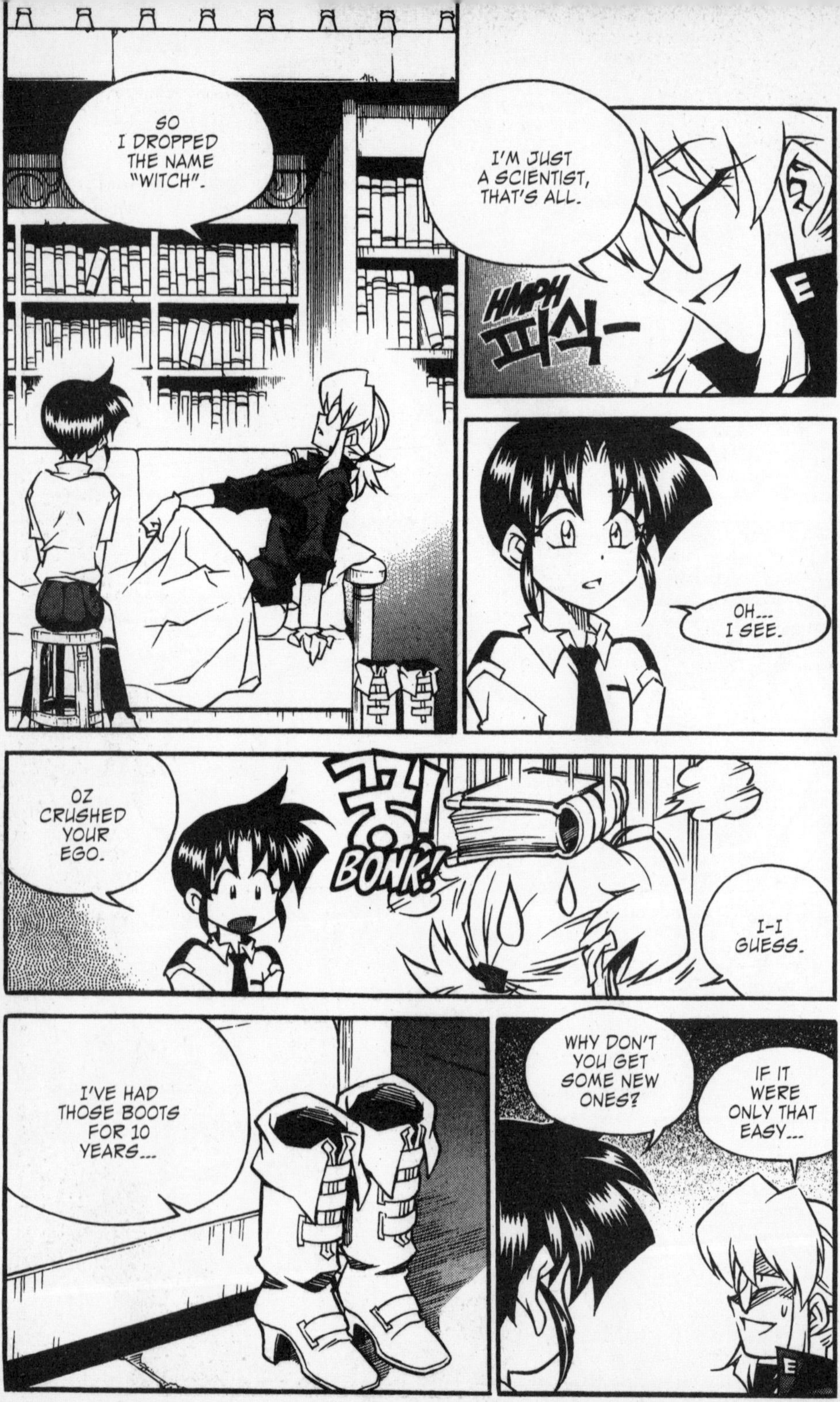
SO I DROPPED THE NAME "WITCH".
I'M JUST A SCIENTIST, THAT'S ALL.
HMPH
피식-
OH... I SEE.
OZ CRUSHED YOUR EGO.
쿵!
BONK!
I-I GUESS.
I'VE HAD THOSE BOOTS FOR 10 YEARS...
WHY DON'T YOU GET SOME NEW ONES?
IF IT WERE ONLY THAT EASY...

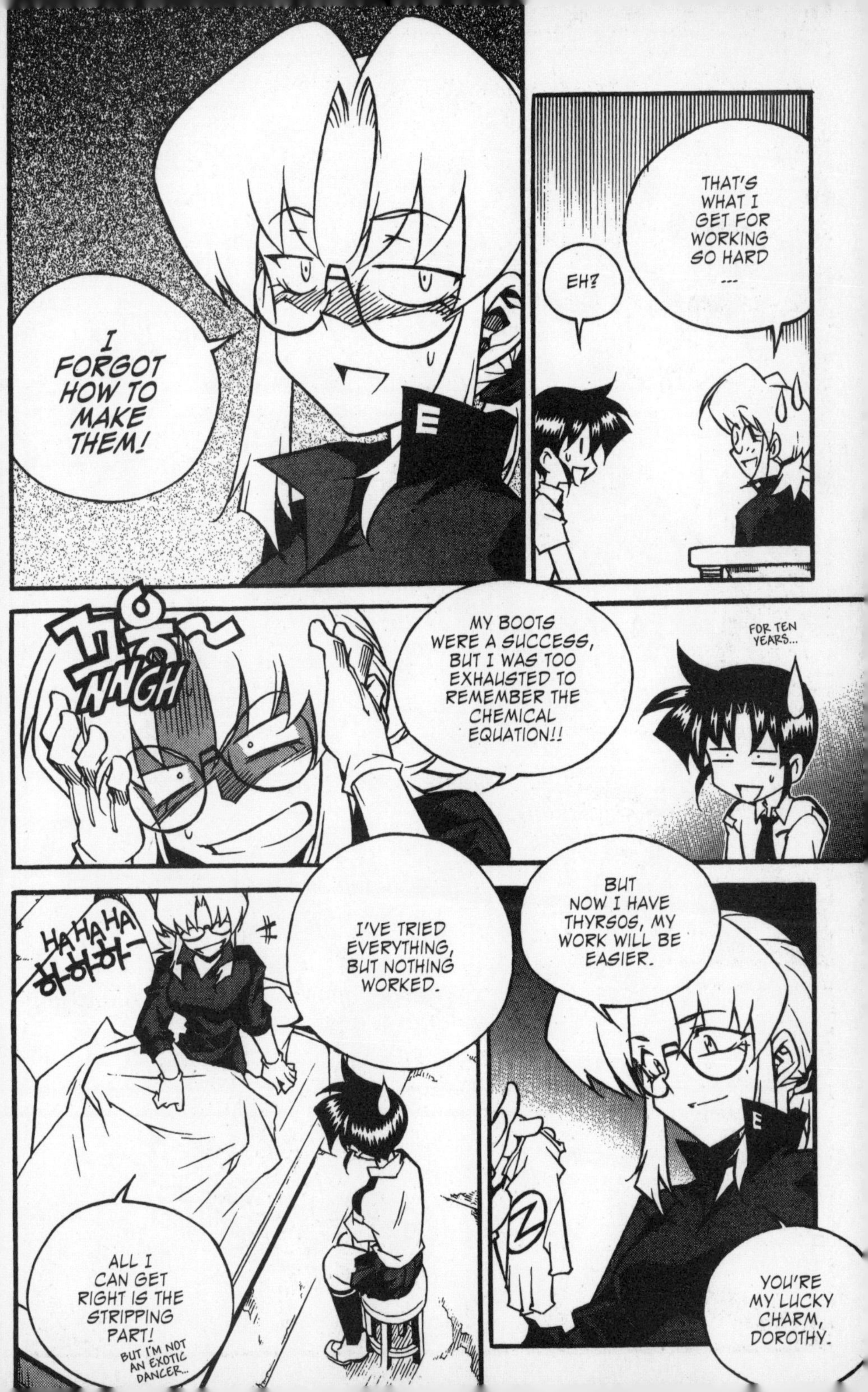
THAT'S WHAT I GET FOR WORKING SO HARD ---
EH?
I FORGOT HOW TO MAKE THEM!
FOR TEN YEARS...
MY BOOTS WERE A SUCCESS, BUT I WAS TOO EXHAUSTED TO REMEMBER THE CHEMICAL EQUATION!!
NNGH
I'VE TRIED EVERYTHING, BUT NOTHING WORKED.
HA HA HA
하하하
ALL I CAN GET RIGHT IS THE STRIPPING PART!
BUT I'M NOT AN EXOTIC DANCER...
BUT NOW I HAVE THYRSOS, MY WORK WILL BE EASIER.
YOU'RE MY LUCKY CHARM, DOROTHY.

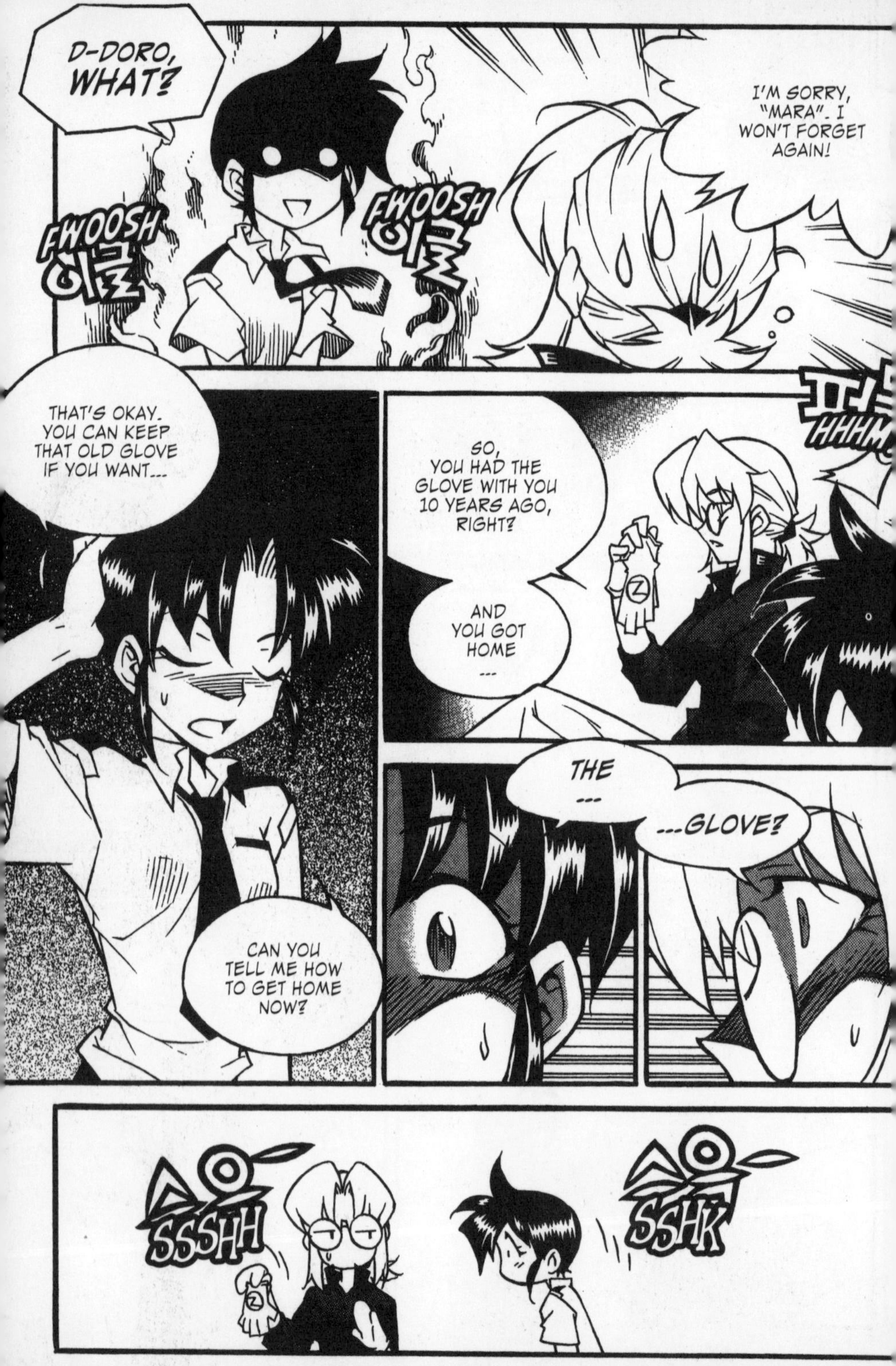
D-DORO, WHAT?
FWOOSH
이글
FWOOSH
이글
I'M SORRY, "MARA". I WON'T FORGET AGAIN!
THAT'S OKAY. YOU CAN KEEP THAT OLD GLOVE IF YOU WANT...
CAN YOU TELL ME HOW TO GET HOME NOW?
SO, YOU HAD THE GLOVE WITH YOU 10 YEARS AGO, RIGHT?
AND YOU GOT HOME ...
THE ...
...GLOVE?
SSSHH
SSHK

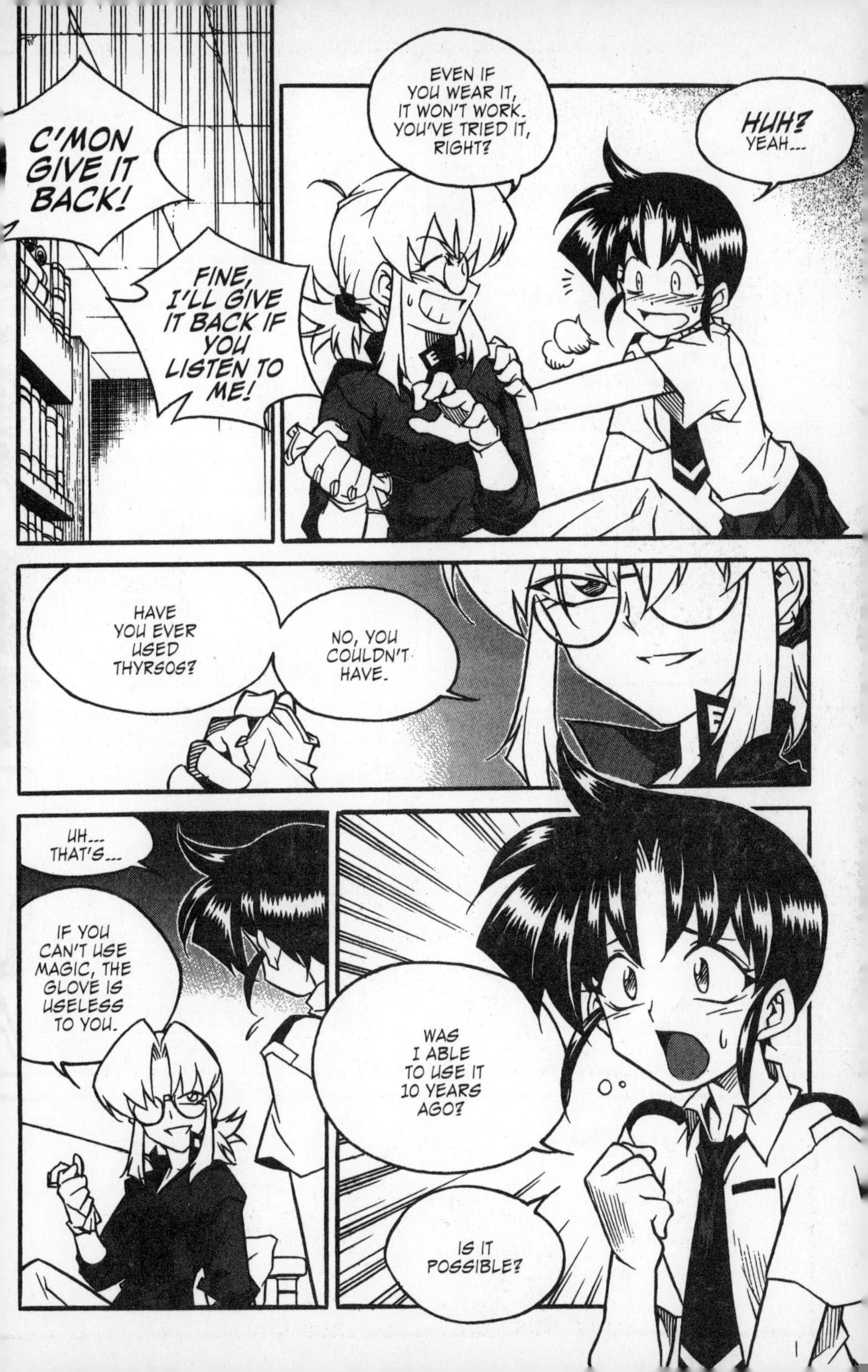
C'MON GIVE IT BACK!
EVEN IF YOU WEAR IT, IT WON'T WORK. YOU'VE TRIED IT, RIGHT?
HUH? YEAH...
FINE, I'LL GIVE IT BACK IF YOU LISTEN TO ME!
HAVE YOU EVER USED THYRSOS?
NO, YOU COULDN'T HAVE.
UH... THAT'S...
IF YOU CAN'T USE MAGIC, THE GLOVE IS USELESS TO YOU.
WAS I ABLE TO USE IT 10 YEARS AGO?
IS IT POSSIBLE?

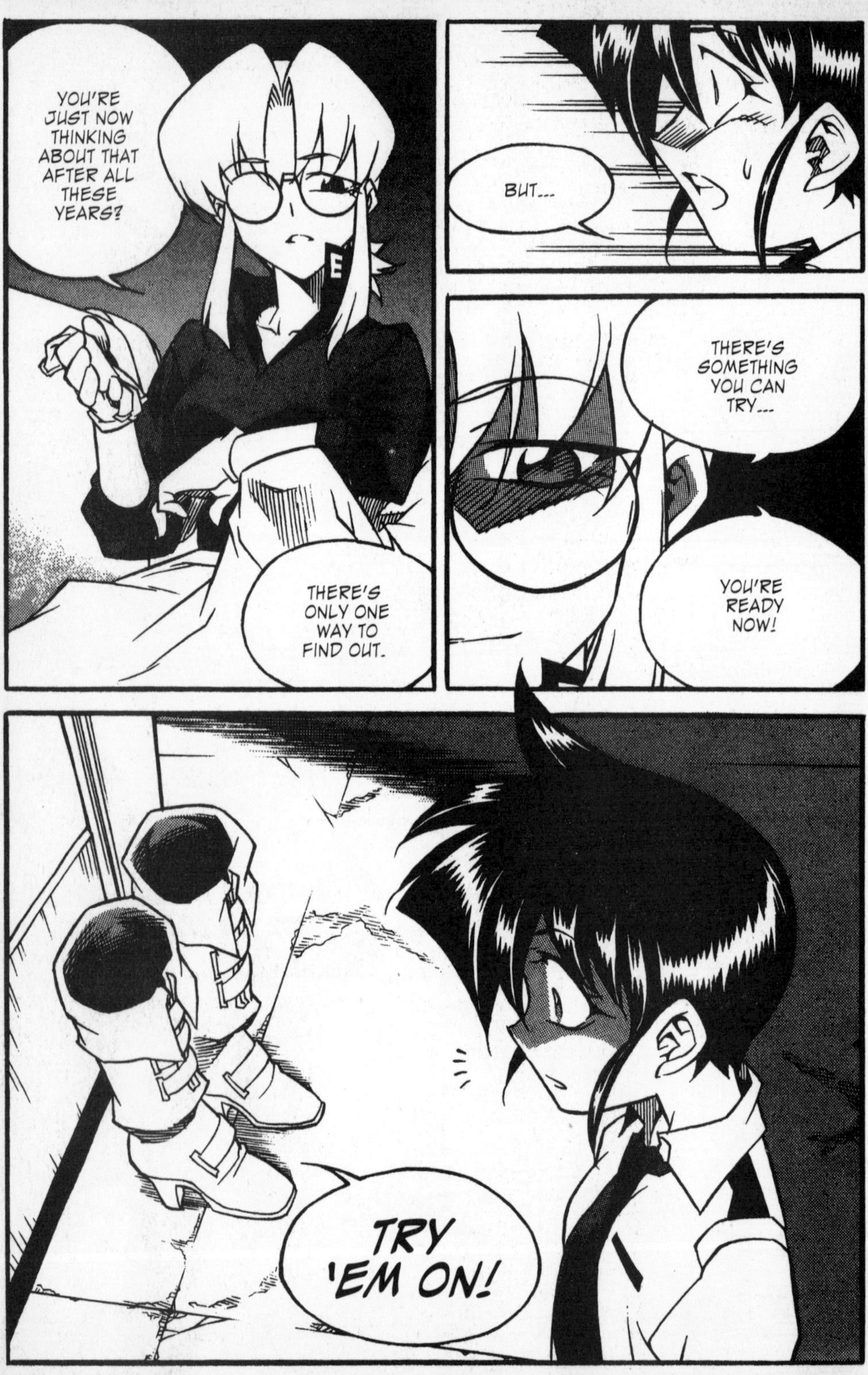
YOU'RE JUST NOW THINKING ABOUT THAT AFTER ALL THESE YEARS?
BUT...
THERE'S ONLY ONE WAY TO FIND OUT.
THERE'S SOMETHING YOU CAN TRY...
YOU'RE READY NOW!
TRY 'EM ON!

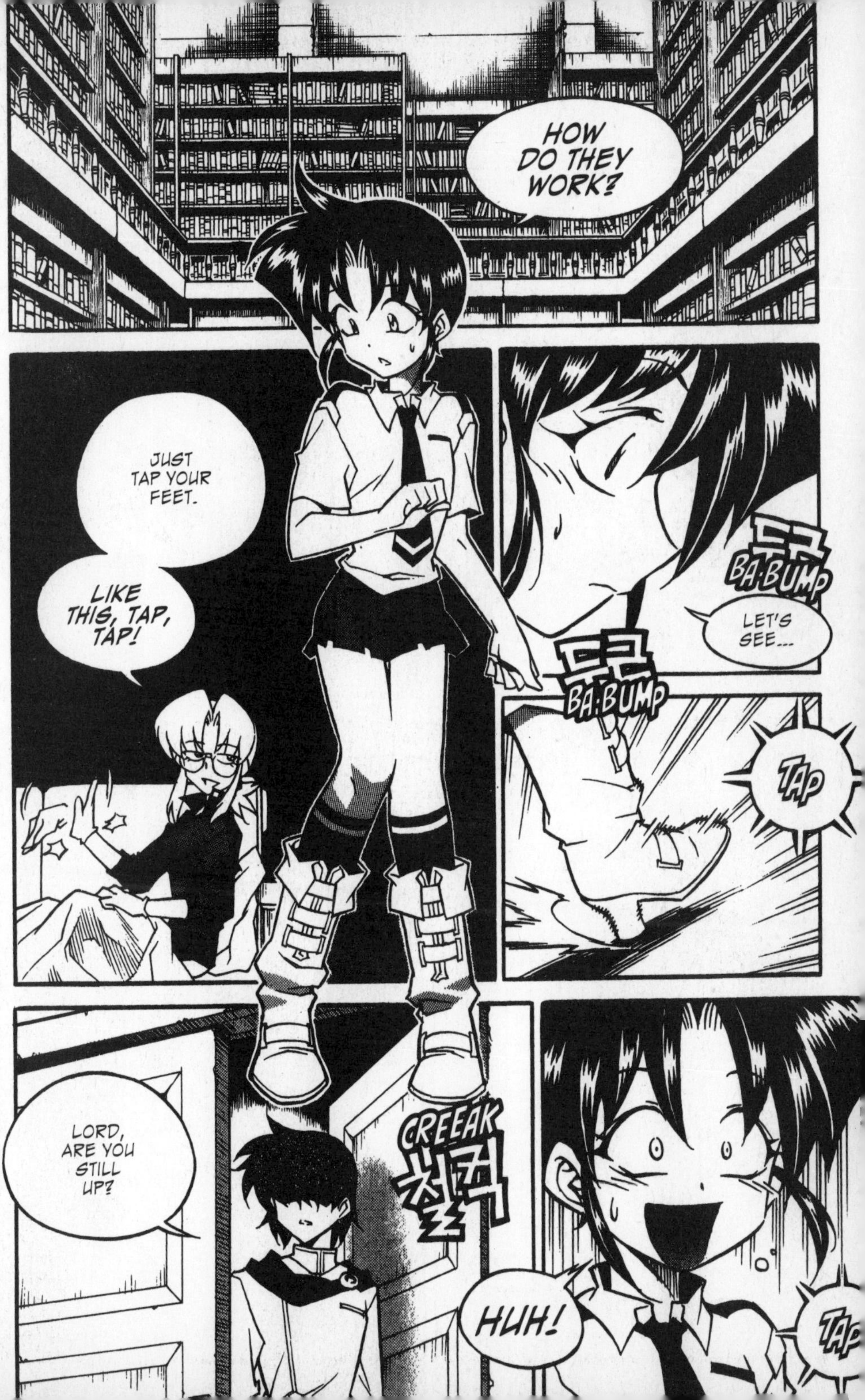
HOW DO THEY WORK?
JUST TAP YOUR FEET.
LIKE THIS, TAP, TAP!
BA-BUMP
LET'S SEE...
BA-BUMP
TAP
LORD, ARE YOU STILL UP?
CREEAK
HUH!
TAP

Step 10 LEAVE!

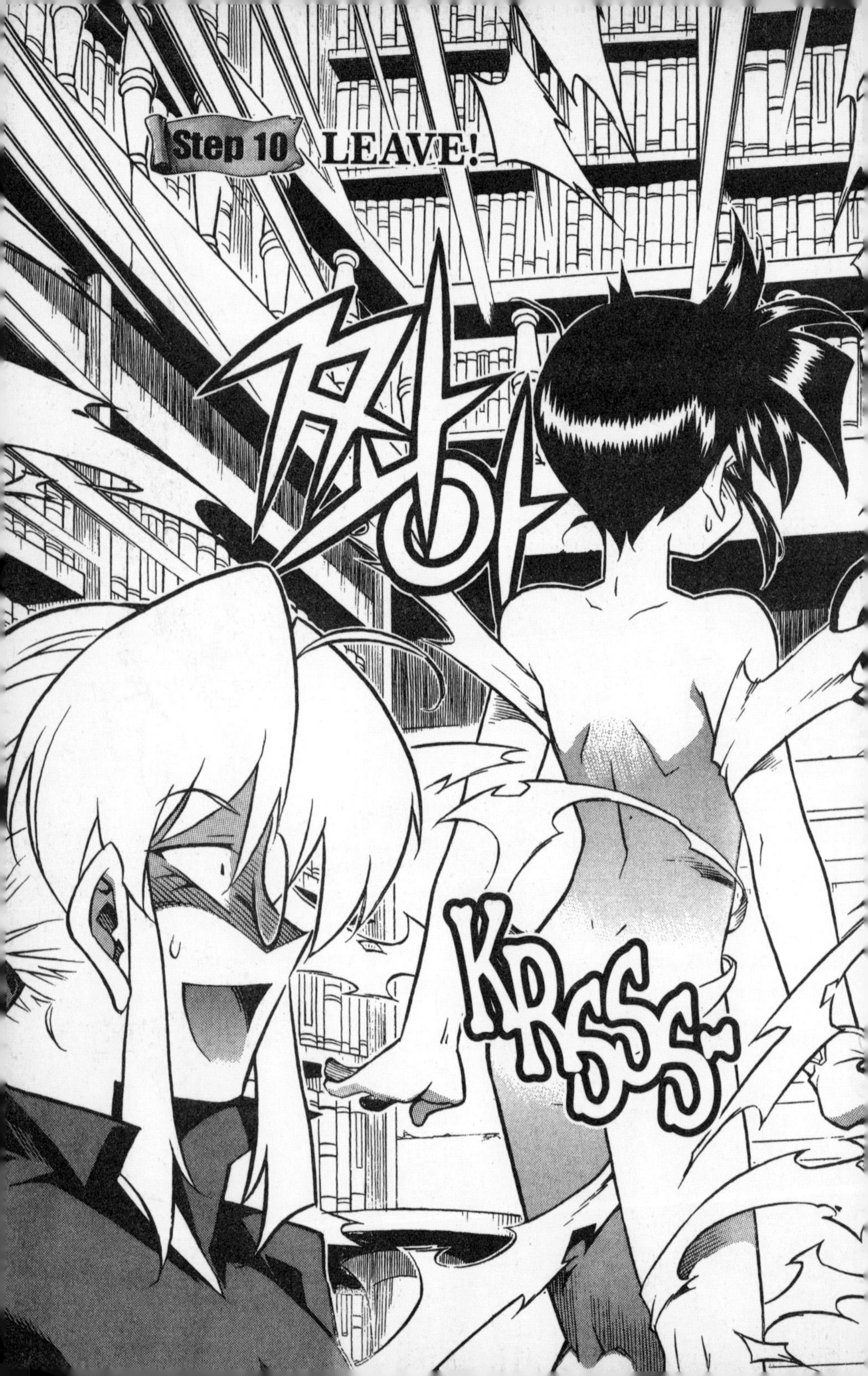
KRSSS

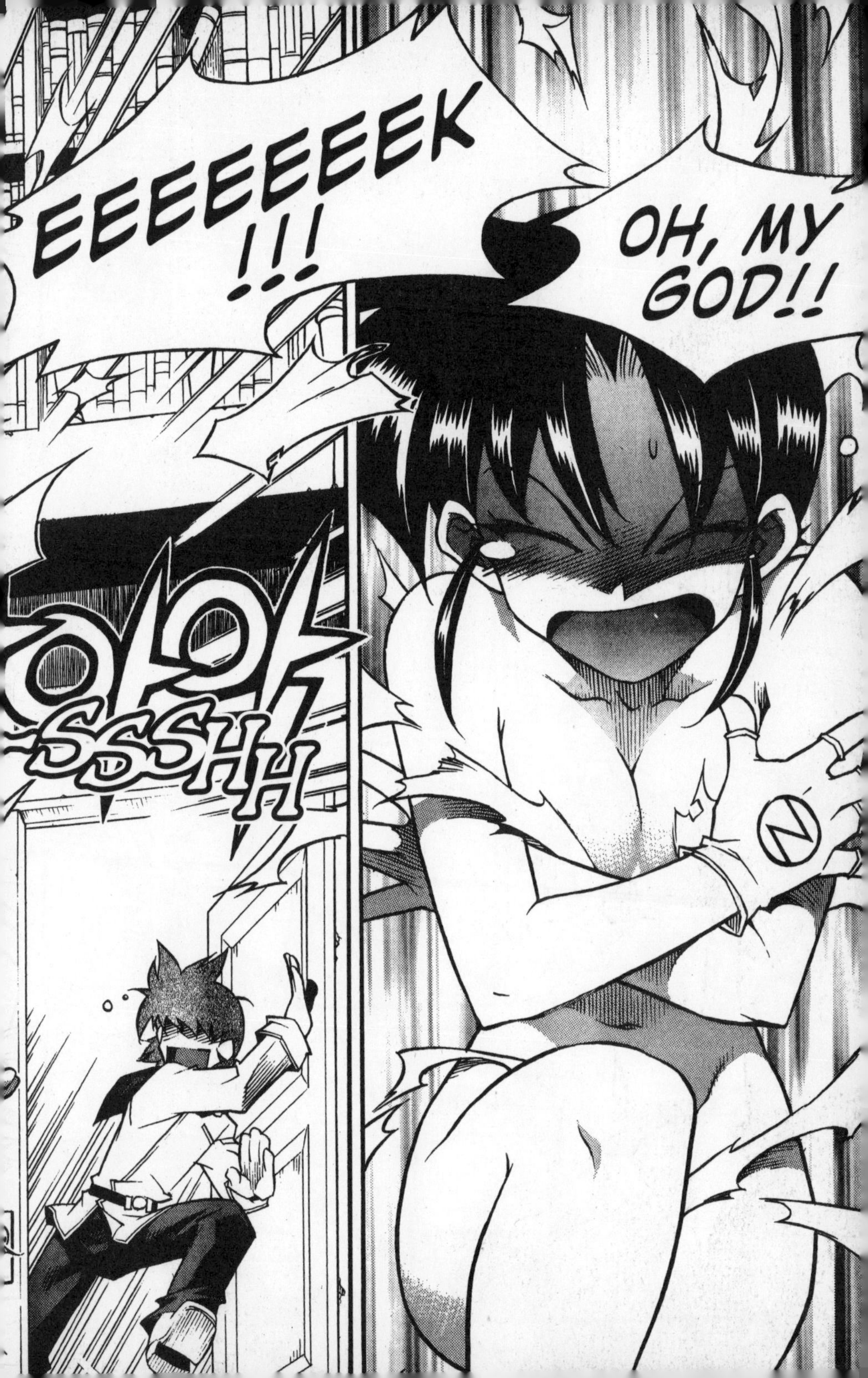
OH, MY GOD!!
EEEEEEEEK !!!
SSSHH

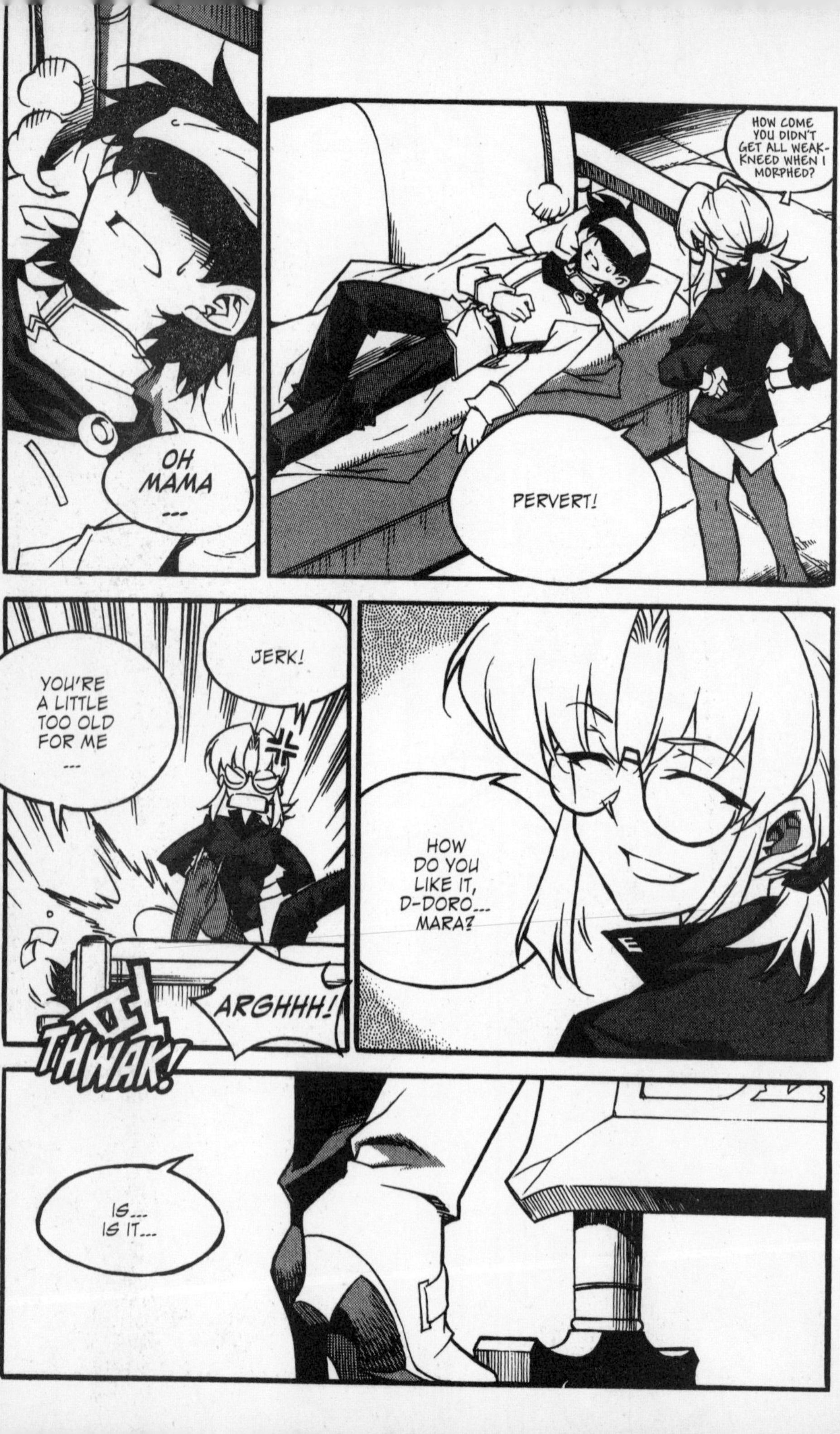
HOW COME YOU DIDN'T GET ALL WEAK-KNEED WHEN I MORPHED?
OH MAMA ...
PERVERT!
JERK!
YOU'RE A LITTLE TOO OLD FOR ME ...
ARGHHH!
THWAK!
HOW DO YOU LIKE IT, D-DORO... MARA?
IS... IS IT...

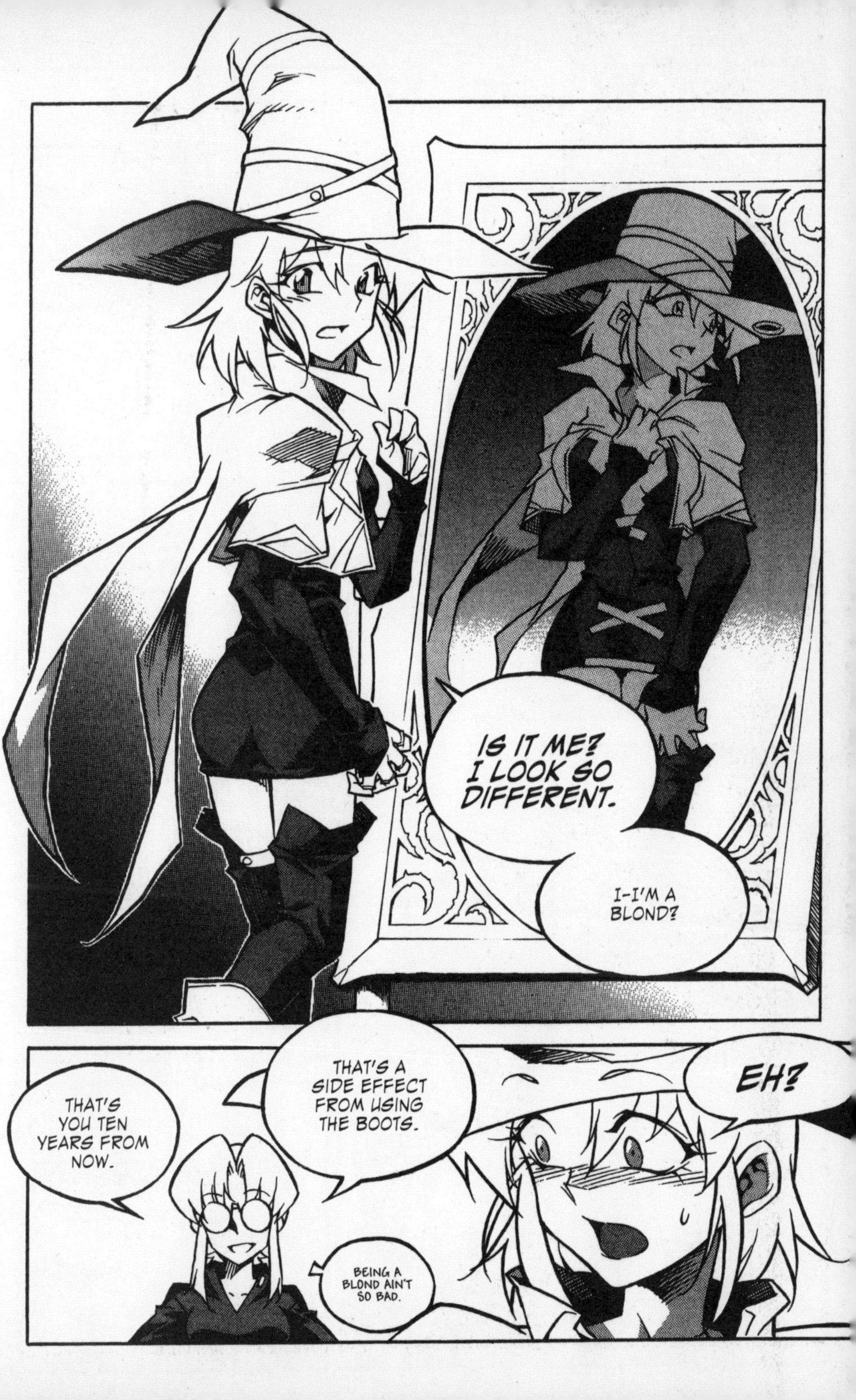
IS IT ME? I LOOK SO DIFFERENT.
I-I'M A BLOND?
EH?
THAT'S A SIDE EFFECT FROM USING THE BOOTS.
THAT'S YOU TEN YEARS FROM NOW.
BEING A BLOND AIN'T SO BAD.

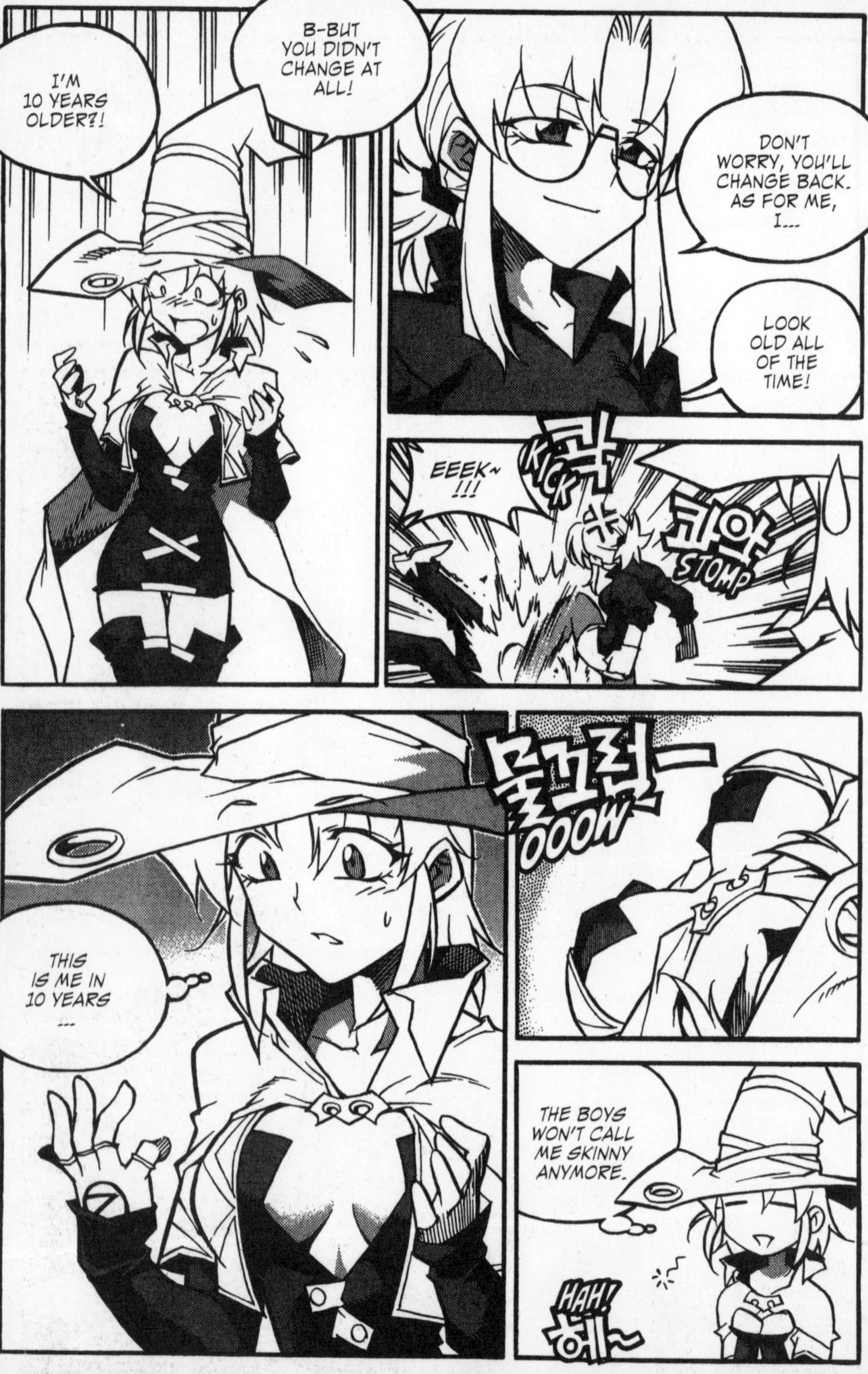
I'M 10 YEARS OLDER?!
B-BUT YOU DIDN'T CHANGE AT ALL!
DON'T WORRY, YOU'LL CHANGE BACK. AS FOR ME, I...
LOOK OLD ALL OF THE TIME!
EEEK~ !!!
KICK
STOMP
OOOW
THIS IS ME IN 10 YEARS ...
THE BOYS WON'T CALL ME SKINNY ANYMORE.
HAH!
헤~

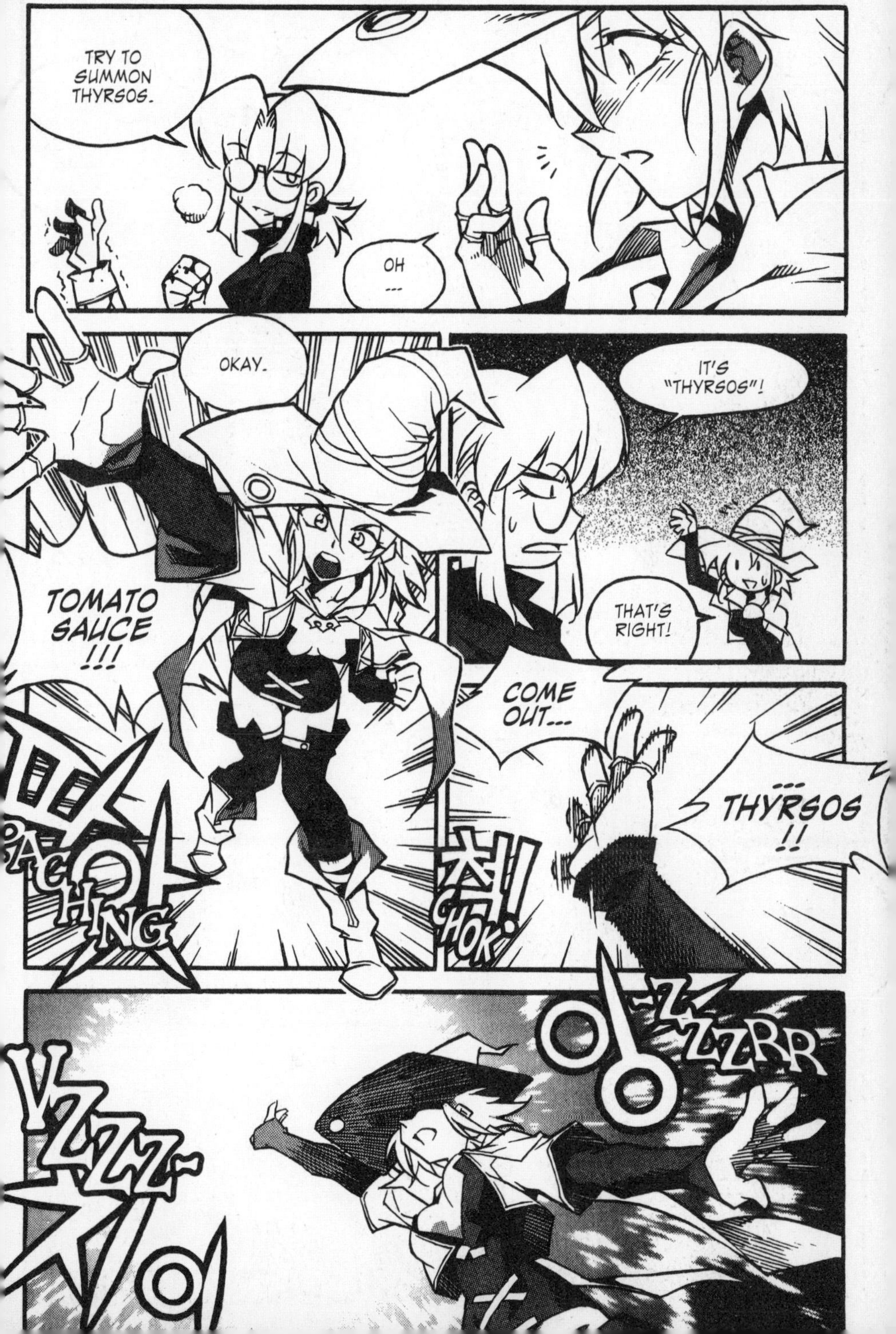
TRY TO SUMMON THYRSOS.
OH ...
OKAY.
TOMATO SAUCE !!!
PACHING
IT'S "THYRSOS"!
THAT'S RIGHT!
COME OUT...
...THYRSOS !!
CHOK!
VZZZ
ZZZRR

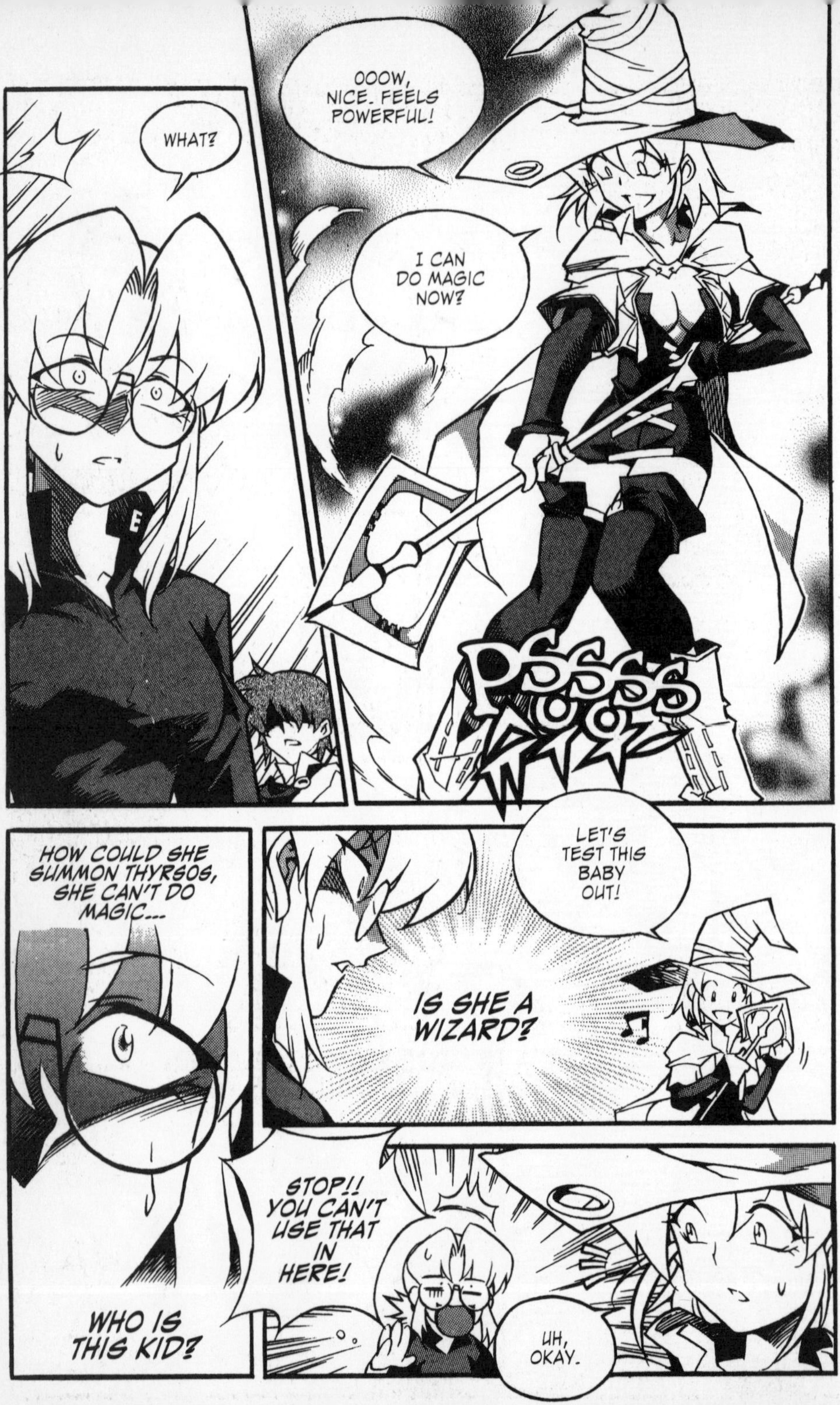
WHAT?
OOOW, NICE. FEELS POWERFUL!
I CAN DO MAGIC NOW?
PSSSS
HOW COULD SHE SUMMON THYRSOS, SHE CAN'T DO MAGIC...
LET'S TEST THIS BABY OUT!
IS SHE A WIZARD?
STOP!! YOU CAN'T USE THAT IN HERE!
UH, OKAY.
WHO IS THIS KID?

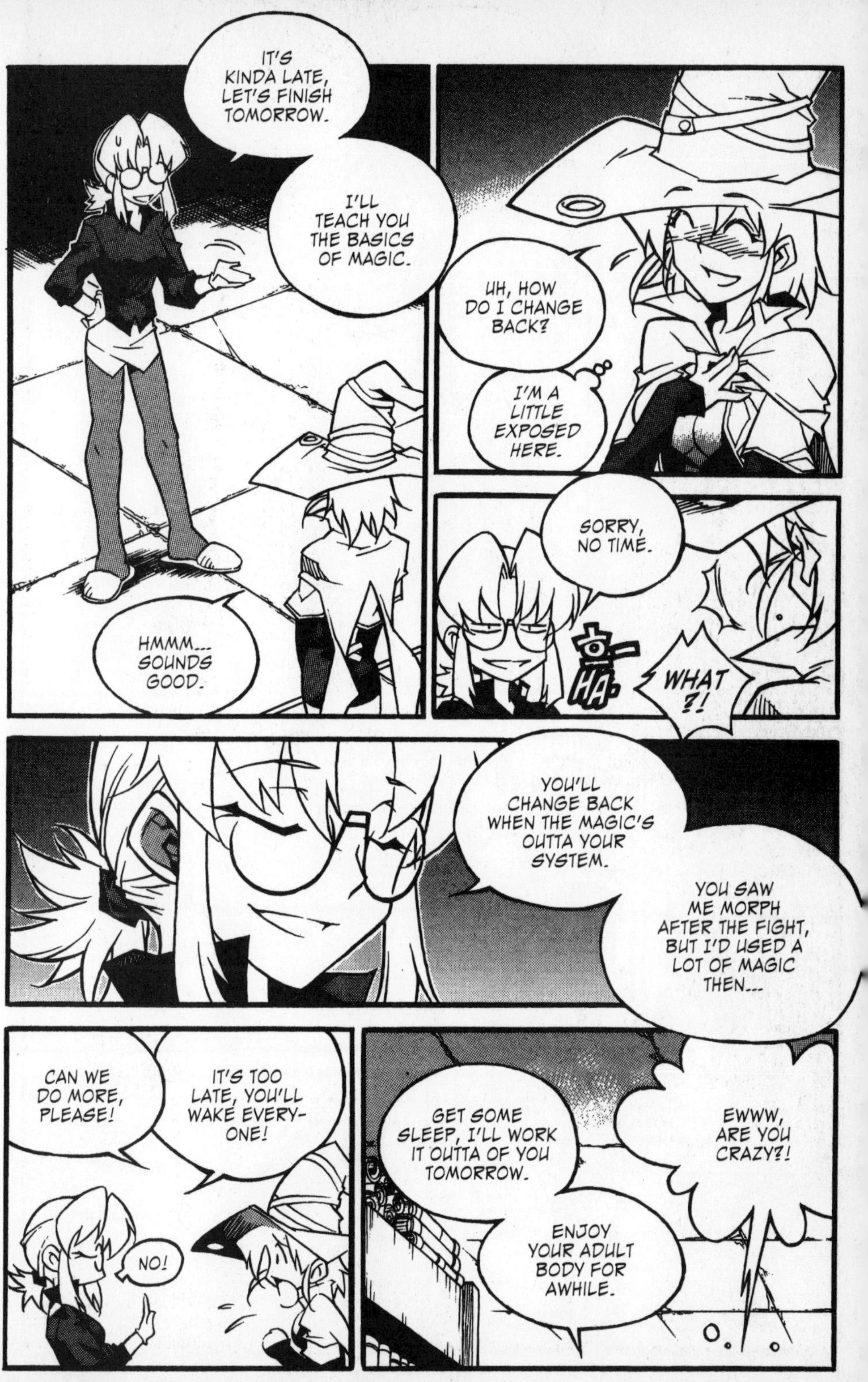
IT'S KINDA LATE, LET'S FINISH TOMORROW.
I'LL TEACH YOU THE BASICS OF MAGIC.
HMMM... SOUNDS GOOD.
UH, HOW DO I CHANGE BACK?
I'M A LITTLE EXPOSED HERE.
SORRY, NO TIME.
HA
WHAT ?!
YOU'LL CHANGE BACK WHEN THE MAGIC'S OUTTA YOUR SYSTEM.
YOU SAW ME MORPH AFTER THE FIGHT, BUT I'D USED A LOT OF MAGIC THEN...
CAN WE DO MORE, PLEASE!
IT'S TOO LATE, YOU'LL WAKE EVERY-ONE!
NO!
GET SOME SLEEP, I'LL WORK IT OUTTA OF YOU TOMORROW.
ENJOY YOUR ADULT BODY FOR AWHILE.
EWWW, ARE YOU CRAZY?!

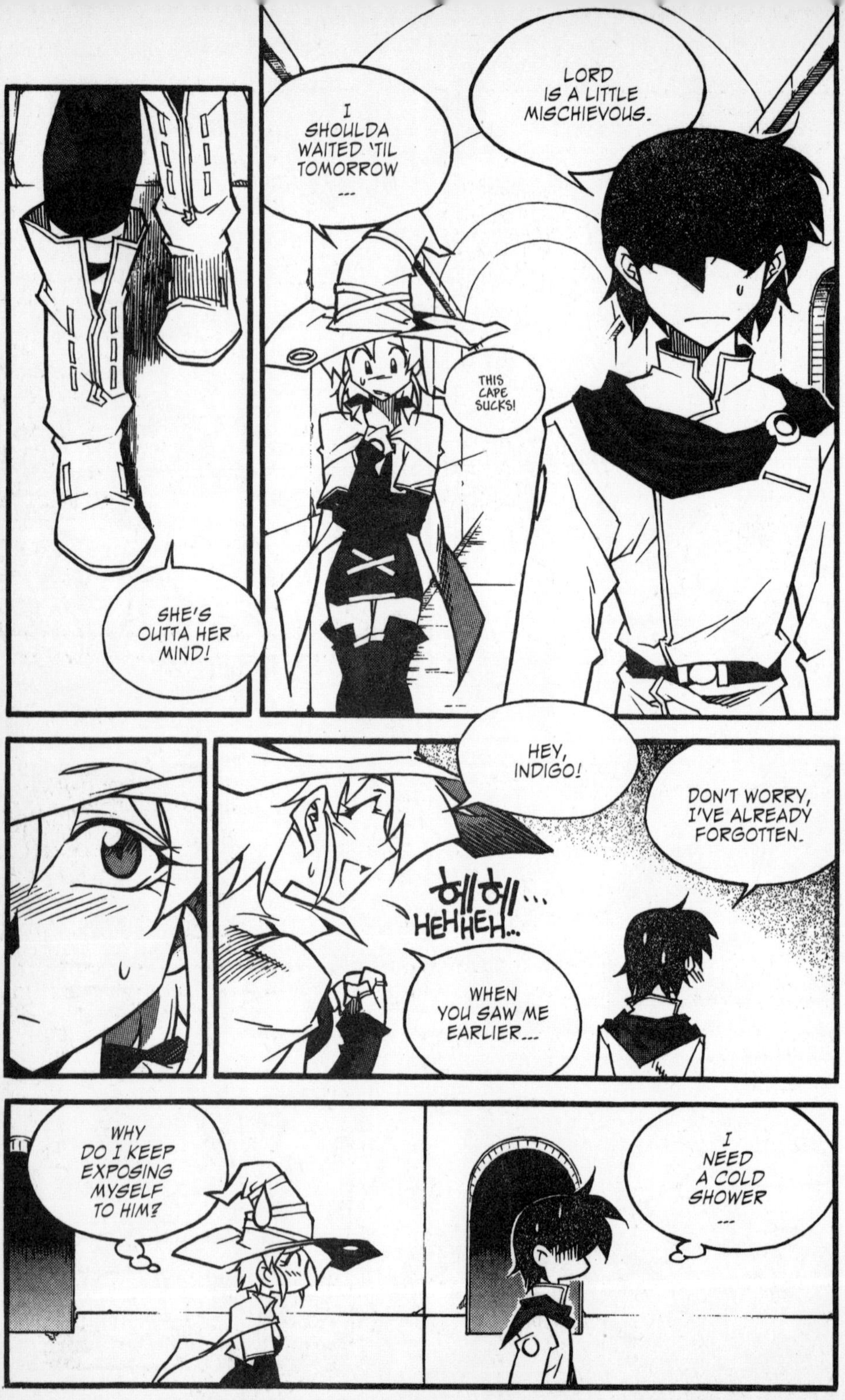
LORD IS A LITTLE MISCHIEVOUS.
I SHOULDA WAITED 'TIL TOMORROW ...
THIS CAPE SUCKS!
SHE'S OUTTA HER MIND!
HEY, INDIGO!
DON'T WORRY, I'VE ALREADY FORGOTTEN.
헤헤...
HEHHEH...
WHEN YOU SAW ME EARLIER...
I NEED A COLD SHOWER ...
WHY DO I KEEP EXPOSING MYSELF TO HIM?

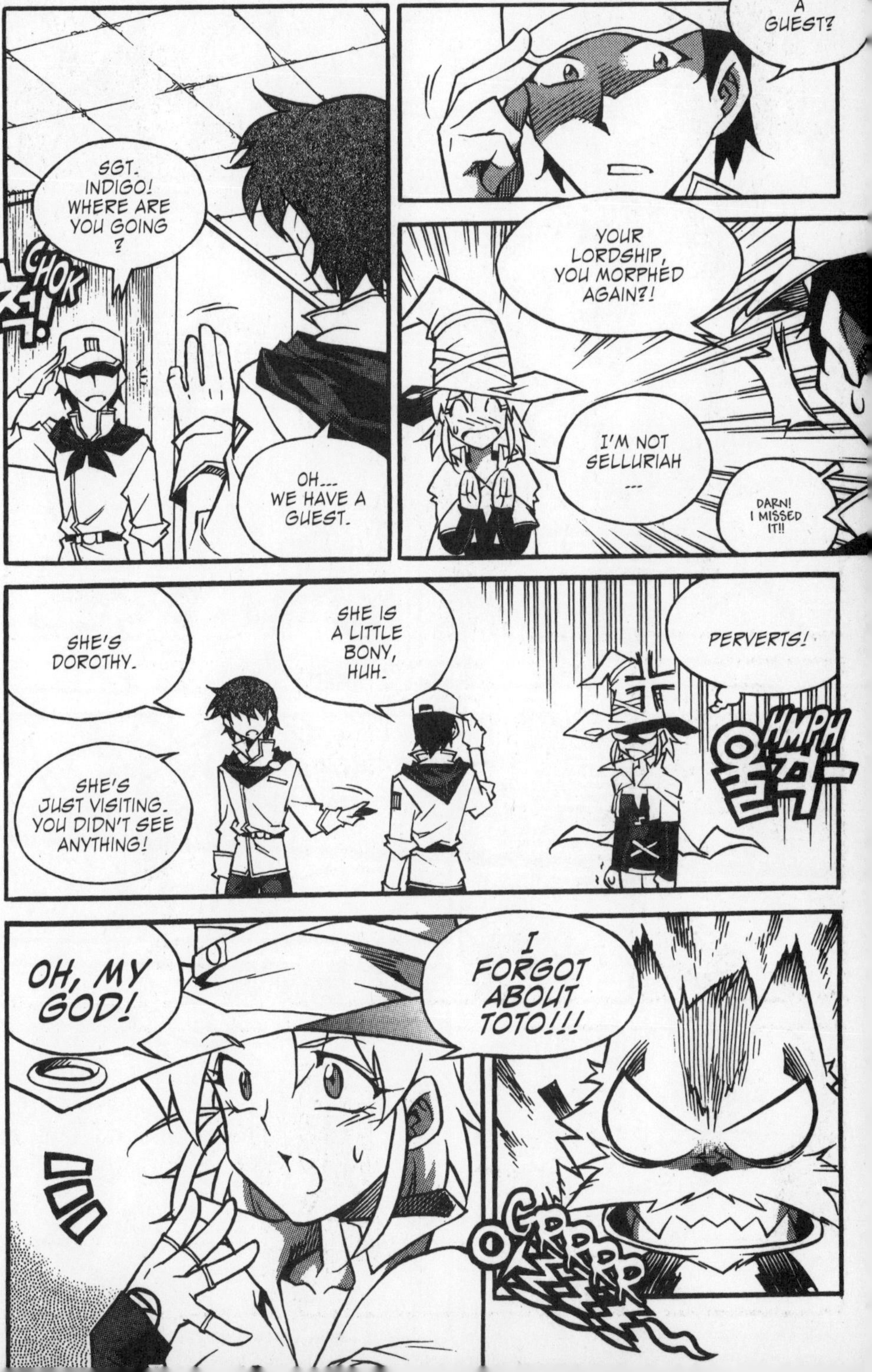
SGT. INDIGO! WHERE ARE YOU GOING ?
CHOK
OH... WE HAVE A GUEST.
A GUEST?
YOUR LORDSHIP, YOU MORPHED AGAIN?!
I'M NOT SELLURIAH ...
DARN! I MISSED IT!!
SHE'S DOROTHY.
SHE'S JUST VISITING. YOU DIDN'T SEE ANYTHING!
SHE IS A LITTLE BONY, HUH.
PERVERTS!
HMPH
OH, MY GOD!
I FORGOT ABOUT TOTO!!!

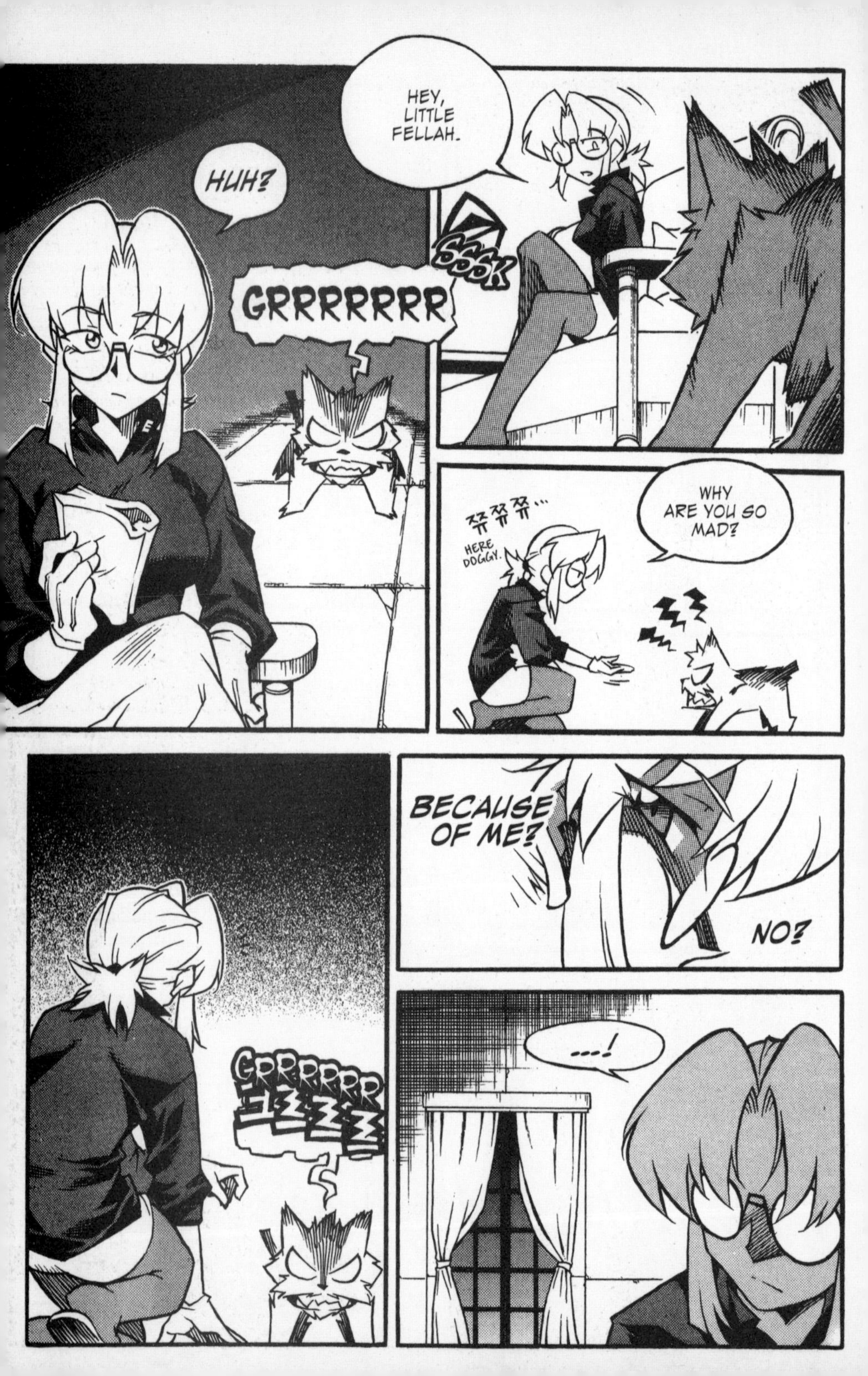
HUH?
GRRRRRRR
HEY, LITTLE FELLAH.
SSSK
쭈쭈쭈...
HERE DOGGY.
WHY ARE YOU SO MAD?
BECAUSE OF ME?
NO?
GRRRRRRR
...!

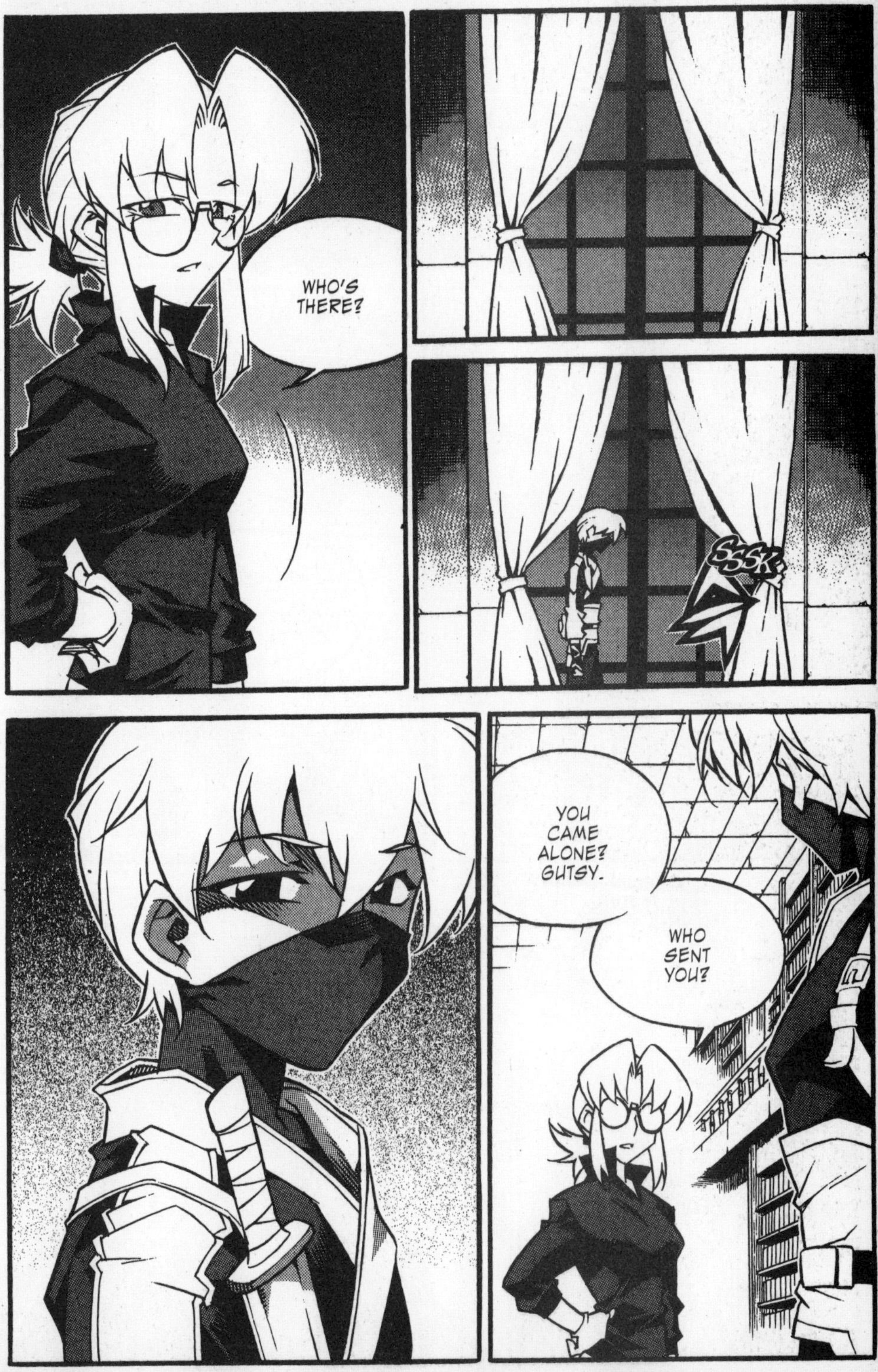
WHO'S THERE?
SSSK
YOU CAME ALONE? GUTSY.
WHO SENT YOU?

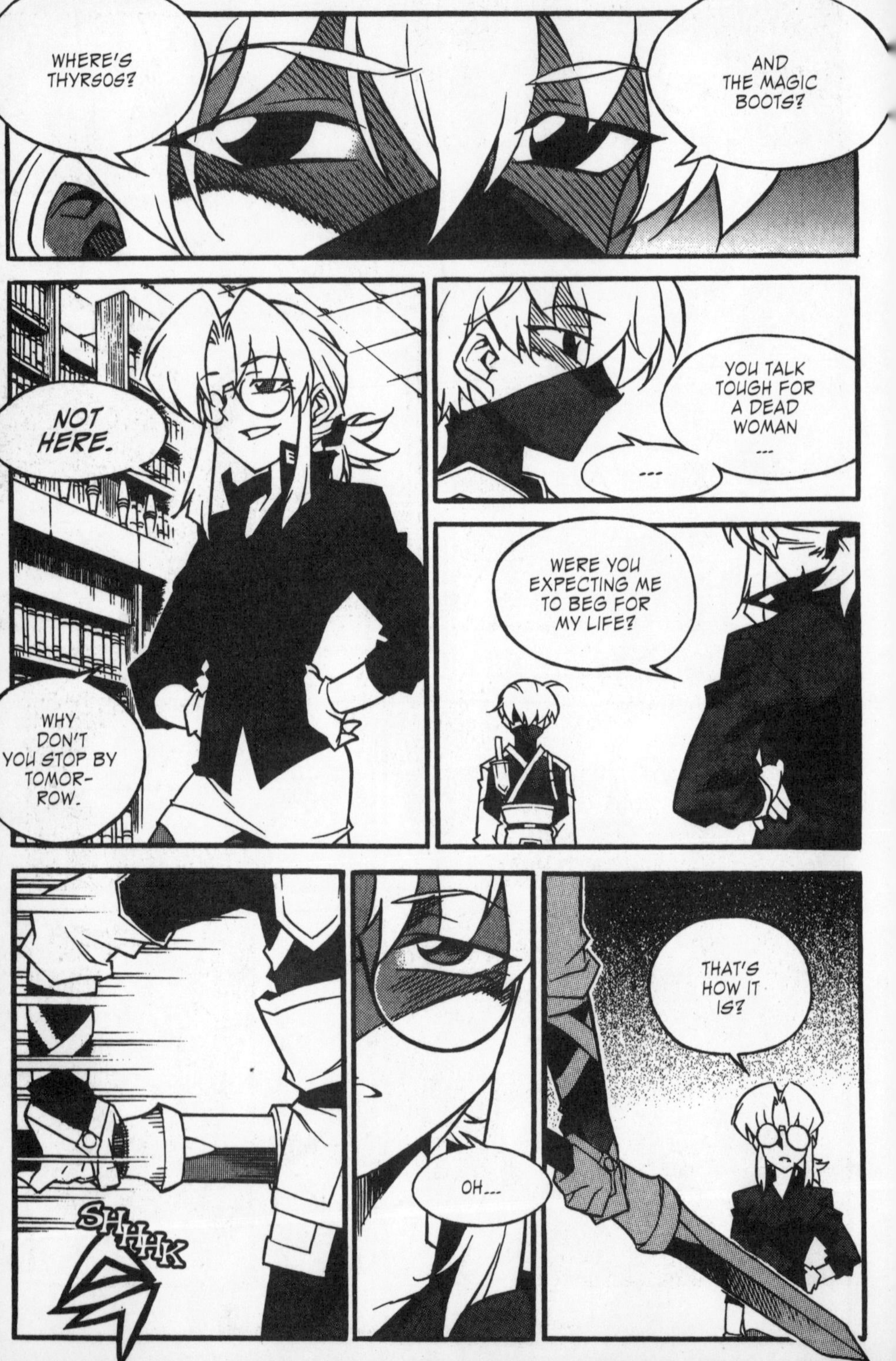
WHERE'S THYRSOS?
AND THE MAGIC BOOTS?
NOT HERE.
WHY DON'T YOU STOP BY TOMOR- ROW.
YOU TALK TOUGH FOR A DEAD WOMAN ...
...
WERE YOU EXPECTING ME TO BEG FOR MY LIFE?
SHHHK
OH...
THAT'S HOW IT IS?

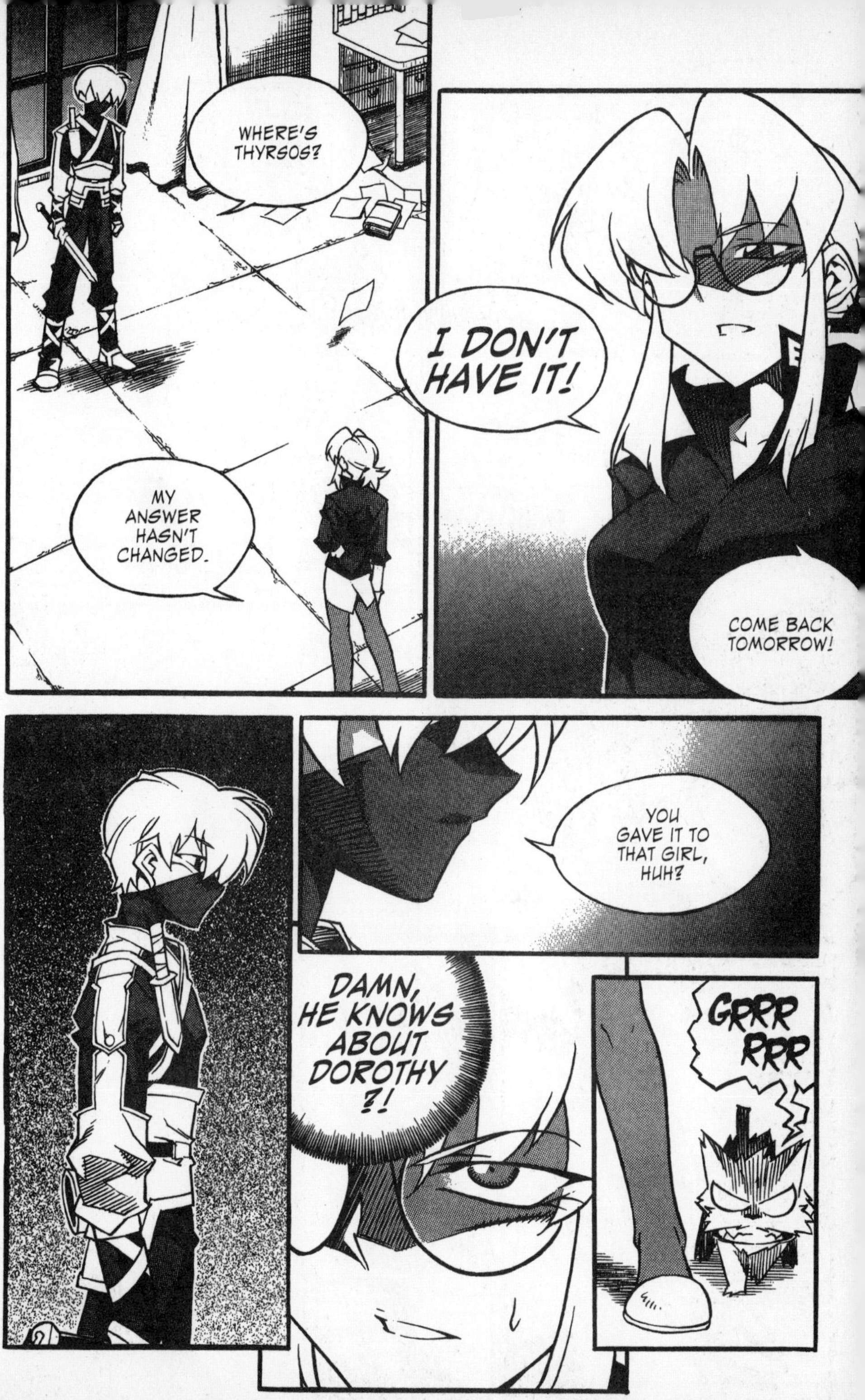
WHERE'S THYRSOS?
MY ANSWER HASN'T CHANGED.
I DON'T HAVE IT!
COME BACK TOMORROW!
YOU GAVE IT TO THAT GIRL, HUH?
DAMN, HE KNOWS ABOUT DOROTHY ?!
GRRR RRR

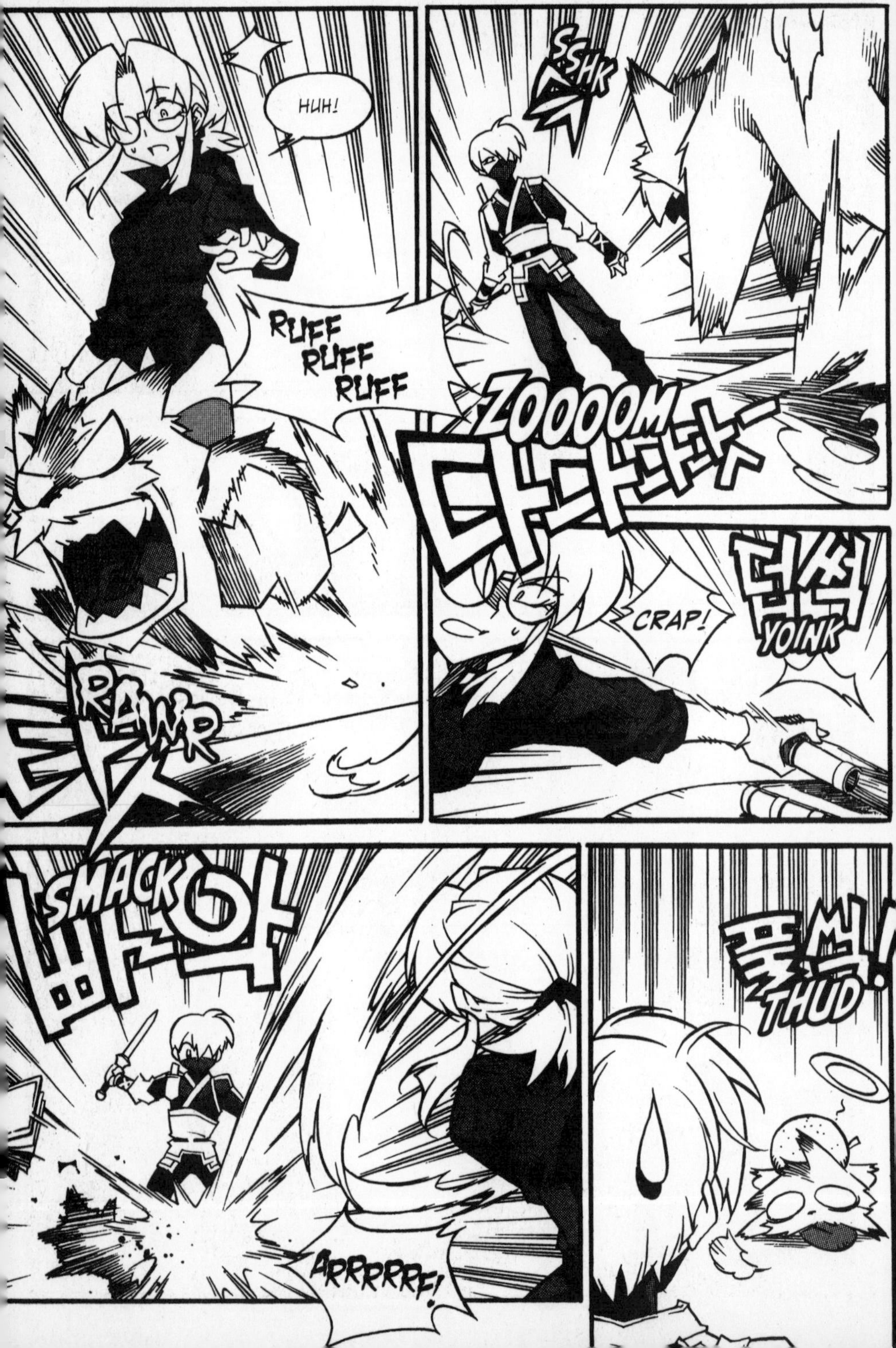

HUH!
RUFF RUFF RUFF
RAWR
SSHK
ZOOOOM
CRAP!
덥석
YOINK
SMACK
빠악
ARRRRRF!
풀썩!
THUD

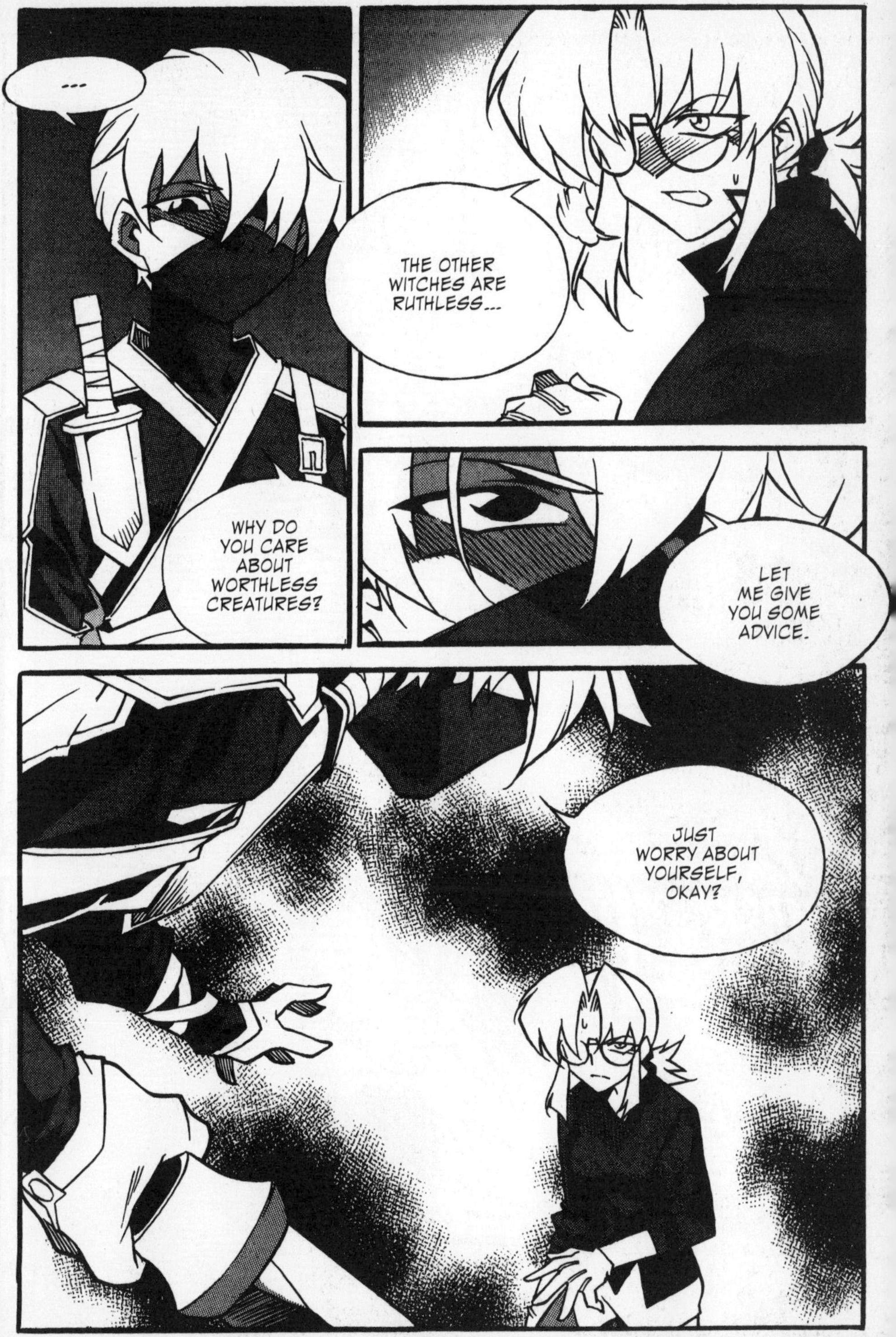
...
THE OTHER WITCHES ARE RUTHLESS...
WHY DO YOU CARE ABOUT WORTHLESS CREATURES?
LET ME GIVE YOU SOME ADVICE.
JUST WORRY ABOUT YOURSELF, OKAY?

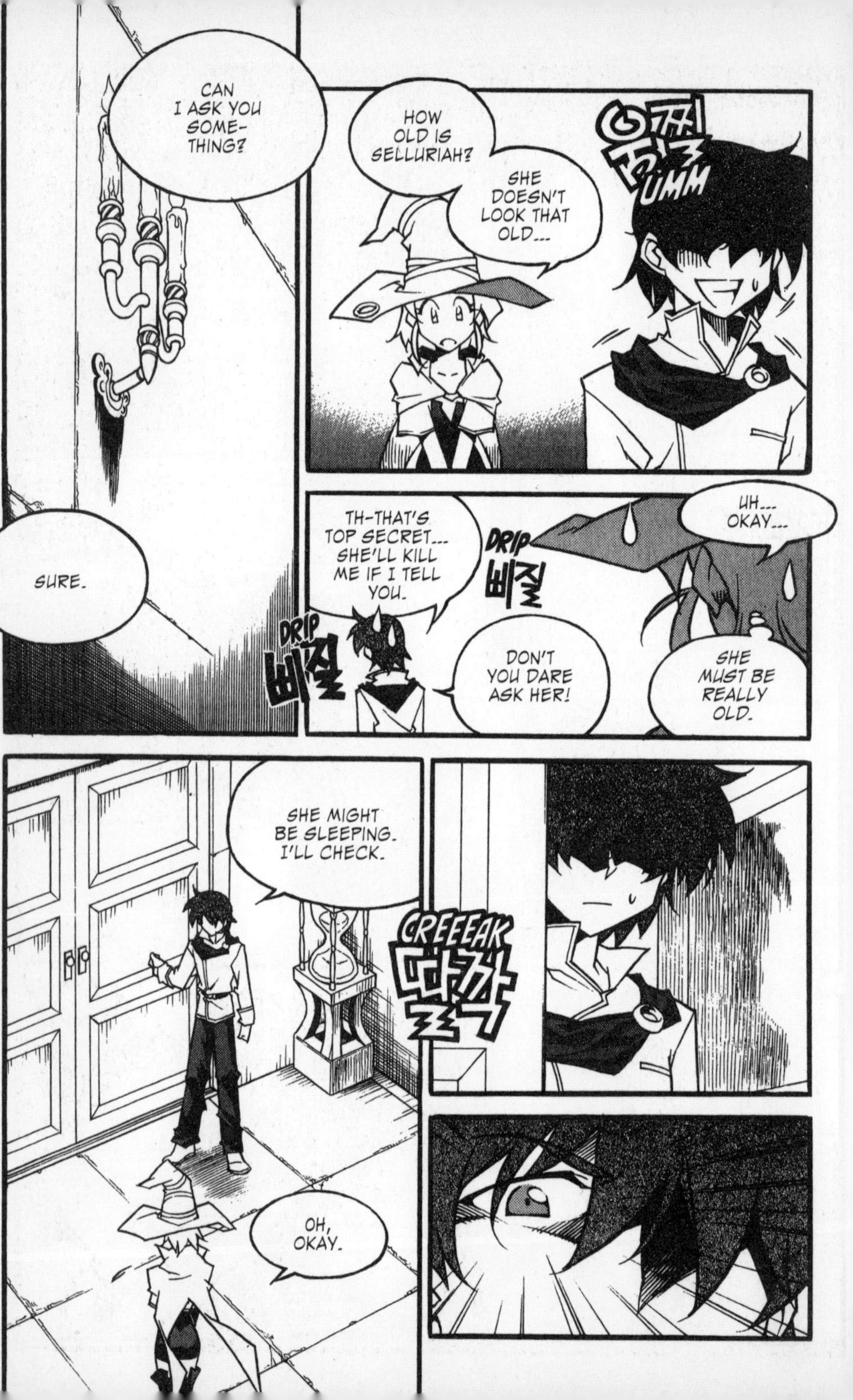
CAN I ASK YOU SOME-THING?
HOW OLD IS SELLURIAH?
SHE DOESN'T LOOK THAT OLD...
UMM
SURE.
TH-THAT'S TOP SECRET... SHE'LL KILL ME IF I TELL YOU.
DRIP
UH... OKAY...
DRIP
DON'T YOU DARE ASK HER!
SHE MUST BE REALLY OLD.
SHE MIGHT BE SLEEPING. I'LL CHECK.
CREEEAK
OH, OKAY.

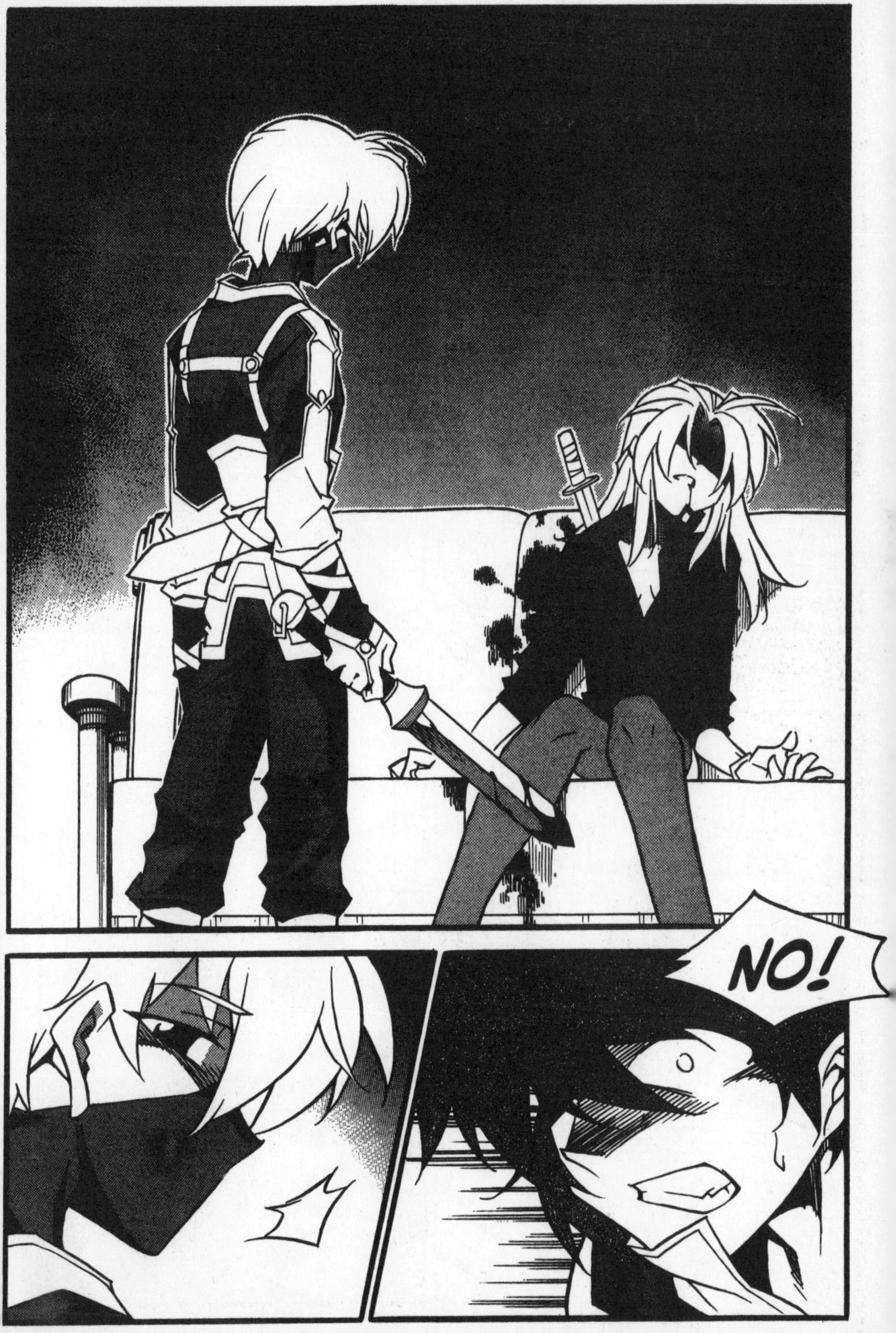
NO!

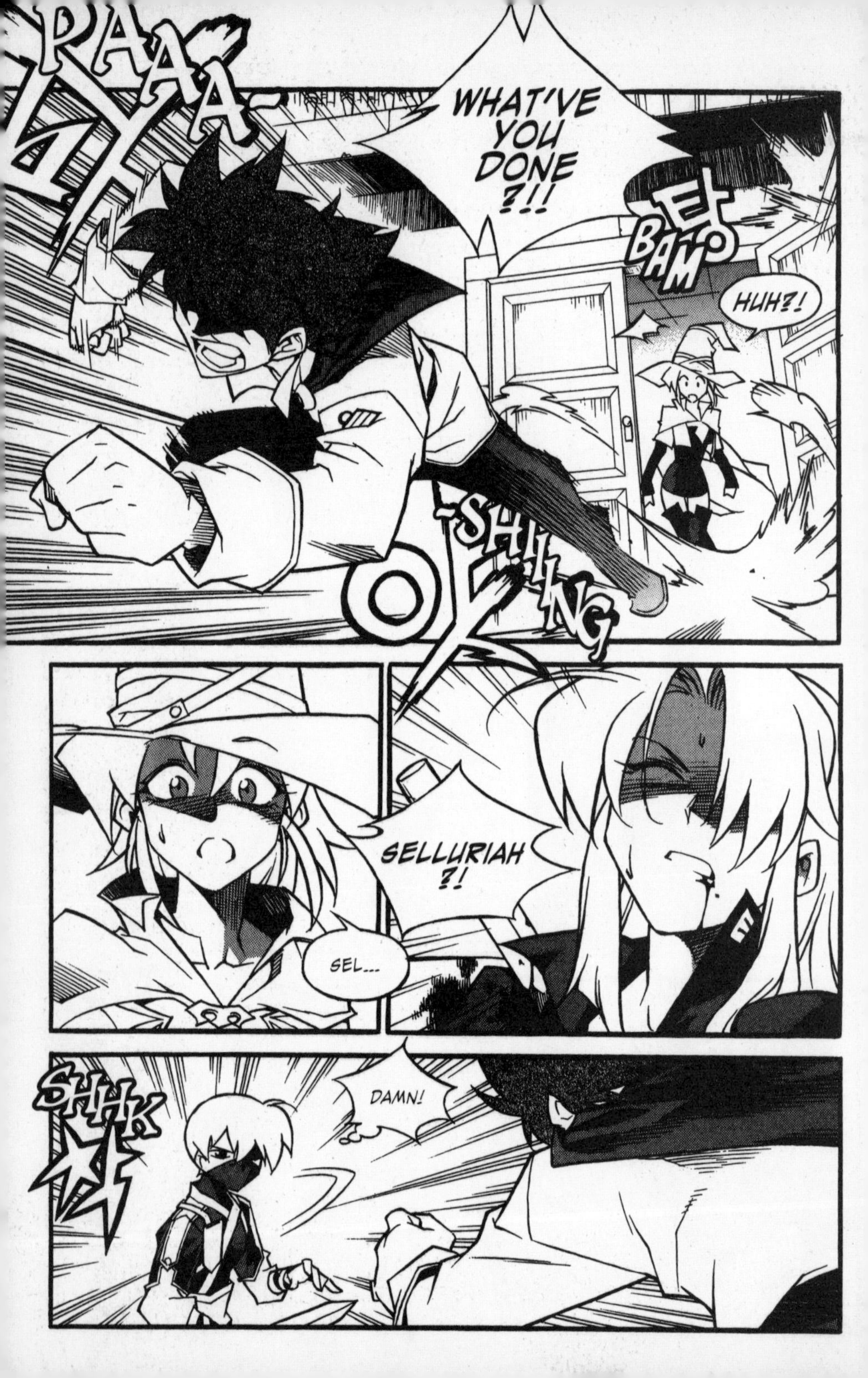
PAAAAYA
WHAT'VE YOU DONE ?!!
탁
BAM
HUH?!
-SHIING
SELLURIAH ?!
SEL...
SHHK
DAMN!

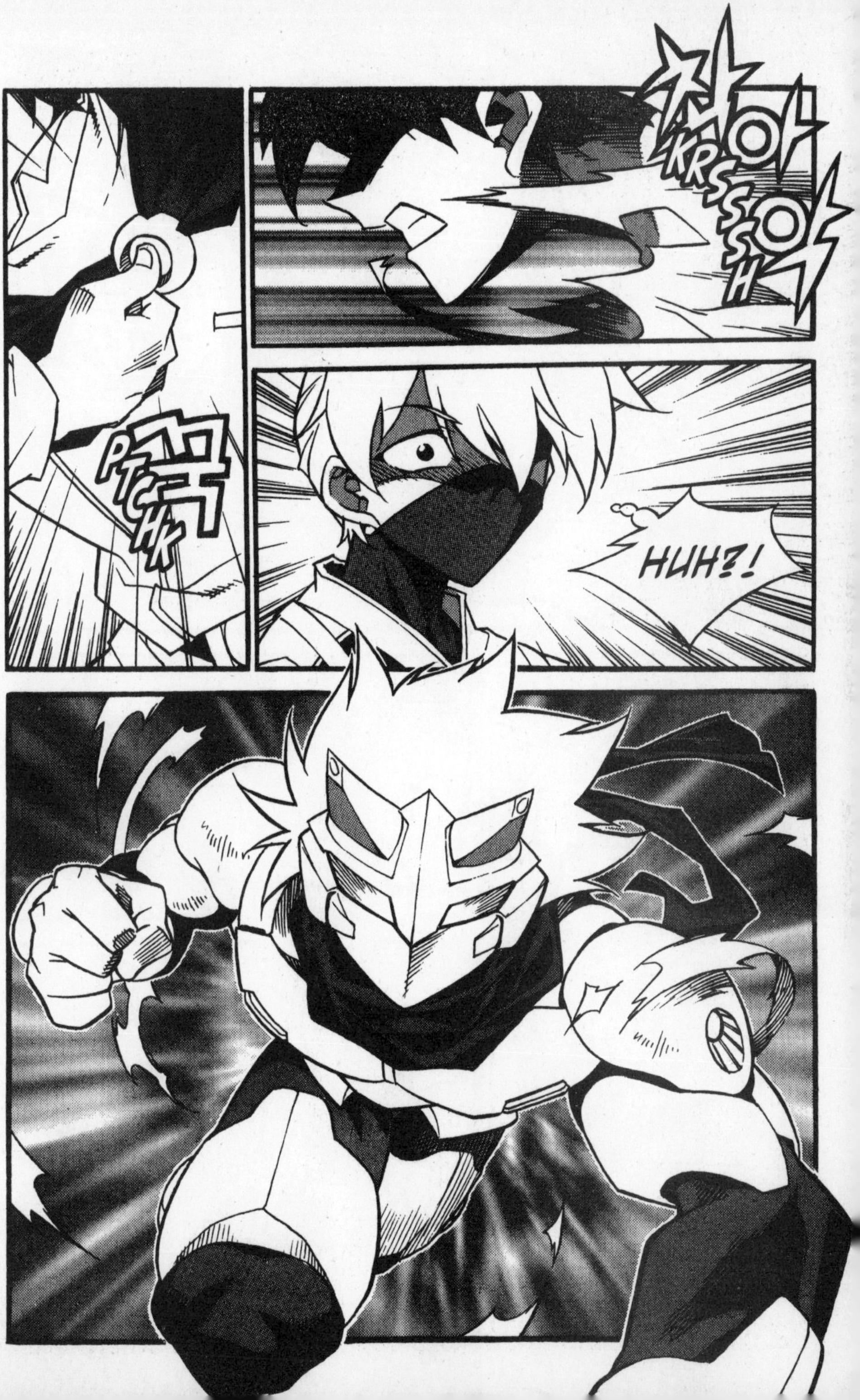
KRSSSH
PTCHK
HUH?!

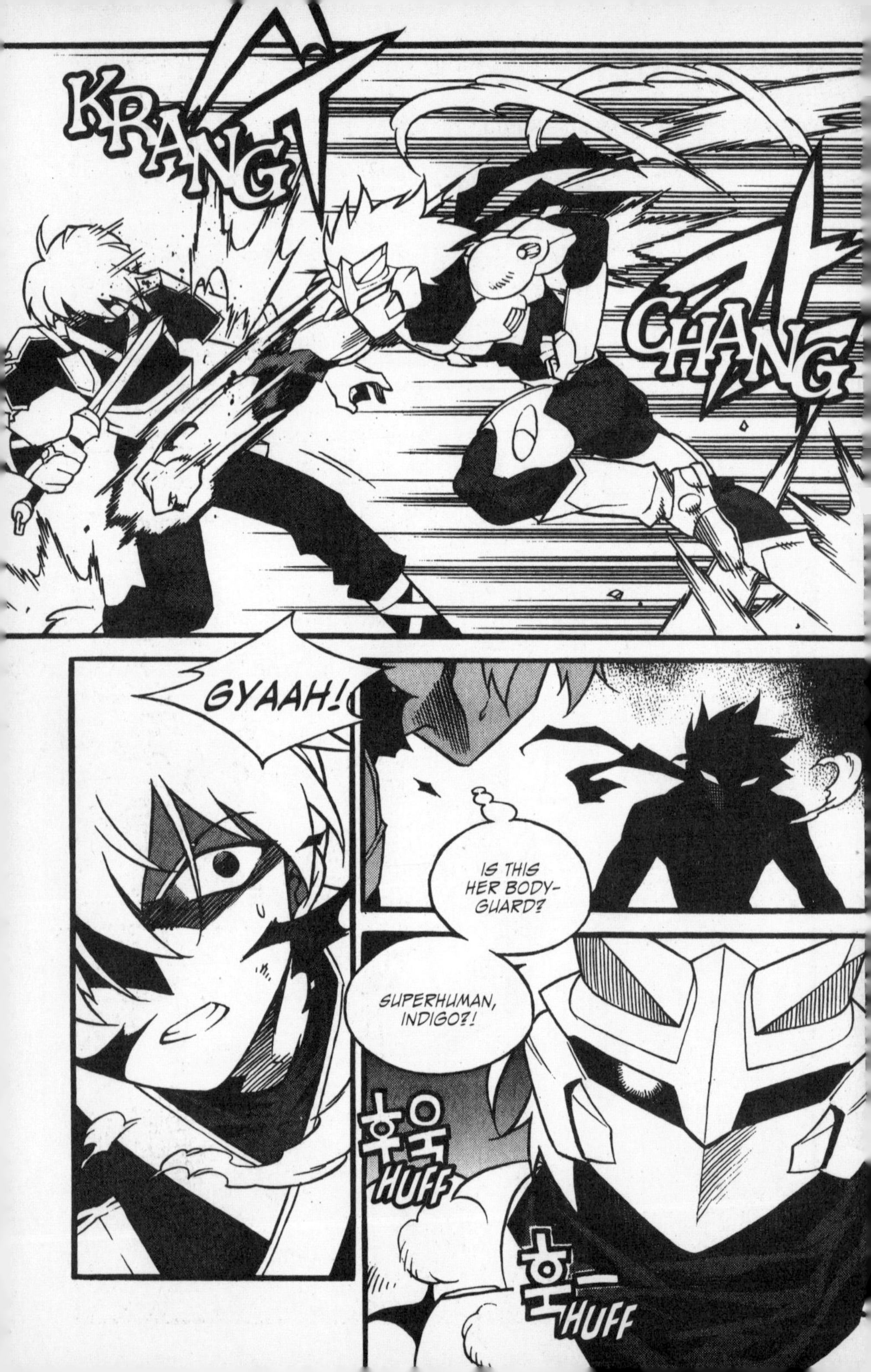
KRANG
CHANG
GYAAH!
IS THIS HER BODY-GUARD?
SUPERHUMAN, INDIGO?!
후욱
HUFF
후-
HUFF

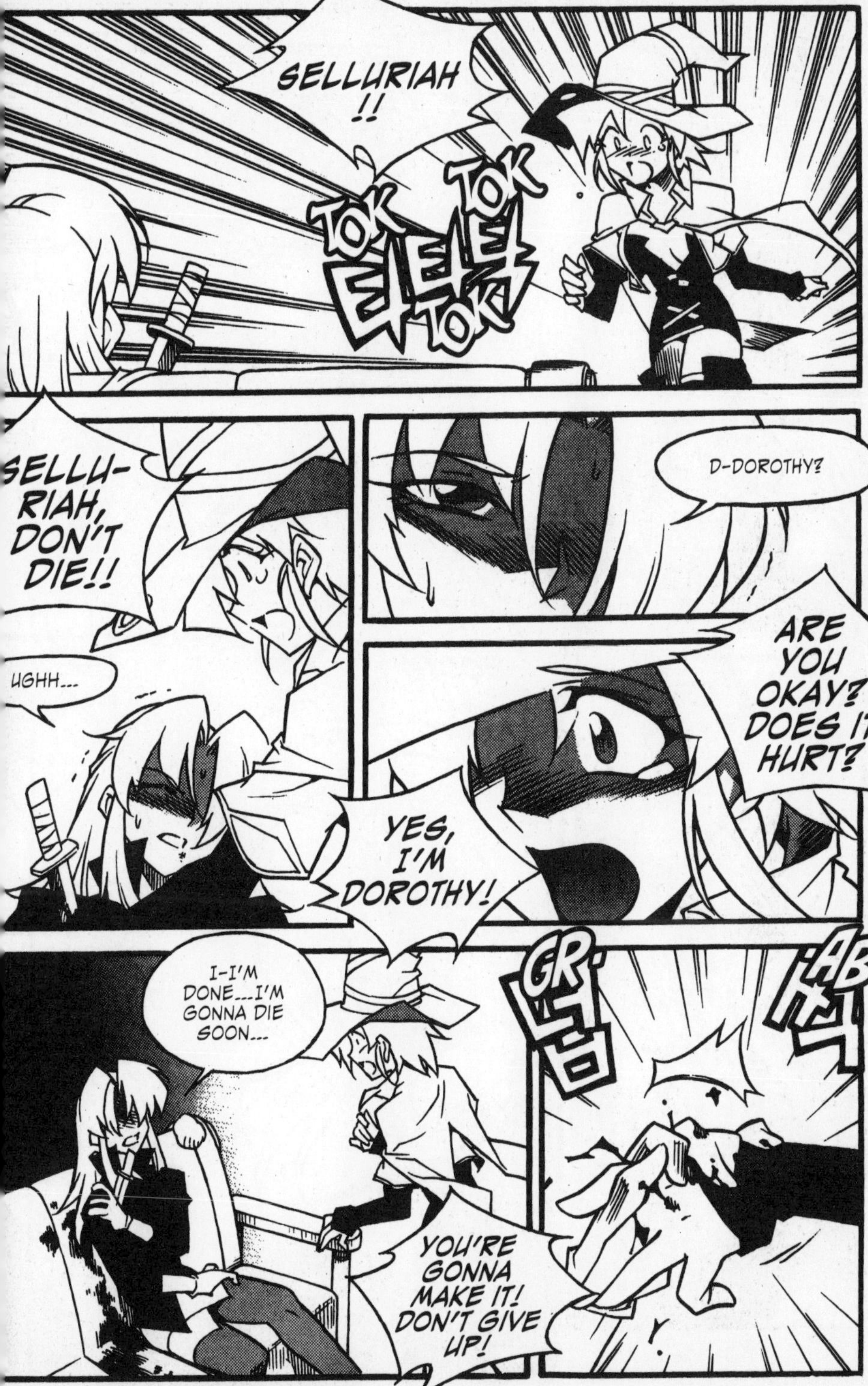
SELLURIAH !!
TOK TOK
TOK TOK
SELLU-RIAH, DON'T DIE!!
D-DOROTHY?
UGHH...
ARE YOU OKAY? DOES IT HURT?
YES, I'M DOROTHY!
I-I'M DONE...I'M GONNA DIE SOON...
GRAB
YOU'RE GONNA MAKE IT! DON'T GIVE UP!

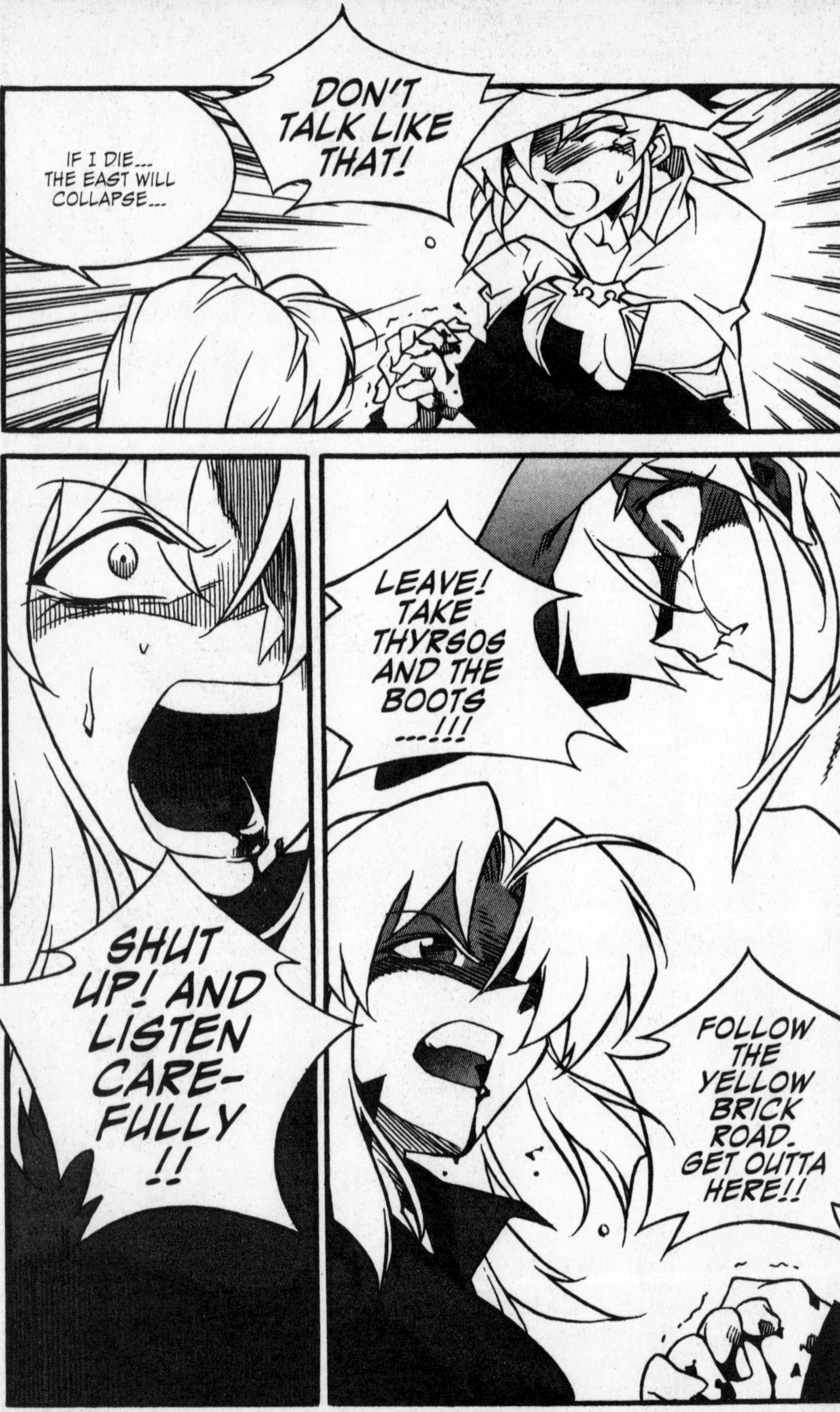
IF I DIE... THE EAST WILL COLLAPSE...
DON'T TALK LIKE THAT!
LEAVE! TAKE THYRSOS AND THE BOOTS ---!!!
FOLLOW THE YELLOW BRICK ROAD. GET OUTTA HERE!!
SHUT UP! AND LISTEN CARE-FULLY !!

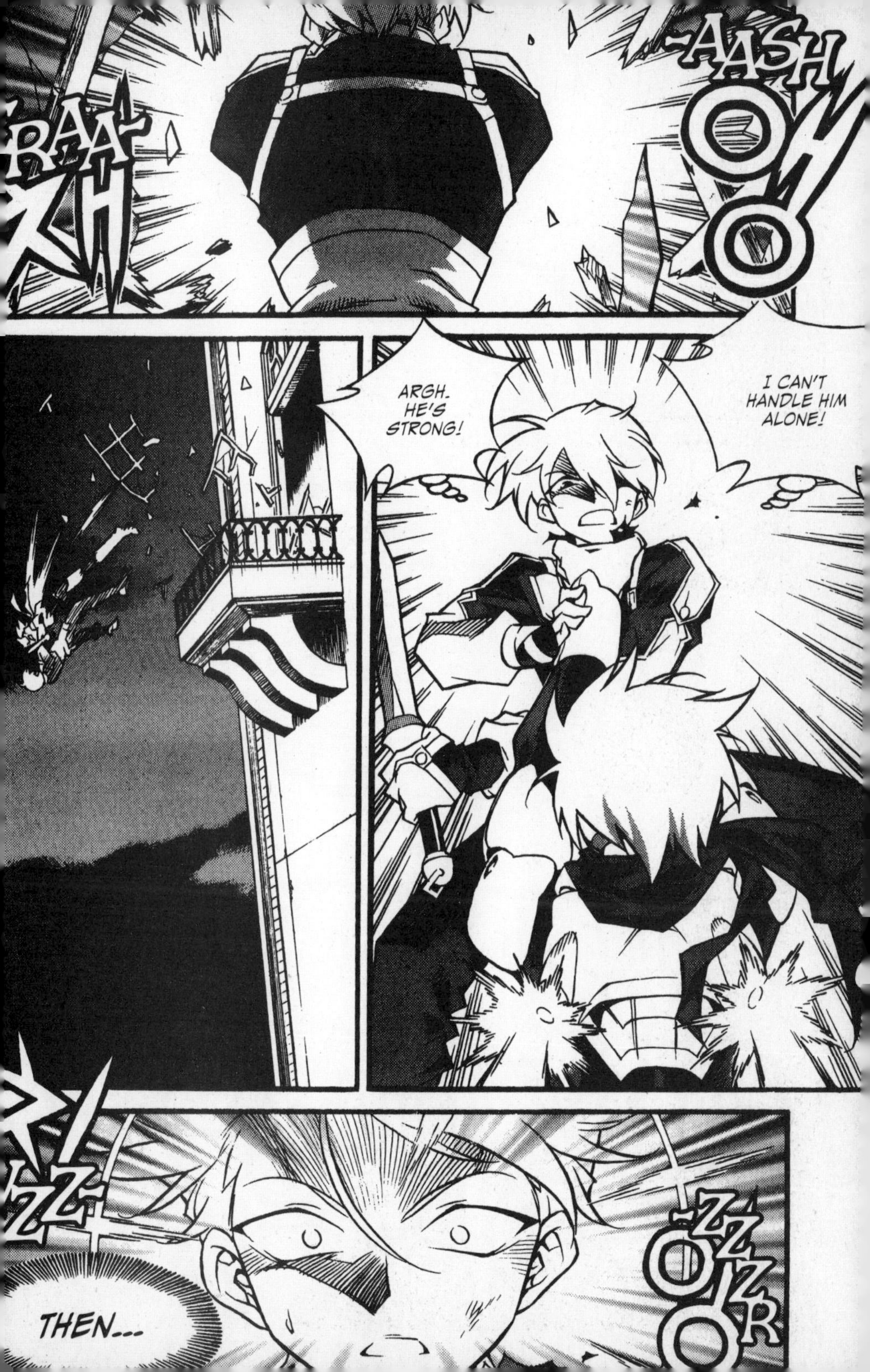
RAA-ZH
-AASH
OOO
ARGH. HE'S STRONG!
I CAN'T HANDLE HIM ALONE!
ZZ-
-ZZZR
THEN...

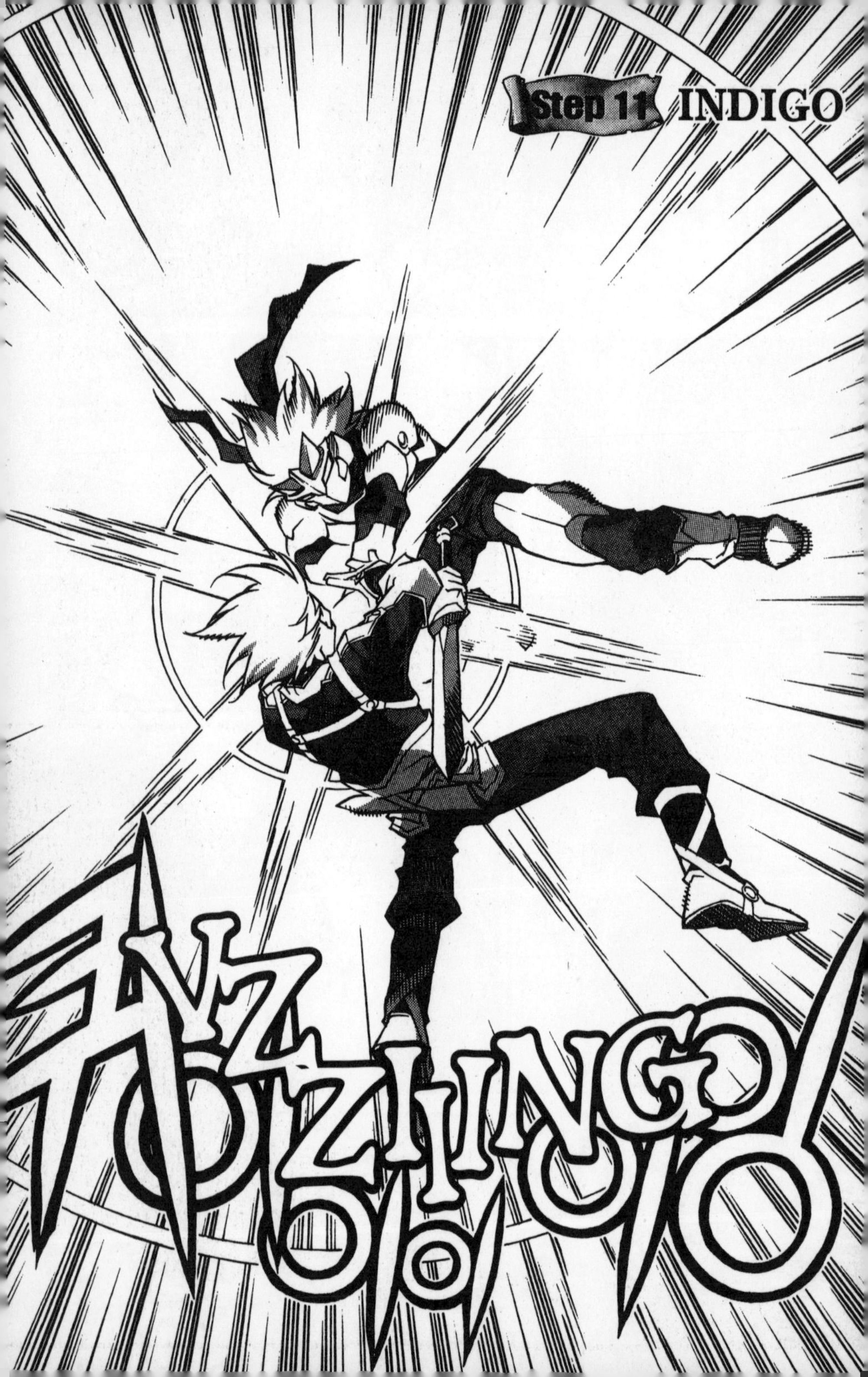
Step 11 INDIGO

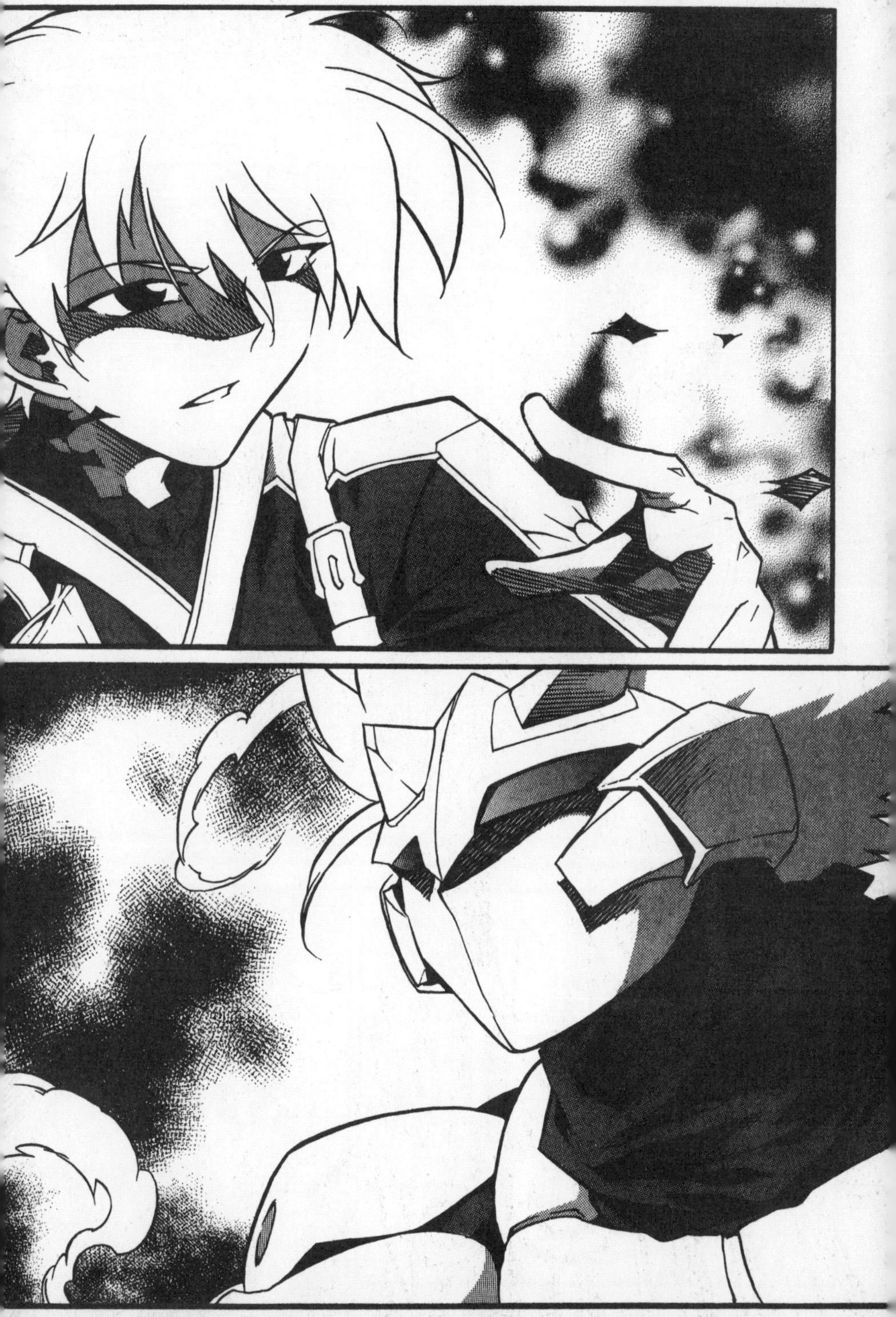

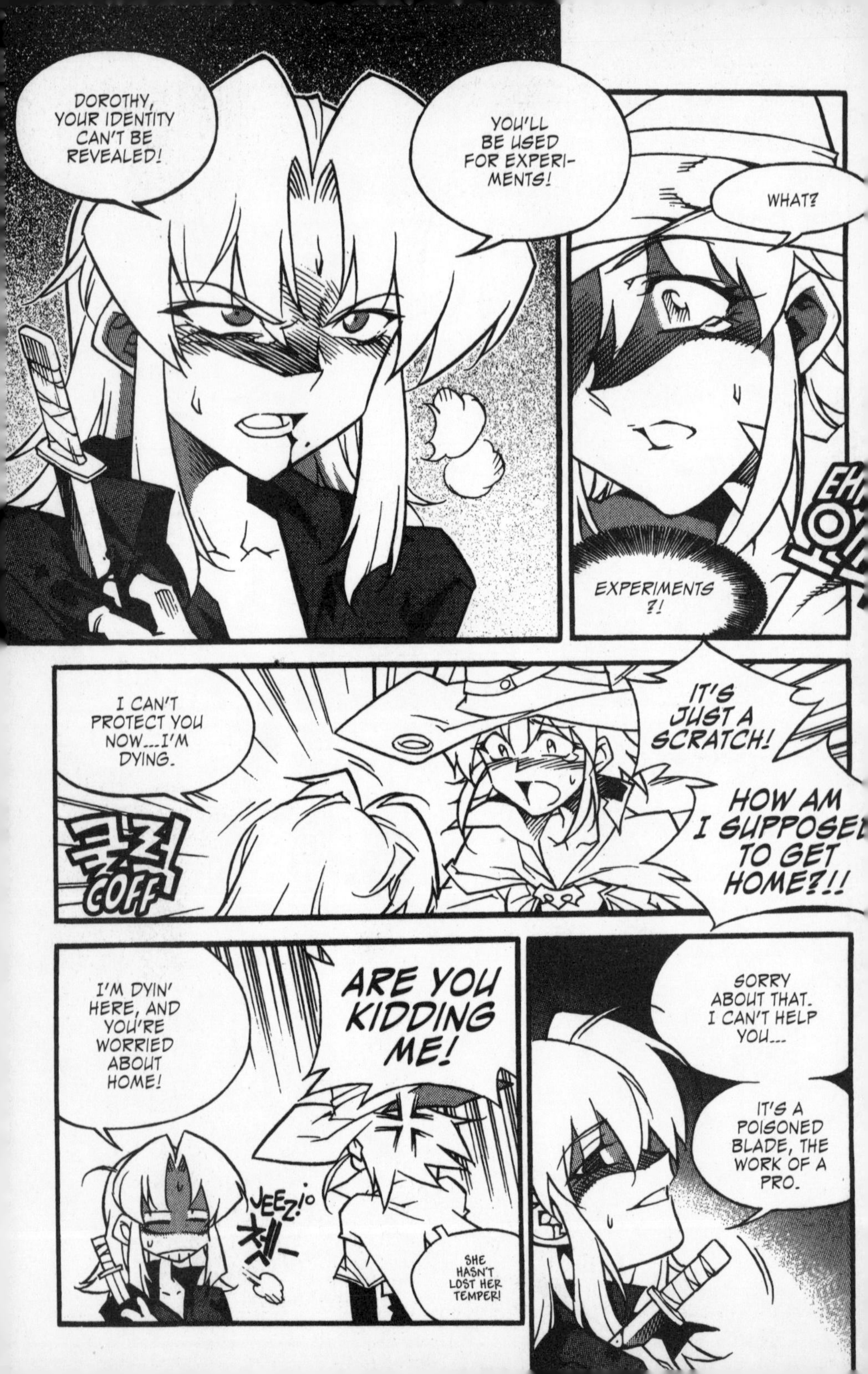
DOROTHY, YOUR IDENTITY CAN'T BE REVEALED!
YOU'LL BE USED FOR EXPERI- MENTS!
WHAT?
EXPERIMENTS ?!
I CAN'T PROTECT YOU NOW...I'M DYING.
GOFF
IT'S JUST A SCRATCH!
HOW AM I SUPPOSED TO GET HOME?!!
I'M DYIN' HERE, AND YOU'RE WORRIED ABOUT HOME!
ARE YOU KIDDING ME!
JEEZ!
SHE HASN'T LOST HER TEMPER!
SORRY ABOUT THAT. I CAN'T HELP YOU...
IT'S A POISONED BLADE, THE WORK OF A PRO.

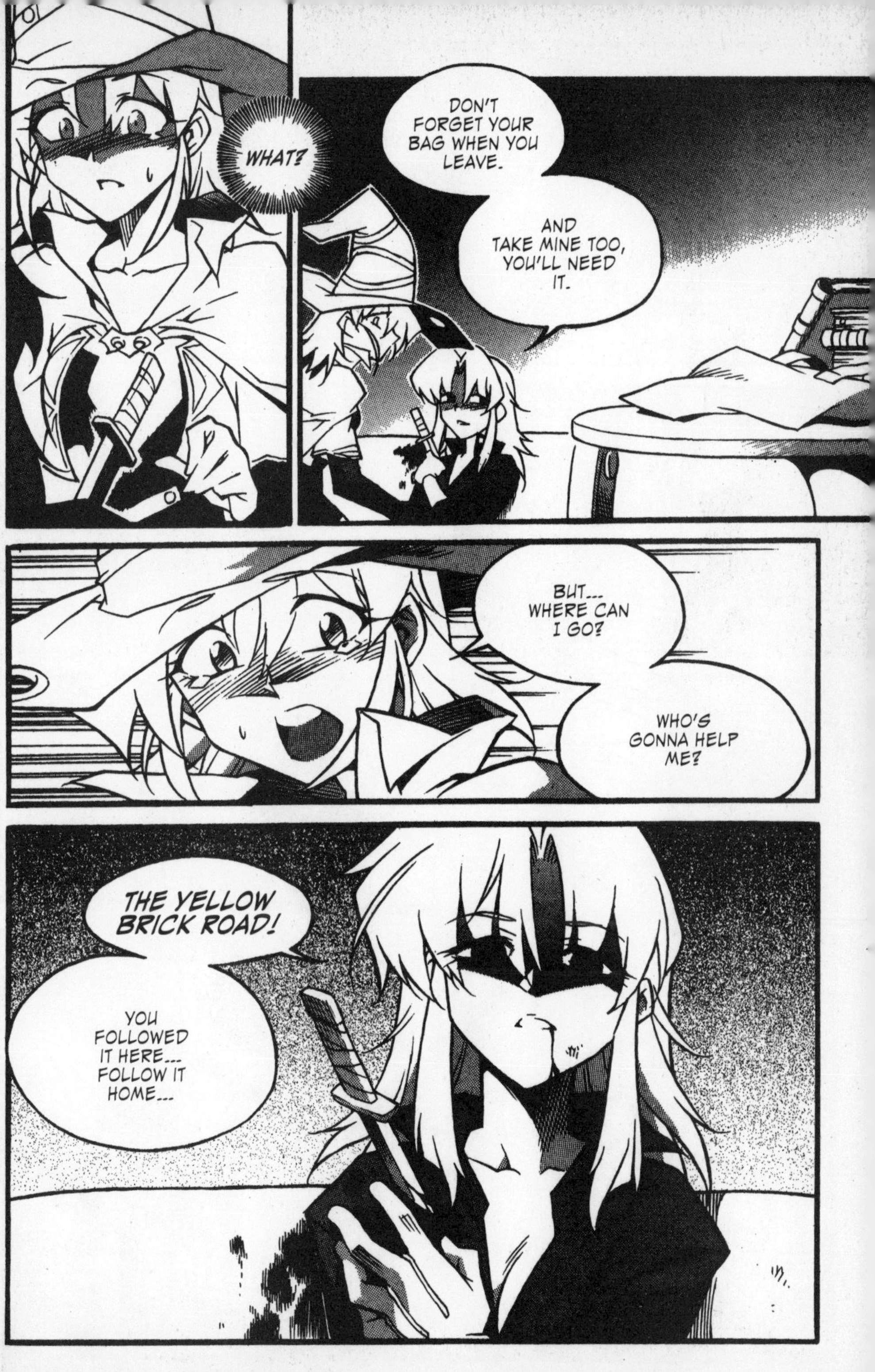
WHAT?
DON'T FORGET YOUR BAG WHEN YOU LEAVE.
AND TAKE MINE TOO, YOU'LL NEED IT.
BUT... WHERE CAN I GO?
WHO'S GONNA HELP ME?
THE YELLOW BRICK ROAD!
YOU FOLLOWED IT HERE... FOLLOW IT HOME...

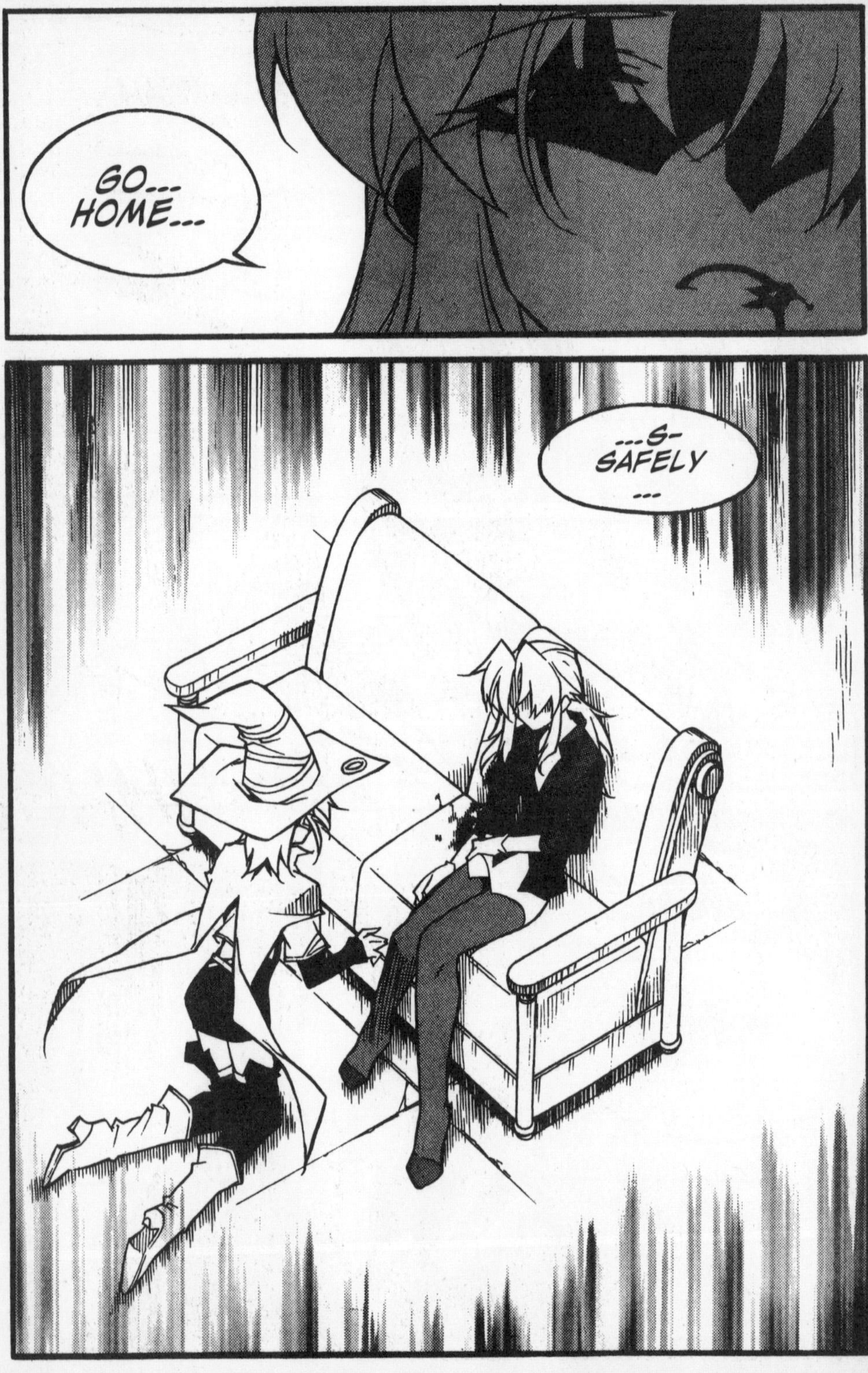
GO... HOME...
...S- SAFELY ...

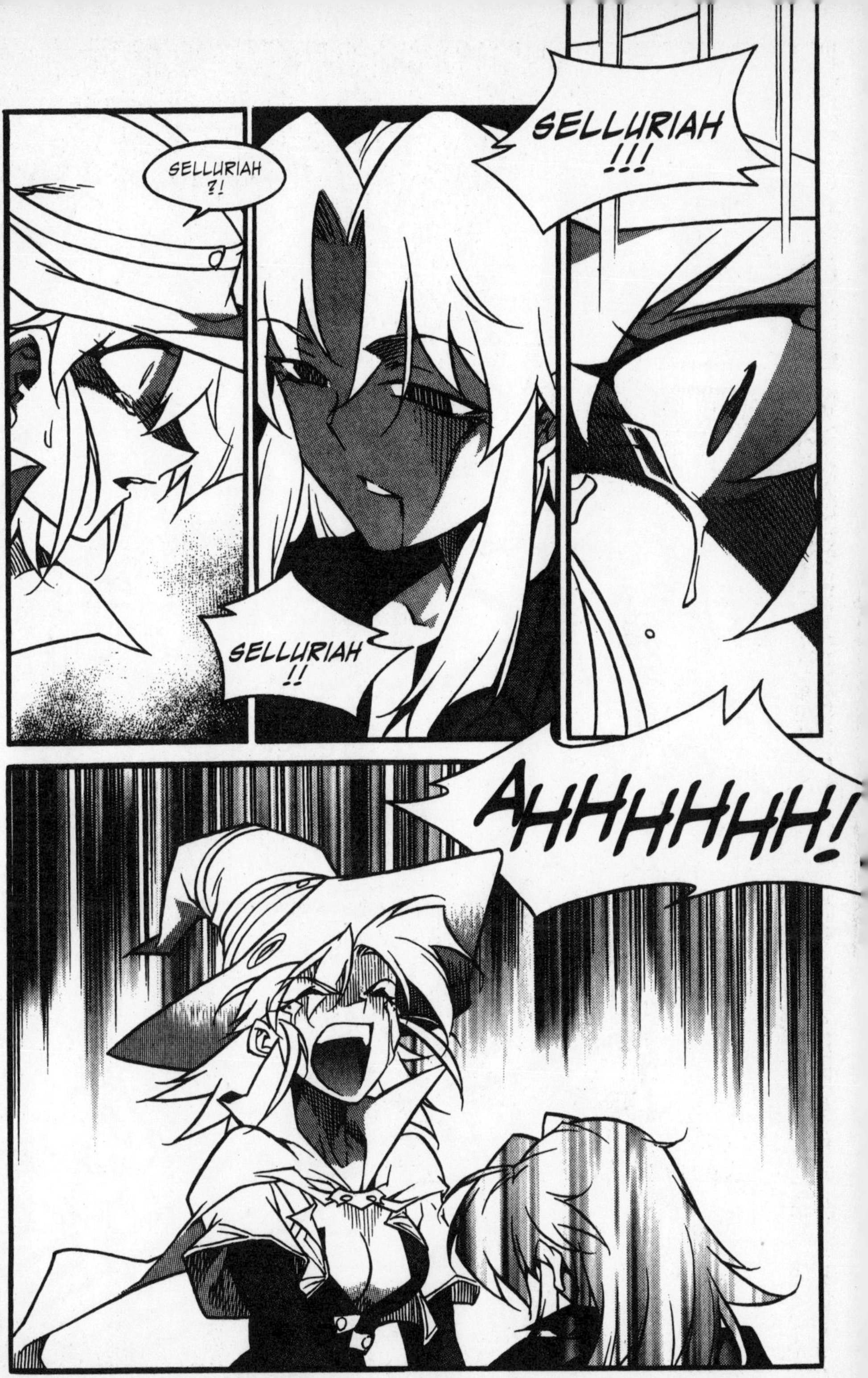
SELLURIAH ?!
SELLURIAH !!
SELLURIAH !!!
AHHHHHH!

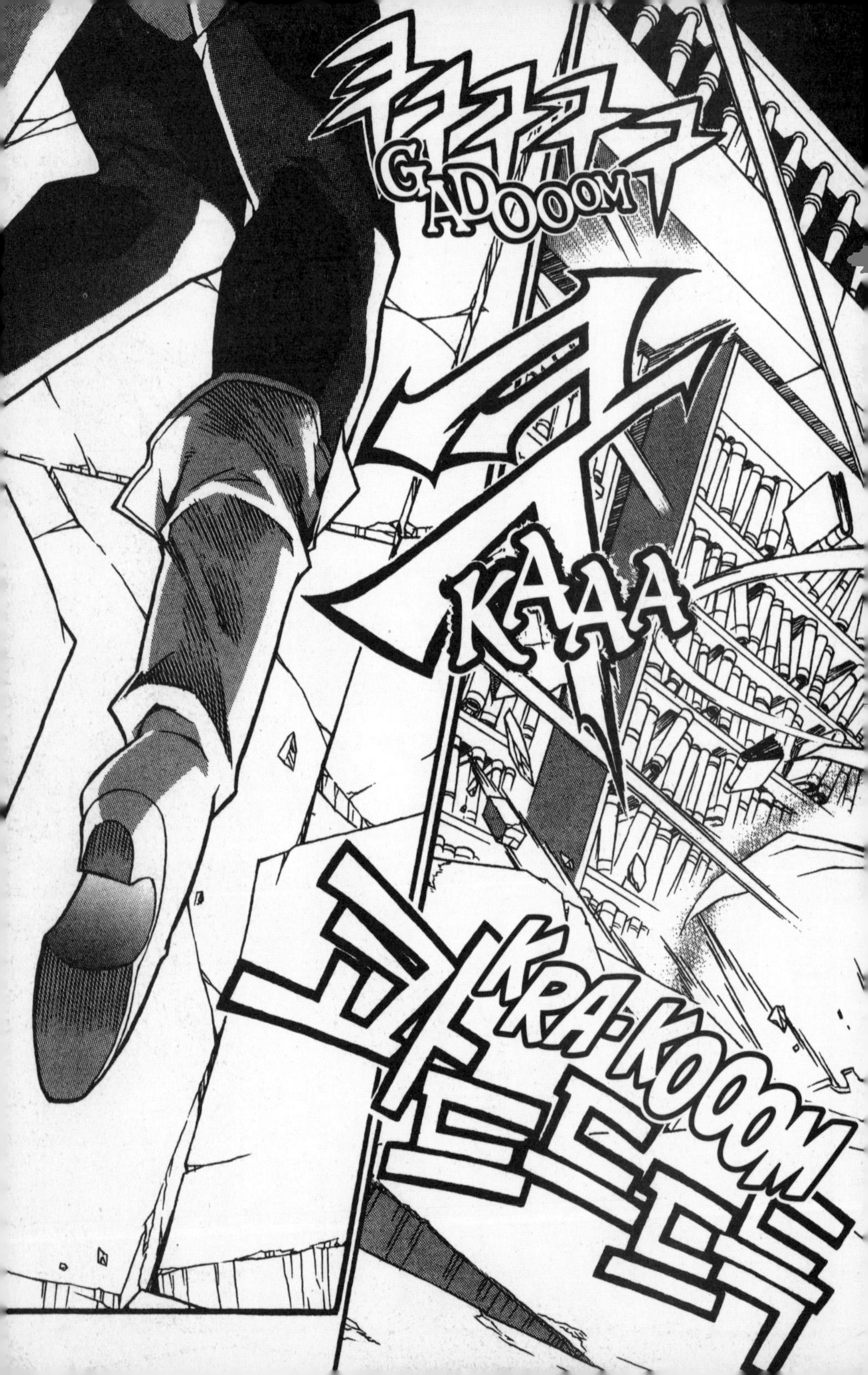
GADOOOM
KAAA
KRA-KOOOM

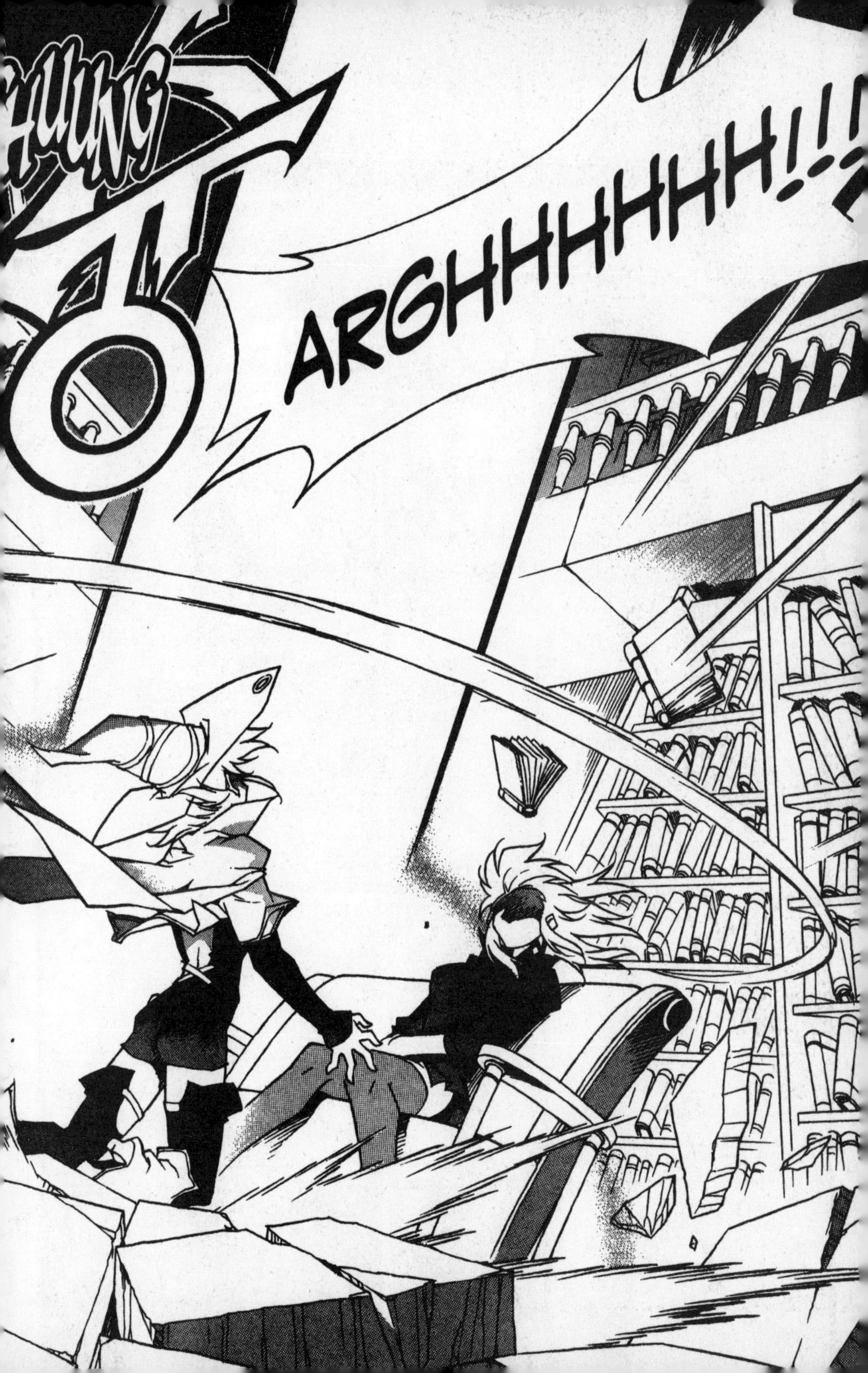
ARGHHHHHHH!!!

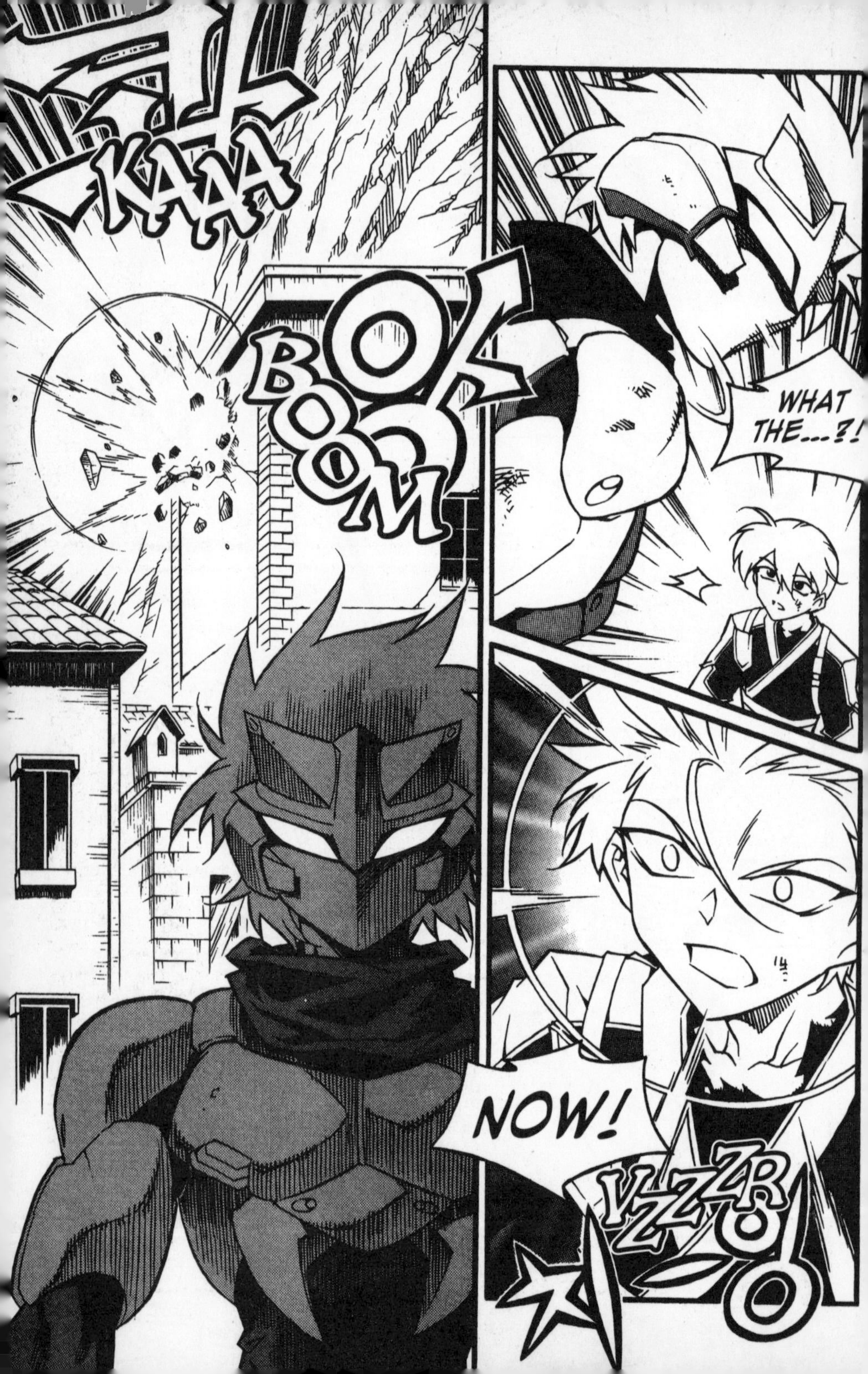
KAAA
BOOOOM
WHAT THE...?!
NOW!
VZZZR

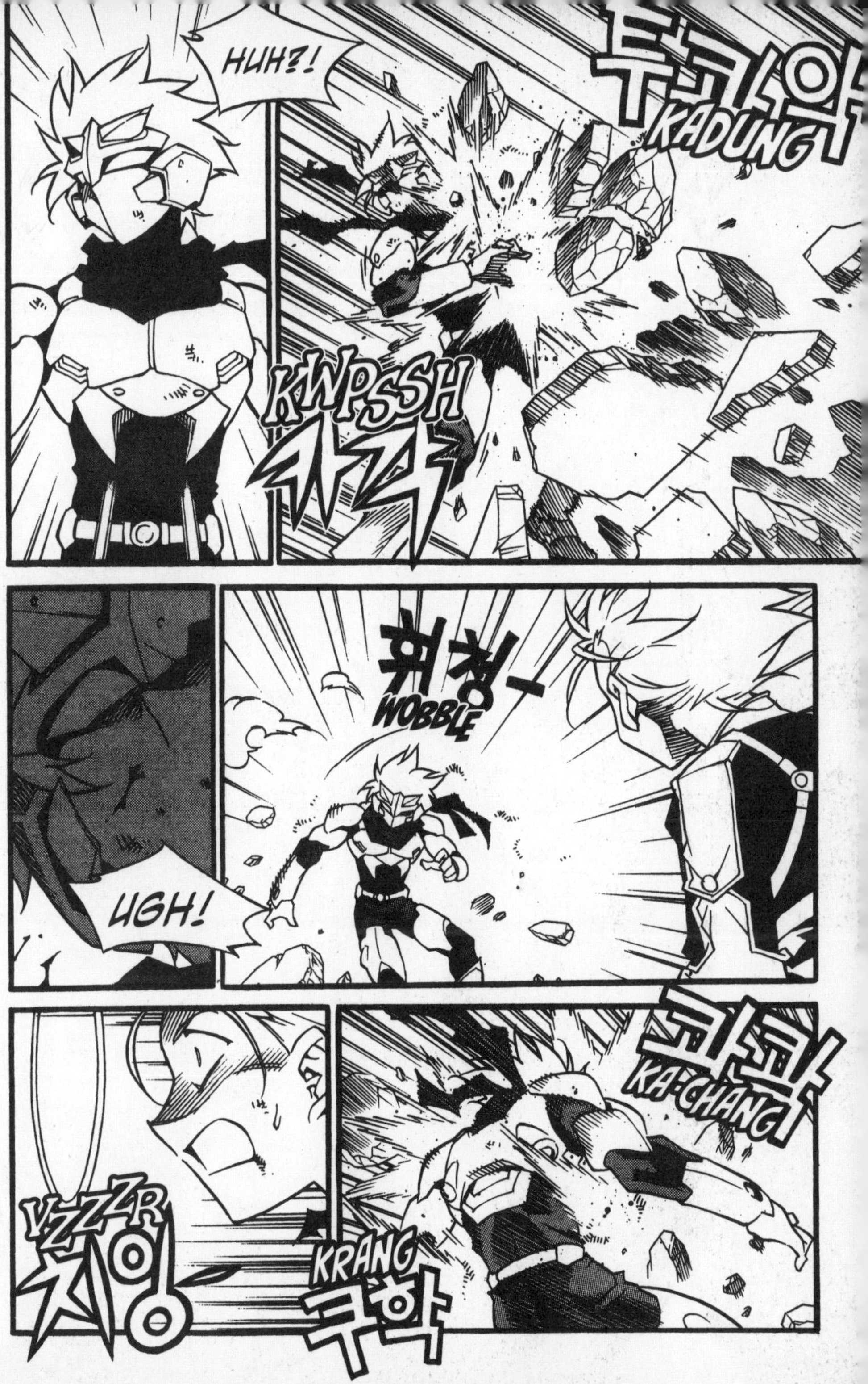
HUH?!
KADUNG
KWPSSH
휘청-
WOBBLE
UGH!
KA-CHANG
VZZZR
KRANG

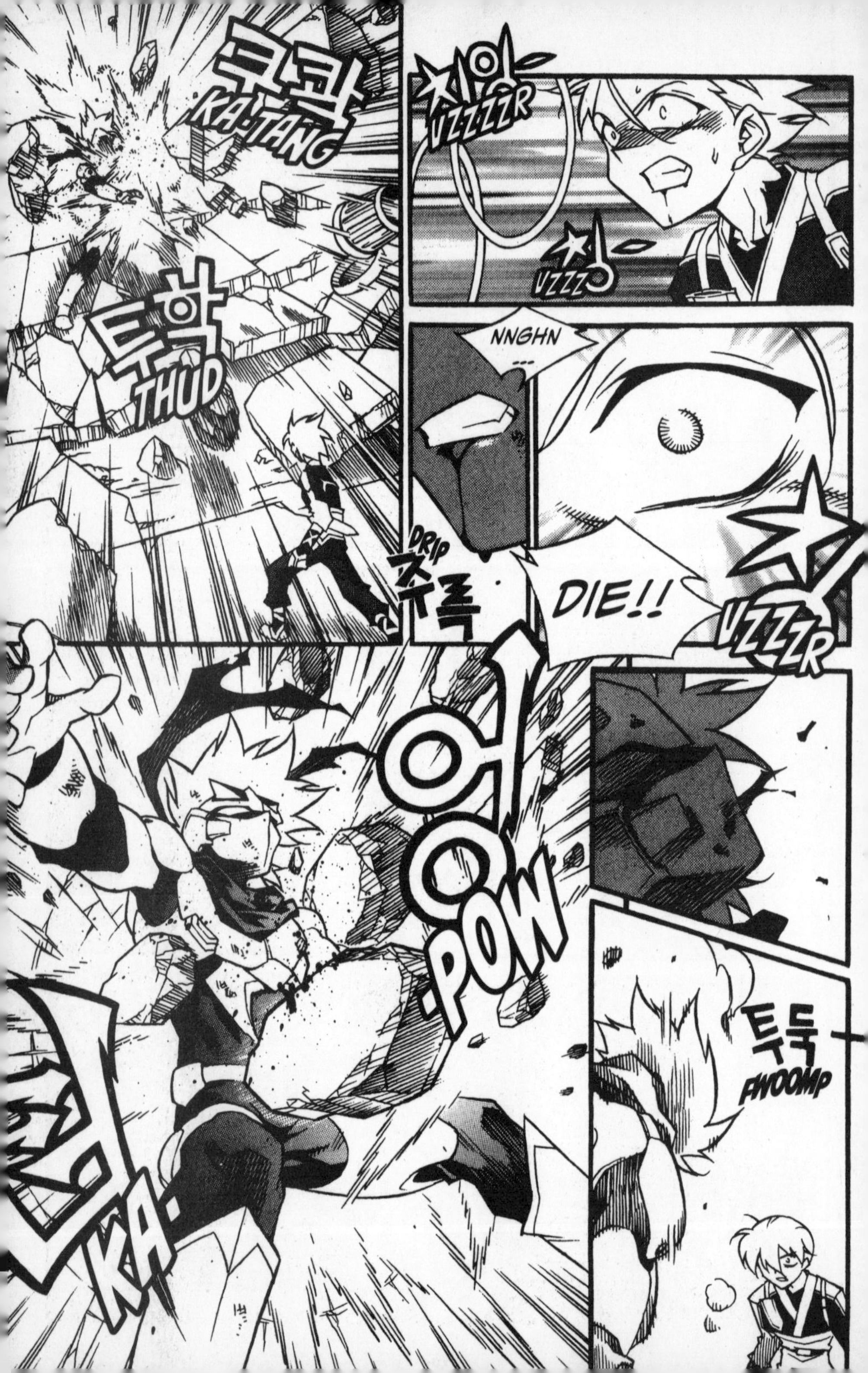
KA-TANG
THUD
VZZZZR
VZZZ
NNGHN ---
DRIP
DIE!!
VZZZR
KA-
POW
FWOOMP

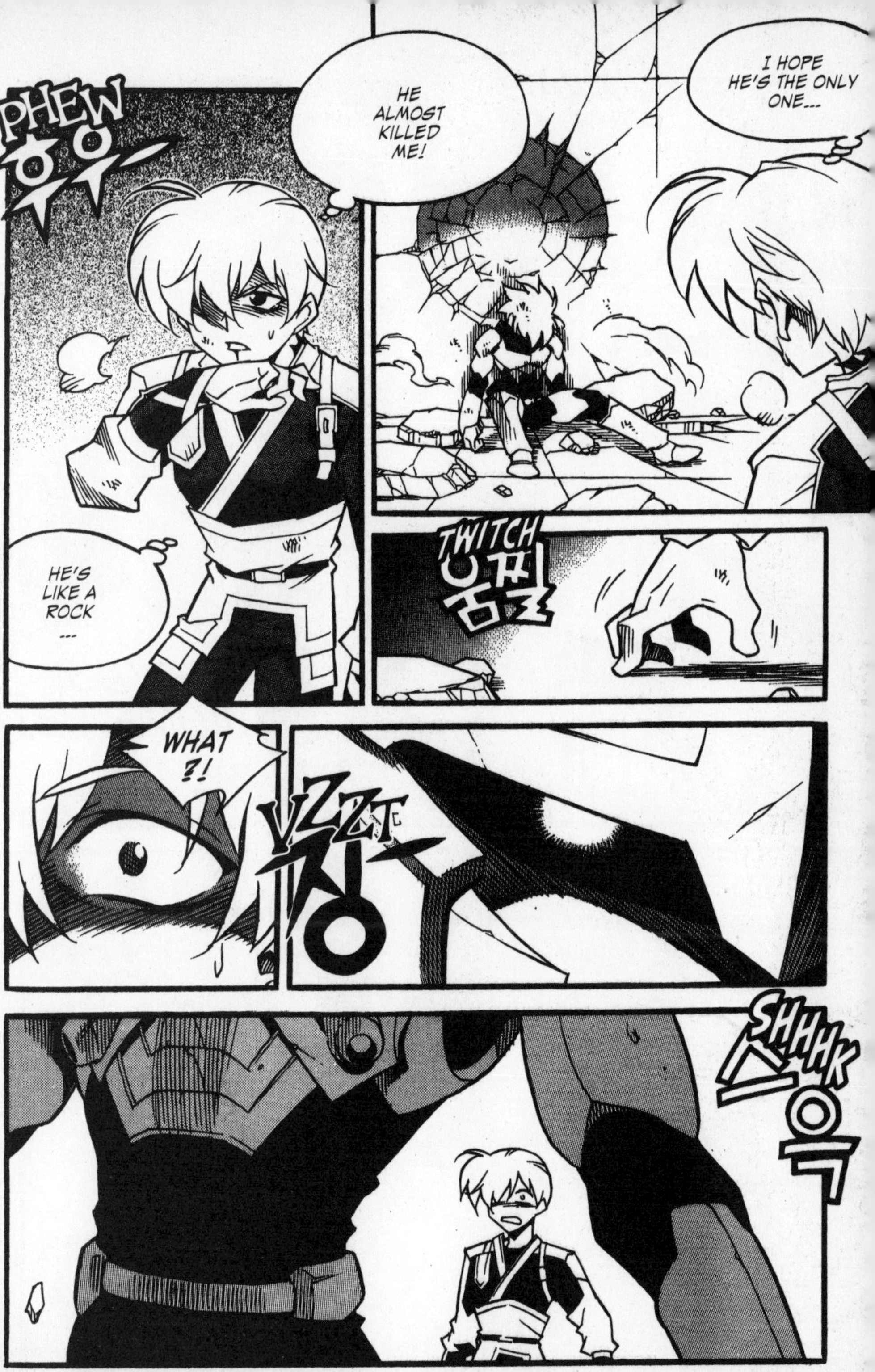
PHEW
흥어
HE ALMOST KILLED ME!
HE'S LIKE A ROCK ...
I HOPE HE'S THE ONLY ONE...
TWITCH
움찔
WHAT ?!
VZZT
지잉
SHHHK
스윽

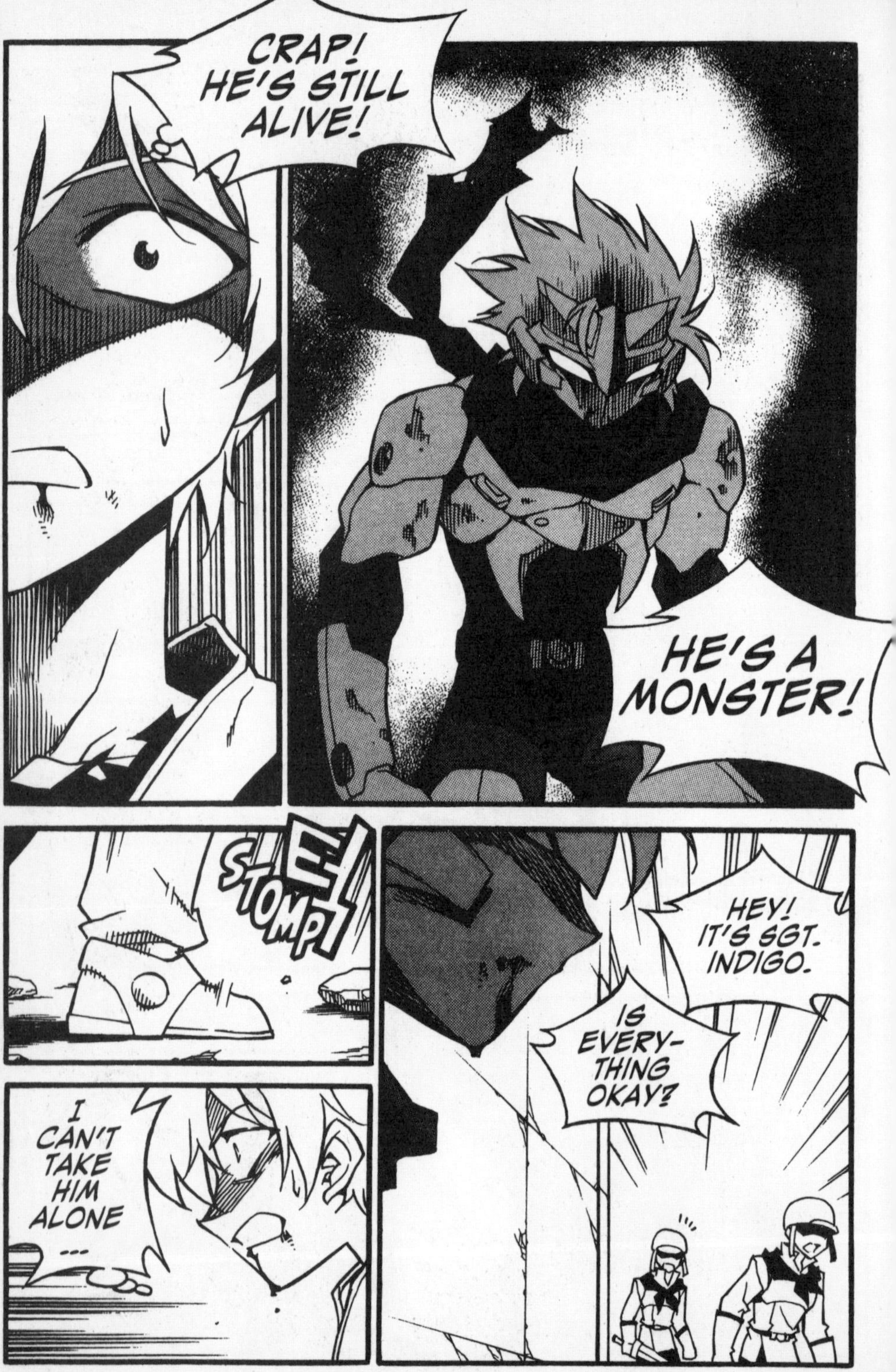
CRAP! HE'S STILL ALIVE!
HE'S A MONSTER!
STOMP
HEY! IT'S SGT. INDIGO.
IS EVERYTHING OKAY?
I CAN'T TAKE HIM ALONE ...

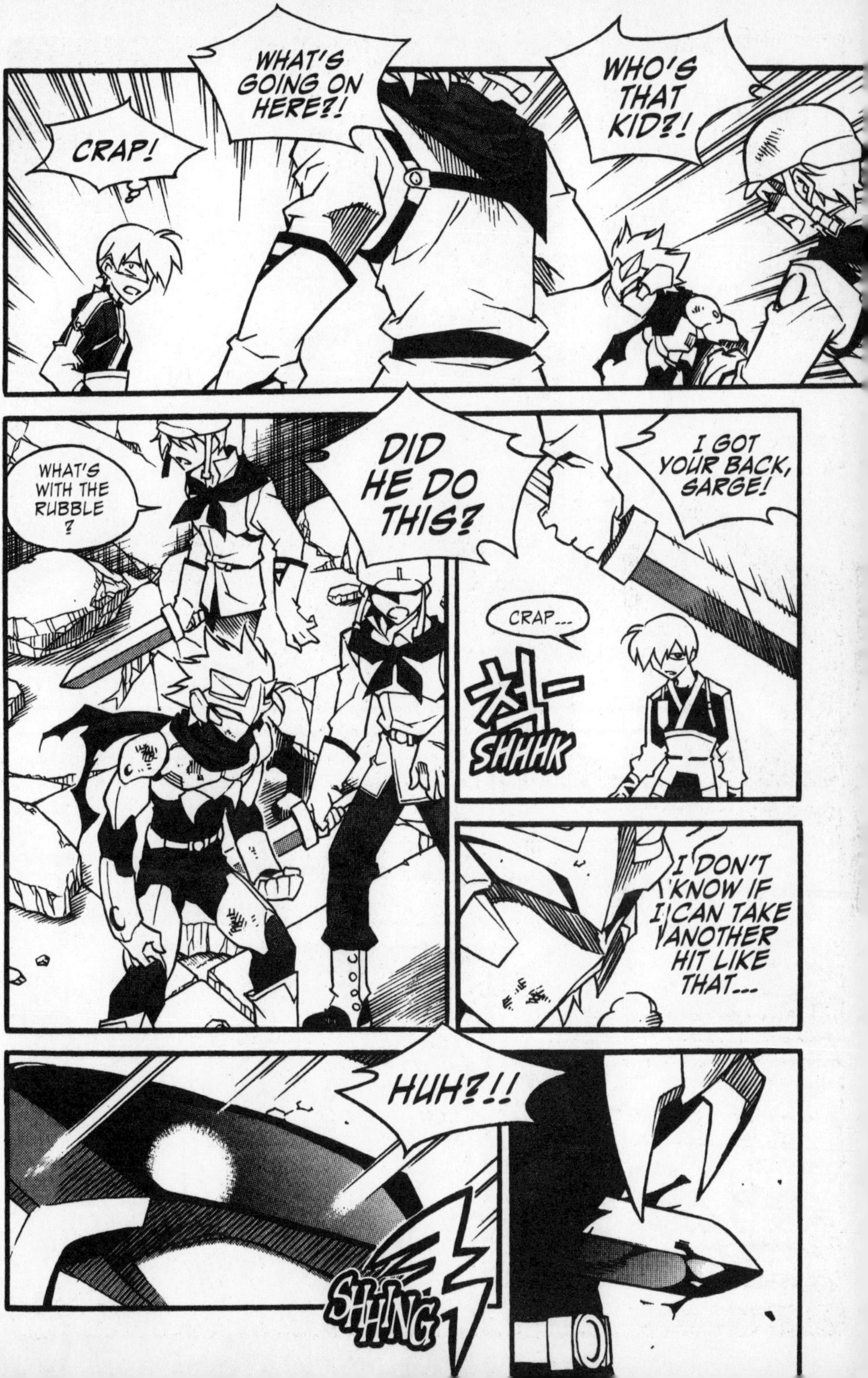
CRAP!
WHAT'S GOING ON HERE?!
WHO'S THAT KID?!
WHAT'S WITH THE RUBBLE?
DID HE DO THIS?
I GOT YOUR BACK, SARGE!
CRAP...
SHHHK
I DON'T KNOW IF I CAN TAKE ANOTHER HIT LIKE THAT...
HUH?!!
SHING

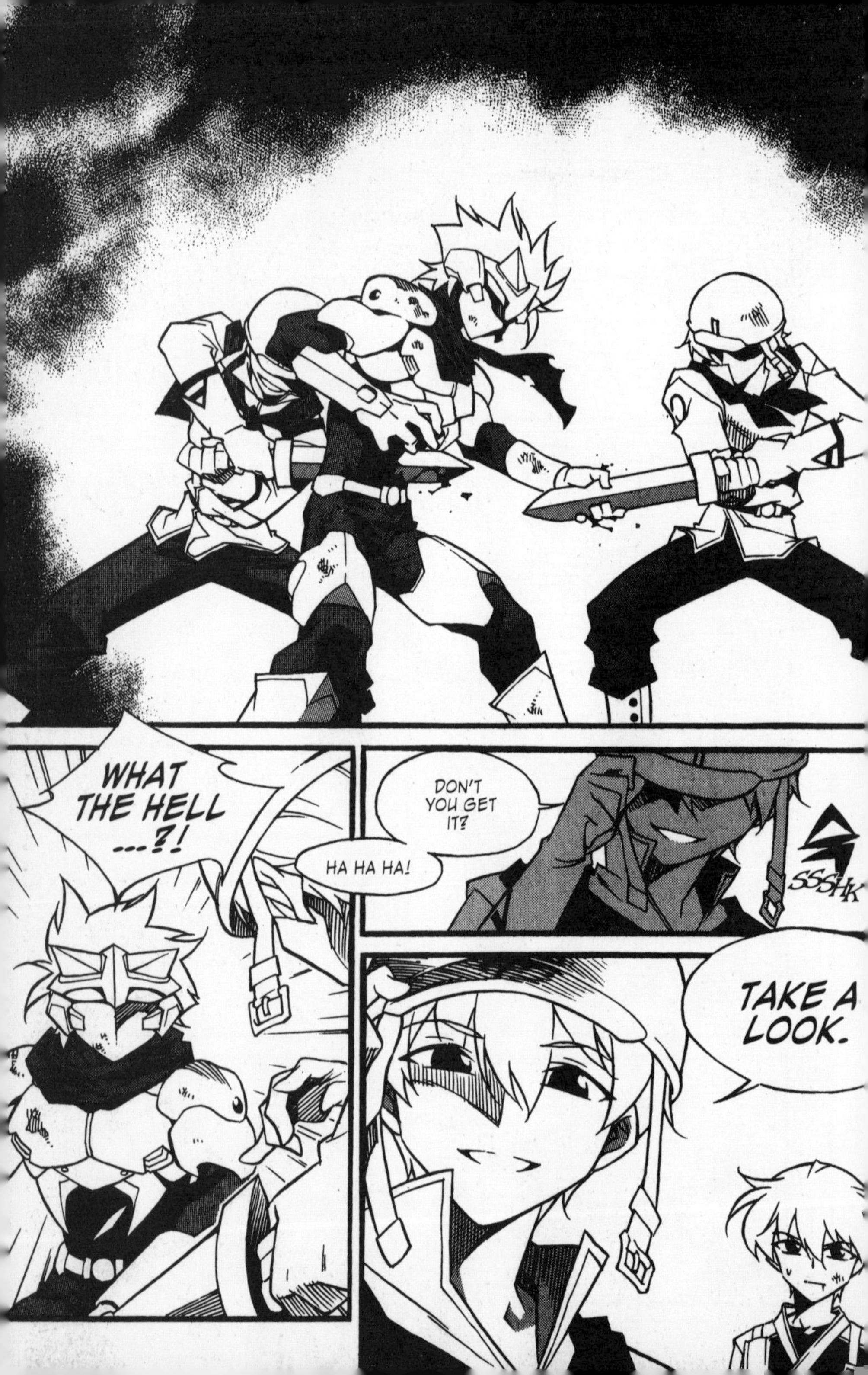
WHAT THE HELL ---?!
DON'T YOU GET IT?
HA HA HA!
SSSHK
TAKE A LOOK.

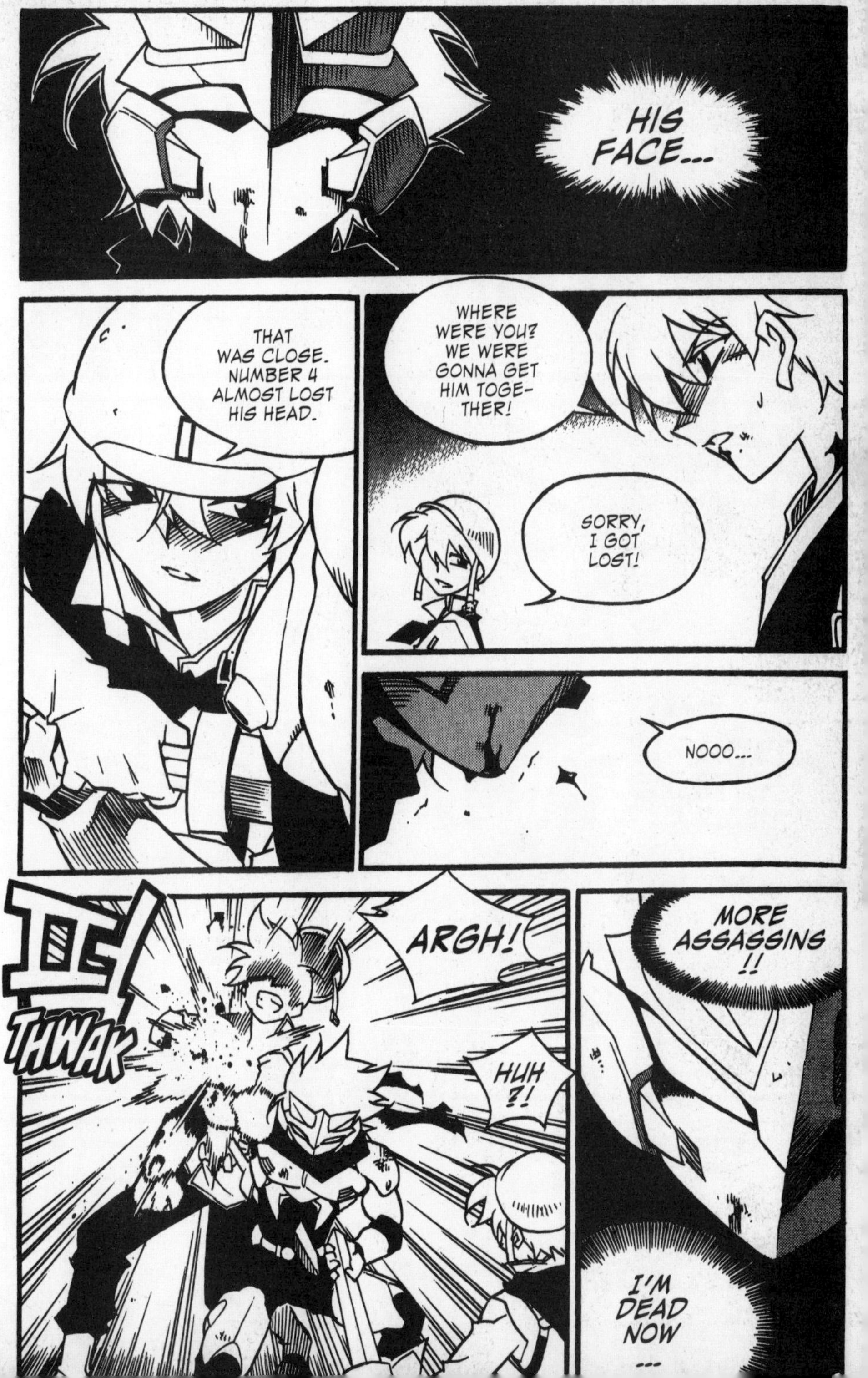
HIS FACE...
THAT WAS CLOSE. NUMBER 4 ALMOST LOST HIS HEAD.
WHERE WERE YOU? WE WERE GONNA GET HIM TOGE-THER!
SORRY, I GOT LOST!
NOOO...
THWAK
ARGH!
HUH ?!
MORE ASSASSINS !!
I'M DEAD NOW ...

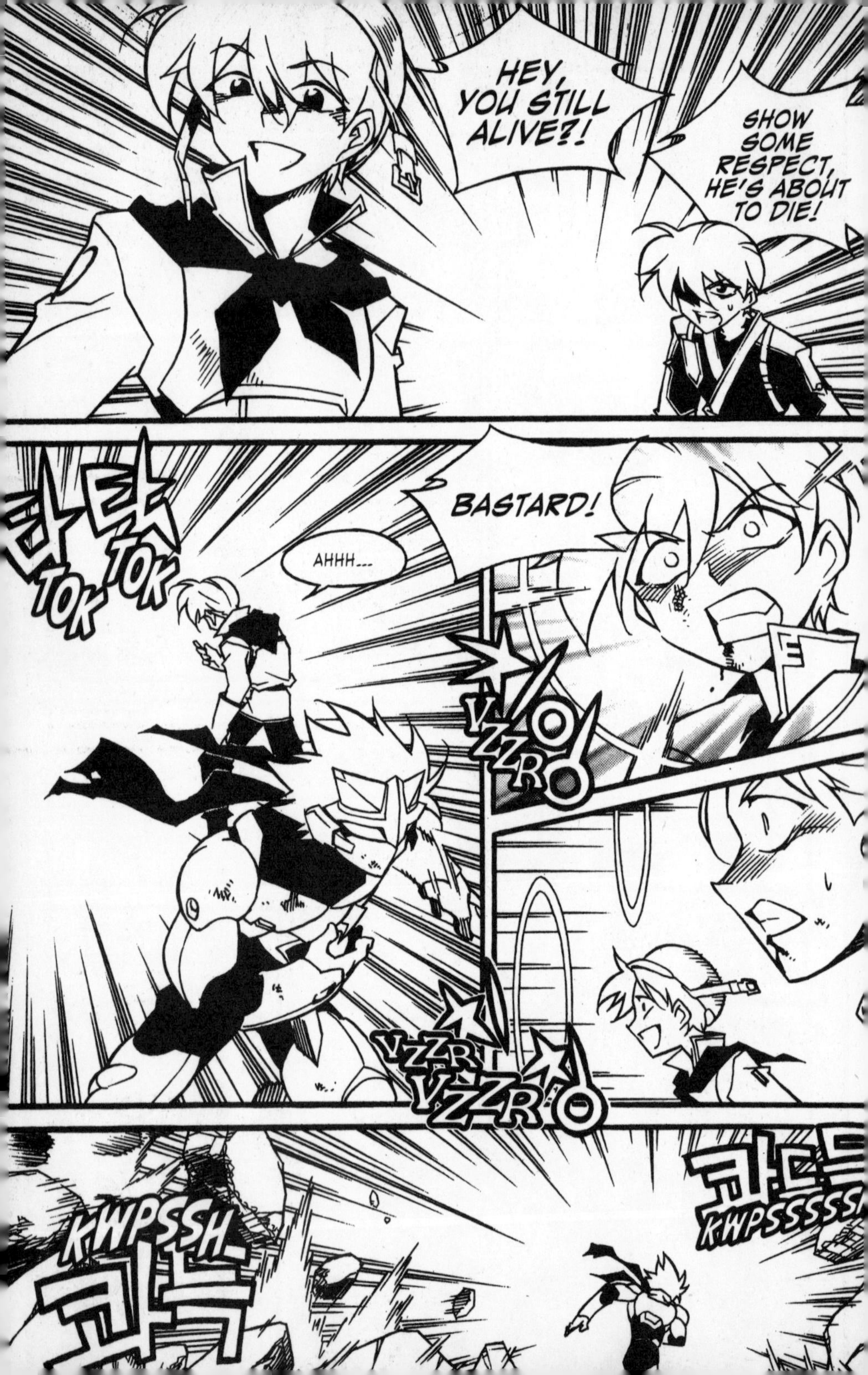

HEY, YOU STILL ALIVE?!
SHOW SOME RESPECT, HE'S ABOUT TO DIE!
BASTARD!
AHHH...
TOK TOK
VZZRO
VZZR
VZZRO
KWPSSH
KWPSSSSS

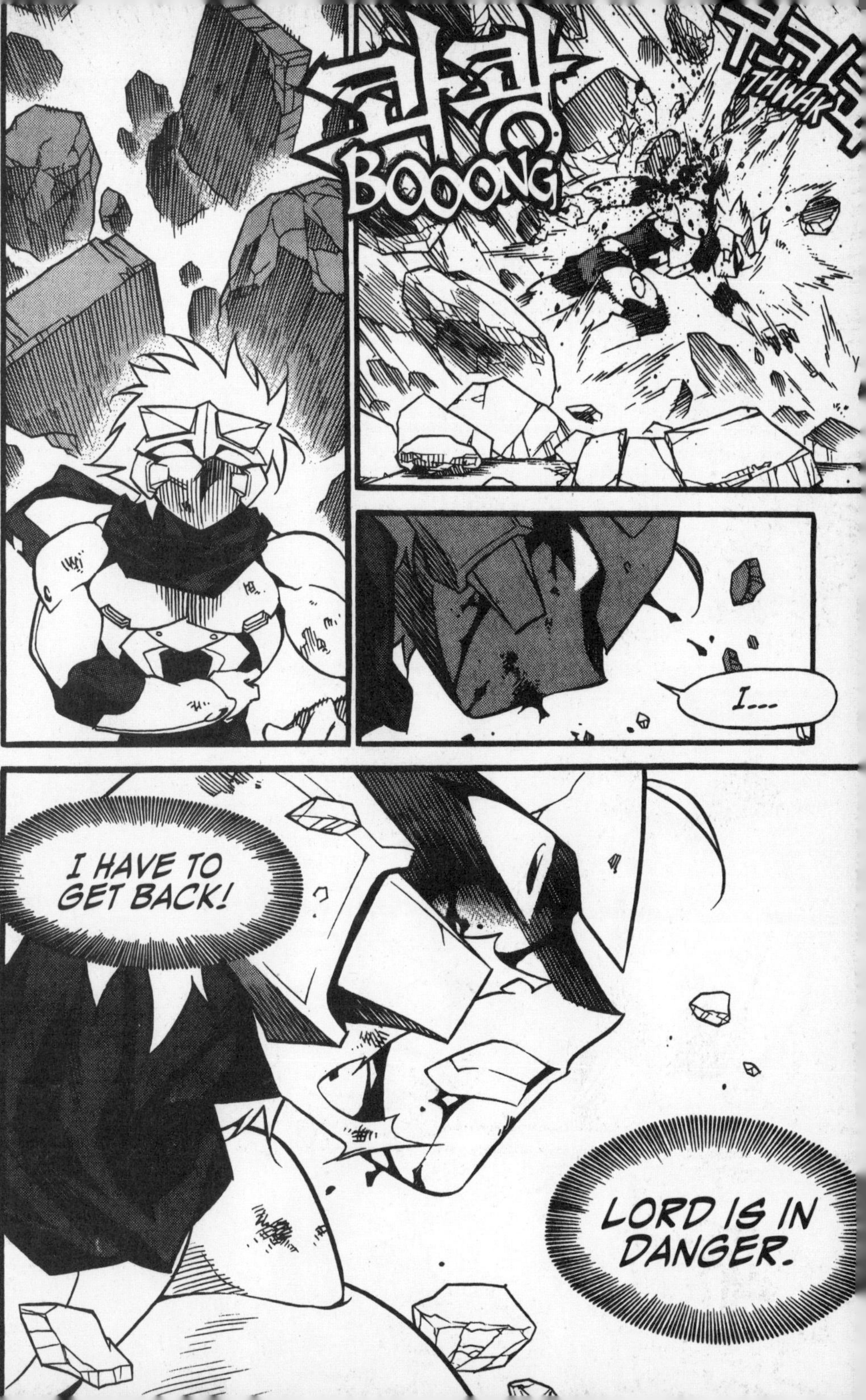

BOOONG
THWAK
I...
I HAVE TO GET BACK!
LORD IS IN DANGER.

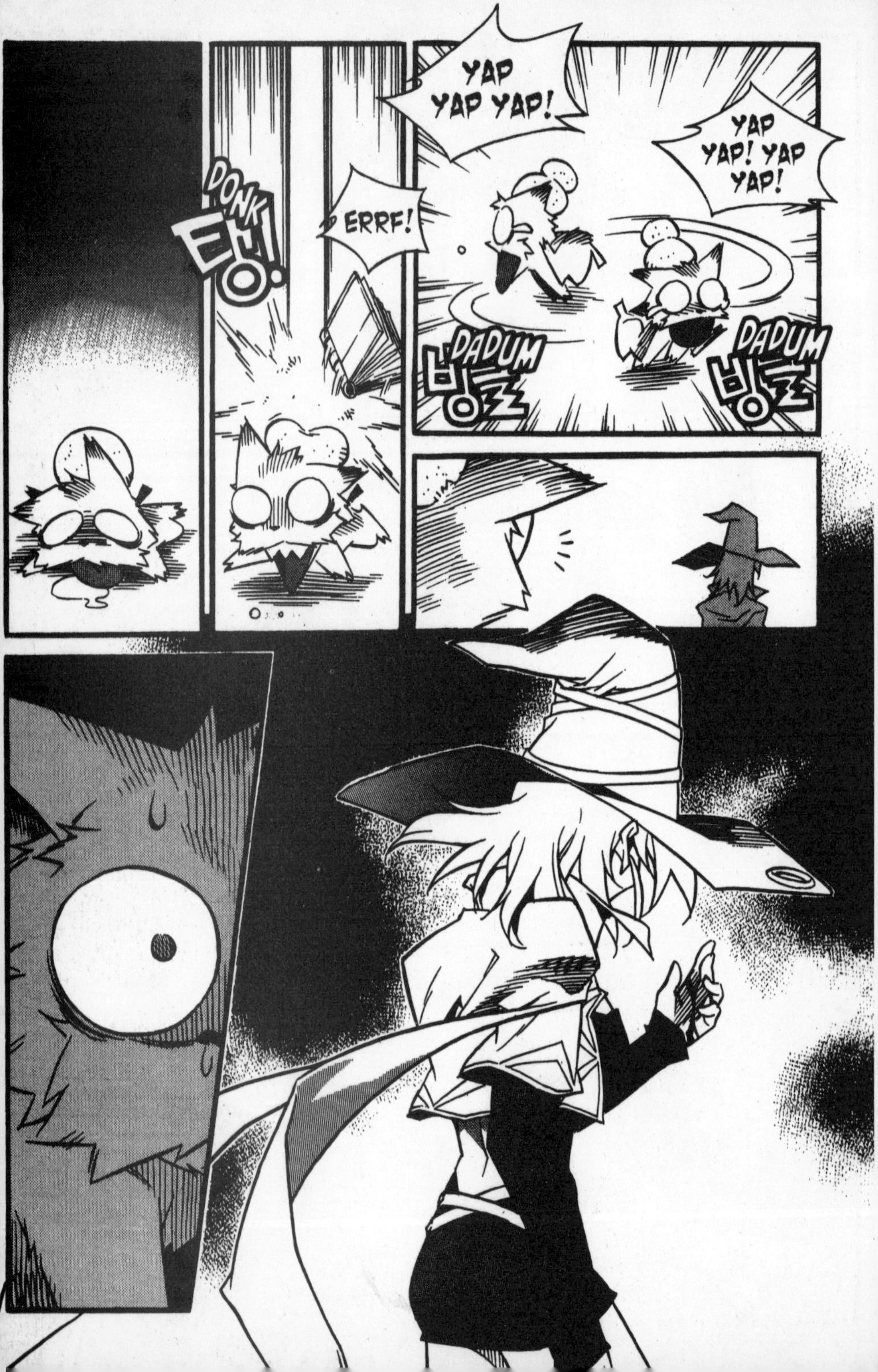
DONK
ERRF!
YAP YAP YAP!
YAP YAP! YAP YAP!
DADUM
DADUM

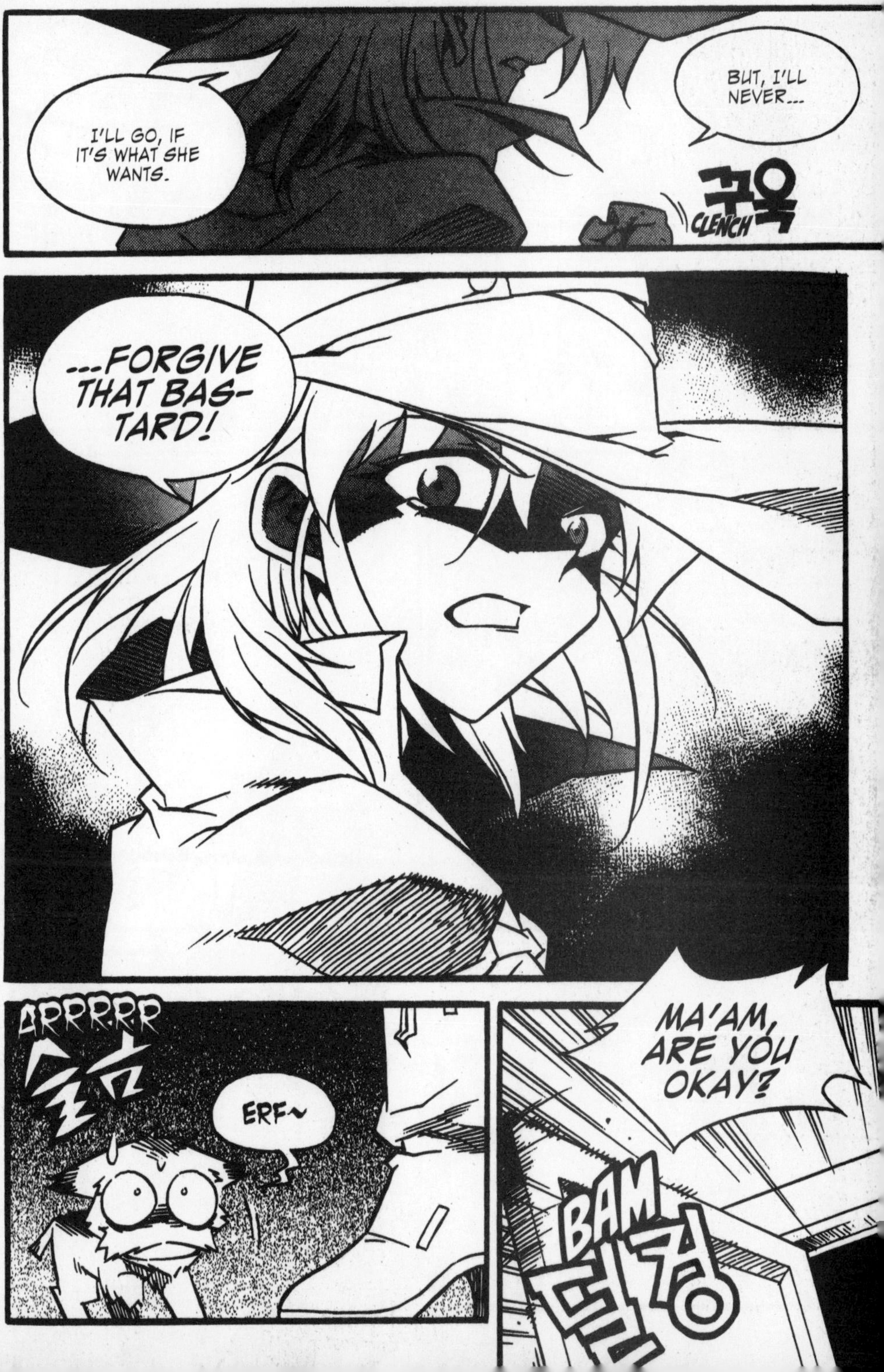
I'LL GO, IF IT'S WHAT SHE WANTS.
BUT, I'LL NEVER...
구욱
CLENCH
...FORGIVE THAT BAS-TARD!
MA'AM, ARE YOU OKAY?
BAM
덜컹
ARRRRR
ERF~

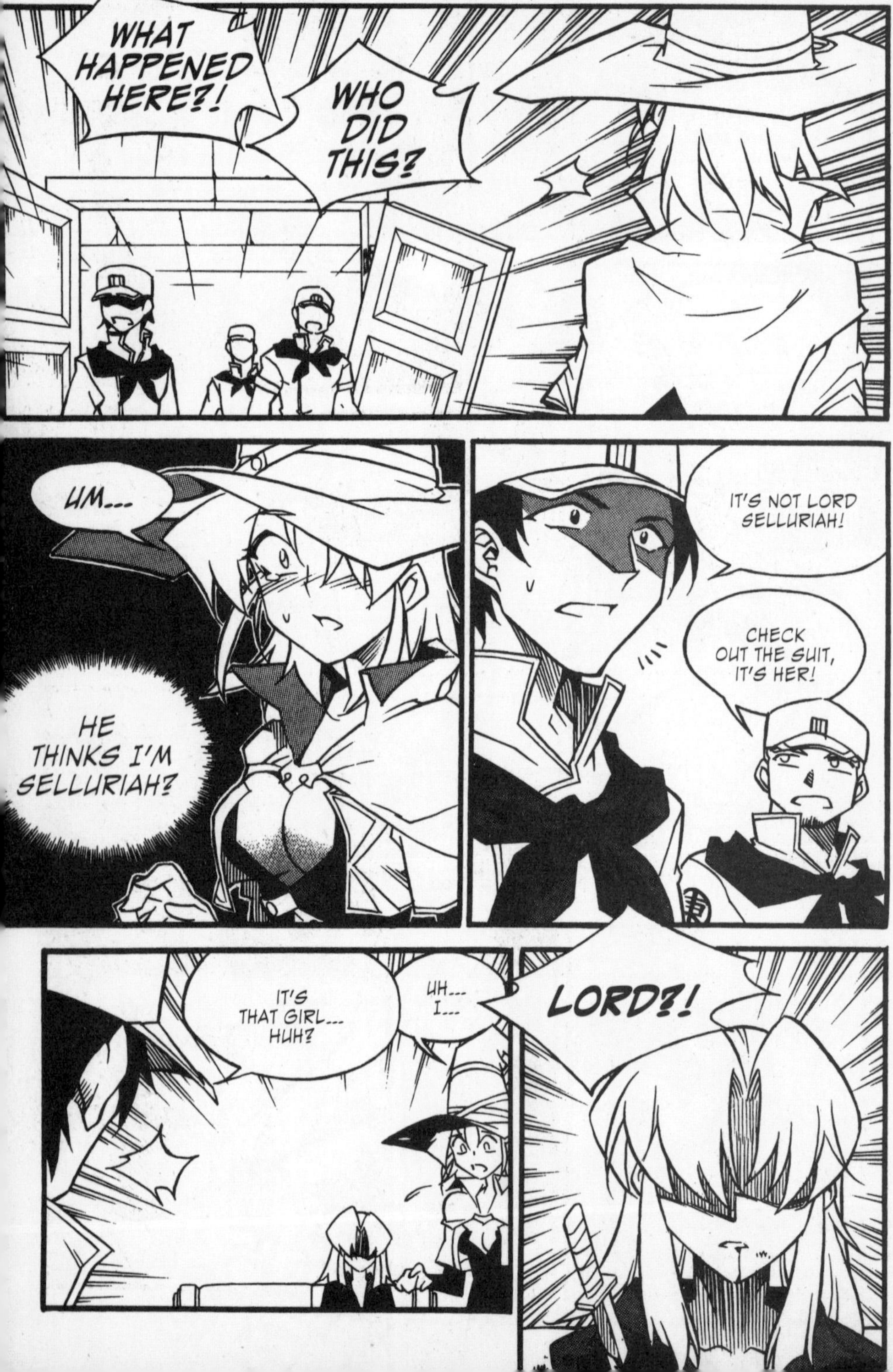
WHAT HAPPENED HERE?!
WHO DID THIS?
UM...
HE THINKS I'M SELLURIAH?
IT'S NOT LORD SELLURIAH!
CHECK OUT THE SUIT, IT'S HER!
IT'S THAT GIRL... HUH?
UH... I...
LORD?!

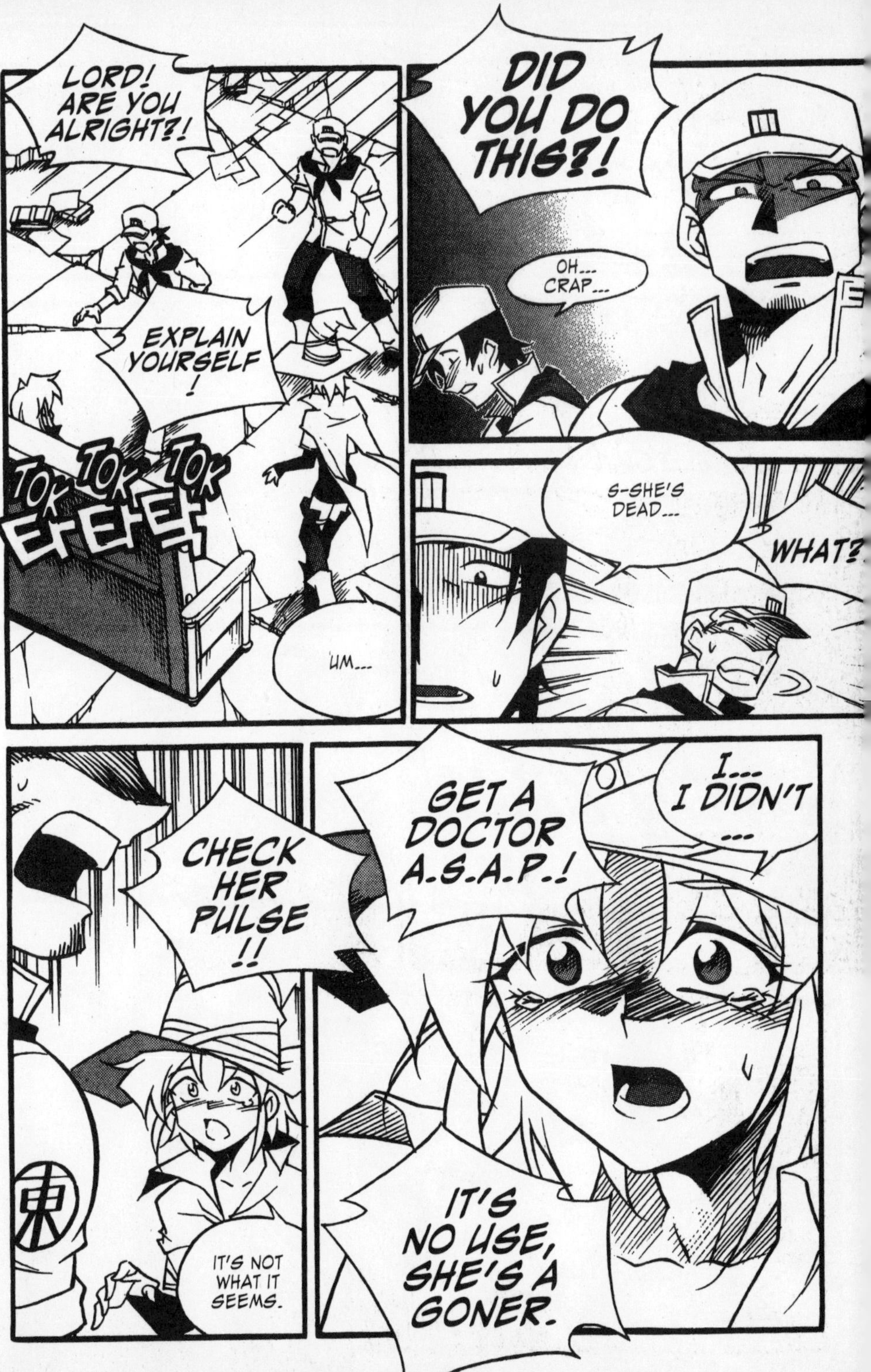
LORD! ARE YOU ALRIGHT?!
EXPLAIN YOURSELF!
TOK TOK TOK
탁탁탁
UM...
DID YOU DO THIS?!
OH... CRAP...
S-SHE'S DEAD...
WHAT?
CHECK HER PULSE!!
IT'S NOT WHAT IT SEEMS.
I... I DIDN'T...
GET A DOCTOR A.S.A.P.!
IT'S NO USE, SHE'S A GONER.

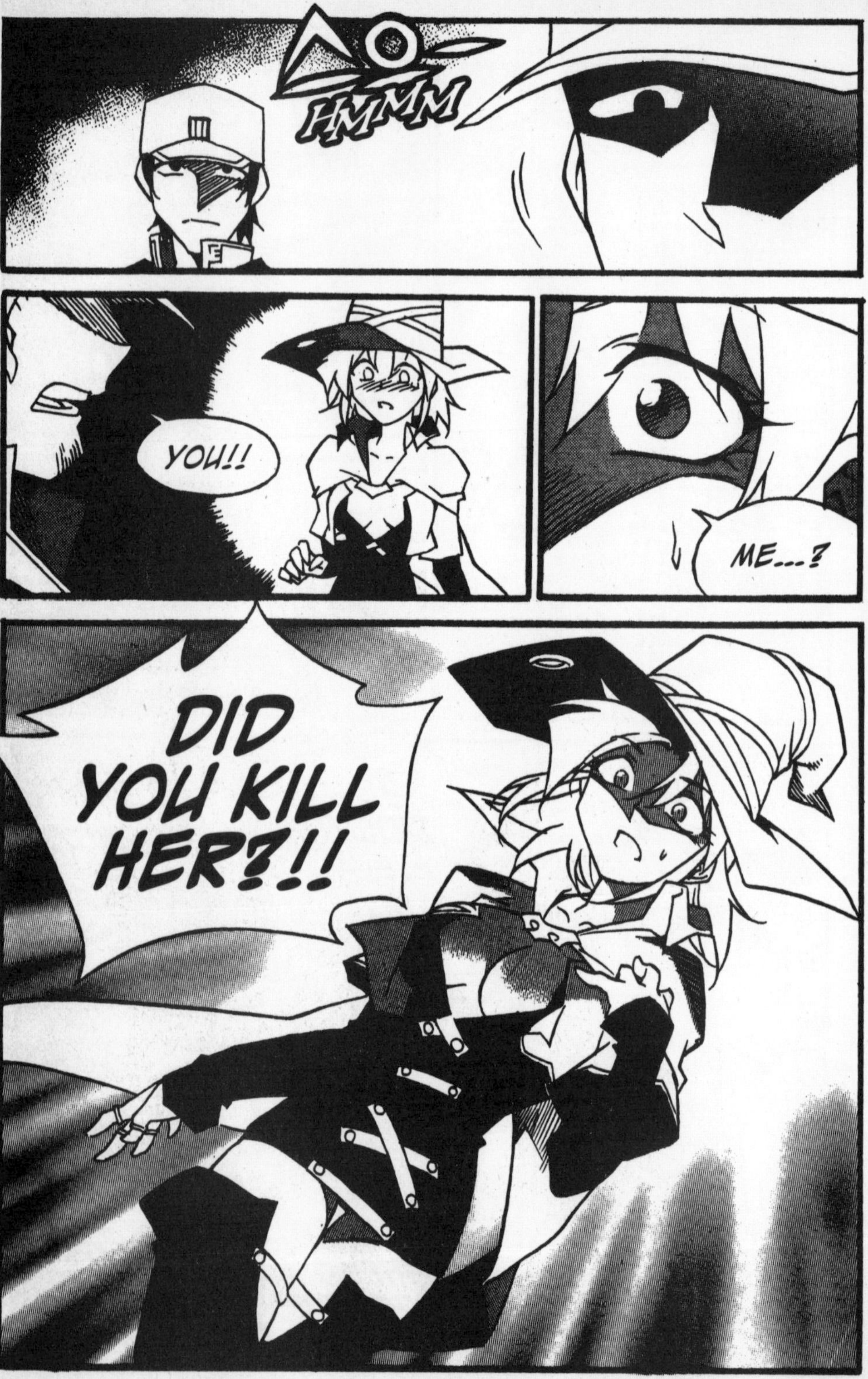
HMMM
YOU!!
ME...?
DID YOU KILL HER?!!

Step 12 IT WASN'T ME!

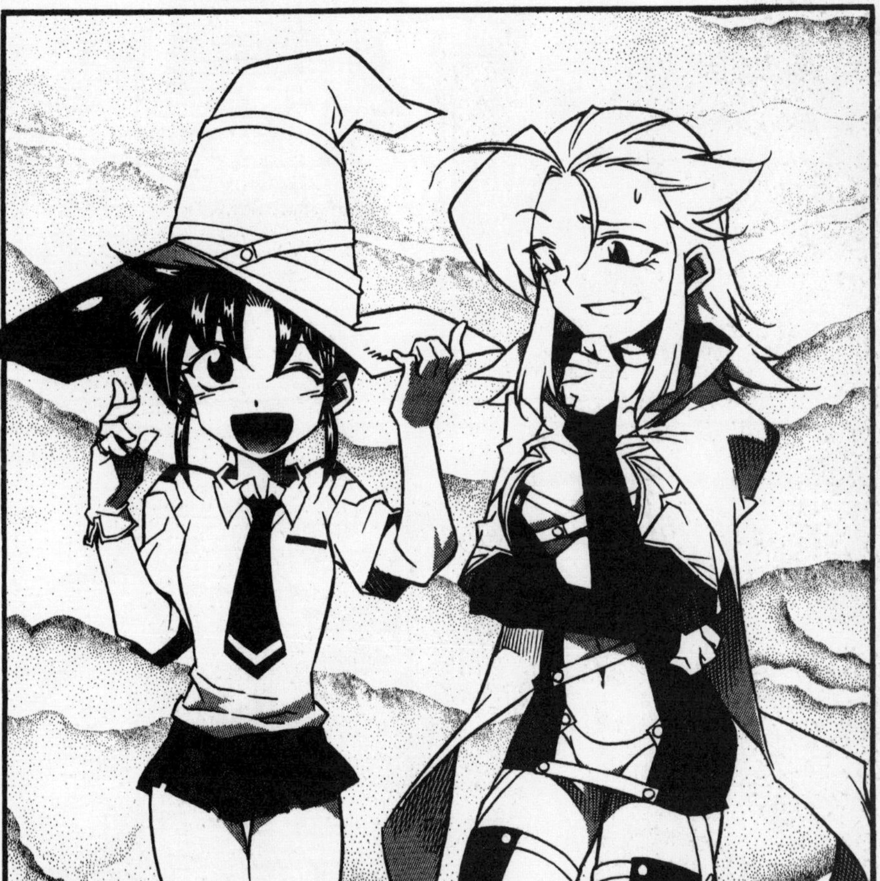

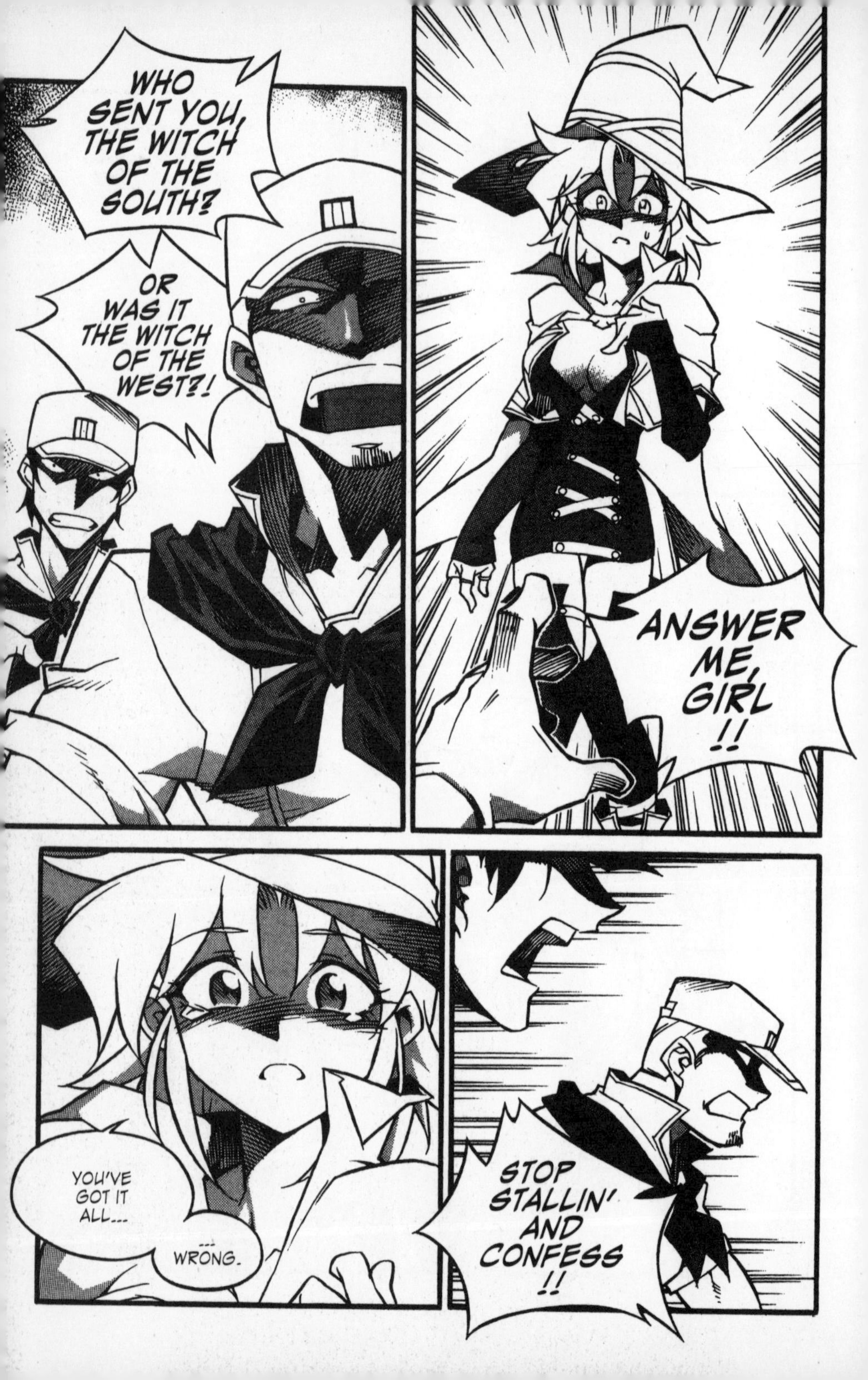
WHO SENT YOU, THE WITCH OF THE SOUTH?
OR WAS IT THE WITCH OF THE WEST?!
ANSWER ME, GIRL!!
YOU'VE GOT IT ALL...
...WRONG.
STOP STALLIN' AND CONFESS!!

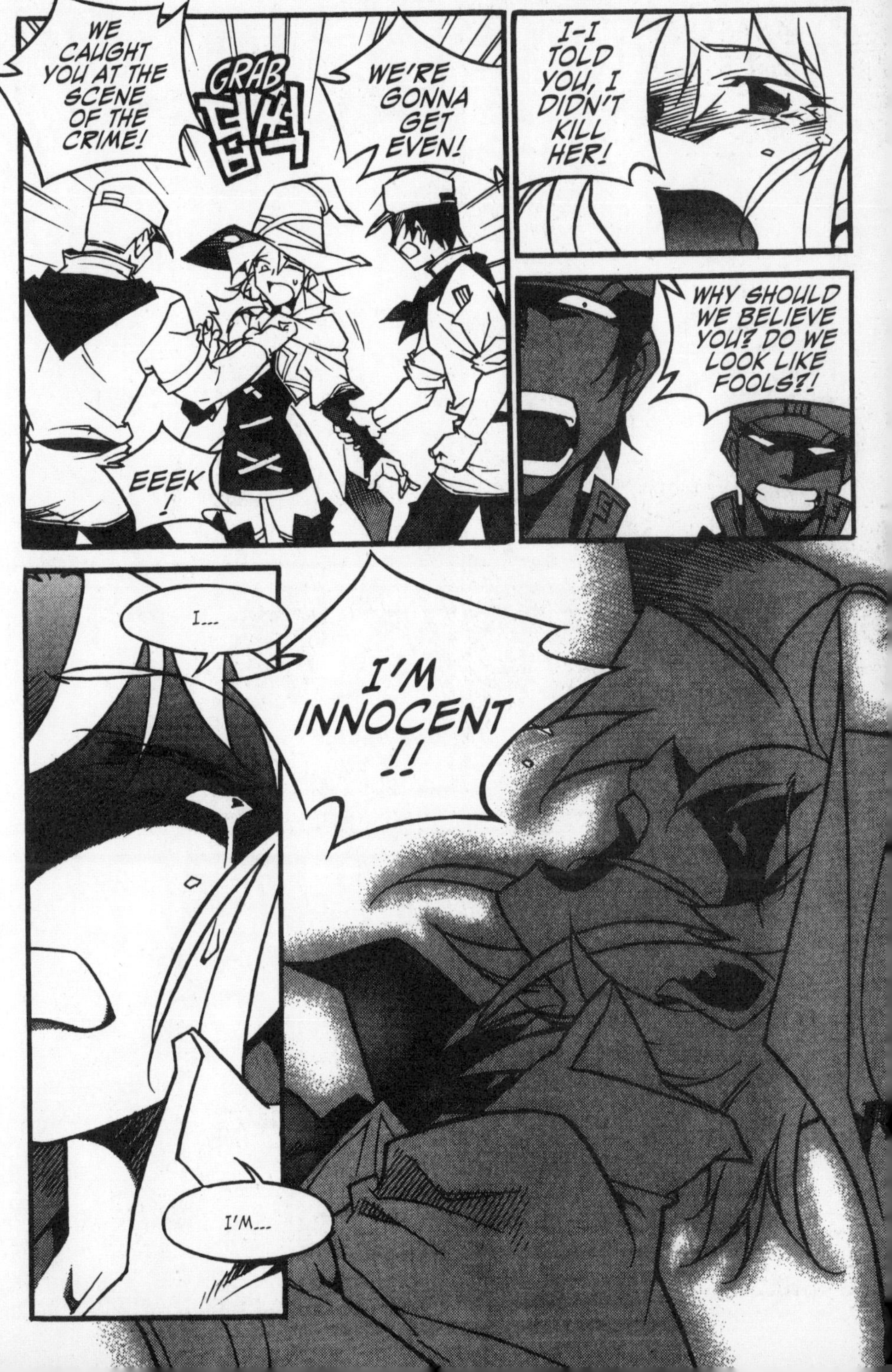

WE CAUGHT YOU AT THE SCENE OF THE CRIME!
GRAB
WE'RE GONNA GET EVEN!
EEEK!
I-I TOLD YOU, I DIDN'T KILL HER!
WHY SHOULD WE BELIEVE YOU? DO WE LOOK LIKE FOOLS?!
I...
I'M...
I'M INNOCENT!!

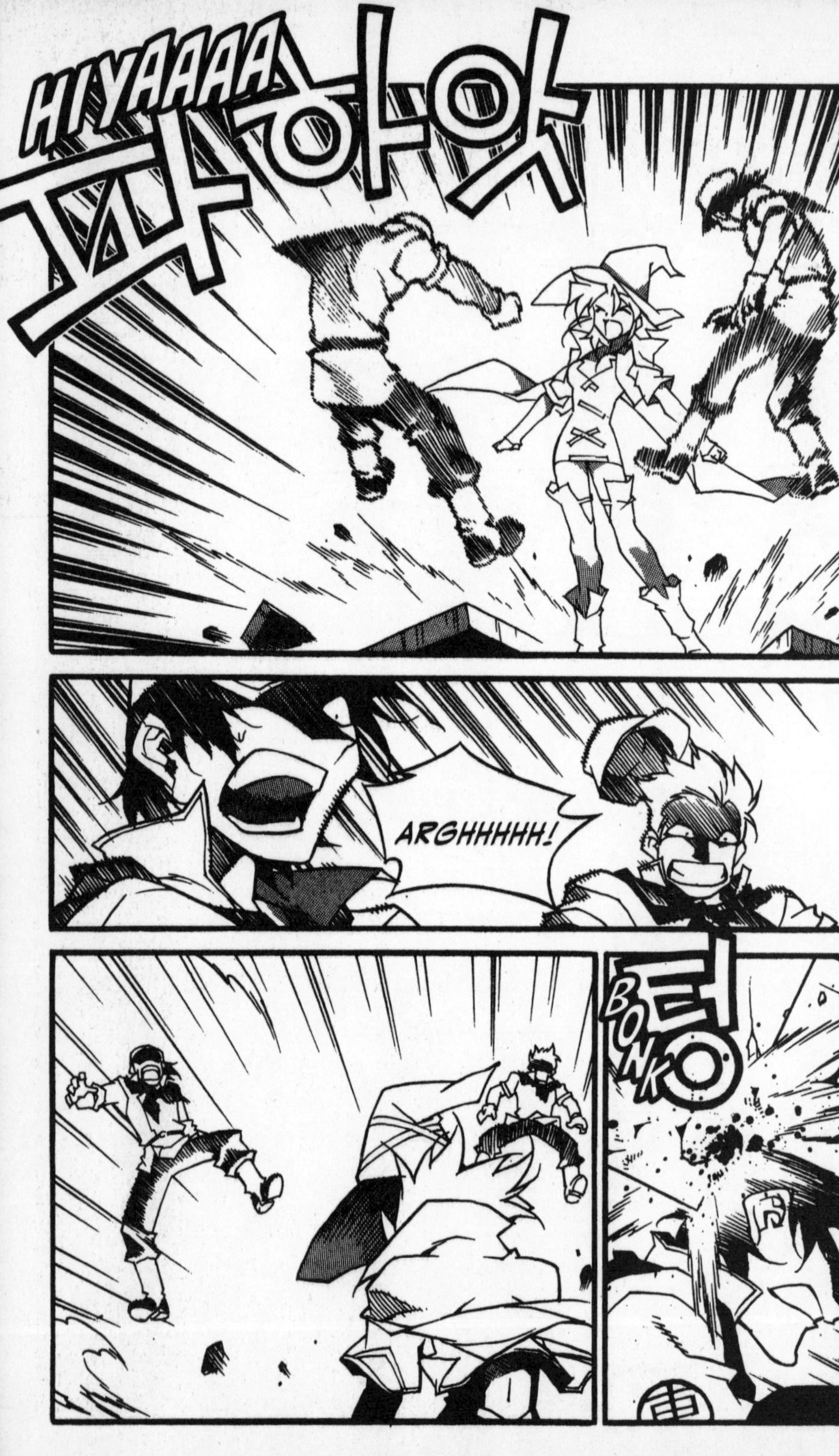
HIYAAAA
파야아앗
ARGHHHHH!
BONK

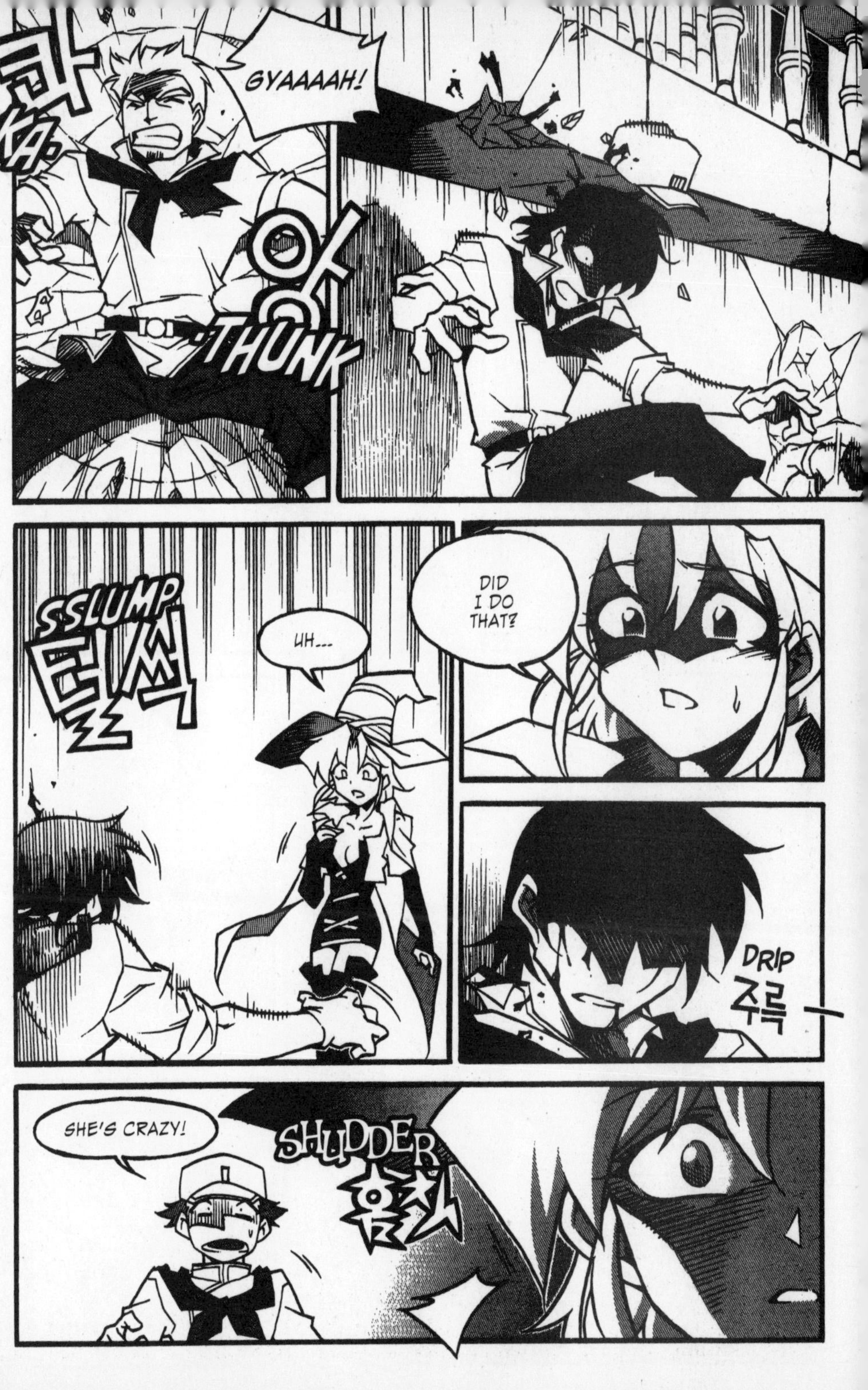
KA
GYAAAAH!
THUNK
SSLUMP
UH...
DID I DO THAT?
DRIP
주륵
SHE'S CRAZY!
SHUDDER

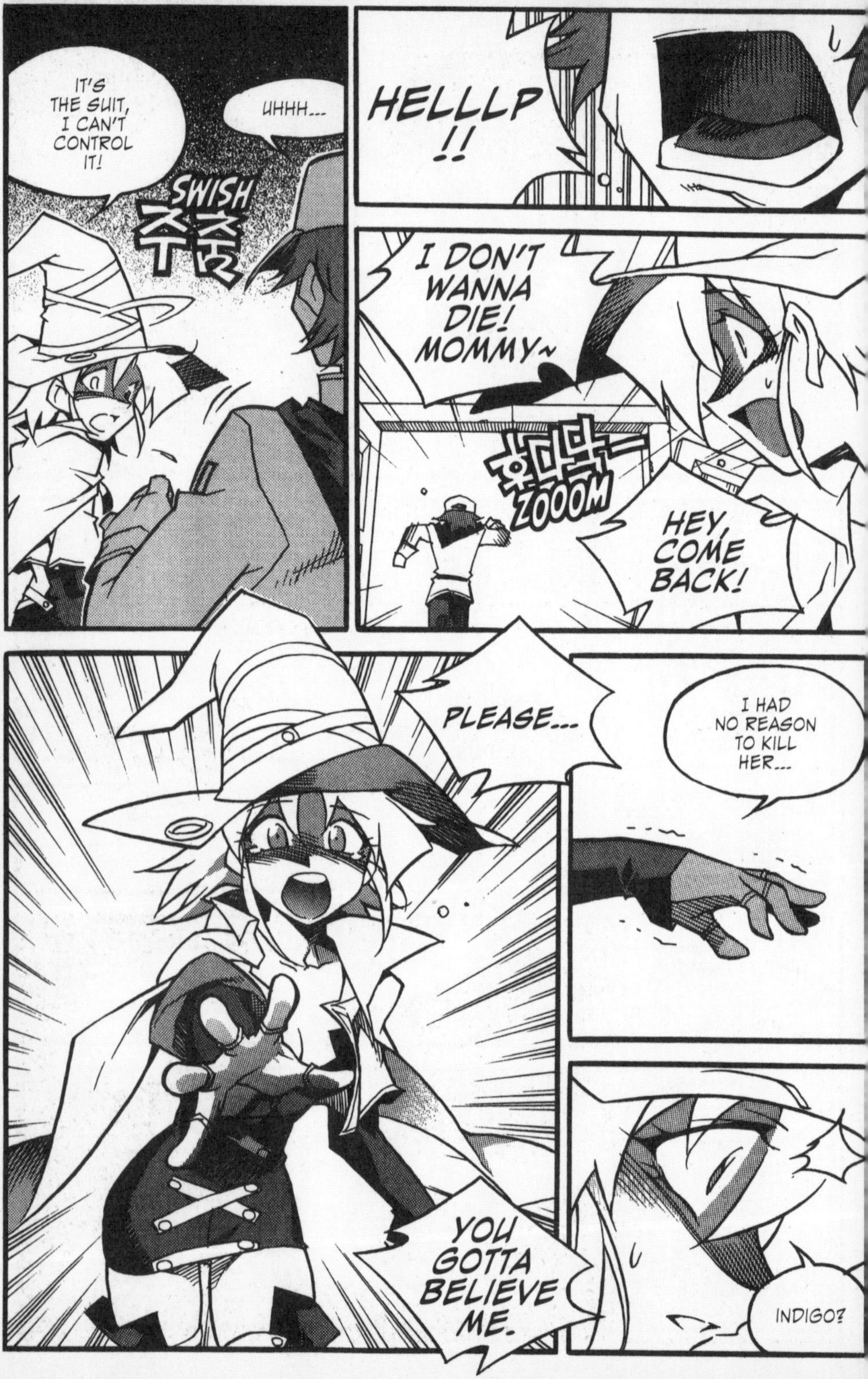

UHHH...
IT'S THE SUIT, I CAN'T CONTROL IT!
SWISH
주죽
HELLLP !!
I DON'T WANNA DIE! MOMMY~
후다닥
ZOOOM
HEY, COME BACK!
PLEASE...
YOU GOTTA BELIEVE ME.
I HAD NO REASON TO KILL HER...
INDIGO?

HE TOOK A BIG DIVE OUTTA THE WINDOW THOUGH.

INDIGO CAN SORT THIS MESS OUT!

IS HE EVEN ALIVE?

HE CAN PROVE MY INNOCENCE!

—WHAT?

THAT IMAGE ...

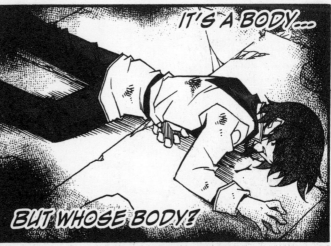

IT'S A BODY...

BUT WHOSE BODY?

INDIGO?

IS HE DEAD?

NO, HE'S STILL ALIVE!

WHO ARE THOSE GUYS?

THAT UNIFORM.... THE ASSASSIN!!

ARE THE SOLDIERS WITH HIM?!

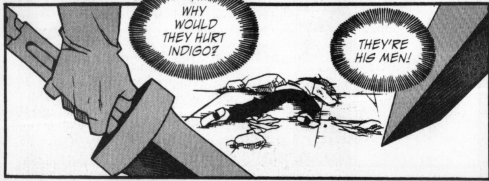

WHY WOULD THEY HURT INDIGO?

THEY'RE HIS MEN!

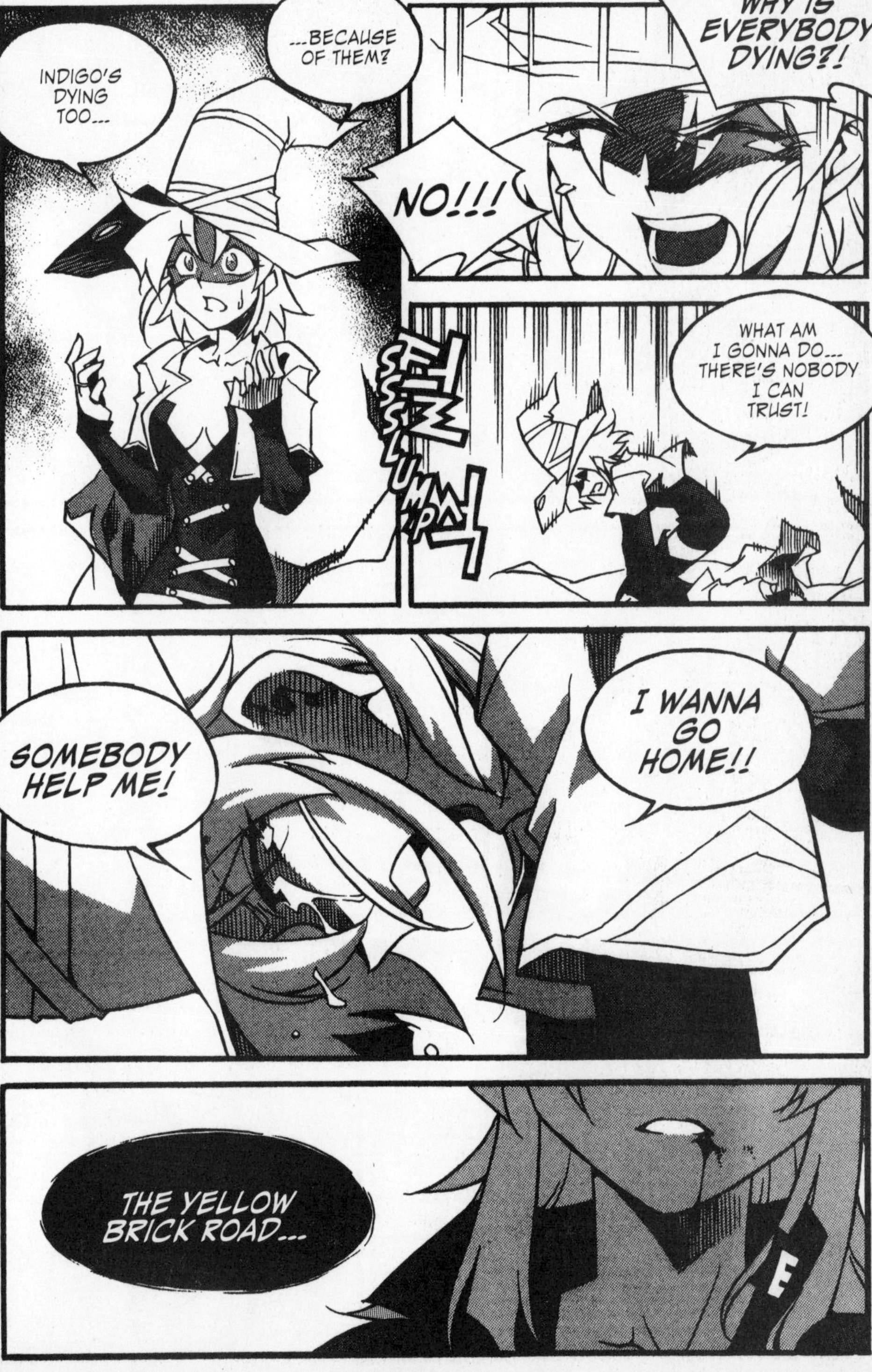

INDIGO'S DYING TOO...
...BECAUSE OF THEM?
WHY IS EVERYBODY DYING?!
NO!!!
FFSSSZZ
SLUMMP
WHAT AM I GONNA DO... THERE'S NOBODY I CAN TRUST!
SOMEBODY HELP ME!
I WANNA GO HOME!!
THE YELLOW BRICK ROAD...

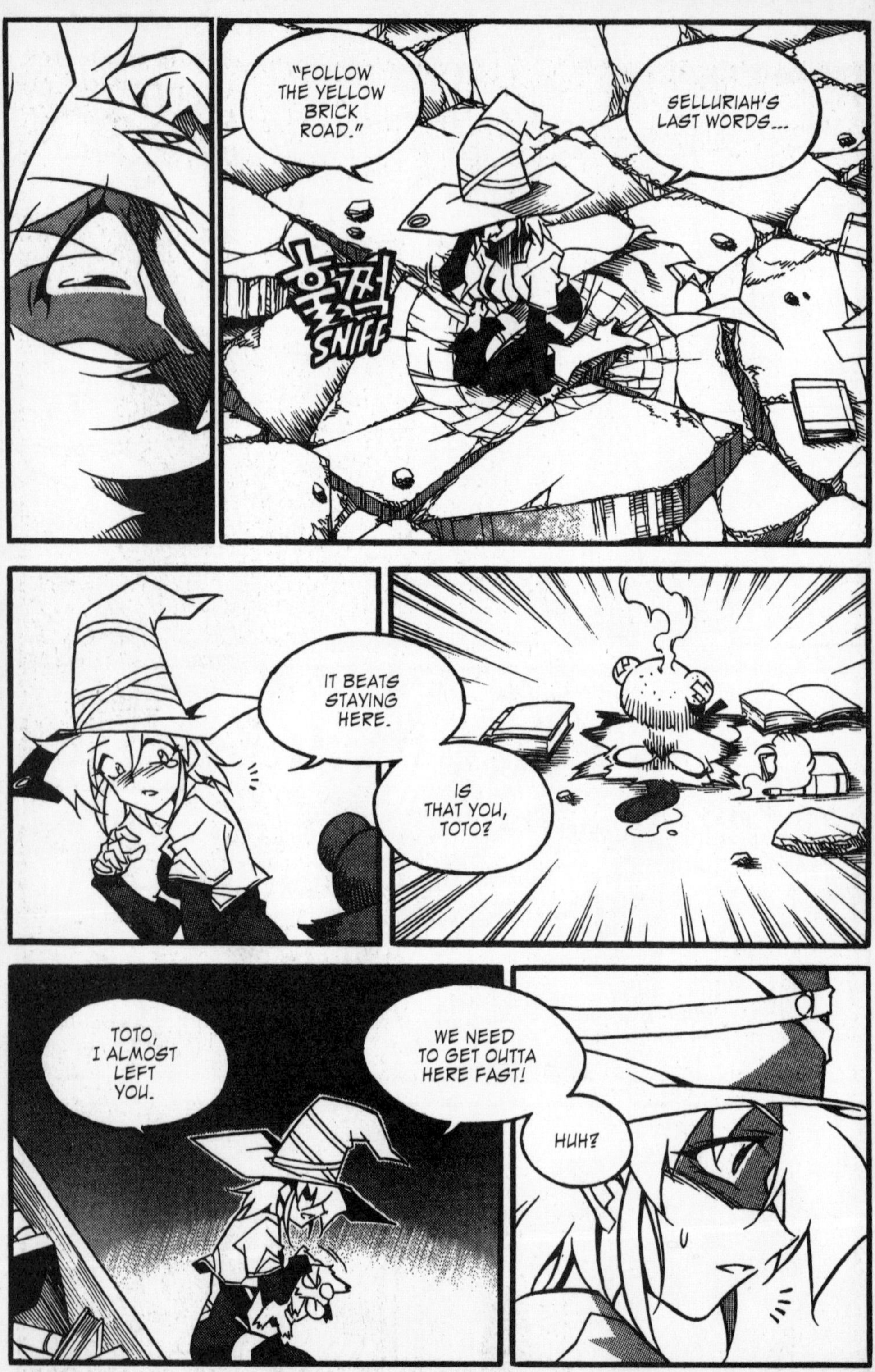
"FOLLOW THE YELLOW BRICK ROAD."
SELLURIAH'S LAST WORDS...
SNIFF
IT BEATS STAYING HERE.
IS THAT YOU, TOTO?
TOTO, I ALMOST LEFT YOU.
WE NEED TO GET OUTTA HERE FAST!
HUH?

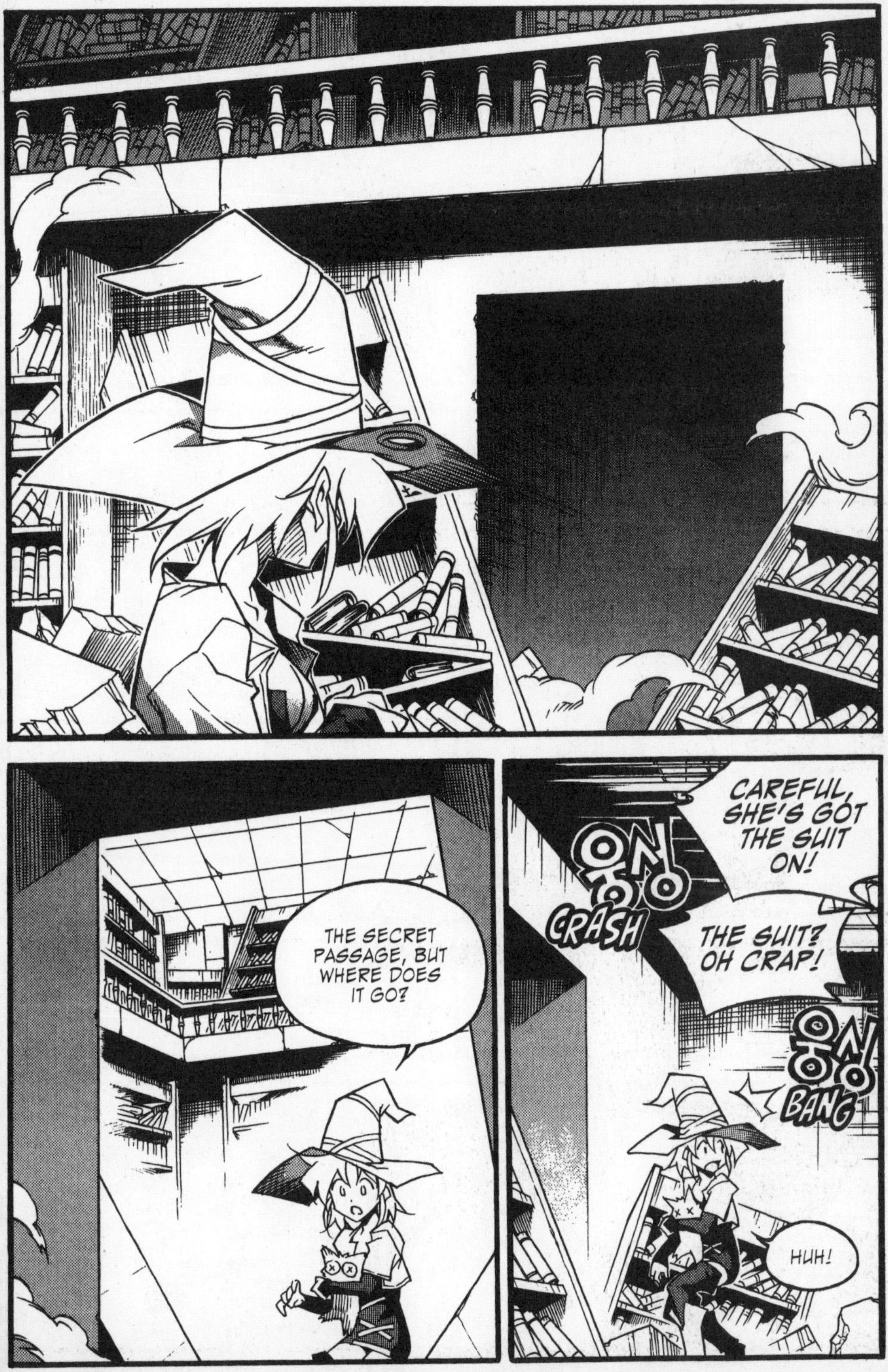
THE SECRET PASSAGE, BUT WHERE DOES IT GO?
CRASH
CAREFUL, SHE'S GOT THE SUIT ON!
THE SUIT? OH CRAP!
BANG
HUH!

GET HER BEFORE SHE ESCAPES!

타타타—
TOK TOK TOK

I GOTTA GET OUTTA HERE!

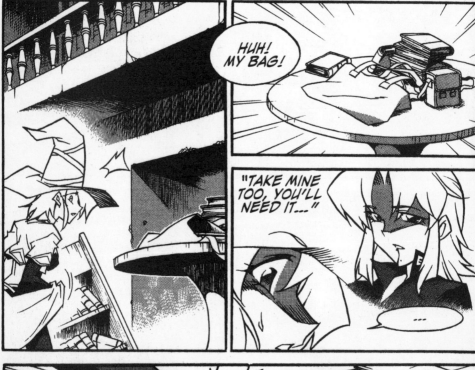

HUH! MY BAG!

"TAKE MINE TOO, YOU'LL NEED IT...."

...

YOINK 터

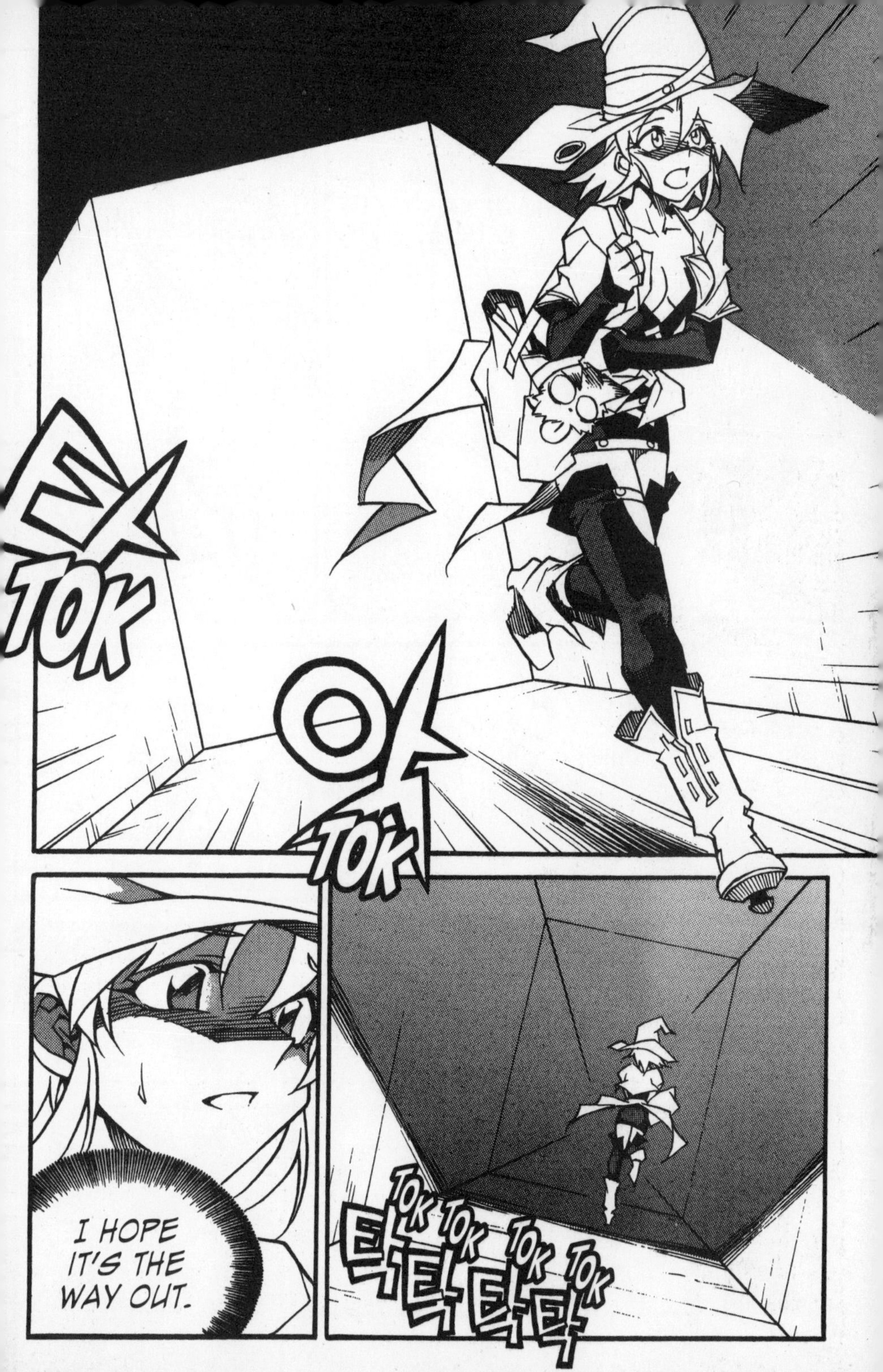
TOK
TOK
I HOPE IT'S THE WAY OUT.
TOK TOK TOK TOK

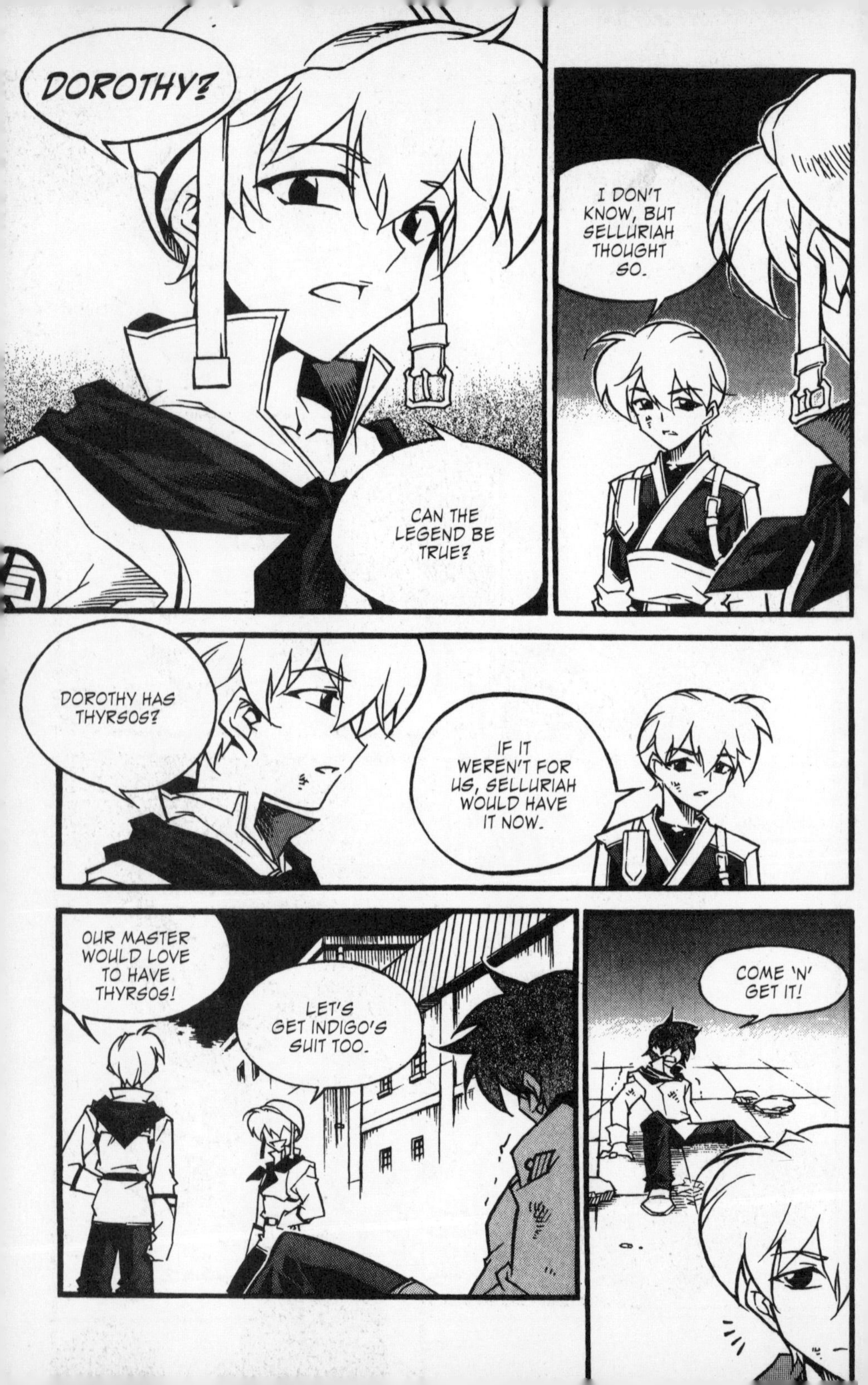
DOROTHY?
CAN THE LEGEND BE TRUE?
I DON'T KNOW, BUT SELLURIAH THOUGHT SO.
DOROTHY HAS THYRSOS?
IF IT WEREN'T FOR US, SELLURIAH WOULD HAVE IT NOW.
OUR MASTER WOULD LOVE TO HAVE THYRSOS!
LET'S GET INDIGO'S SUIT TOO.
COME 'N' GET IT!

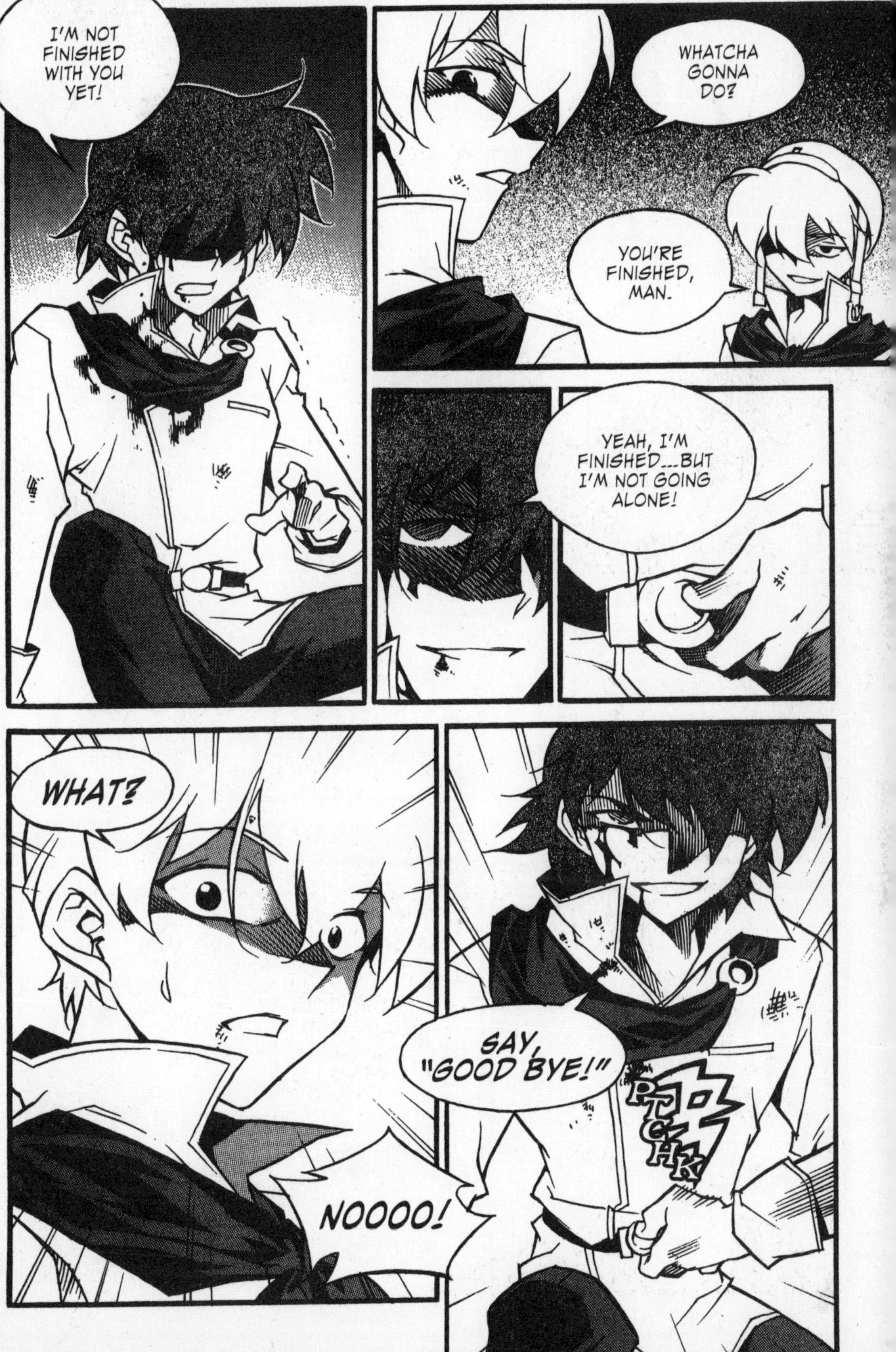
I'M NOT FINISHED WITH YOU YET!
WHATCHA GONNA DO?
YOU'RE FINISHED, MAN.
YEAH, I'M FINISHED...BUT I'M NOT GOING ALONE!
WHAT?
SAY, "GOOD BYE!"
PTCHK
NOOOO!

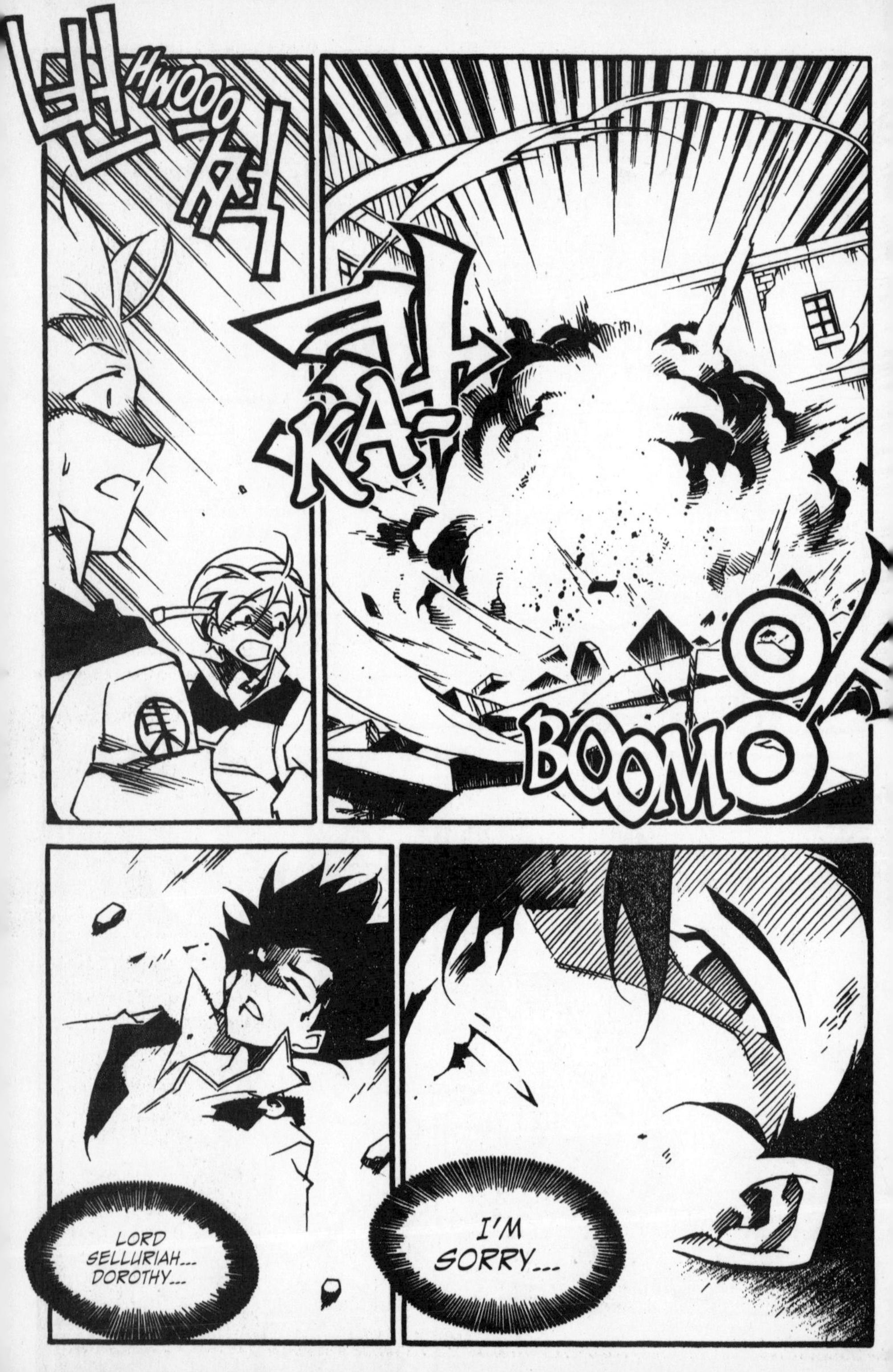
HWOOO
KA-
BOOM
LORD SELLURIAH... DOROTHY...
I'M SORRY...

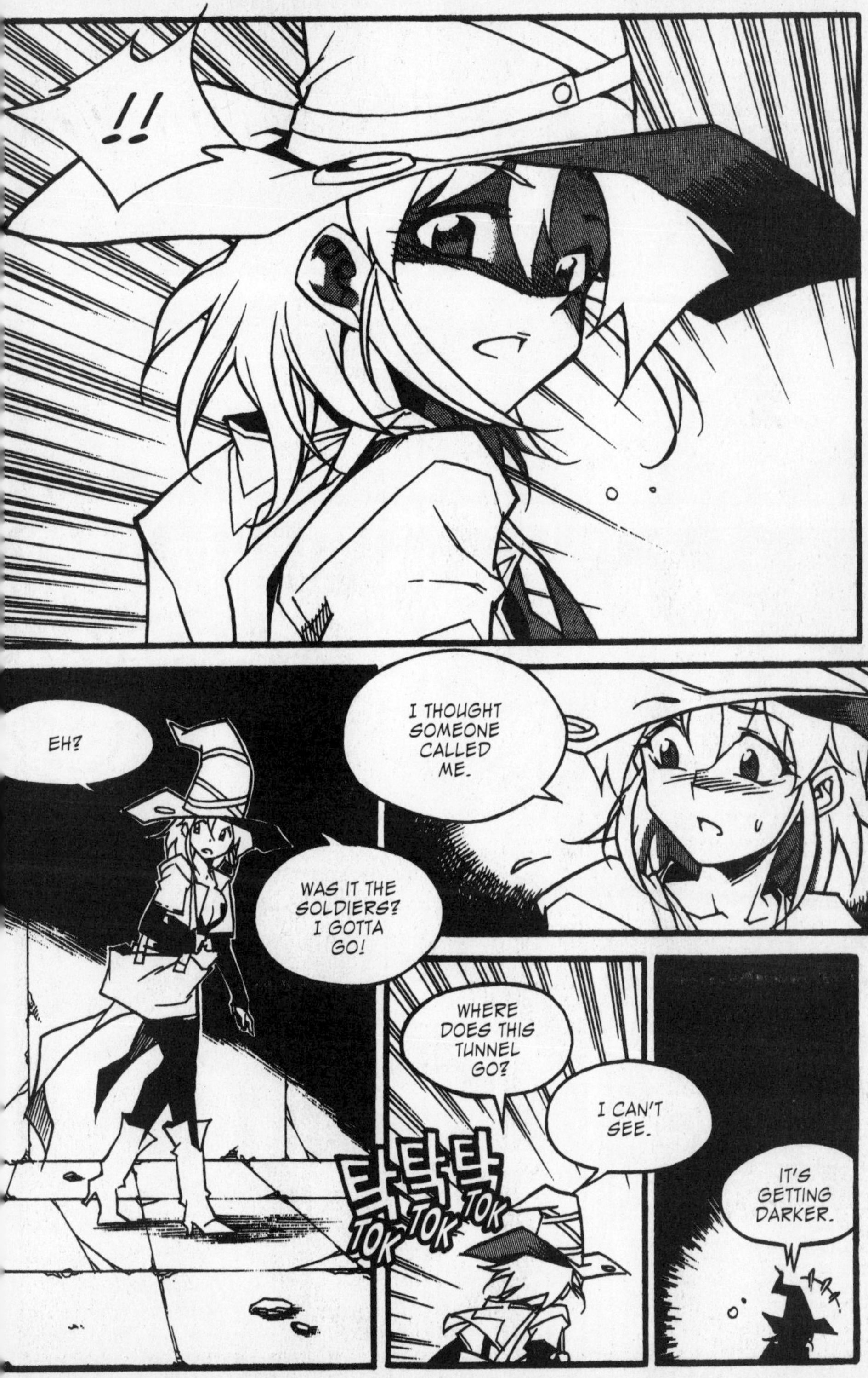
!!
EH?
I THOUGHT SOMEONE CALLED ME.
WAS IT THE SOLDIERS? I GOTTA GO!
WHERE DOES THIS TUNNEL GO?
I CAN'T SEE.
탁 탁 탁
TOK TOK TOK
IT'S GETTING DARKER.

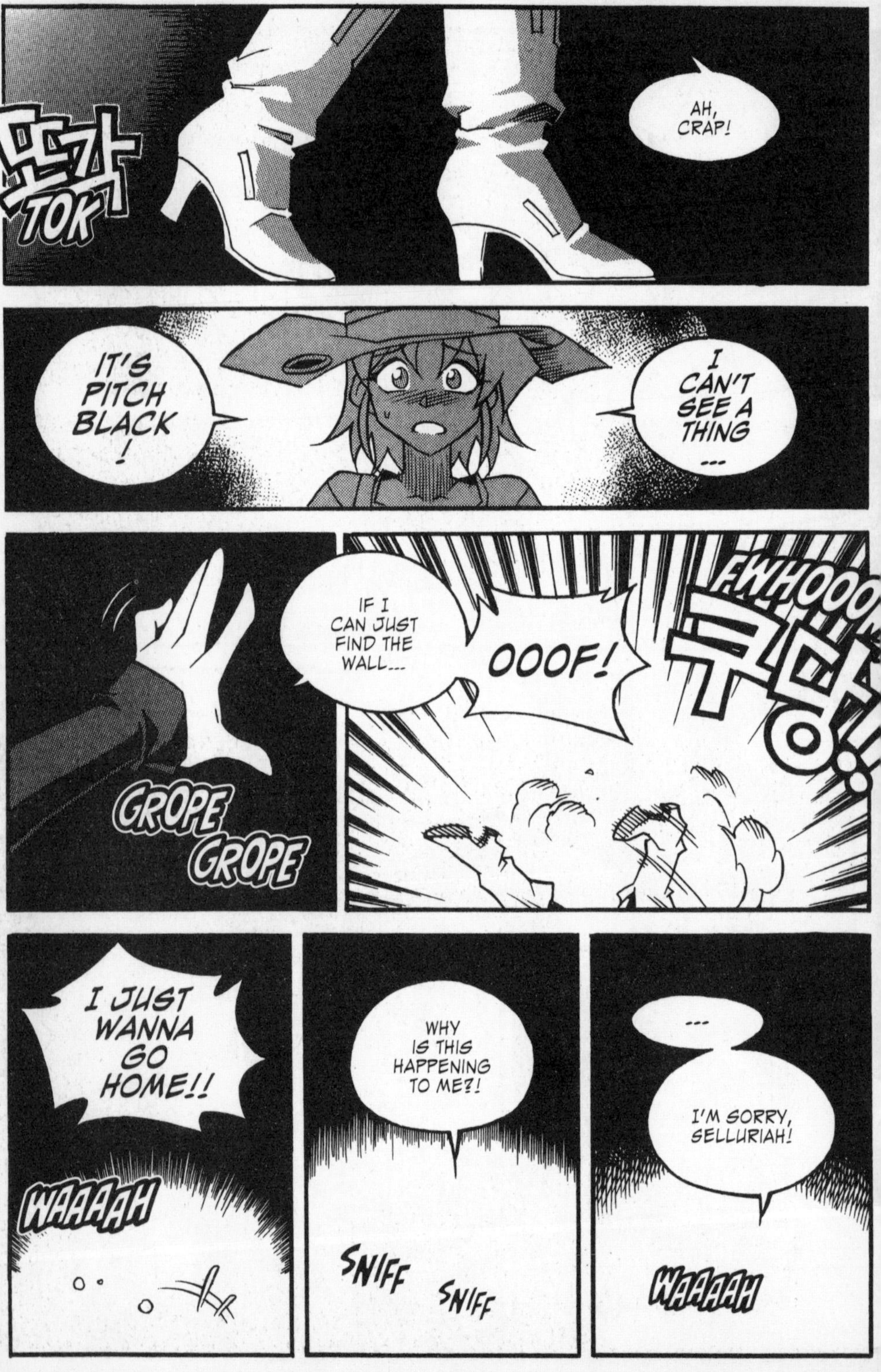

또각
TOK
AH, CRAP!
IT'S PITCH BLACK!
I CAN'T SEE A THING...
IF I CAN JUST FIND THE WALL...
GROPE GROPE
OOOF!
FWHOOO
쿠당!!
I JUST WANNA GO HOME!!
WAAAAH
WHY IS THIS HAPPENING TO ME?!
SNIFF SNIFF
...
I'M SORRY, SELLURIAH!
WAAAAH

HUH?

AN EXIT? IT CAN'T BE!

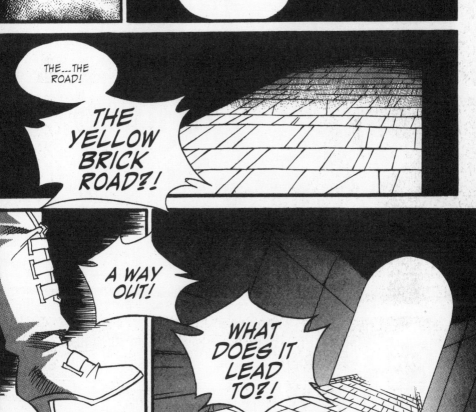

THE....THE ROAD!

THE YELLOW BRICK ROAD?!

A WAY OUT!

WHAT DOES IT LEAD TO?!

TOK TOK TOK TOK
타타타타 타 —

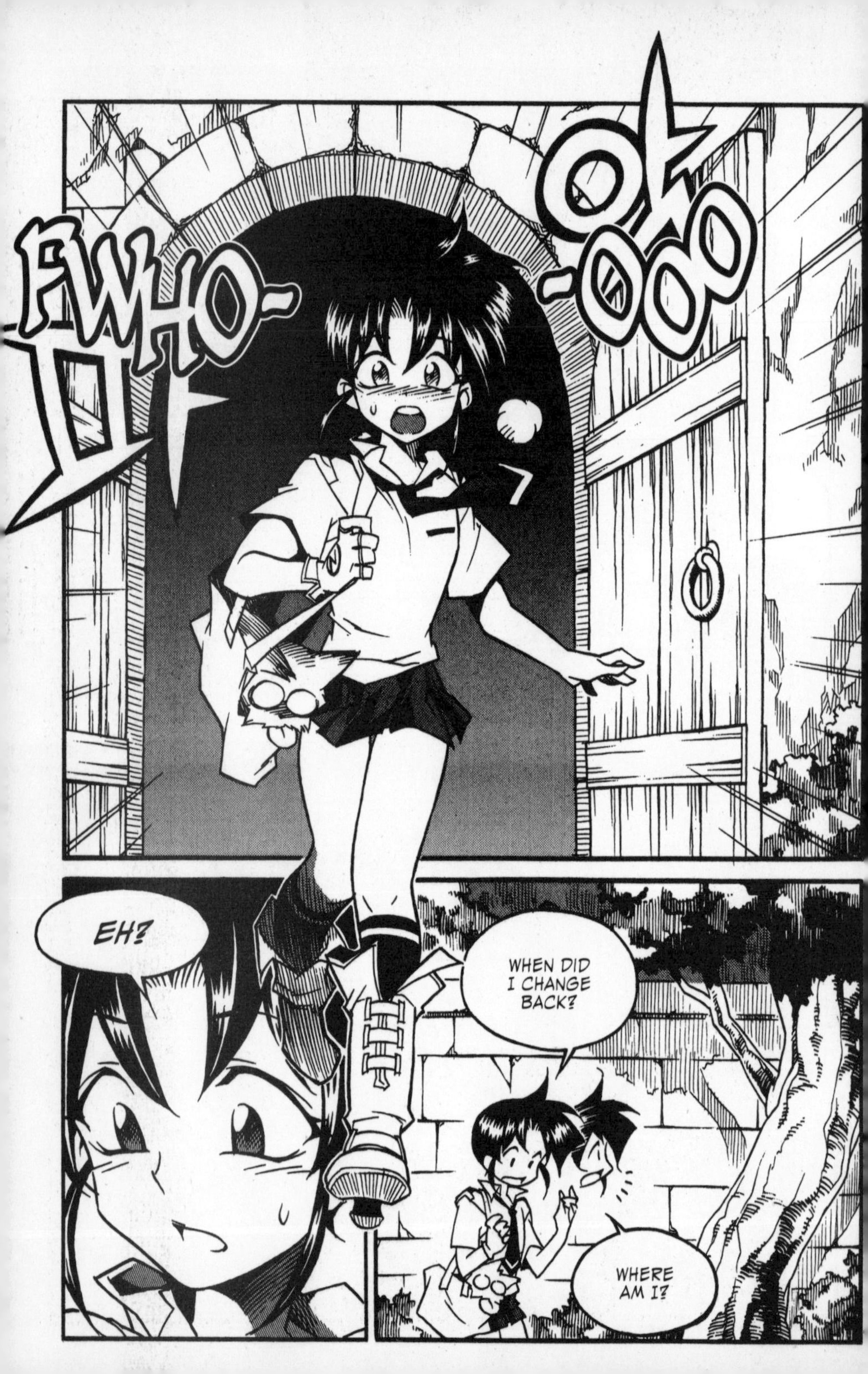
FWHO-II
OK-OOO
EH?
WHEN DID I CHANGE BACK?
WHERE AM I?

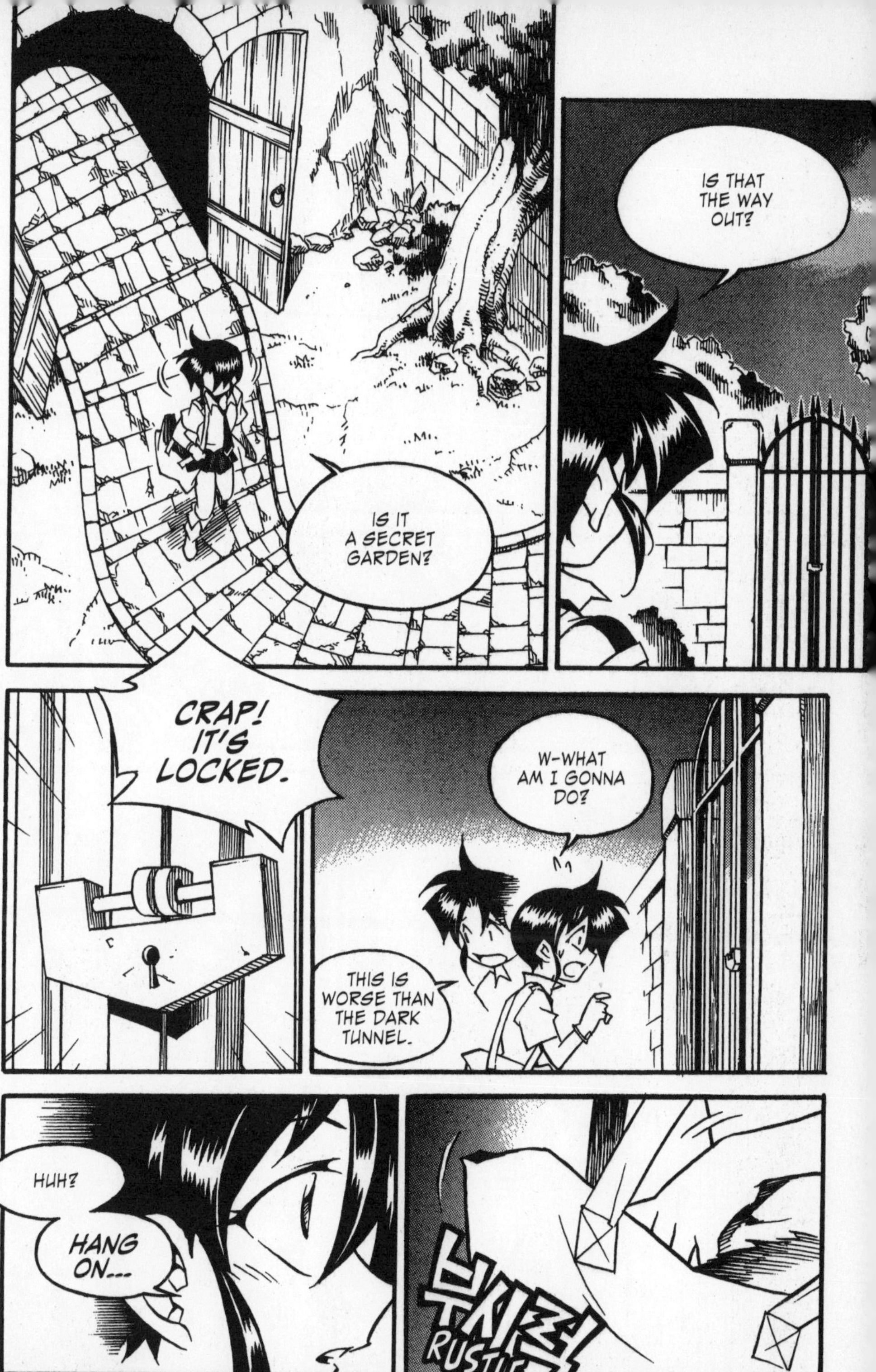
IS IT A SECRET GARDEN?
IS THAT THE WAY OUT?
CRAP! IT'S LOCKED.
W-WHAT AM I GONNA DO?
THIS IS WORSE THAN THE DARK TUNNEL.
HUH?
HANG ON...
RUSTLE

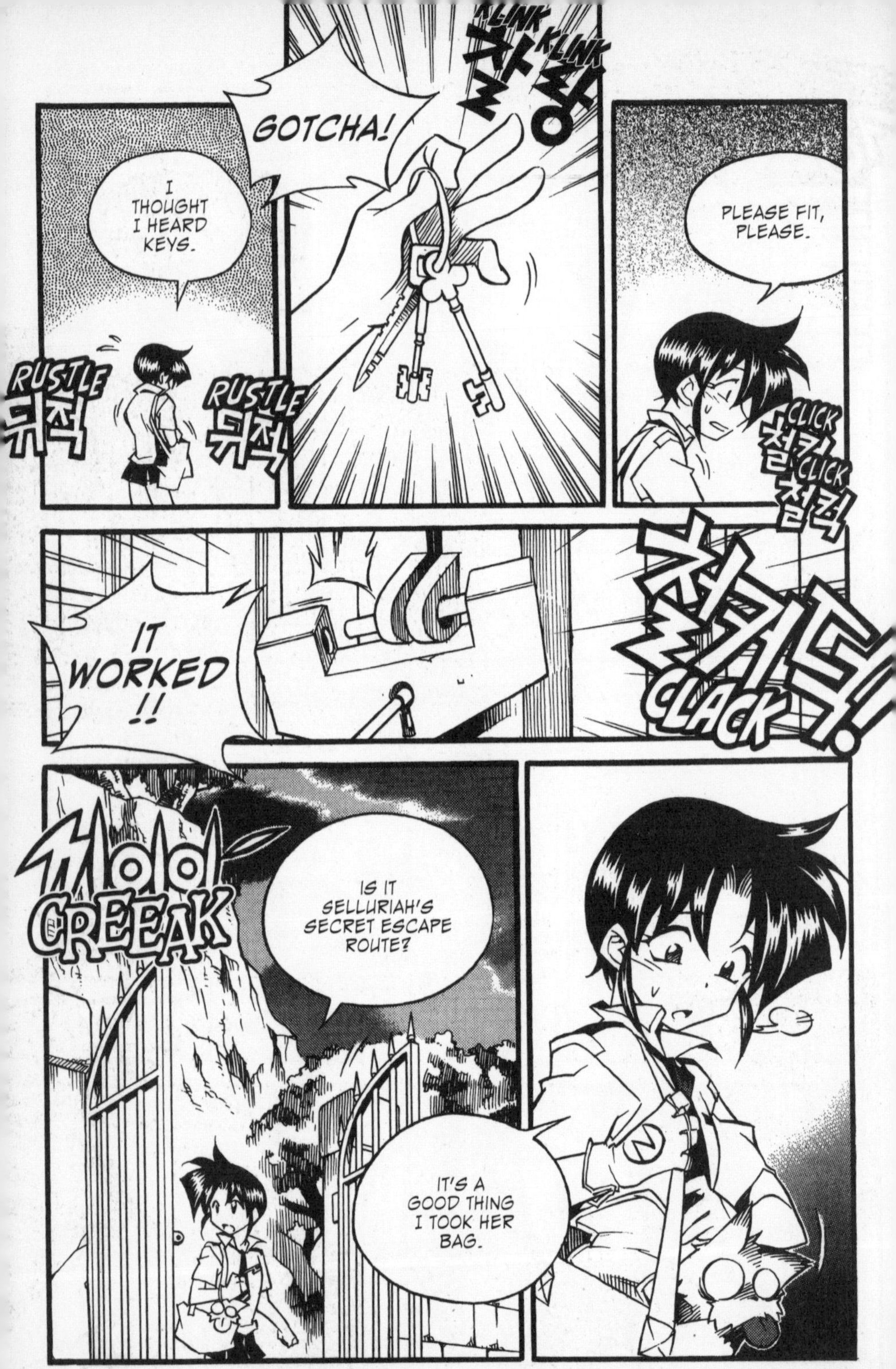

I THOUGHT I HEARD KEYS.
RUSTLE
뒤적
RUSTLE
뒤적
GOTCHA!
KLINK
KLINK
찰랑
PLEASE FIT, PLEASE.
CLICK
철컥
CLICK
철컥
IT WORKED!!
CLACK
철커덕
CREEAK
끼이익
IS IT SELLURIAH'S SECRET ESCAPE ROUTE?
IT'S A GOOD THING I TOOK HER BAG.

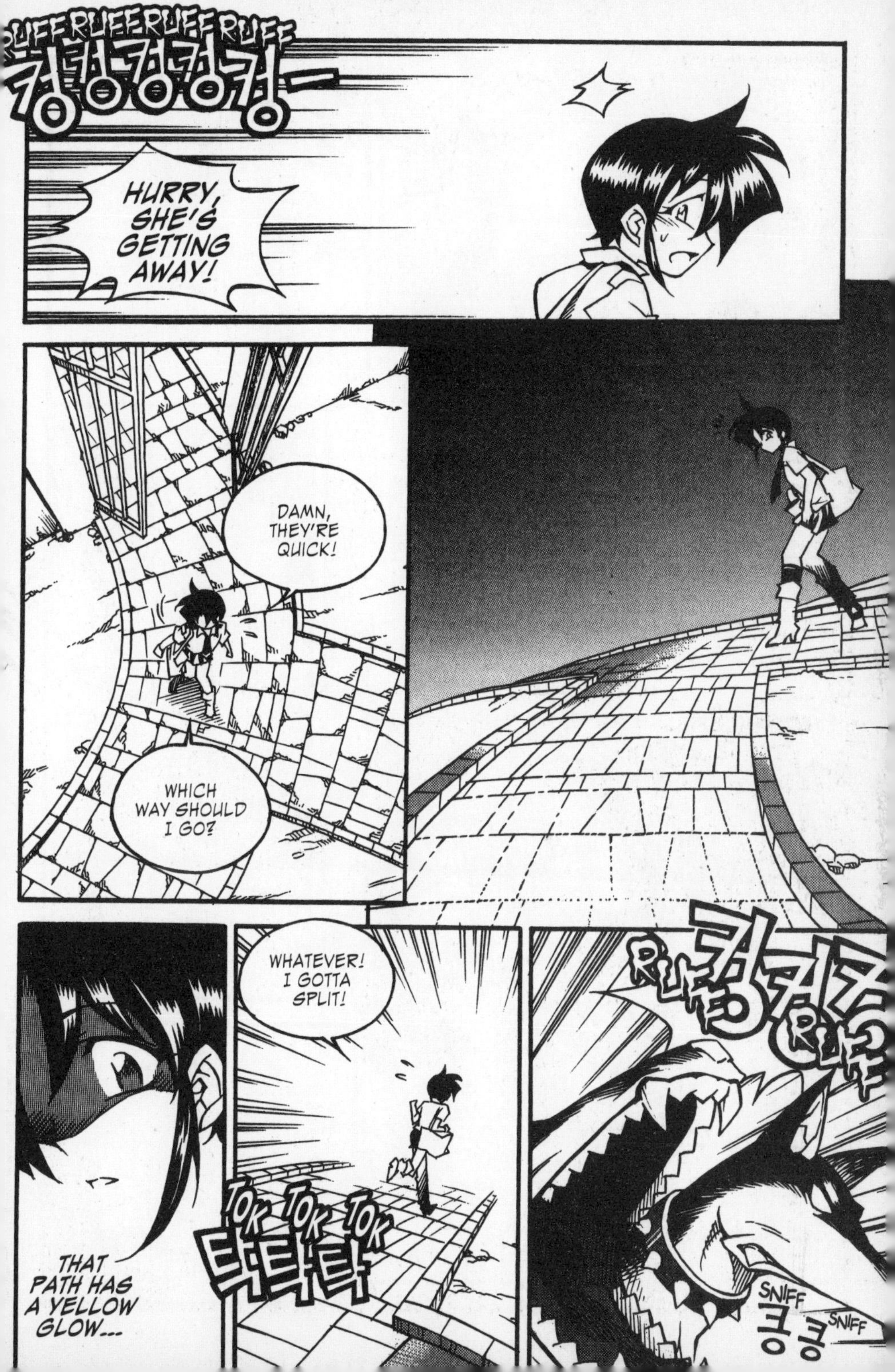
RUFF RUFF RUFF RUFF
컹컹컹컹컹컹—
HURRY, SHE'S GETTING AWAY!
DAMN, THEY'RE QUICK!
WHICH WAY SHOULD I GO?
THAT PATH HAS A YELLOW GLOW...
WHATEVER! I GOTTA SPLIT!
TOK TOK TOK
탁타타
RUFF
컹컹
RUFF
SNIFF
킁킁
SNIFF

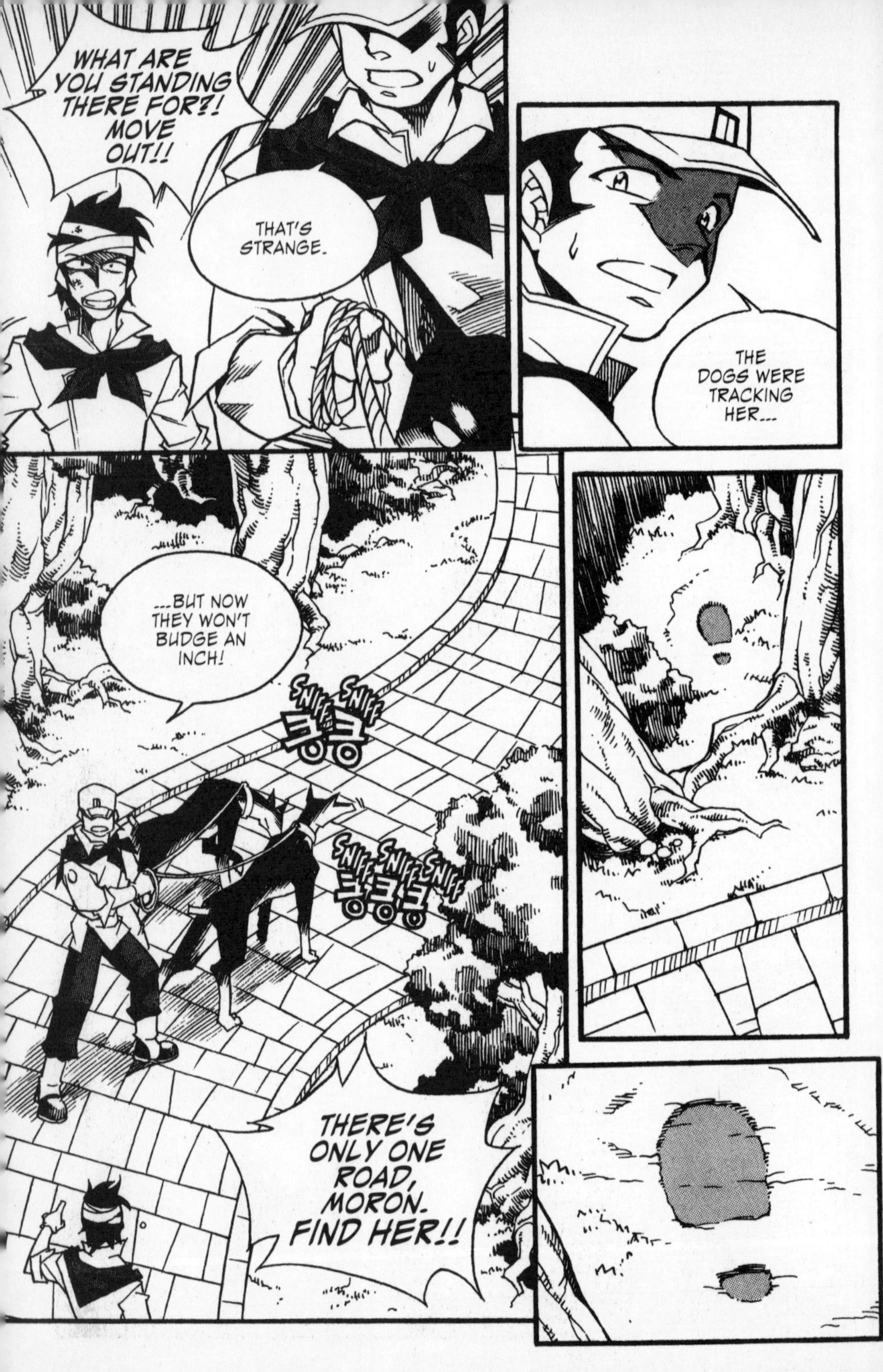
WHAT ARE YOU STANDING THERE FOR?! MOVE OUT!!
THAT'S STRANGE.
THE DOGS WERE TRACKING HER...
...BUT NOW THEY WON'T BUDGE AN INCH!
SNIFF SNIFF
SNIFF SNIFF SNIFF
THERE'S ONLY ONE ROAD, MORON. FIND HER!!

Step 13 DON'T CRY

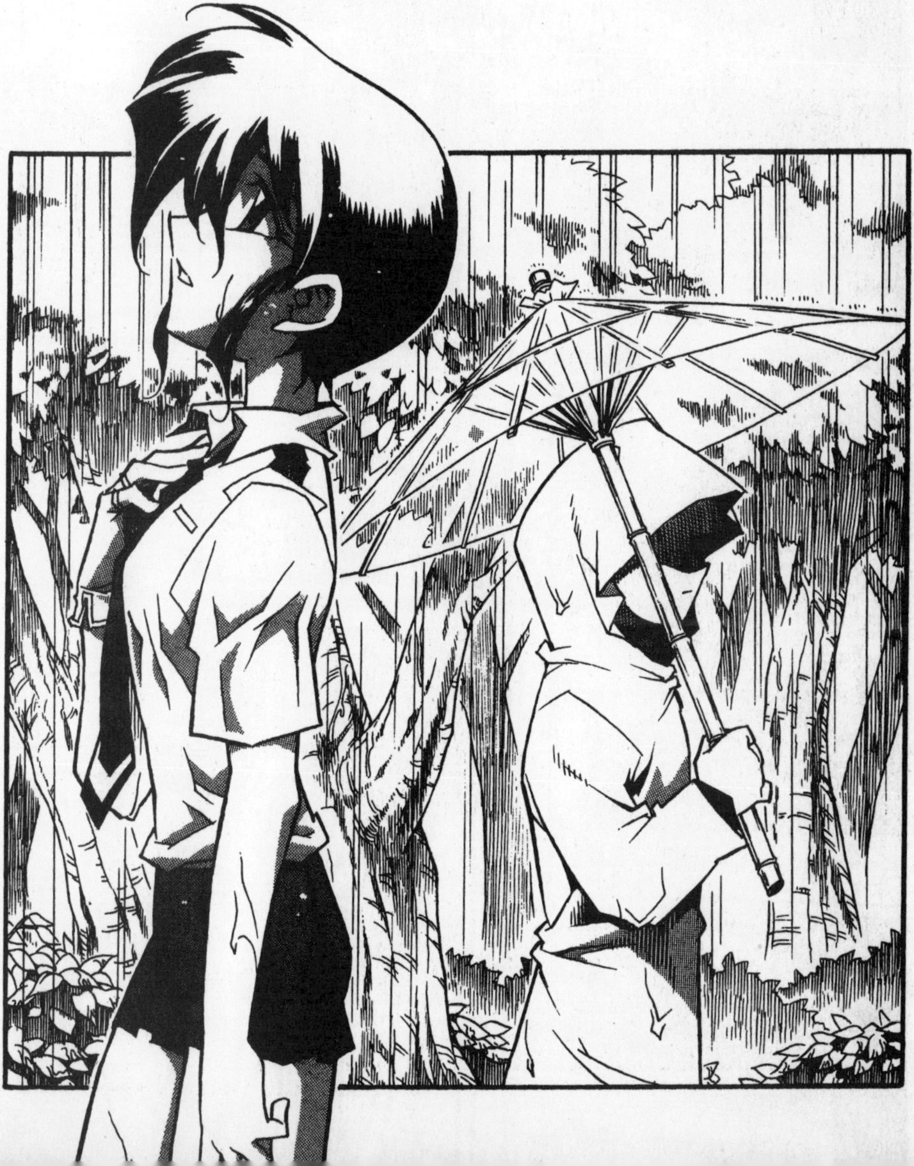

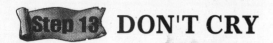

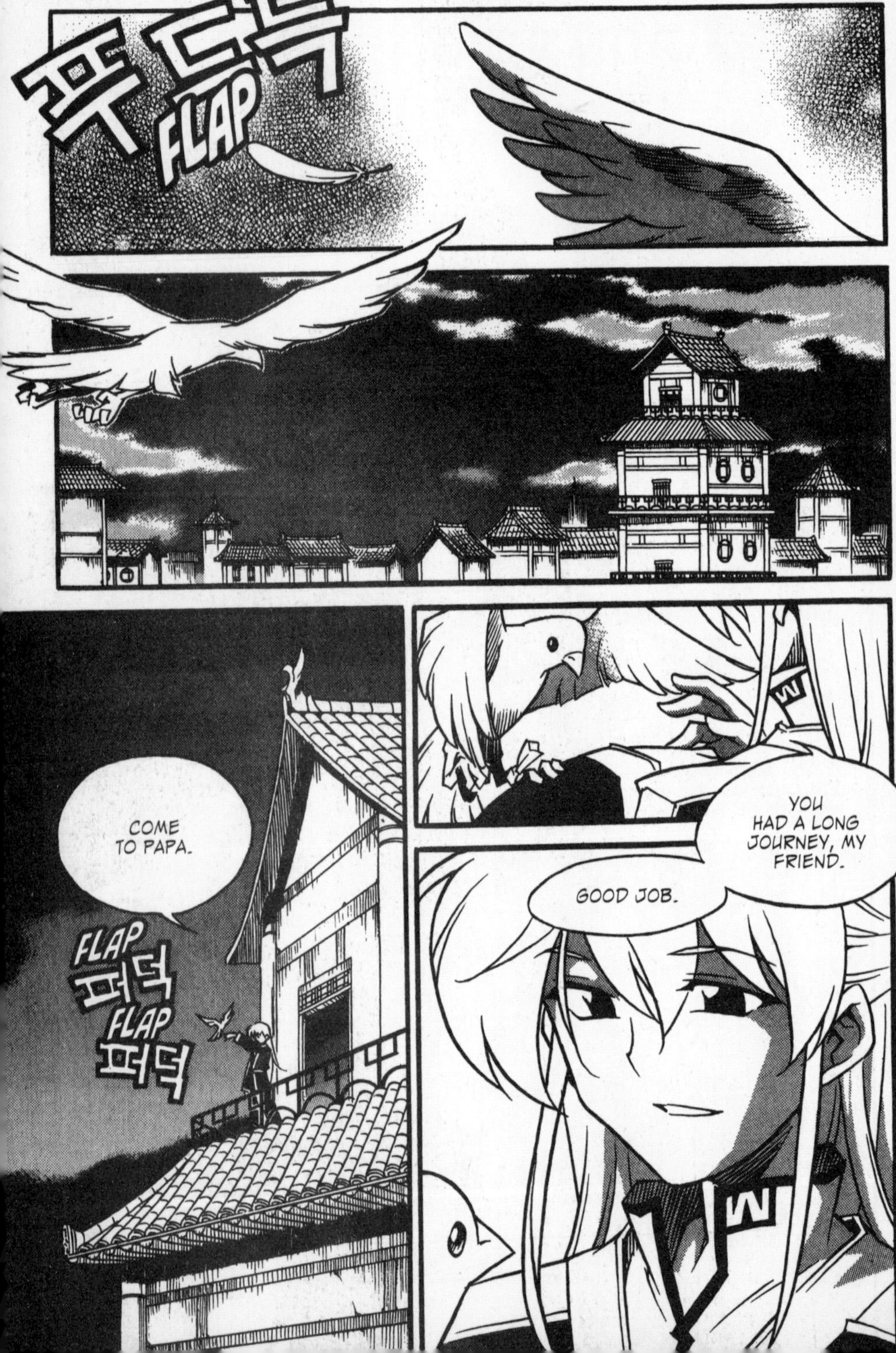

푸드득
FLAP
COME TO PAPA.
FLAP
퍼덕
FLAP
퍼덕
YOU HAD A LONG JOURNEY, MY FRIEND.
GOOD JOB.

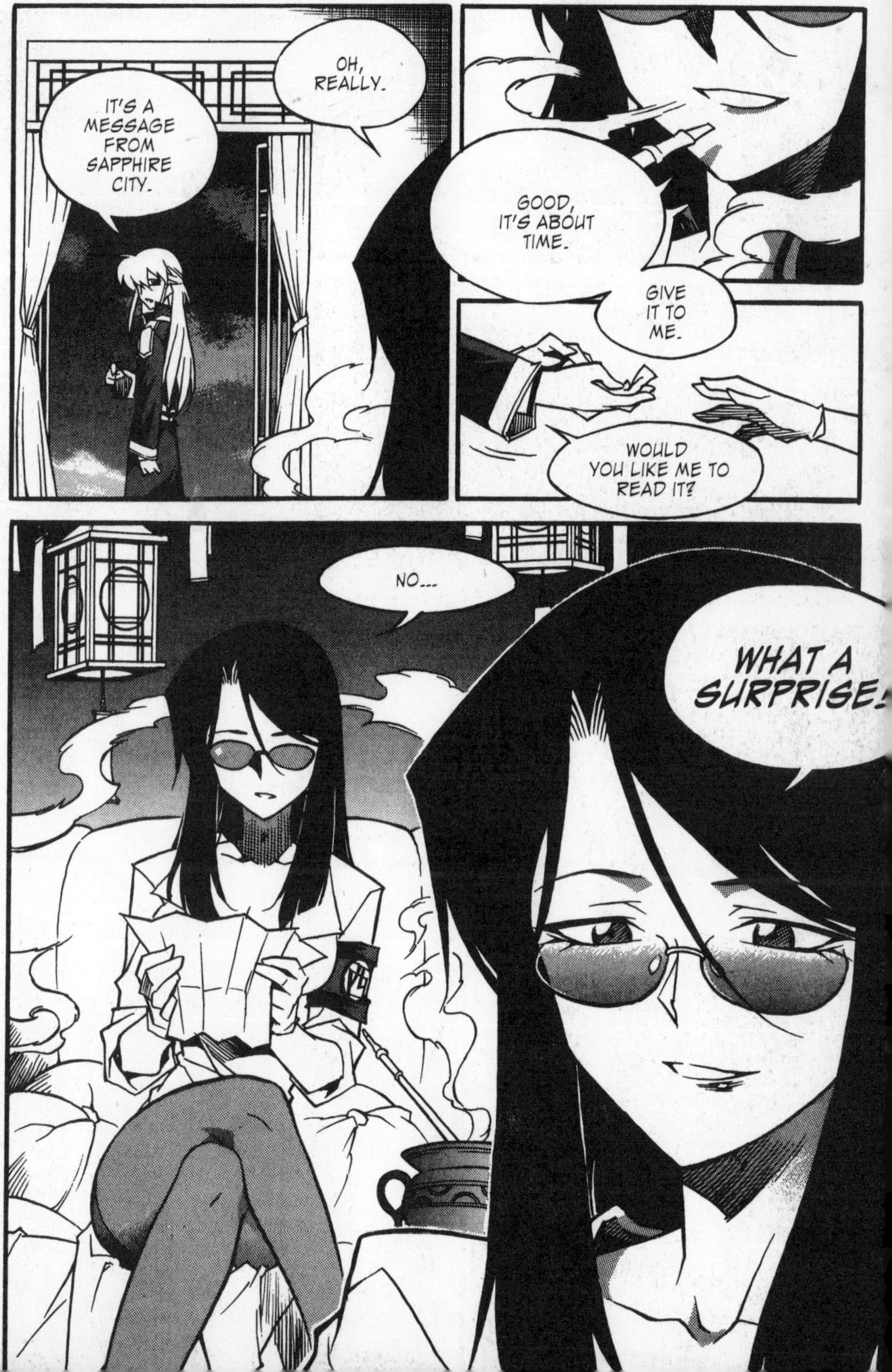
IT'S A MESSAGE FROM SAPPHIRE CITY.
OH, REALLY.
GOOD, IT'S ABOUT TIME.
GIVE IT TO ME.
WOULD YOU LIKE ME TO READ IT?
NO...
WHAT A SURPRISE!

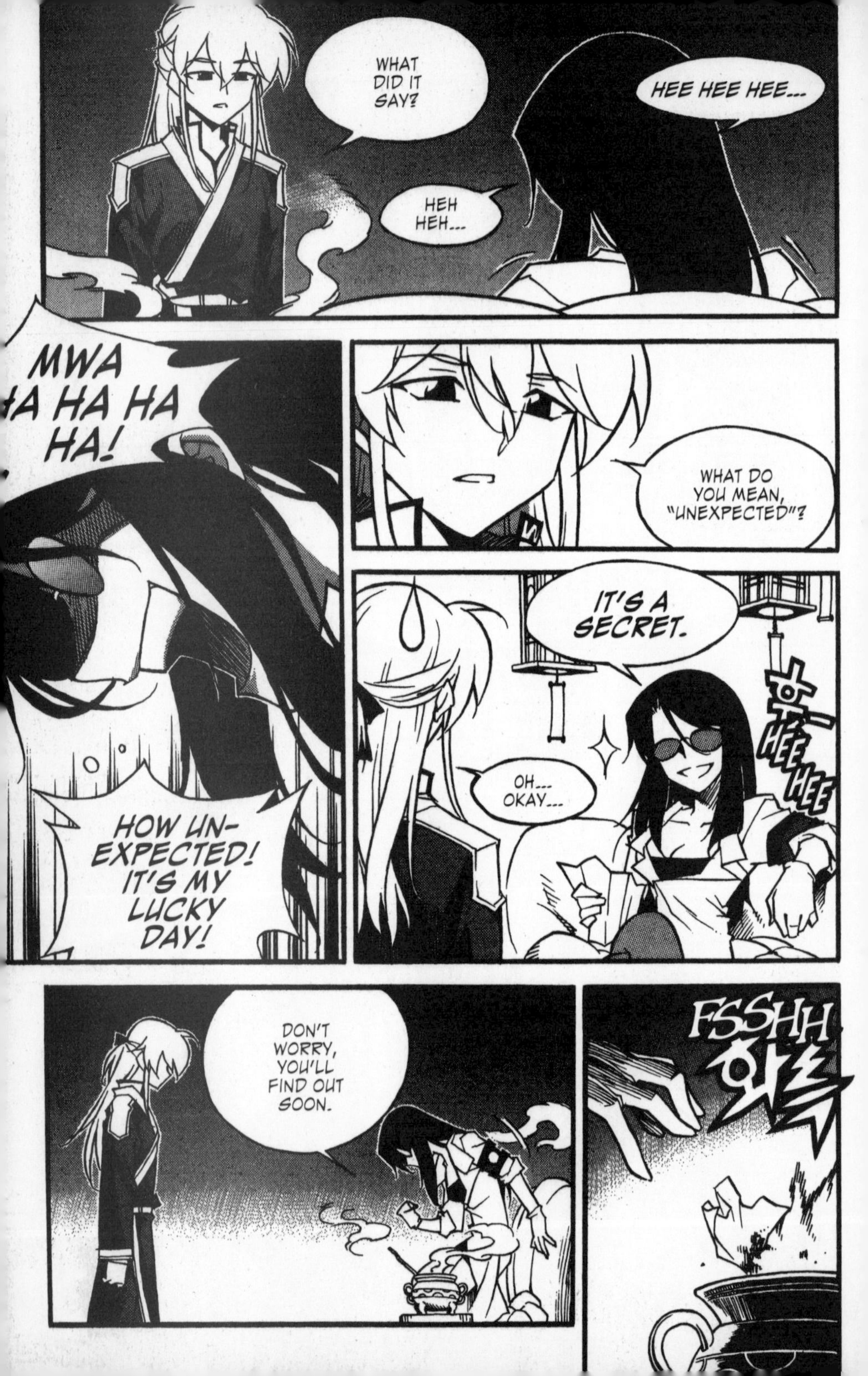
WHAT DID IT SAY?
HEE HEE HEE...
HEH HEH...
MWA HA HA HA HA!
HOW UN-EXPECTED! IT'S MY LUCKY DAY!
WHAT DO YOU MEAN, "UNEXPECTED"?
IT'S A SECRET.
HEE HEE
OH... OKAY...
DON'T WORRY, YOU'LL FIND OUT SOON.
FSSHH

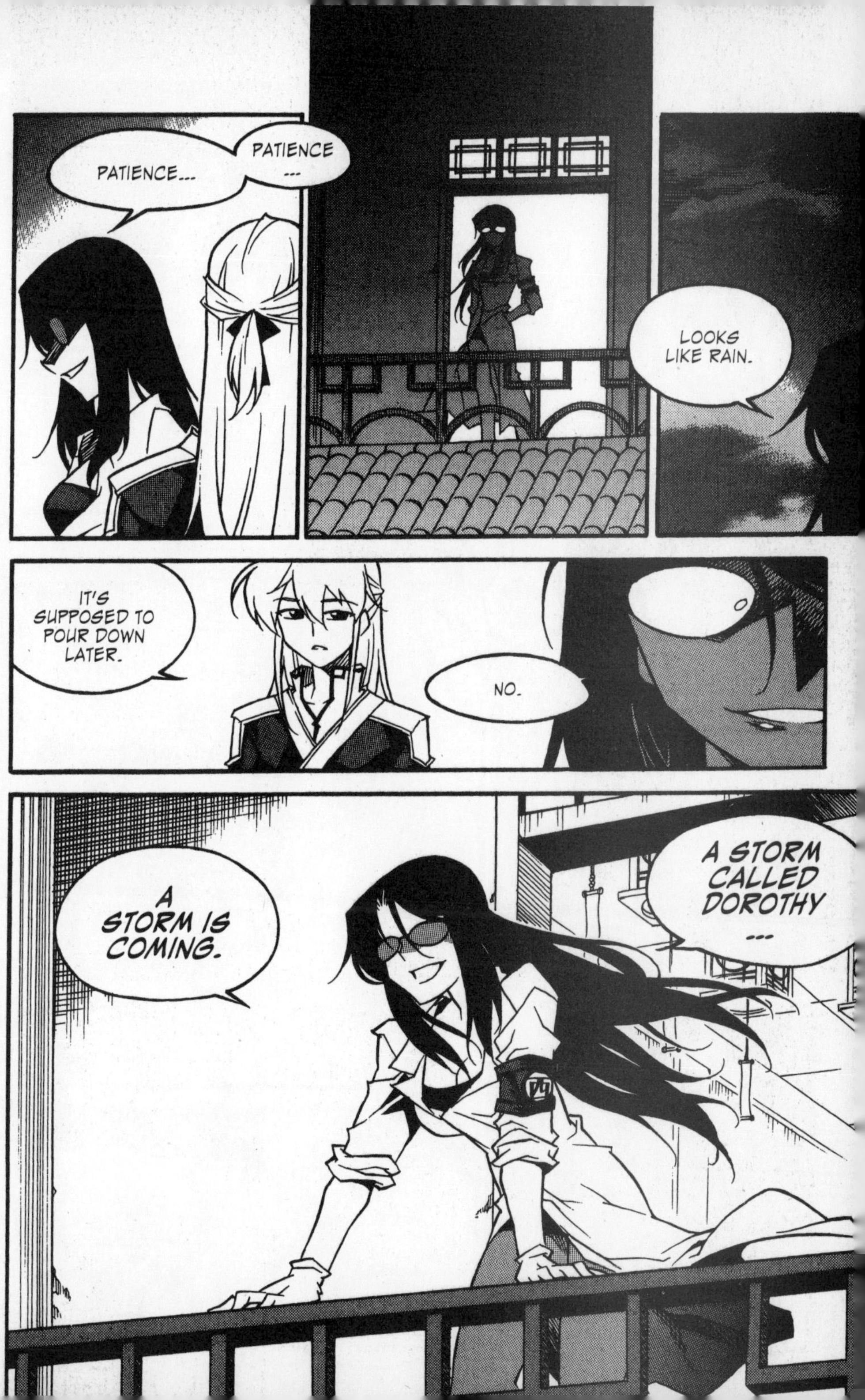
PATIENCE...
PATIENCE ...
LOOKS LIKE RAIN.
IT'S SUPPOSED TO POUR DOWN LATER.
NO.
A STORM IS COMING.
A STORM CALLED DOROTHY ...

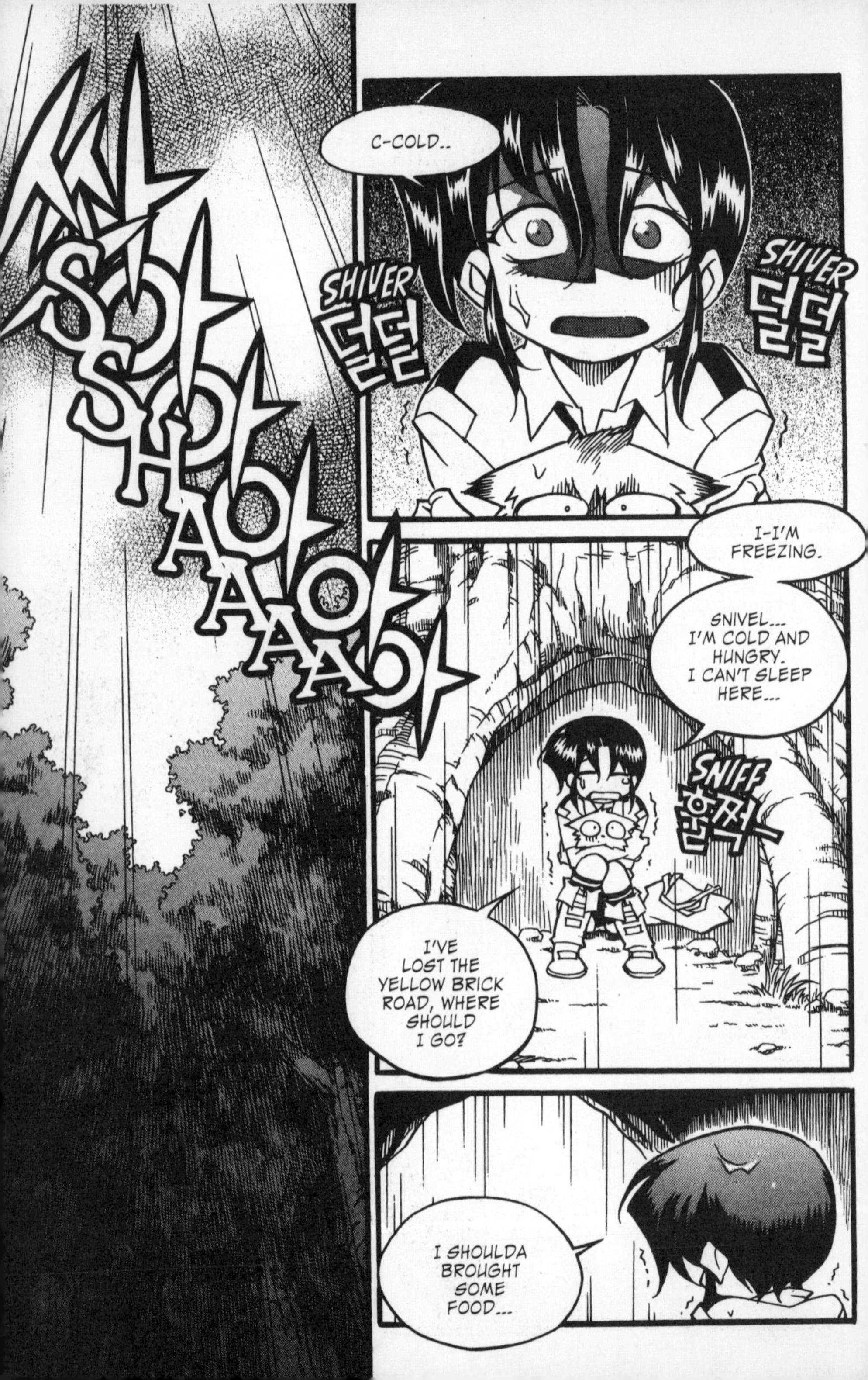

SSSHAAAA
C-COLD..
SHIVER
덜덜
SHIVER
덜덜
I-I'M FREEZING.
SNIVEL... I'M COLD AND HUNGRY. I CAN'T SLEEP HERE...
SNIFF
훌쩍
I'VE LOST THE YELLOW BRICK ROAD, WHERE SHOULD I GO?
I SHOULDA BROUGHT SOME FOOD...

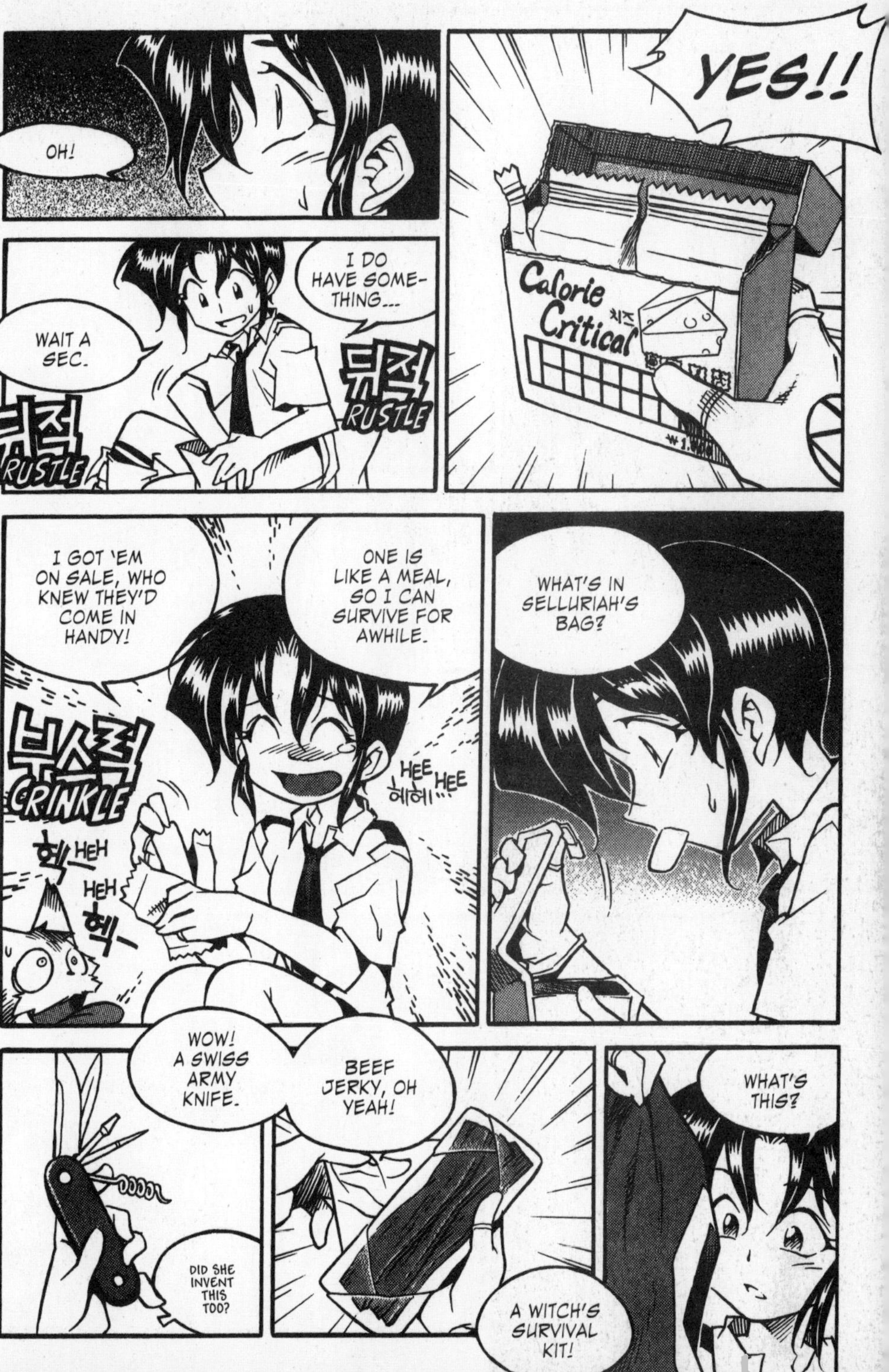
OH!
YES!!
Calorie Critical
치즈
WAIT A SEC.
I DO HAVE SOME-THING...
뒤적 RUSTLE
뒤적 RUSTLE
I GOT 'EM ON SALE, WHO KNEW THEY'D COME IN HANDY!
ONE IS LIKE A MEAL, SO I CAN SURVIVE FOR AWHILE.
부스럭 CRINKLE
HEE HEE 헤헤...
헥 HEH
HEH 헥
WHAT'S IN SELLURIAH'S BAG?
WOW! A SWISS ARMY KNIFE.
DID SHE INVENT THIS TOO?
BEEF JERKY, OH YEAH!
WHAT'S THIS?
A WITCH'S SURVIVAL KIT!

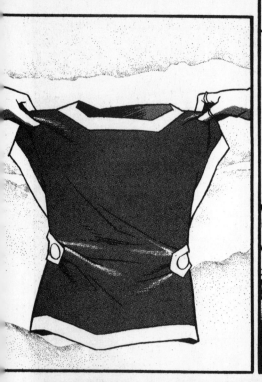

SELLURIAH'S SHIRT...

SNIFF

SNIFF

SOB... SELLURIAH.

NNGH~

ERRR.

HER...

SMELL...

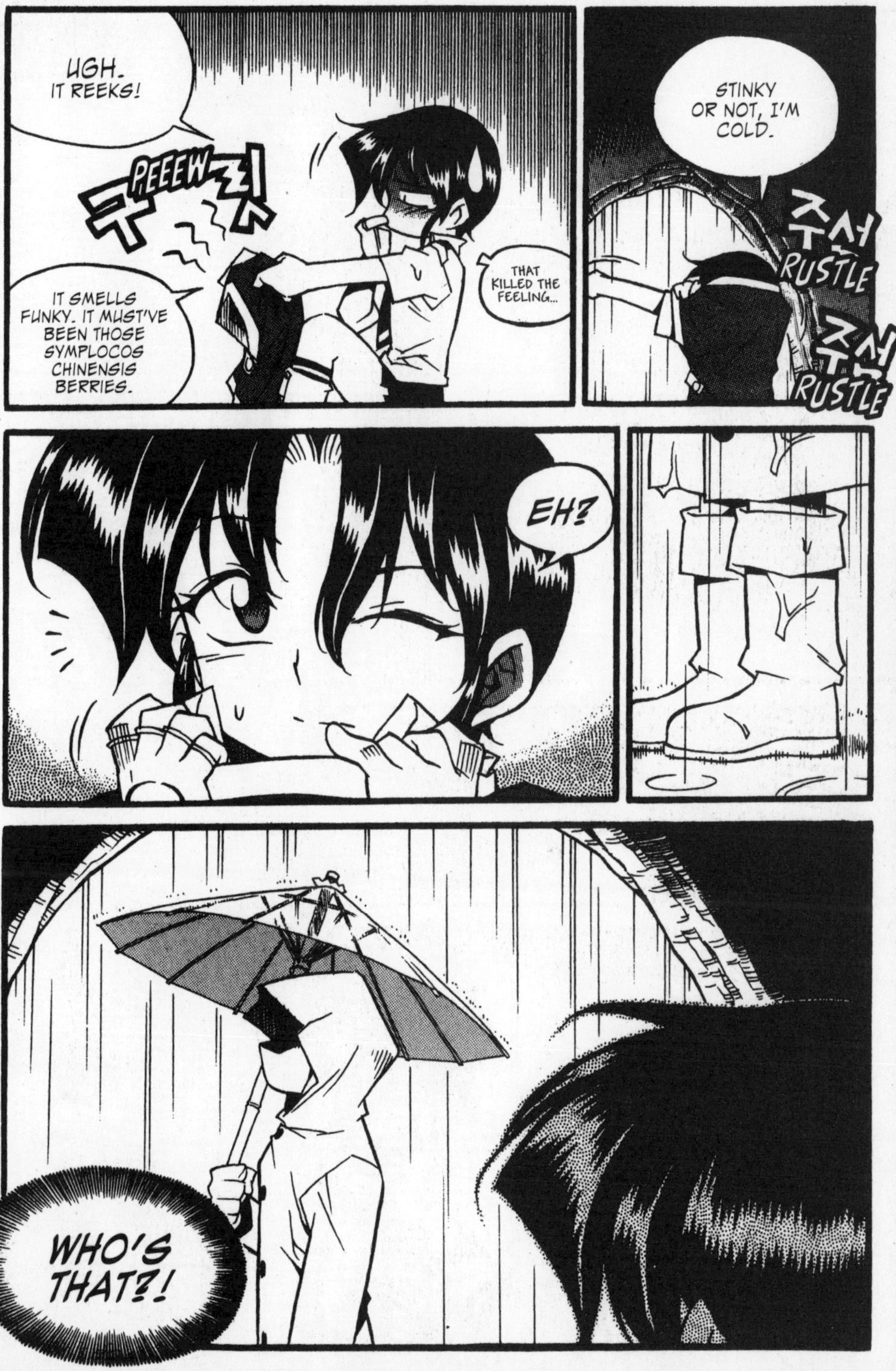
UGH. IT REEKS!
PEEEW
IT SMELLS FUNKY. IT MUST'VE BEEN THOSE SYMPLOCOS CHINENSIS BERRIES.
THAT KILLED THE FEELING...
STINKY OR NOT, I'M COLD.
RUSTLE
RUSTLE
EH?
WHO'S THAT?!

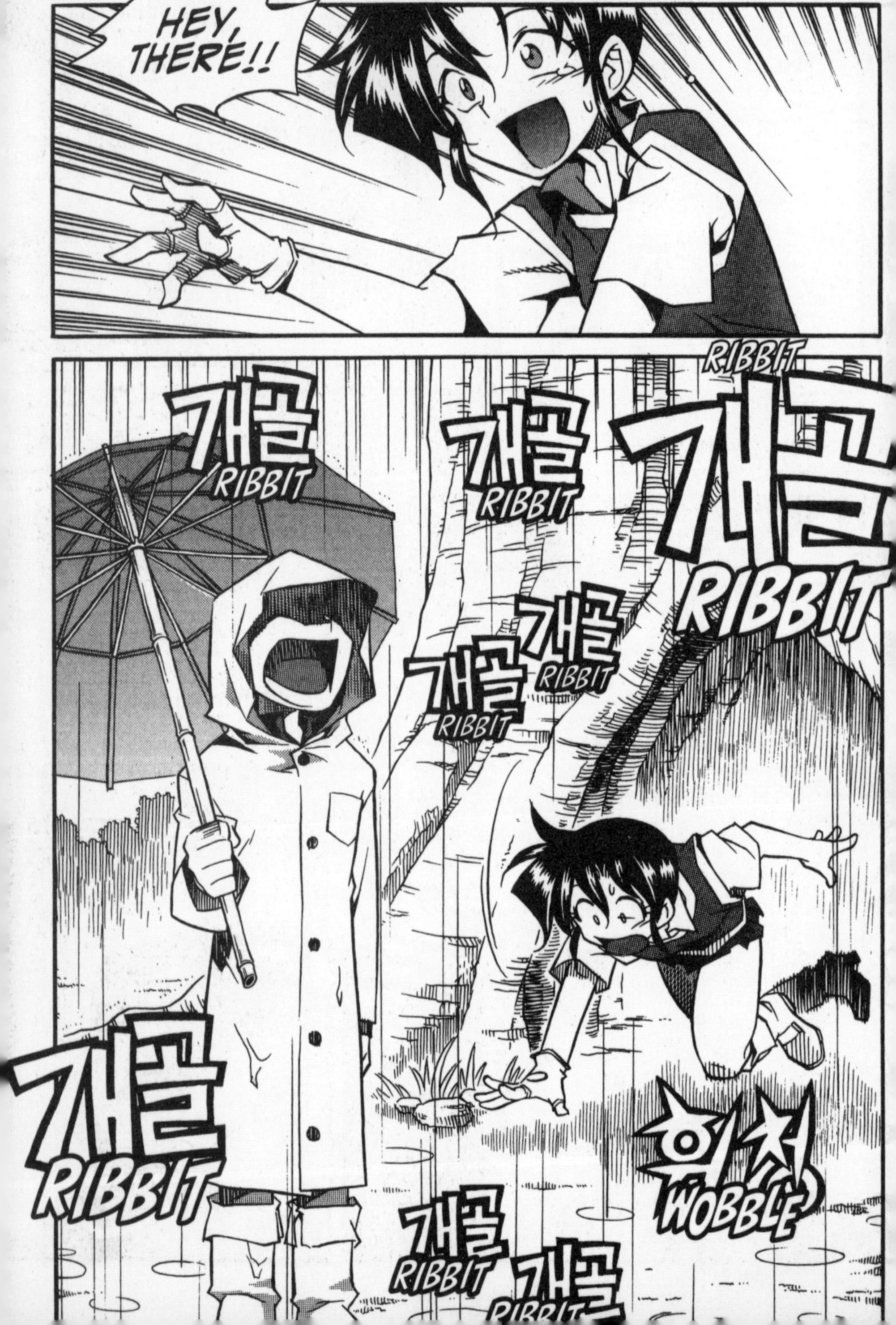
HEY, THERE!!
RIBBIT
개골
RIBBIT
개골
RIBBIT
개골
RIBBIT
개골
RIBBIT
개골
RIBBIT
개골
RIBBIT
휘청
WOBBLE
개골
RIBBIT
개골

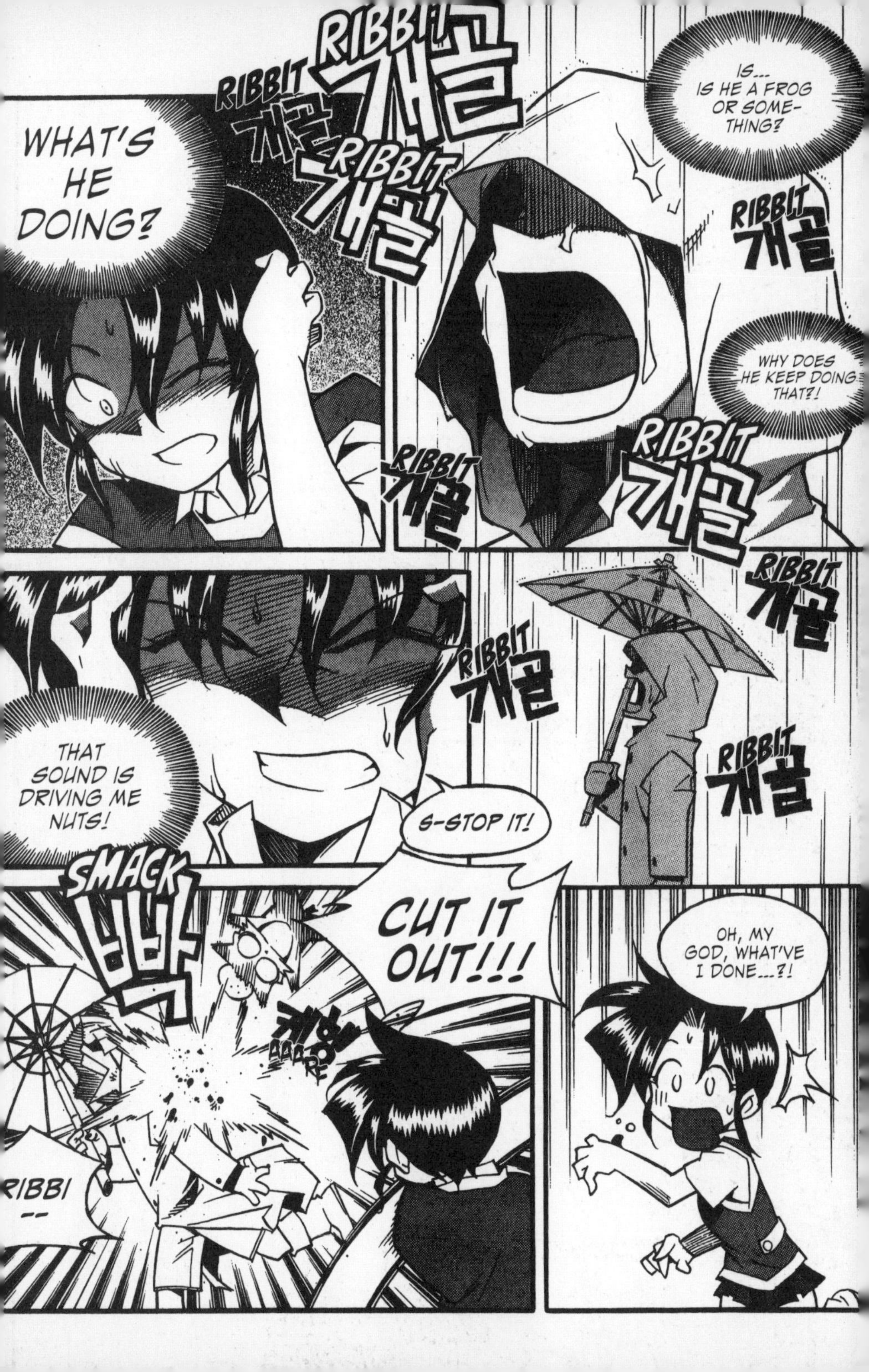
RIBBIT 개골
RIBBIT 개골
RIBBIT 개골
WHAT'S HE DOING?
IS... IS HE A FROG OR SOME-THING?
RIBBIT 개골
WHY DOES HE KEEP DOING THAT?!
RIBBIT 개골
RIBBIT 개골
RIBBIT 개골
RIBBIT 개골
RIBBIT 개골
THAT SOUND IS DRIVING ME NUTS!
S-STOP IT!
SMACK 빠악
CUT IT OUT!!!
RIBBI--
OH, MY GOD, WHAT'VE I DONE...?!

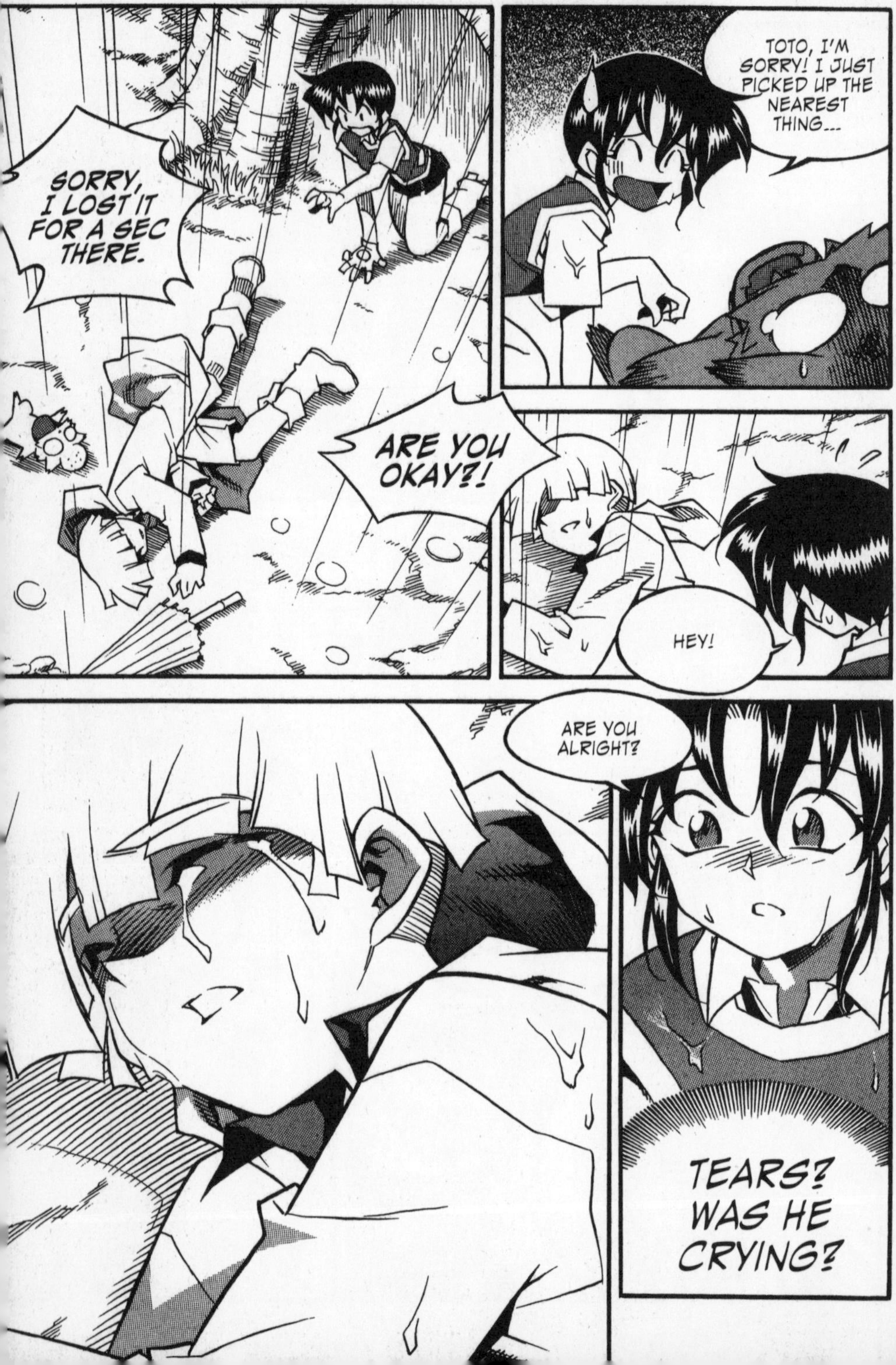
SORRY, I LOST IT FOR A SEC THERE.
TOTO, I'M SORRY! I JUST PICKED UP THE NEAREST THING...
ARE YOU OKAY?!
HEY!
ARE YOU ALRIGHT?
TEARS? WAS HE CRYING?

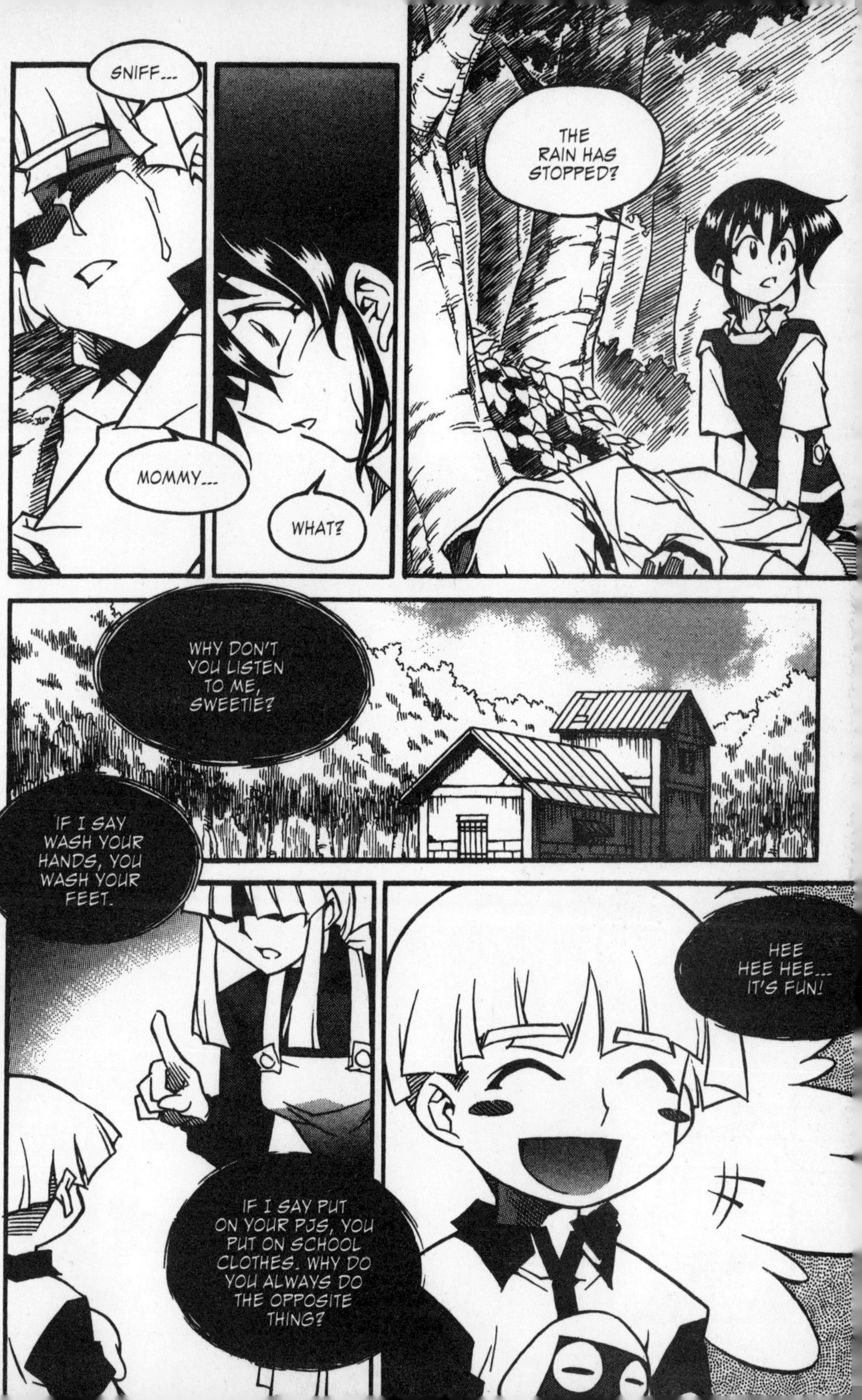
SNIFF...
MOMMY...
WHAT?
THE RAIN HAS STOPPED?
WHY DON'T YOU LISTEN TO ME, SWEETIE?
IF I SAY WASH YOUR HANDS, YOU WASH YOUR FEET.
IF I SAY PUT ON YOUR PJS, YOU PUT ON SCHOOL CLOTHES. WHY DO YOU ALWAYS DO THE OPPOSITE THING?
HEE HEE HEE... IT'S FUN!

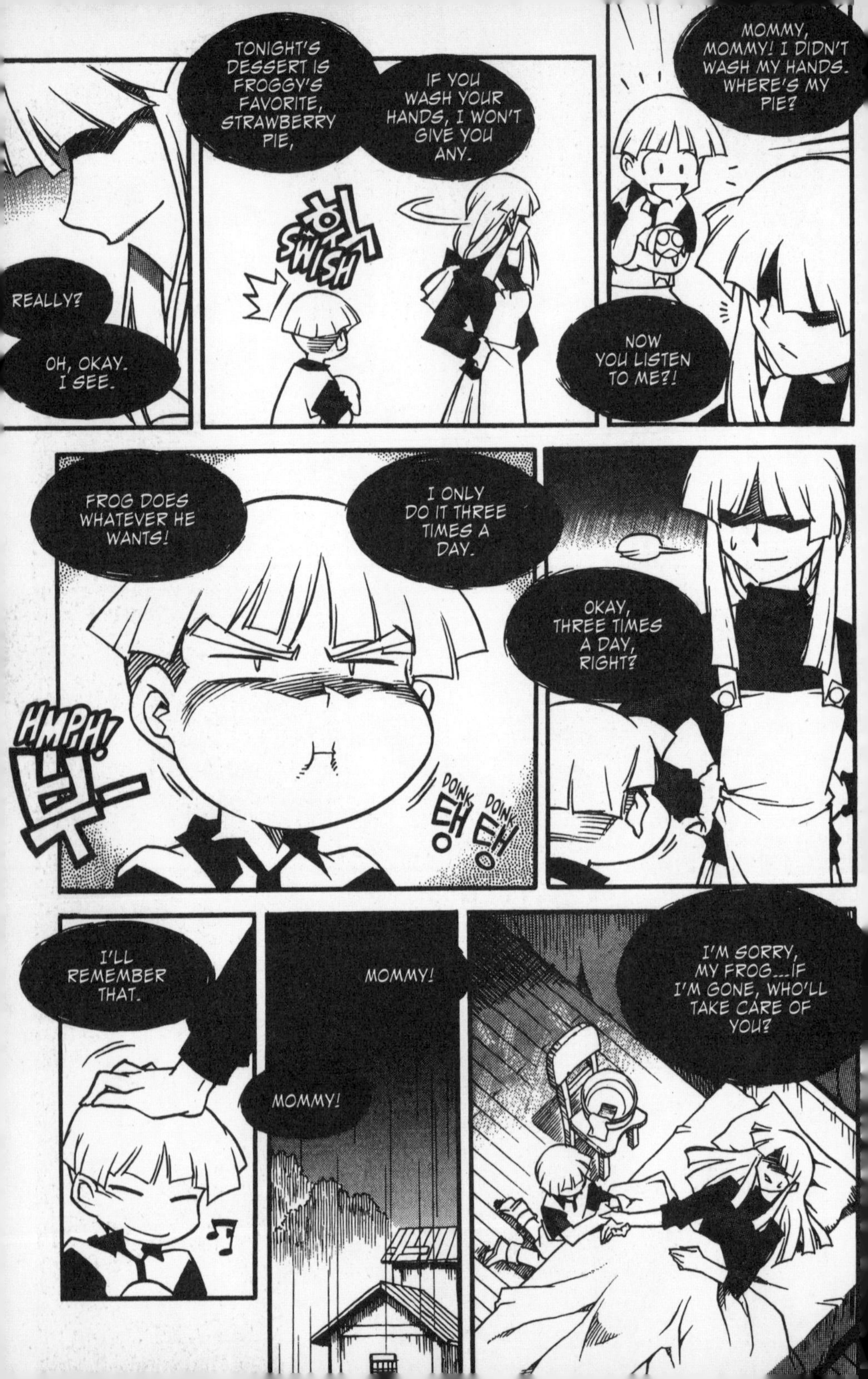
TONIGHT'S DESSERT IS FROGGY'S FAVORITE, STRAWBERRY PIE,
IF YOU WASH YOUR HANDS, I WON'T GIVE YOU ANY.
REALLY?
OH, OKAY. I SEE.
SWISH
MOMMY, MOMMY! I DIDN'T WASH MY HANDS. WHERE'S MY PIE?
NOW YOU LISTEN TO ME?!
FROG DOES WHATEVER HE WANTS!
I ONLY DO IT THREE TIMES A DAY.
HMPH!
DOINK DOINK
OKAY, THREE TIMES A DAY, RIGHT?
I'LL REMEMBER THAT.
MOMMY!
MOMMY!
I'M SORRY, MY FROG...IF I'M GONE, WHO'LL TAKE CARE OF YOU?

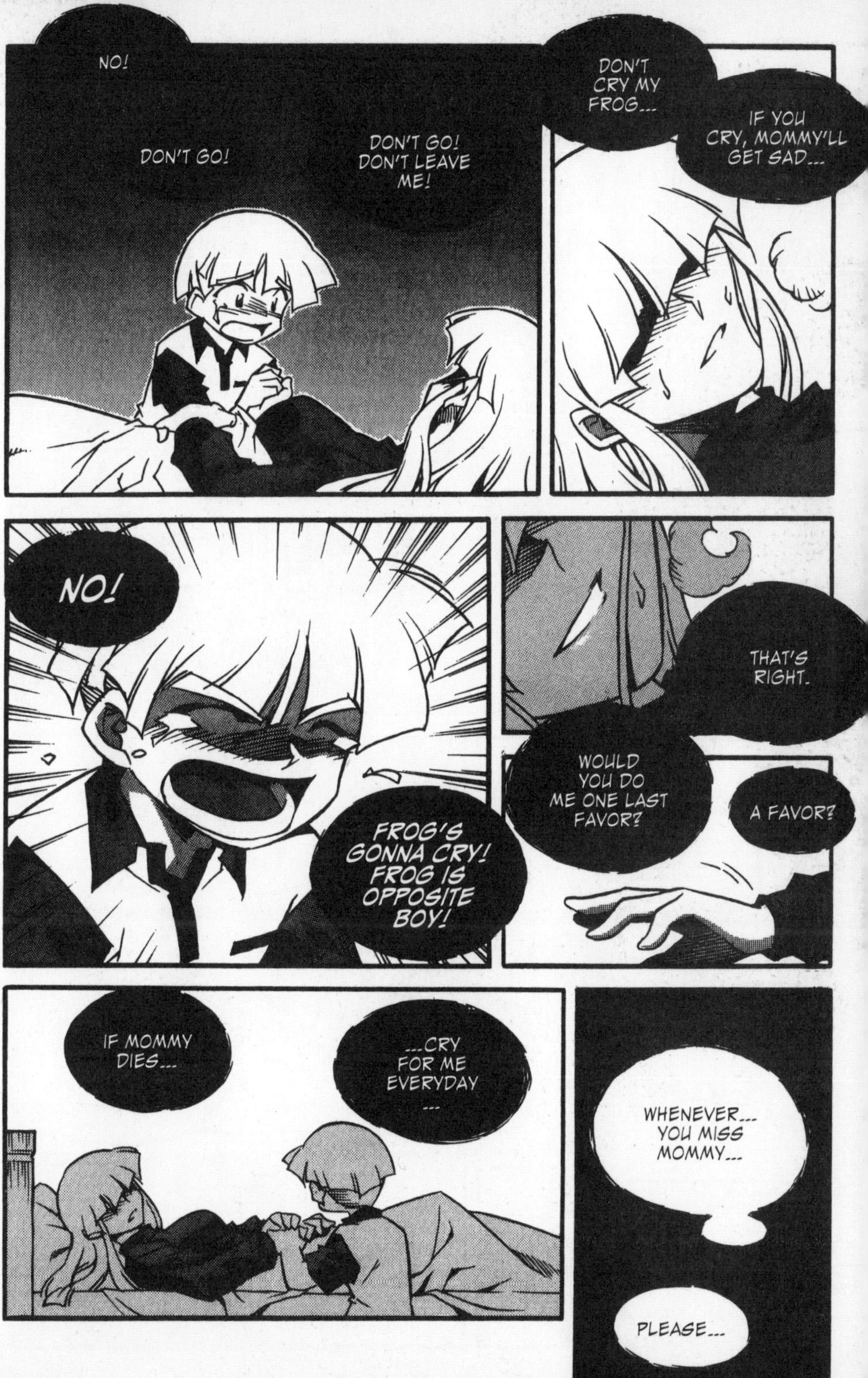
NO!
DON'T GO!
DON'T GO! DON'T LEAVE ME!
DON'T CRY MY FROG...
IF YOU CRY, MOMMY'LL GET SAD...
NO!
FROG'S GONNA CRY! FROG IS OPPOSITE BOY!
THAT'S RIGHT.
WOULD YOU DO ME ONE LAST FAVOR?
A FAVOR?
IF MOMMY DIES...
...CRY FOR ME EVERYDAY ...
WHENEVER... YOU MISS MOMMY...
PLEASE...

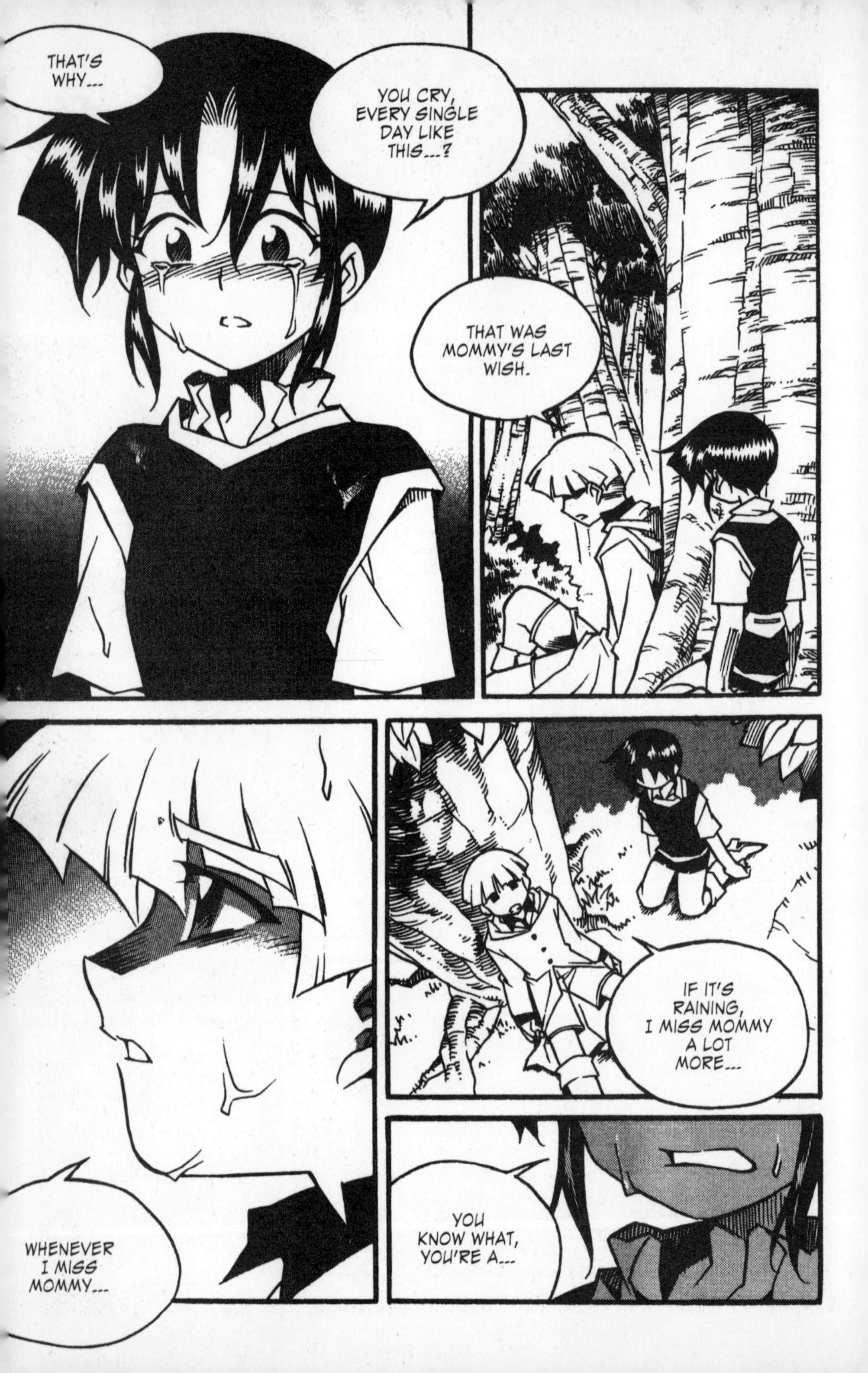
THAT'S WHY...
YOU CRY, EVERY SINGLE DAY LIKE THIS...?
THAT WAS MOMMY'S LAST WISH.
IF IT'S RAINING, I MISS MOMMY A LOT MORE...
WHENEVER I MISS MOMMY...
YOU KNOW WHAT, YOU'RE A...

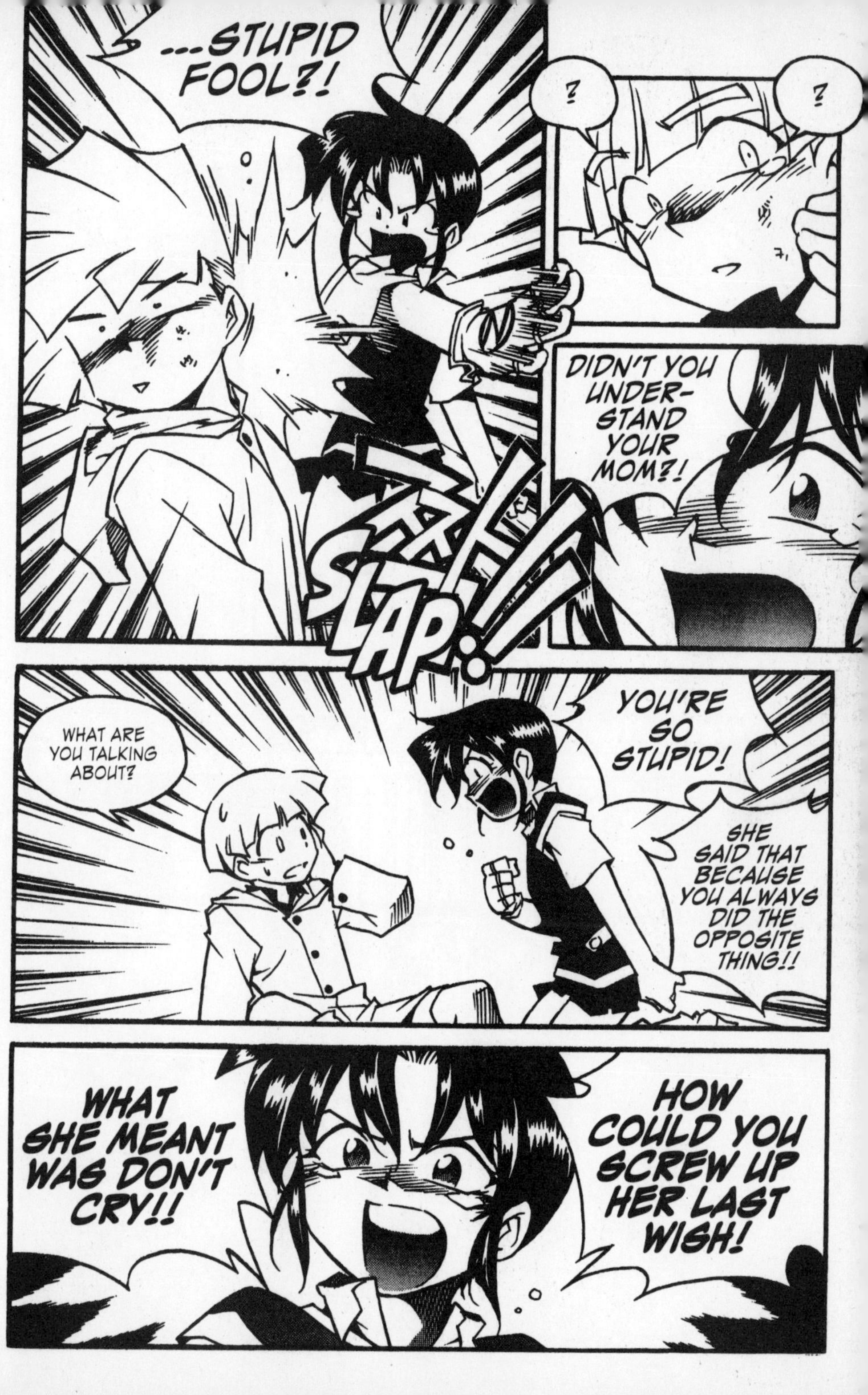
?
?
...STUPID FOOL?!
DIDN'T YOU UNDER-STAND YOUR MOM?!
SLAP!!
YOU'RE SO STUPID!
SHE SAID THAT BECAUSE YOU ALWAYS DID THE OPPOSITE THING!!
WHAT ARE YOU TALKING ABOUT?
HOW COULD YOU SCREW UP HER LAST WISH!
WHAT SHE MEANT WAS DON'T CRY!!

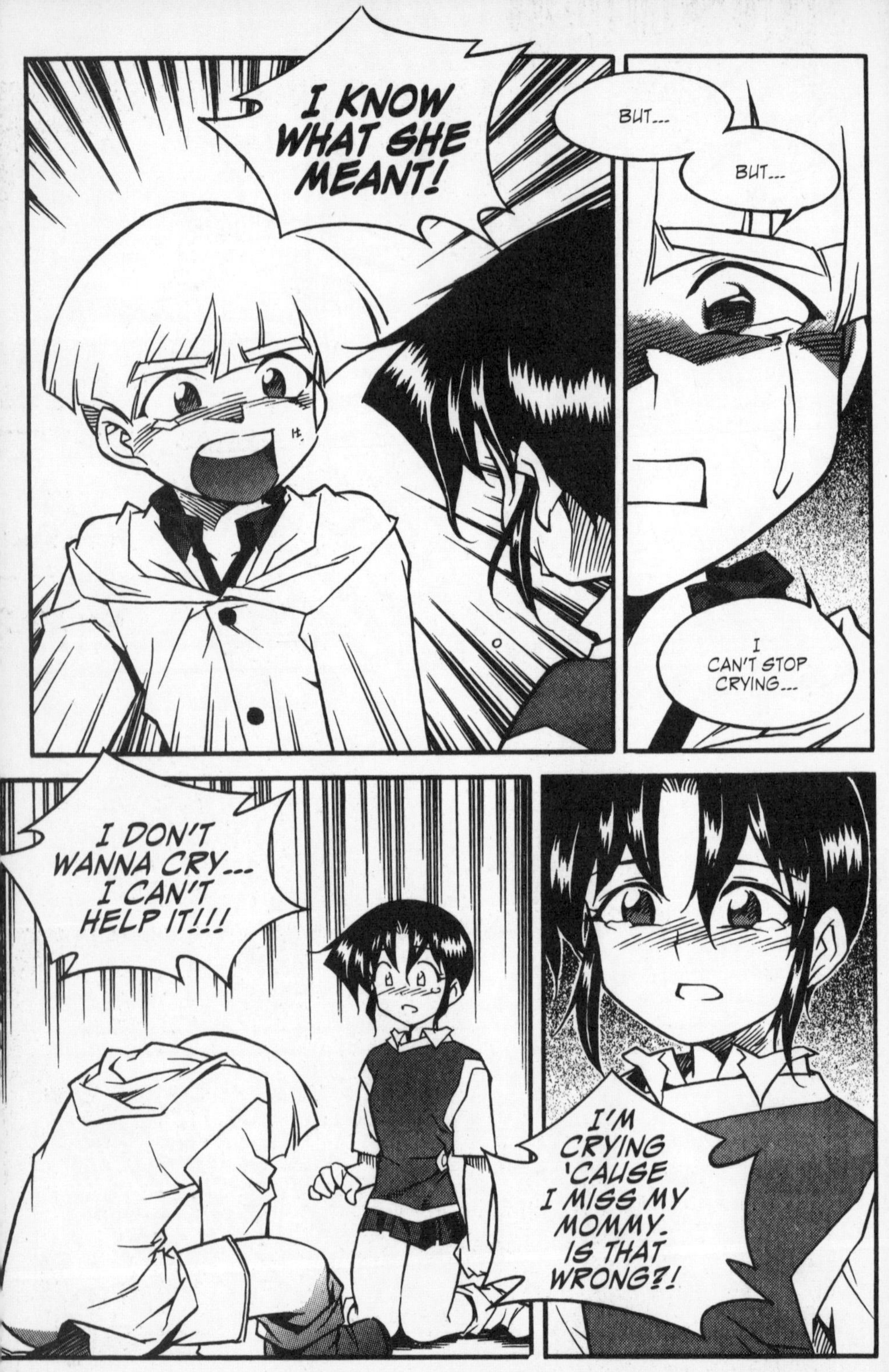

I KNOW WHAT SHE MEANT!
BUT...
BUT...
I CAN'T STOP CRYING...
I DON'T WANNA CRY... I CAN'T HELP IT!!!
I'M CRYING 'CAUSE I MISS MY MOMMY. IS THAT WRONG?!

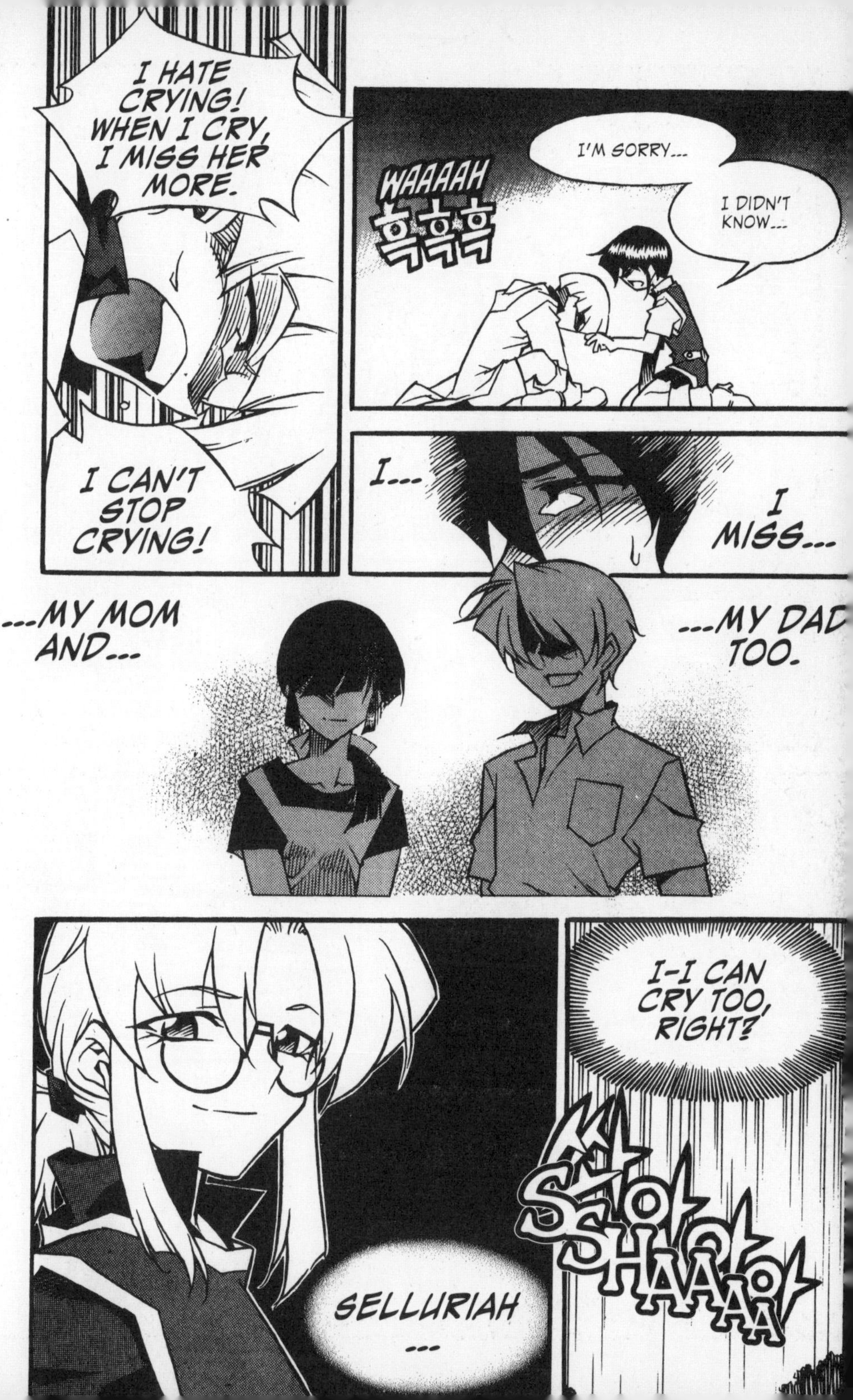
I HATE CRYING! WHEN I CRY, I MISS HER MORE.
I CAN'T STOP CRYING!
WAAAAH
흑흑흑
I'M SORRY...
I DIDN'T KNOW...
I...
I MISS...
...MY MOM AND...
...MY DAD TOO.
SELLURIAH ...
I-I CAN CRY TOO, RIGHT?
SHAAAA

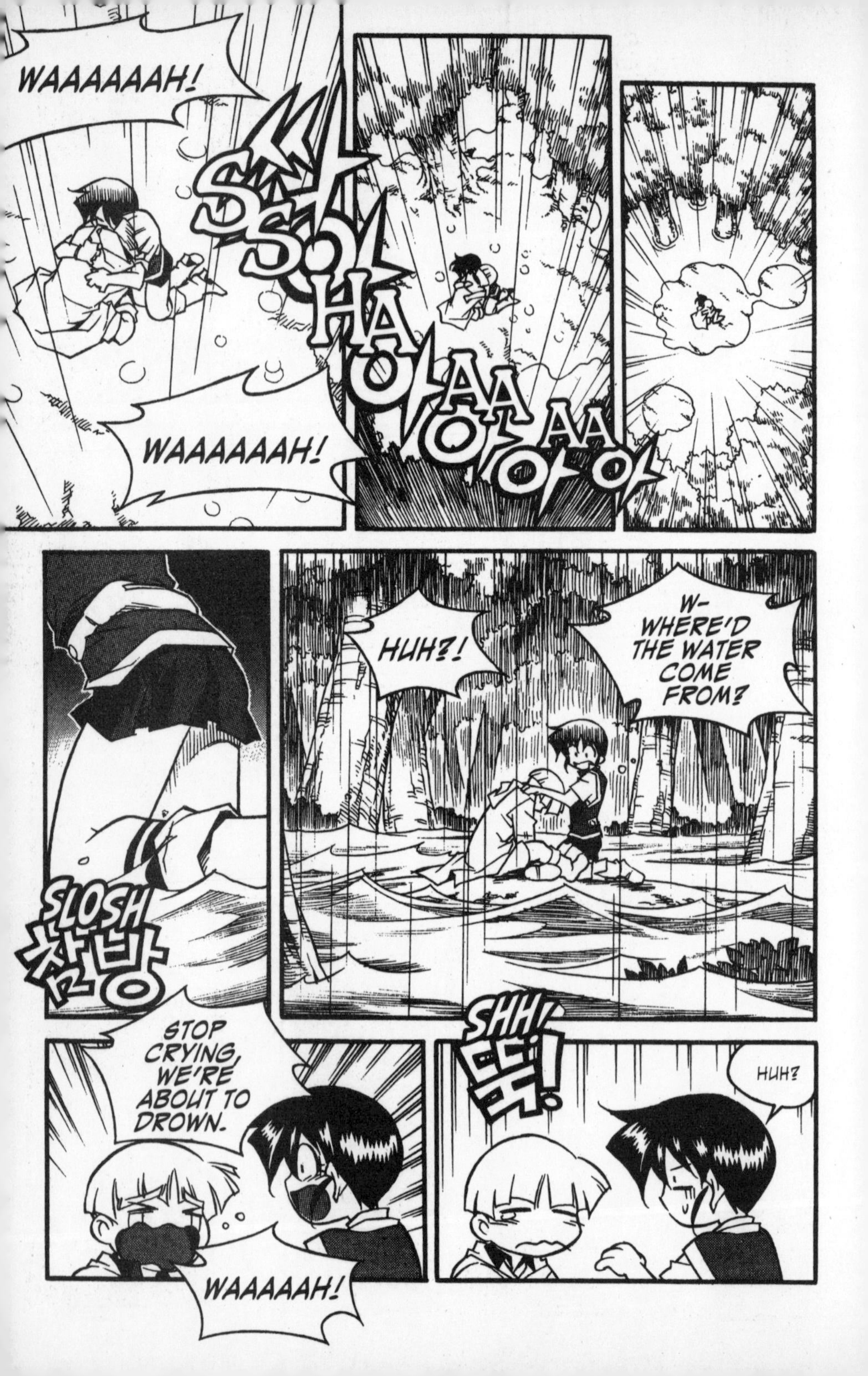

WAAAAAAH!
SSHAOAAAA
WAAAAAAH!
HUH?!
W-WHERE'D THE WATER COME FROM?
SLOSH
찰방
STOP CRYING, WE'RE ABOUT TO DROWN.
WAAAAAH!
SHH!
뚝!
HUH?

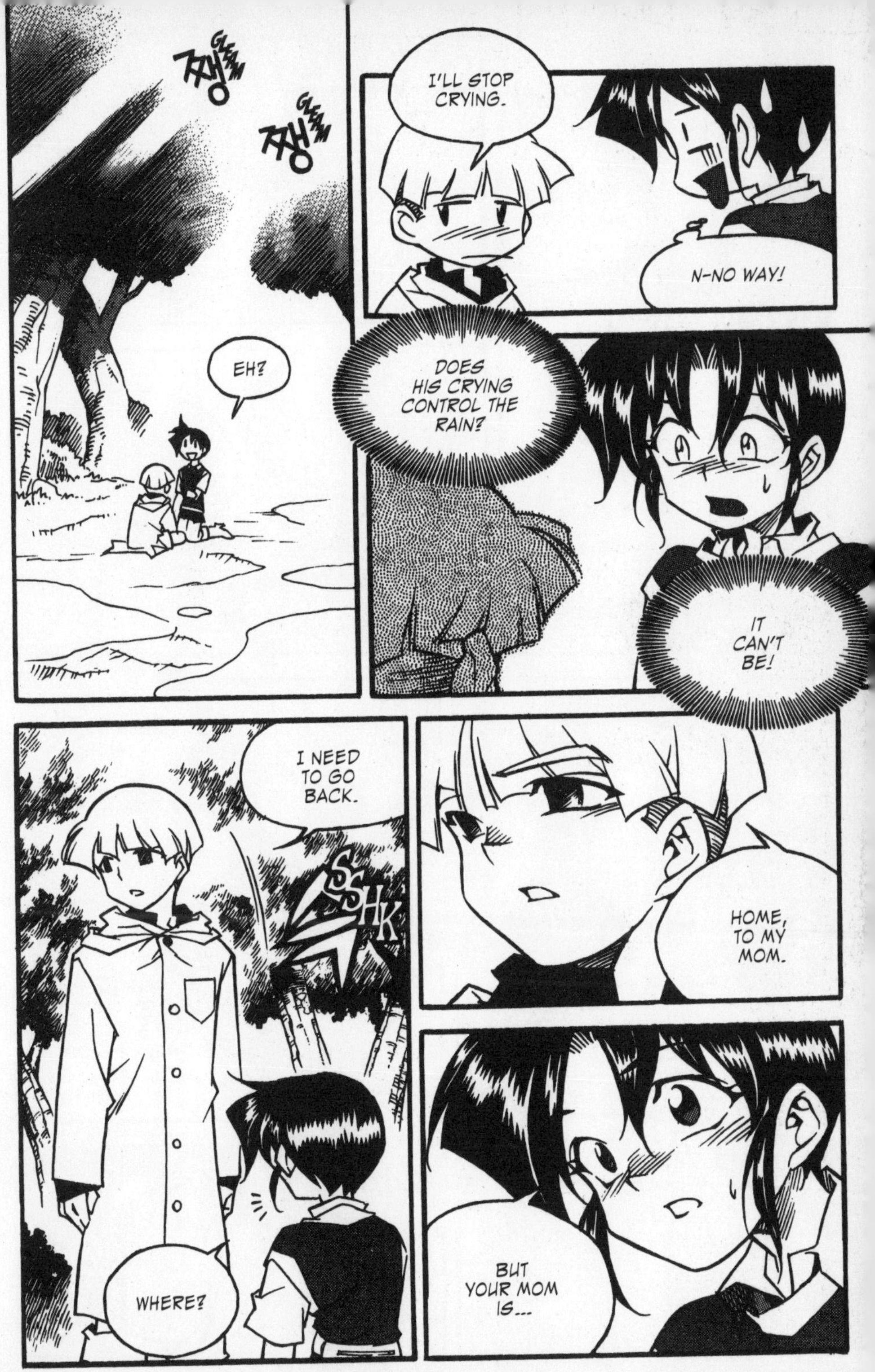

쨍 GLEEM
쨍 GLEEM
EH?
I'LL STOP CRYING.
N-NO WAY!
DOES HIS CRYING CONTROL THE RAIN?
IT CAN'T BE!
I NEED TO GO BACK.
SSHK
WHERE?
HOME, TO MY MOM.
BUT YOUR MOM IS...

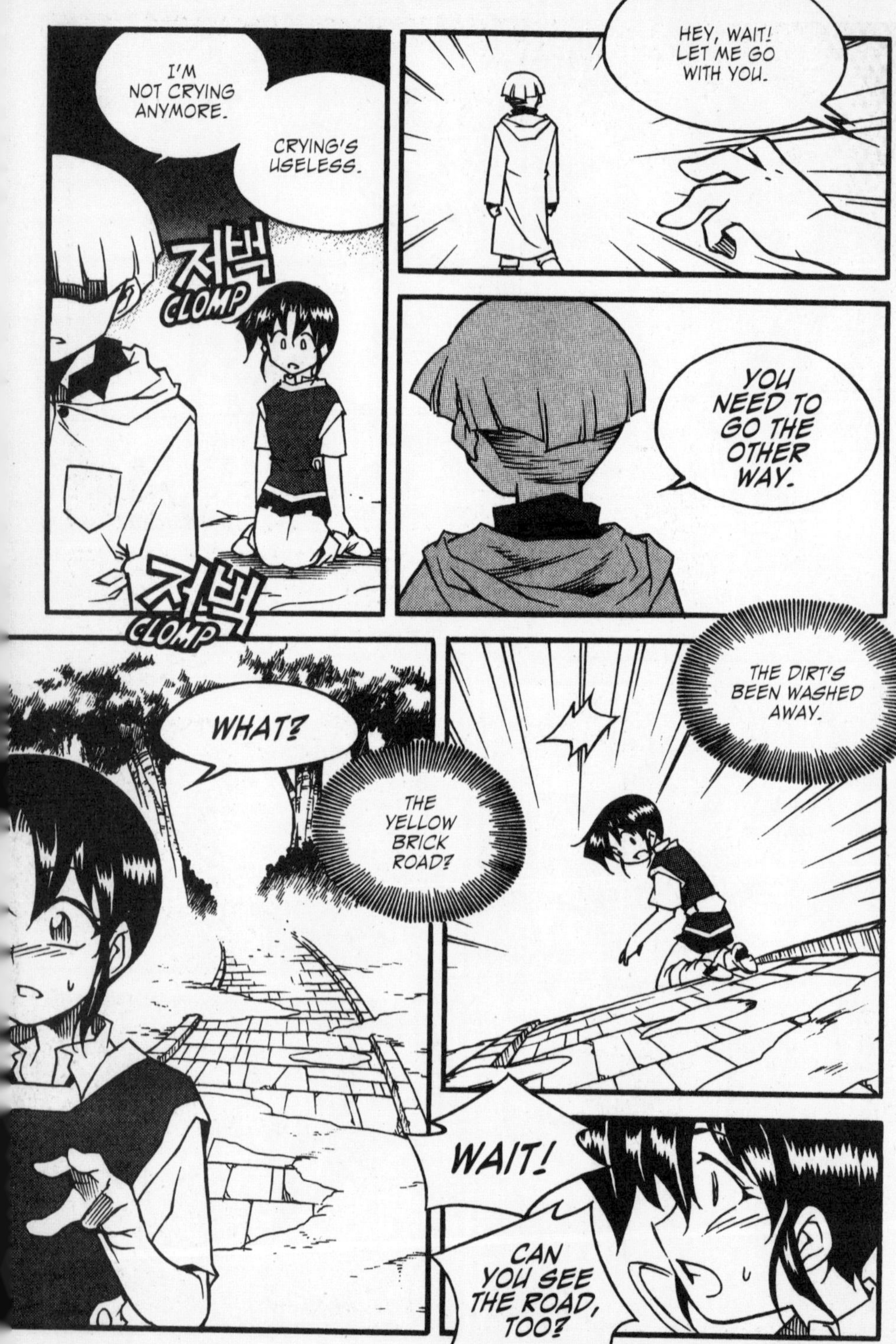
I'M NOT CRYING ANYMORE.
CRYING'S USELESS.
저벅
CLOMP
저벅
CLOMP
HEY, WAIT! LET ME GO WITH YOU.
YOU NEED TO GO THE OTHER WAY.
WHAT?
THE YELLOW BRICK ROAD?
THE DIRT'S BEEN WASHED AWAY.
WAIT!
CAN YOU SEE THE ROAD, TOO?

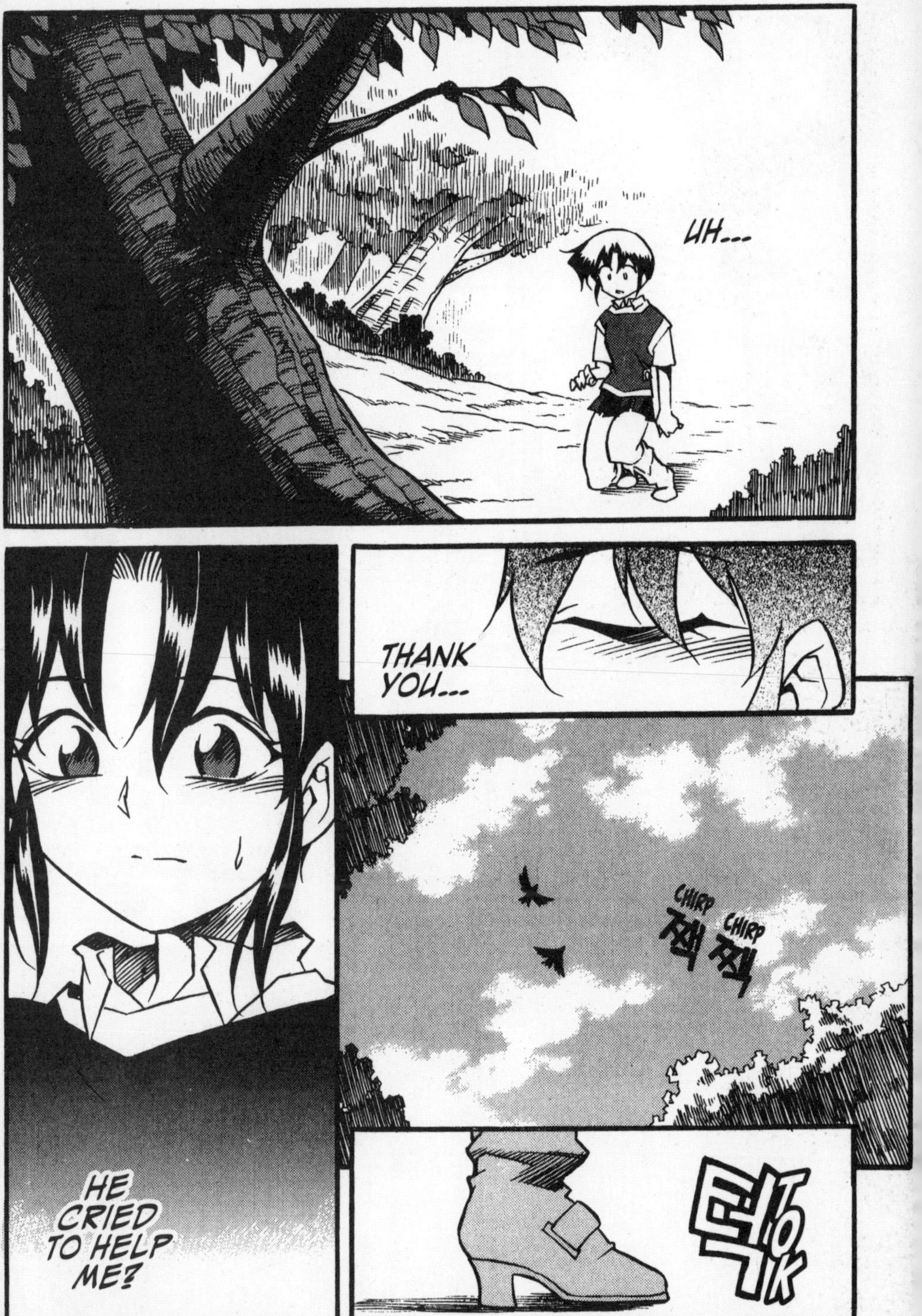
UH...
THANK YOU...
CHIRP 짹 CHIRP 짹
HE CRIED TO HELP ME?
TOK

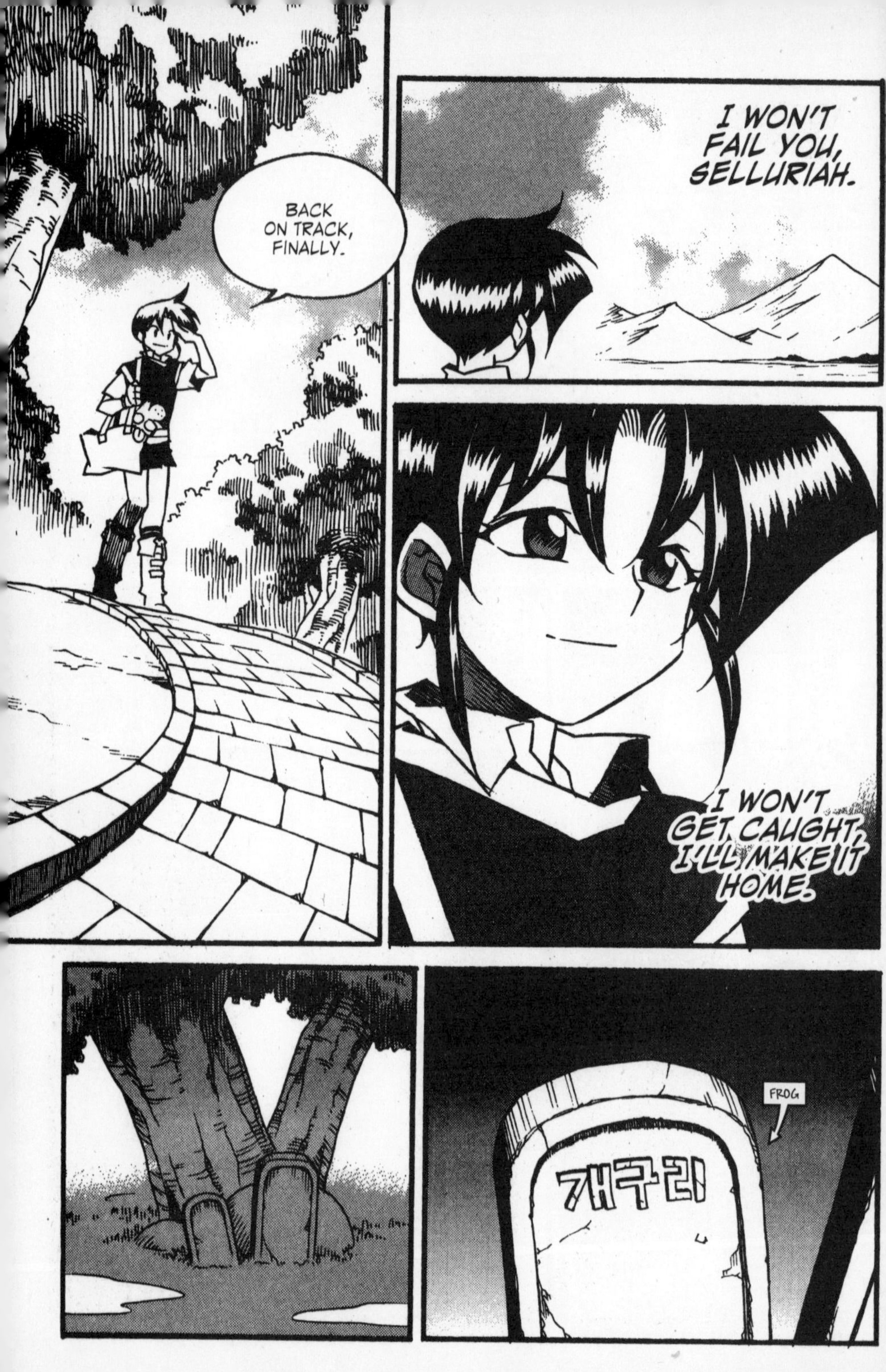
BACK ON TRACK, FINALLY.
I WON'T FAIL YOU, SELLURIAH.
I WON'T GET CAUGHT. I'LL MAKE IT HOME.
FROG
개구리

Step 14 SPY OF THE WEST

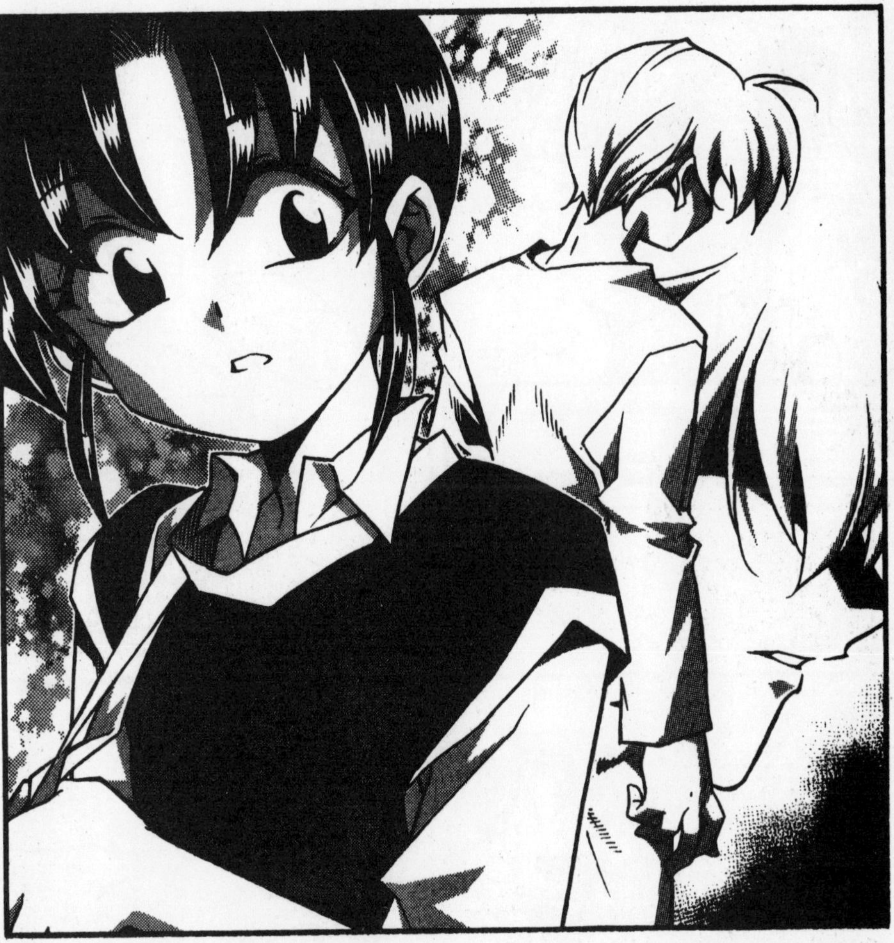

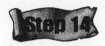

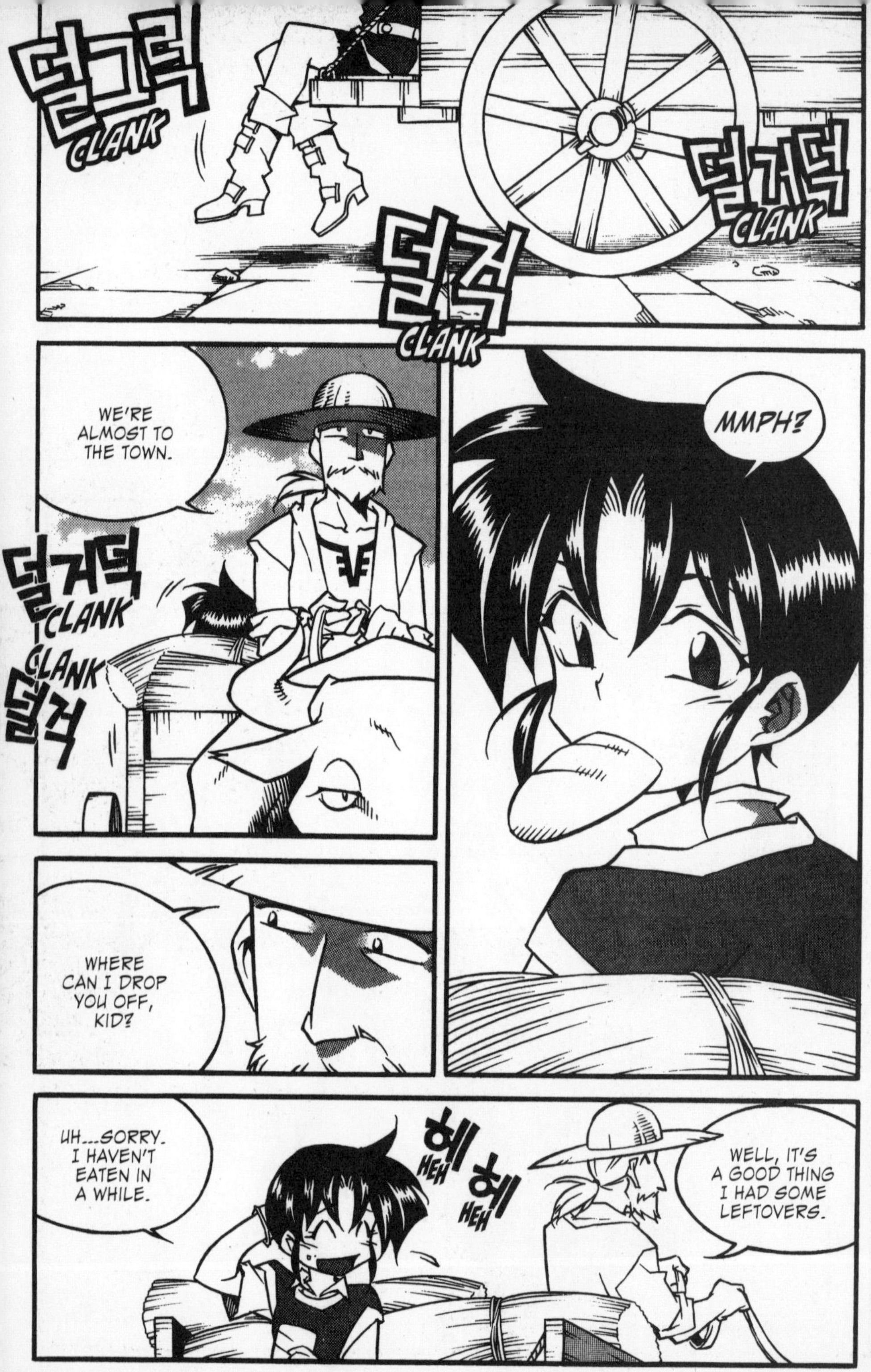
덜그럭
CLANK
덜거덕
CLANK
덜컥
CLANK
WE'RE ALMOST TO THE TOWN.
덜거덕
CLANK
CLANK
덜걱
MMPH?
WHERE CAN I DROP YOU OFF, KID?
UH...SORRY. I HAVEN'T EATEN IN A WHILE.
헤
HEH
헤
HEH
WELL, IT'S A GOOD THING I HAD SOME LEFTOVERS.

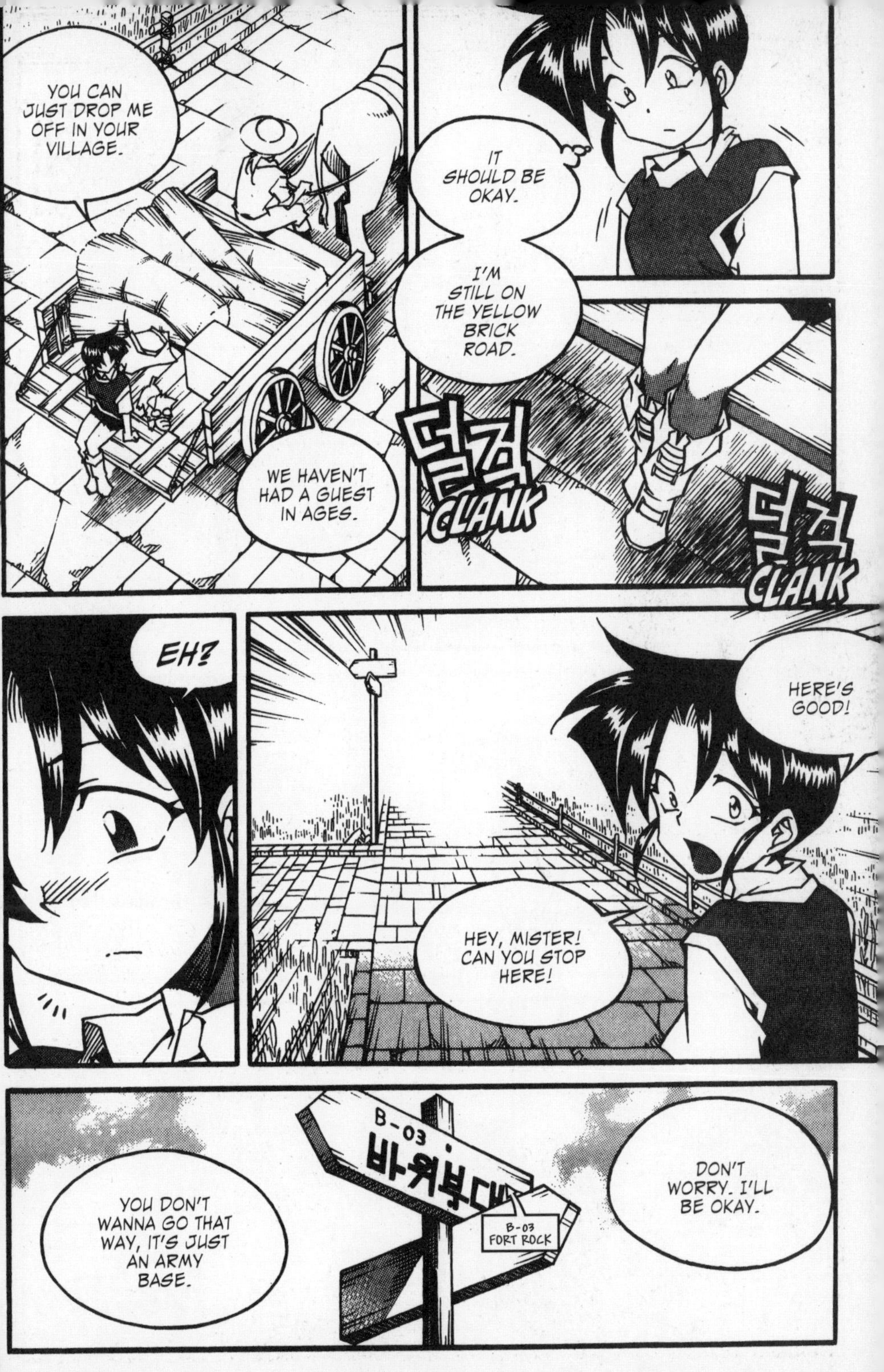

YOU CAN JUST DROP ME OFF IN YOUR VILLAGE.
WE HAVEN'T HAD A GUEST IN AGES.
IT SHOULD BE OKAY.
I'M STILL ON THE YELLOW BRICK ROAD.
덜컹
CLANK
덜컹
CLANK
EH?
HERE'S GOOD!
HEY, MISTER! CAN YOU STOP HERE!
B-03
바위부대
B-03 FORT ROCK
YOU DON'T WANNA GO THAT WAY, IT'S JUST AN ARMY BASE.
DON'T WORRY. I'LL BE OKAY.

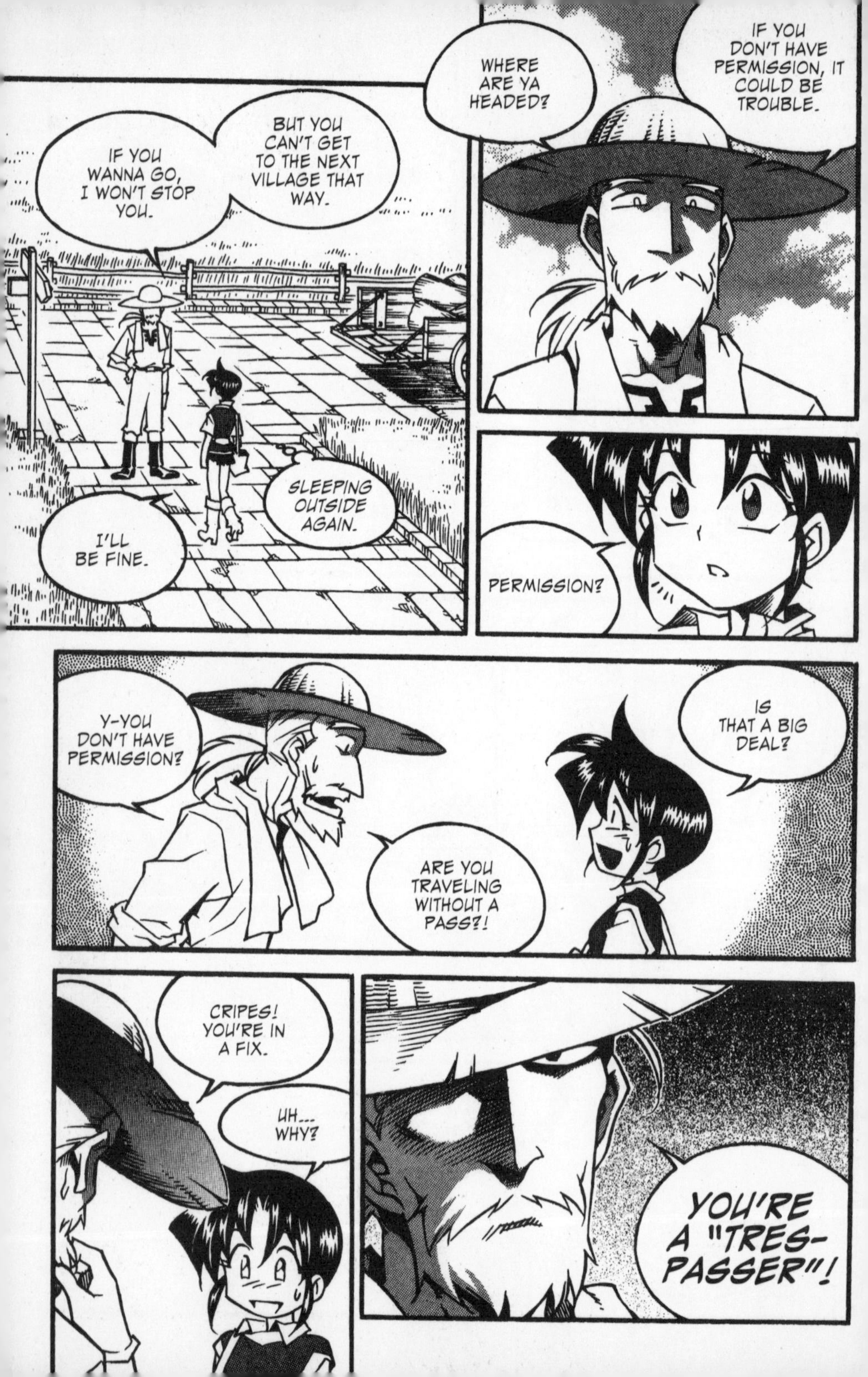
IF YOU WANNA GO, I WON'T STOP YOU.
BUT YOU CAN'T GET TO THE NEXT VILLAGE THAT WAY.
SLEEPING OUTSIDE AGAIN.
I'LL BE FINE.
WHERE ARE YA HEADED?
IF YOU DON'T HAVE PERMISSION, IT COULD BE TROUBLE.
PERMISSION?
Y-YOU DON'T HAVE PERMISSION?
ARE YOU TRAVELING WITHOUT A PASS?!
IS THAT A BIG DEAL?
CRIPES! YOU'RE IN A FIX.
UH... WHY?
YOU'RE A "TRES-PASSER"!

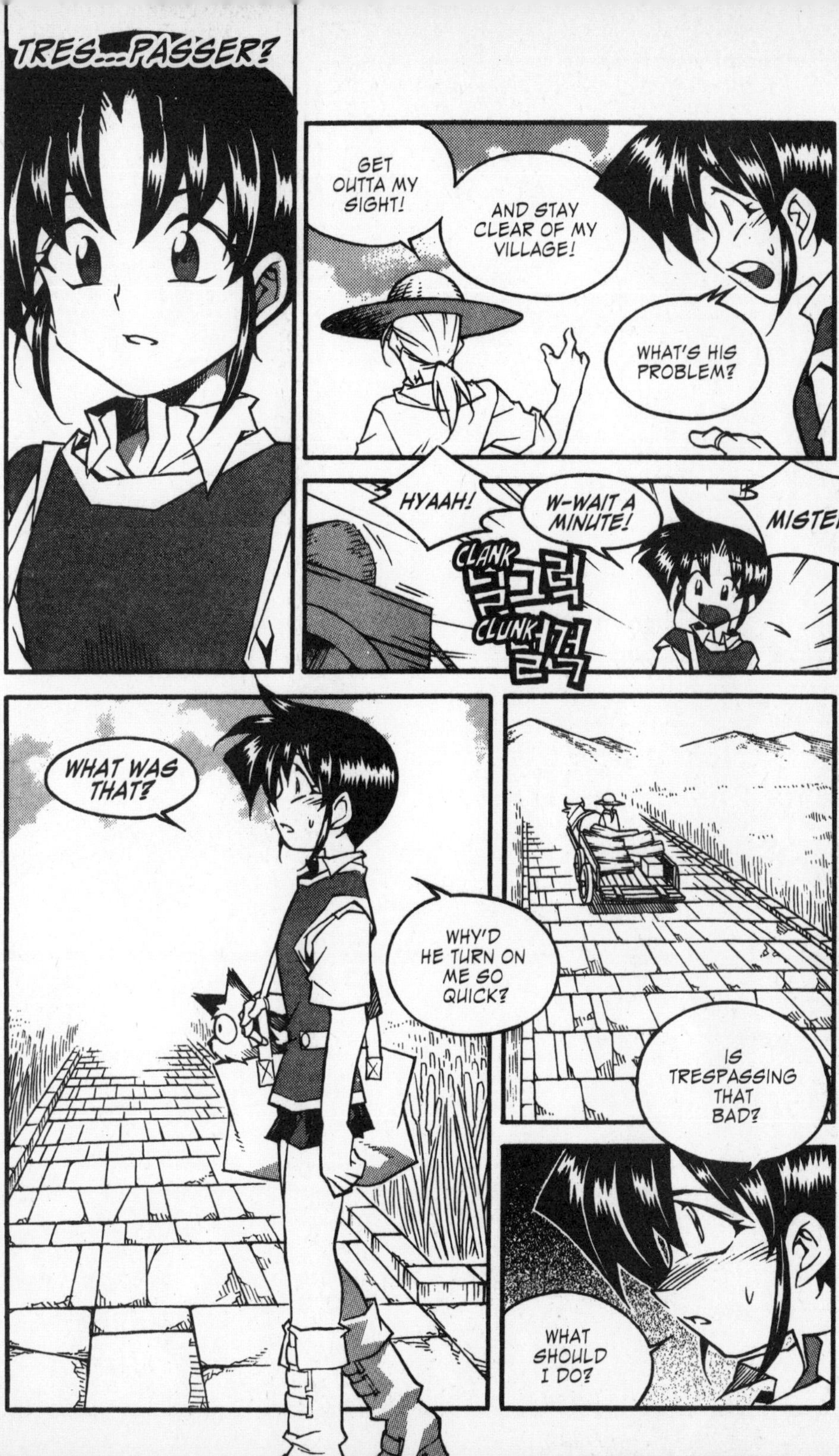
TRES...PASSER?
GET OUTTA MY SIGHT!
AND STAY CLEAR OF MY VILLAGE!
WHAT'S HIS PROBLEM?
HYAAH!
W-WAIT A MINUTE!
MISTER!
CLANK 덜그럭
CLUNK 덜컥
WHAT WAS THAT?
WHY'D HE TURN ON ME SO QUICK?
IS TRESPASSING THAT BAD?
WHAT SHOULD I DO?

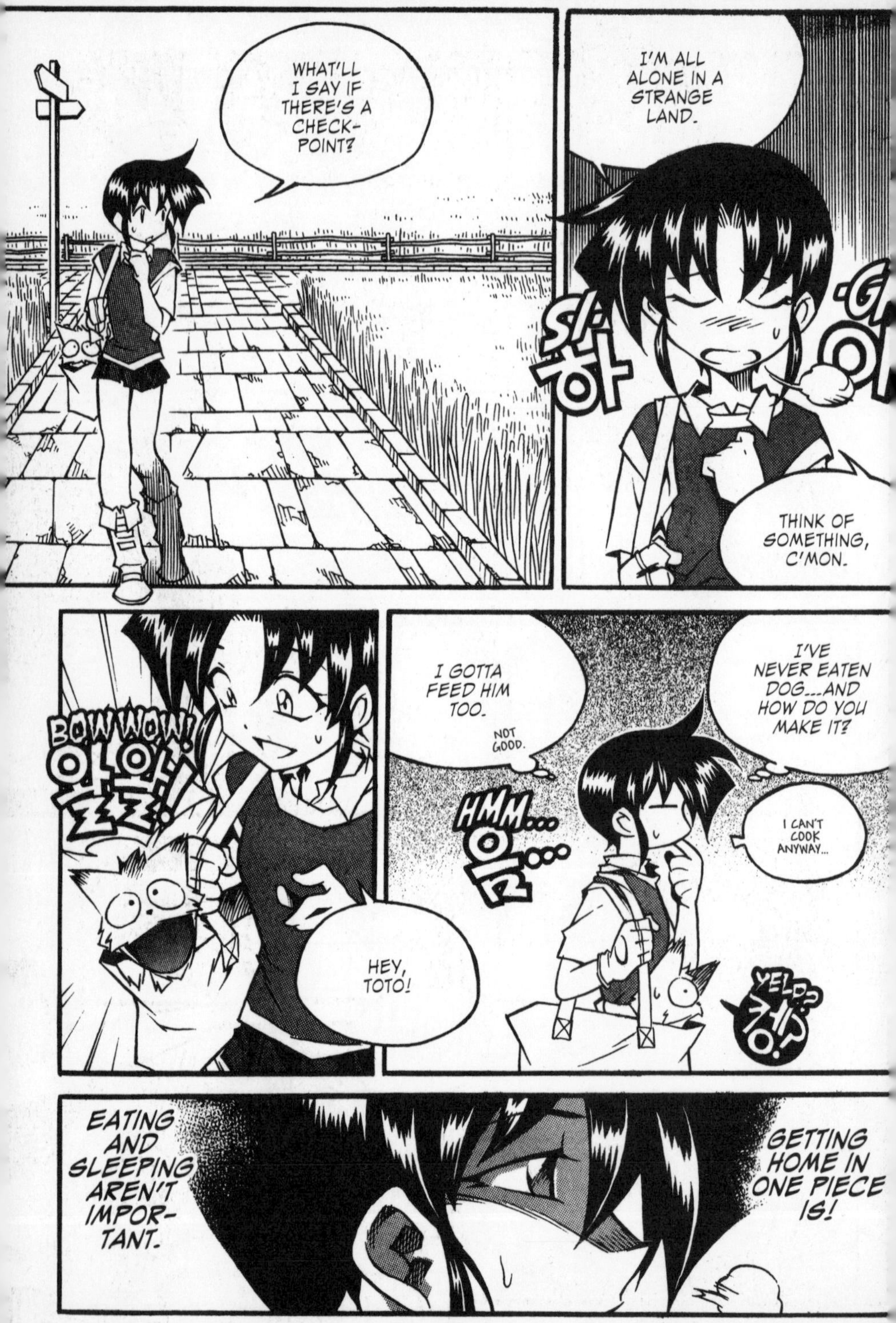
WHAT'LL I SAY IF THERE'S A CHECK-POINT?
I'M ALL ALONE IN A STRANGE LAND.
THINK OF SOMETHING, C'MON.
BOW WOW!
HEY, TOTO!
I GOTTA FEED HIM TOO.
NOT GOOD.
I'VE NEVER EATEN DOG...AND HOW DO YOU MAKE IT?
HMM...
I CAN'T COOK ANYWAY...
YELP?
EATING AND SLEEPING AREN'T IMPOR-TANT.
GETTING HOME IN ONE PIECE IS!

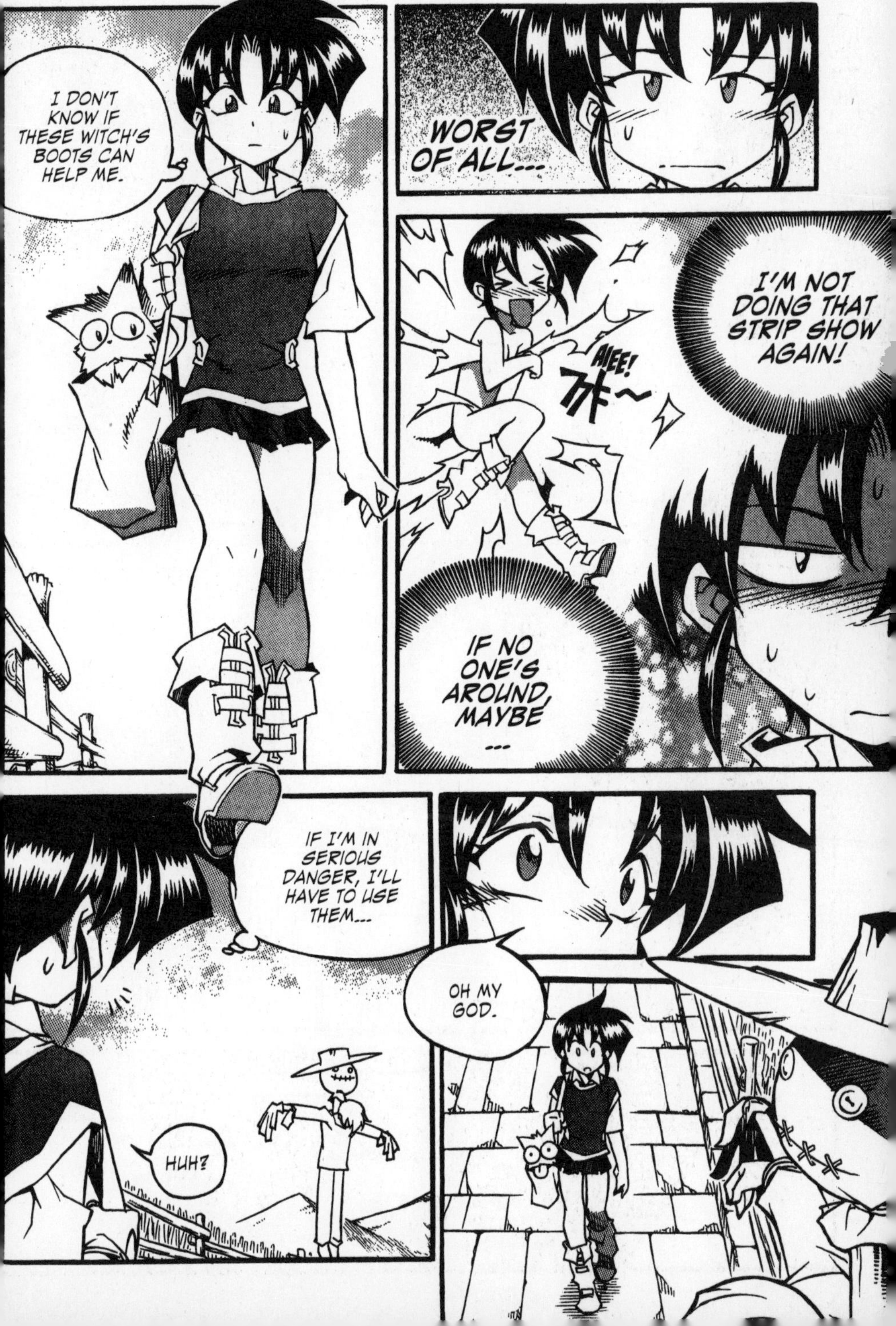

I DON'T KNOW IF THESE WITCH'S BOOTS CAN HELP ME.
WORST OF ALL...
I'M NOT DOING THAT STRIP SHOW AGAIN!
AIEE!
IF NO ONE'S AROUND, MAYBE ...
IF I'M IN SERIOUS DANGER, I'LL HAVE TO USE THEM...
OH MY GOD.
HUH?

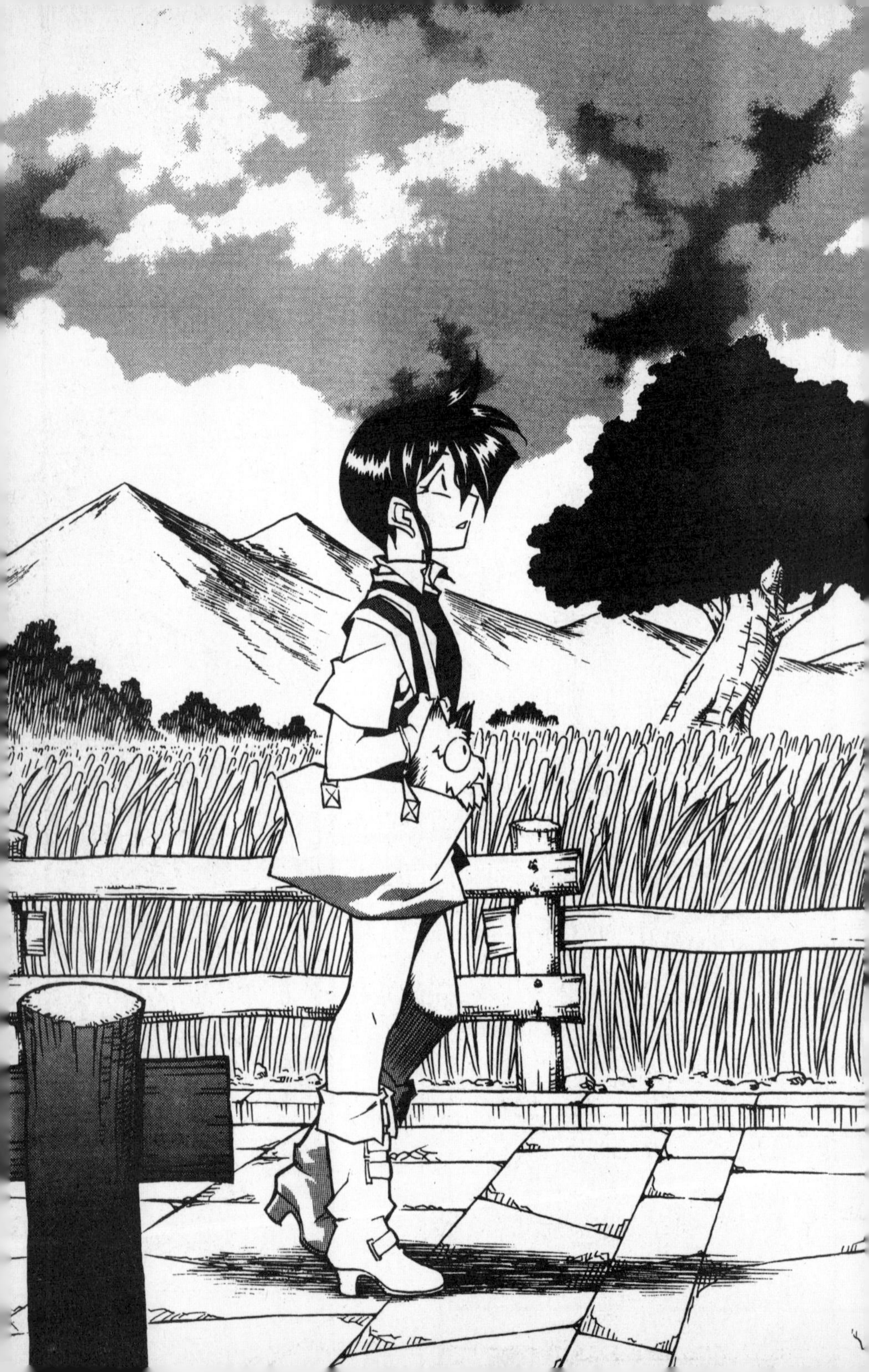

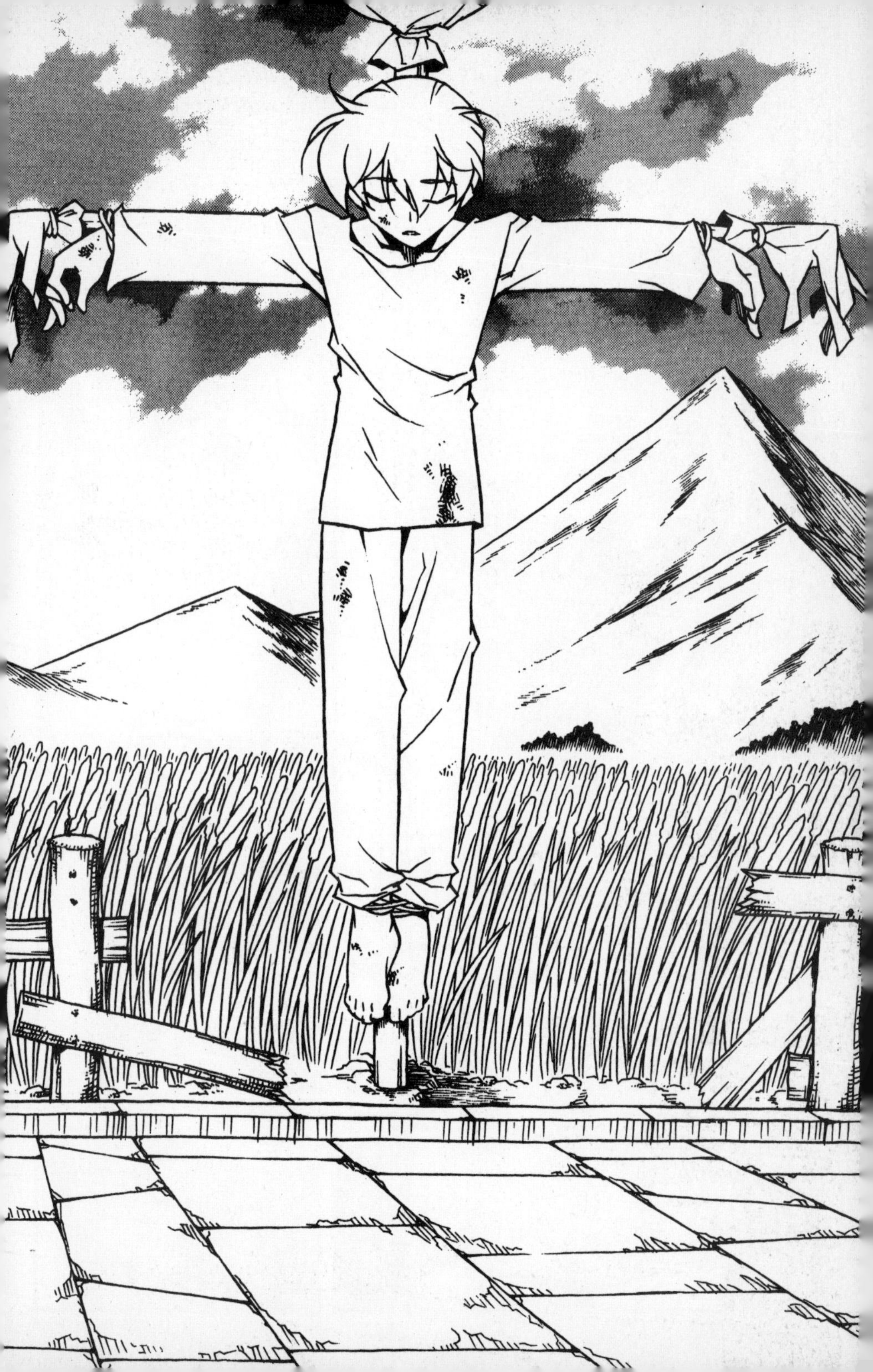

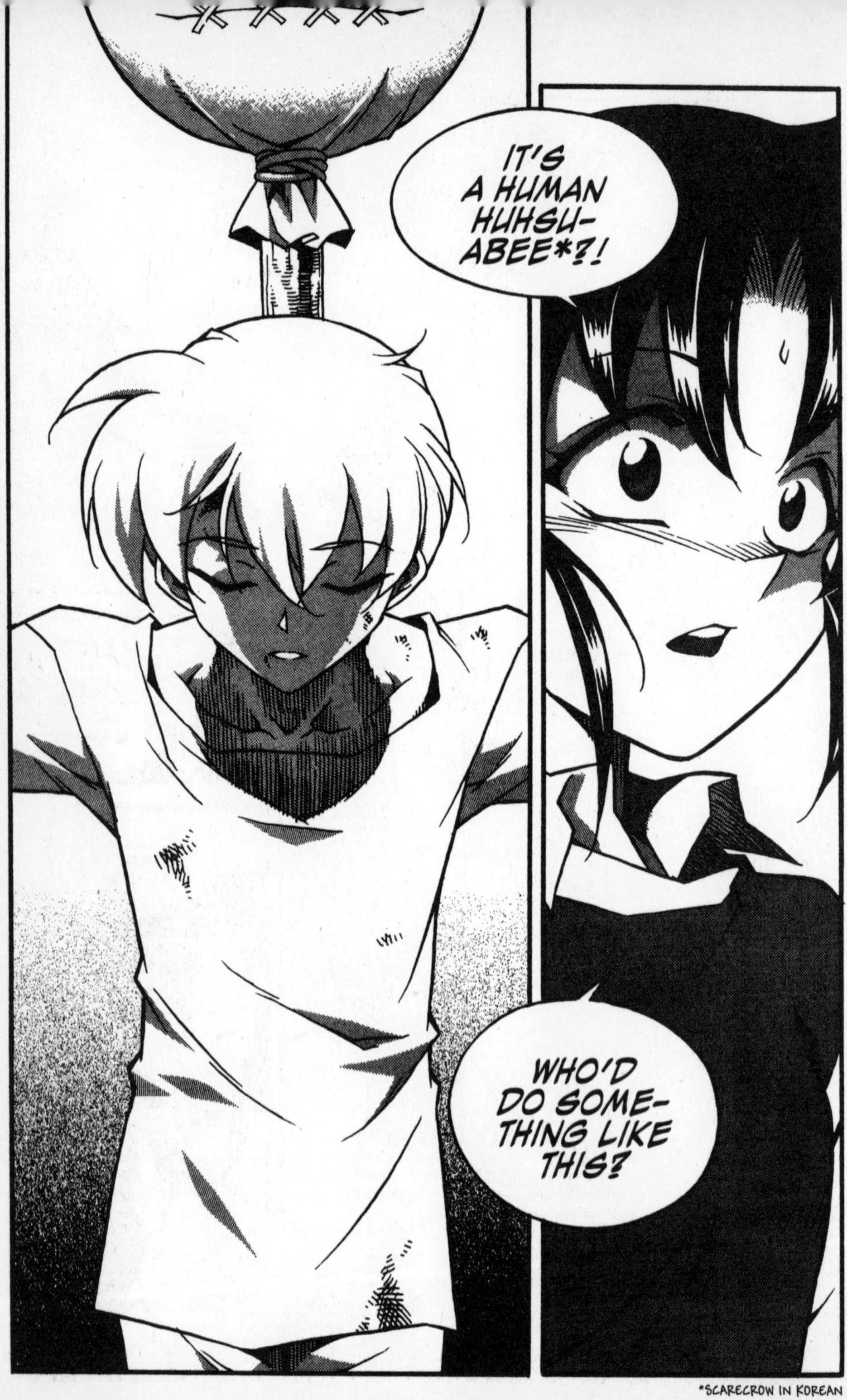
IT'S A HUMAN HUHSU-ABEE*?!
WHO'D DO SOME-THING LIKE THIS?
*SCARECROW IN KOREAN

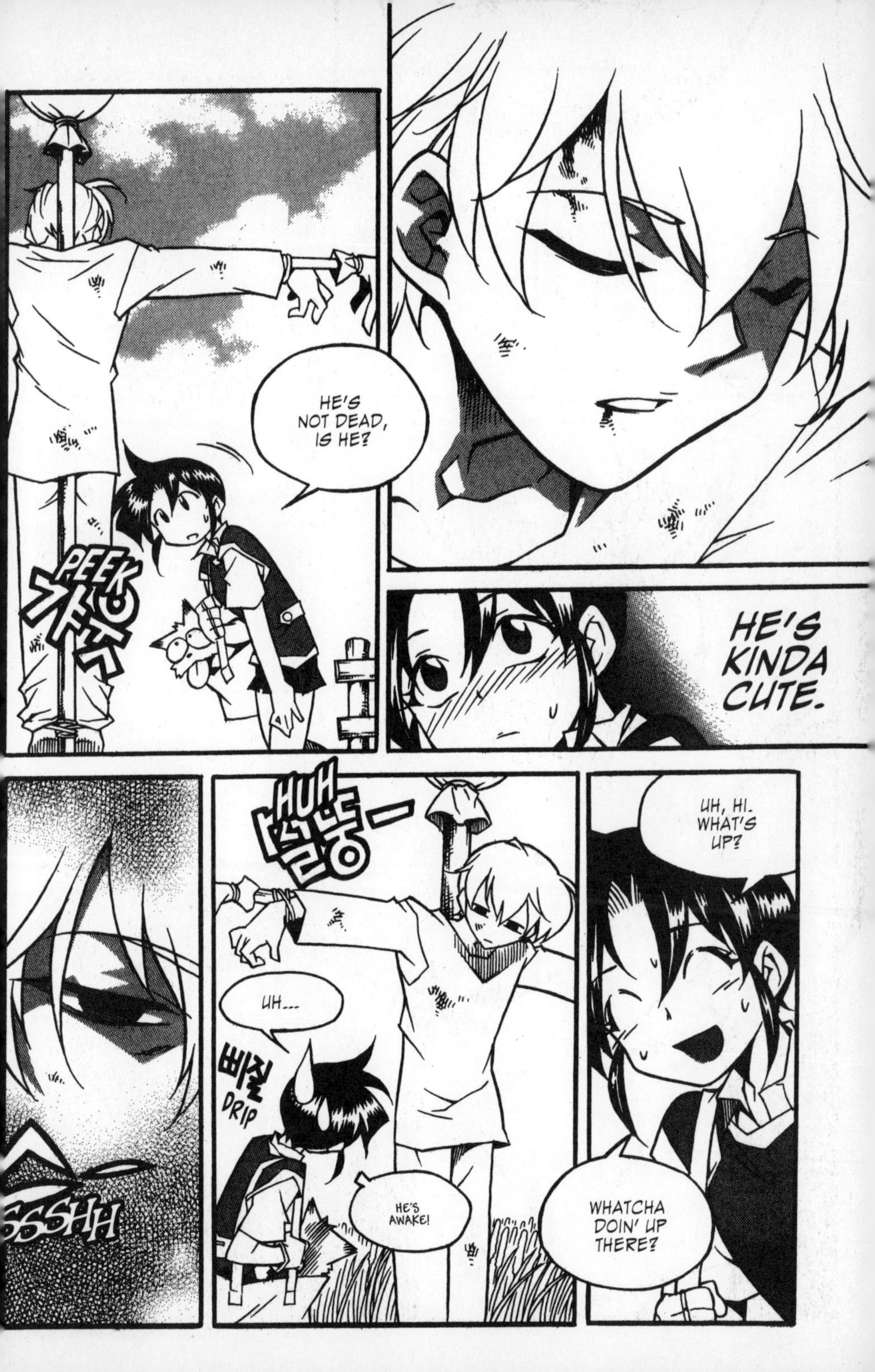
PEEK
HE'S NOT DEAD, IS HE?
HE'S KINDA CUTE.
SSSHH
HUH
UH...
DRIP
HE'S AWAKE!
UH, HI. WHAT'S UP?
WHATCHA DOIN' UP THERE?

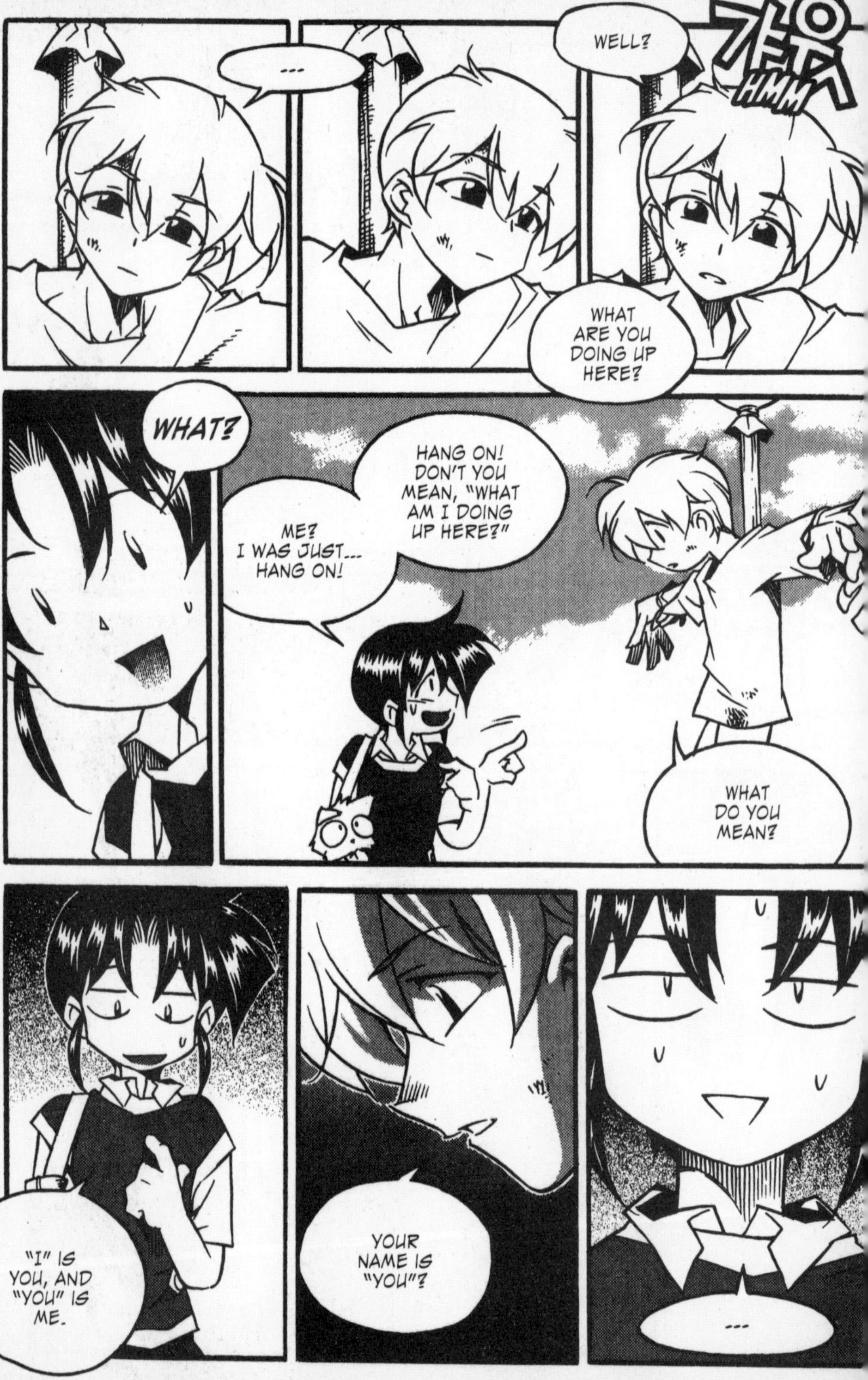

...
WELL?
HMM
WHAT ARE YOU DOING UP HERE?
WHAT?
ME? I WAS JUST... HANG ON!
HANG ON! DON'T YOU MEAN, "WHAT AM I DOING UP HERE?"
WHAT DO YOU MEAN?
"I" IS YOU, AND "YOU" IS ME.
YOUR NAME IS "YOU"?
...

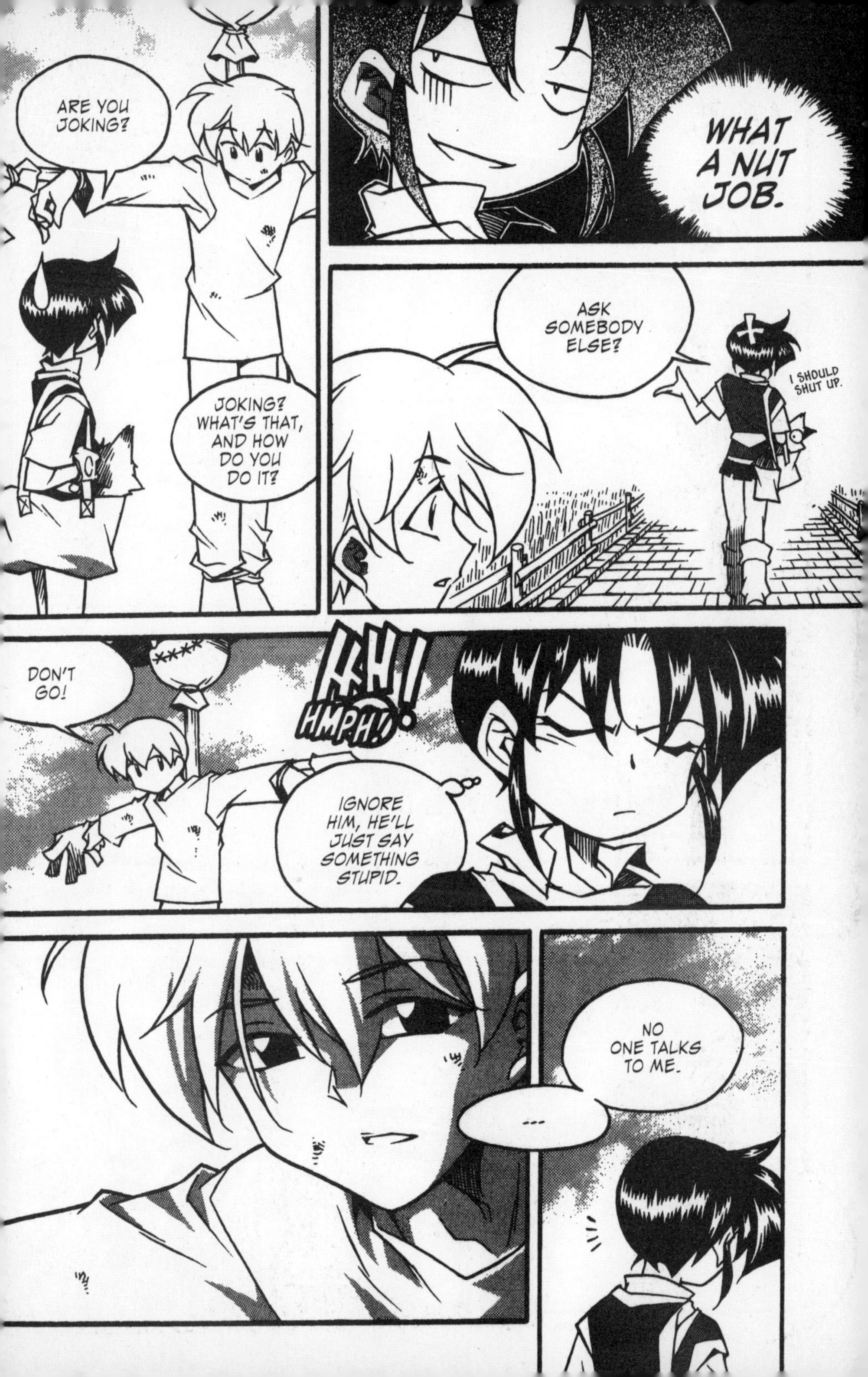
ARE YOU JOKING?
JOKING? WHAT'S THAT, AND HOW DO YOU DO IT?
WHAT A NUT JOB.
ASK SOMEBODY ELSE?
I SHOULD SHUT UP.
DON'T GO!
AH!
HMPH!
IGNORE HIM, HE'LL JUST SAY SOMETHING STUPID.
NO ONE TALKS TO ME.
...

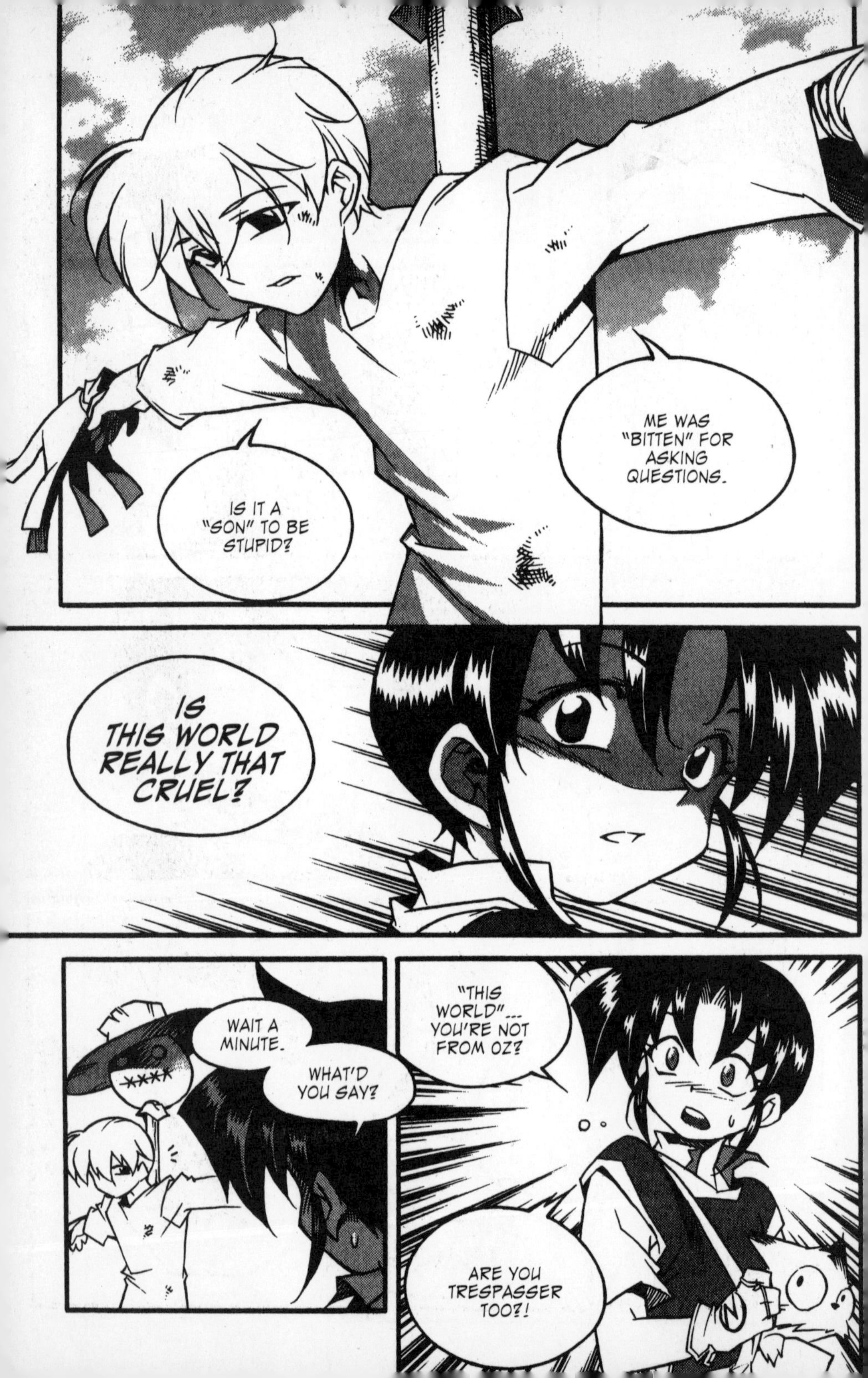
ME WAS "BITTEN" FOR ASKING QUESTIONS.
IS IT A "SON" TO BE STUPID?
IS THIS WORLD REALLY THAT CRUEL?
WAIT A MINUTE.
WHAT'D YOU SAY?
"THIS WORLD"... YOU'RE NOT FROM OZ?
ARE YOU TRESPASSER TOO?!

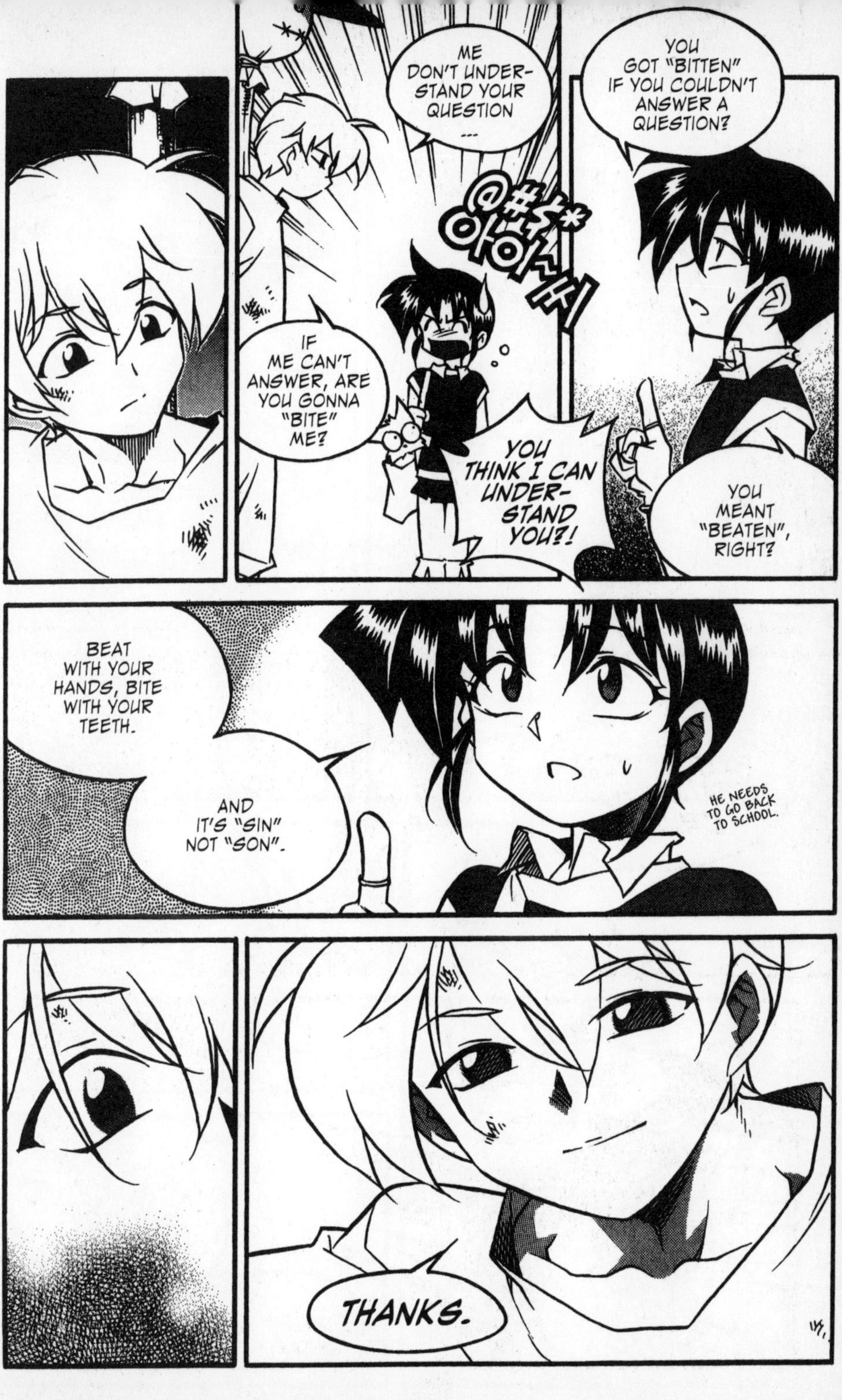
YOU GOT "BITTEN" IF YOU COULDN'T ANSWER A QUESTION?
YOU MEANT "BEATEN", RIGHT?
ME DON'T UNDER-STAND YOUR QUESTION ...
IF ME CAN'T ANSWER, ARE YOU GONNA "BITE" ME?
@#$* AAAAAGH!
YOU THINK I CAN UNDER-STAND YOU?!
BEAT WITH YOUR HANDS, BITE WITH YOUR TEETH.
AND IT'S "SIN" NOT "SON".
HE NEEDS TO GO BACK TO SCHOOL.
THANKS.

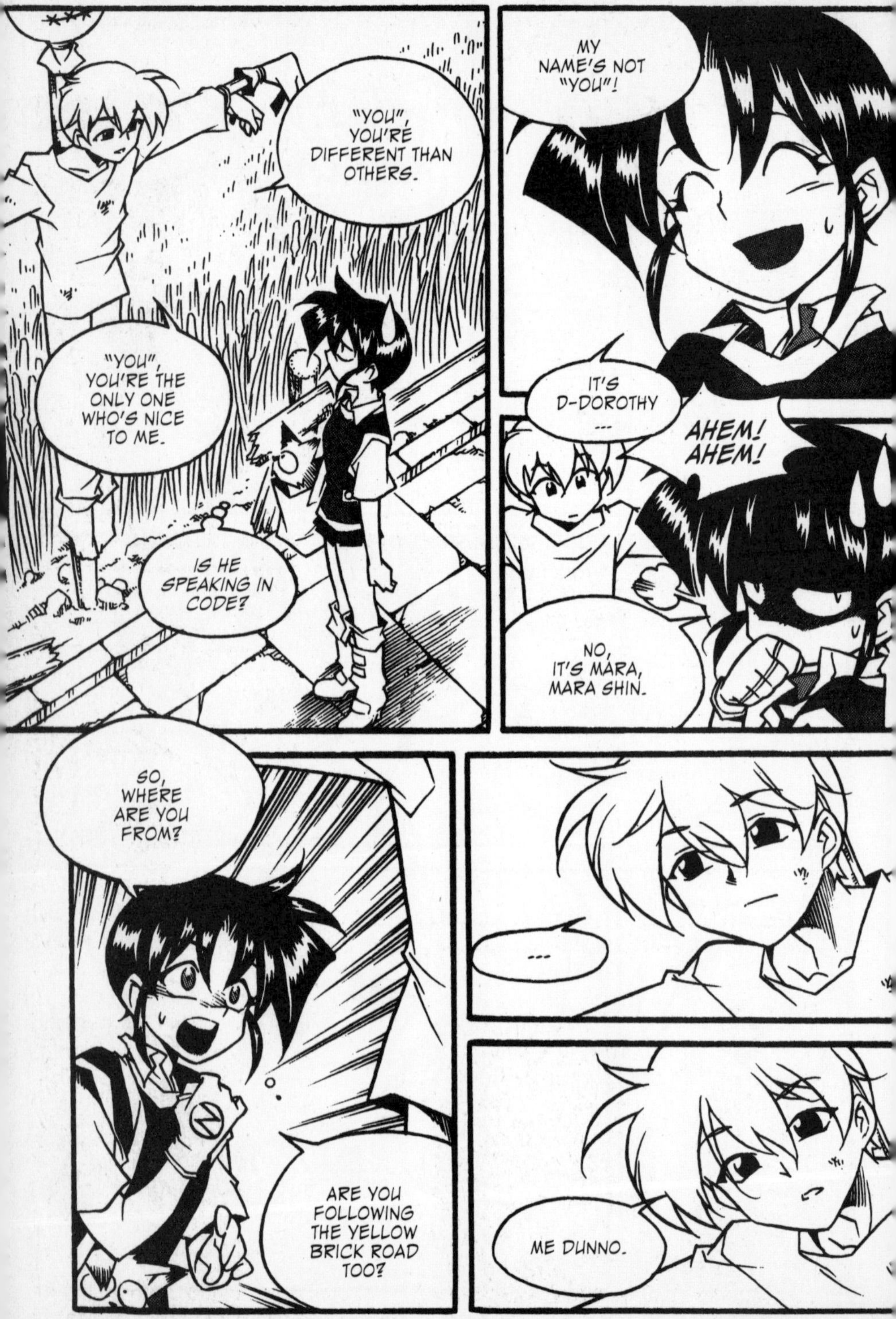
"YOU", YOU'RE DIFFERENT THAN OTHERS.
"YOU", YOU'RE THE ONLY ONE WHO'S NICE TO ME.
IS HE SPEAKING IN CODE?
MY NAME'S NOT "YOU"!
IT'S D-DOROTHY ...
AHEM! AHEM!
NO, IT'S MARA, MARA SHIN.
SO, WHERE ARE YOU FROM?
ARE YOU FOLLOWING THE YELLOW BRICK ROAD TOO?
...
ME DUNNO.

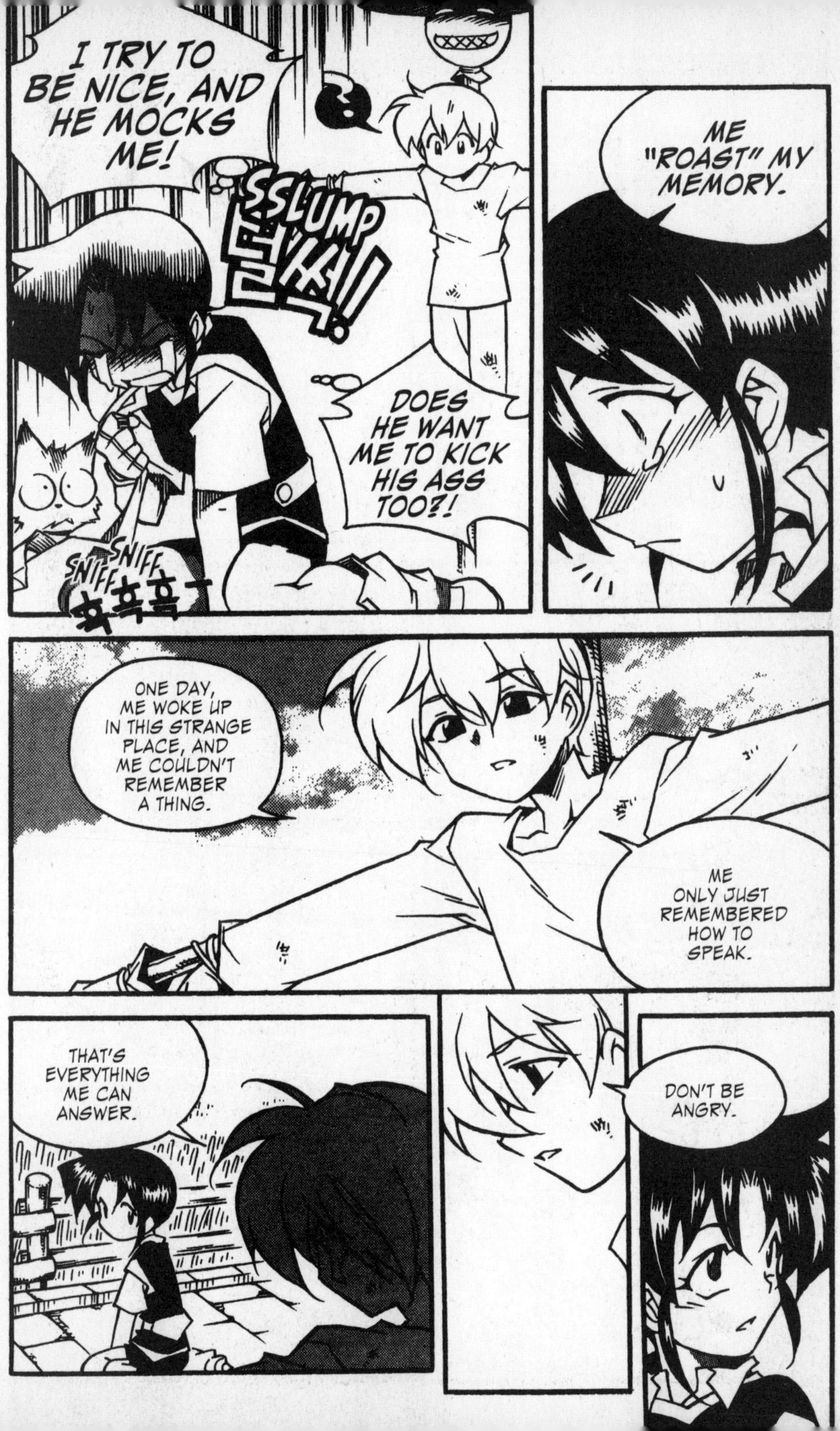
I TRY TO BE NICE, AND HE MOCKS ME!
SSLUMP
DOES HE WANT ME TO KICK HIS ASS TOO?!
SNIFF SNIFF
ME "ROAST" MY MEMORY.
ONE DAY, ME WOKE UP IN THIS STRANGE PLACE, AND ME COULDN'T REMEMBER A THING.
ME ONLY JUST REMEMBERED HOW TO SPEAK.
THAT'S EVERYTHING ME CAN ANSWER.
DON'T BE ANGRY.

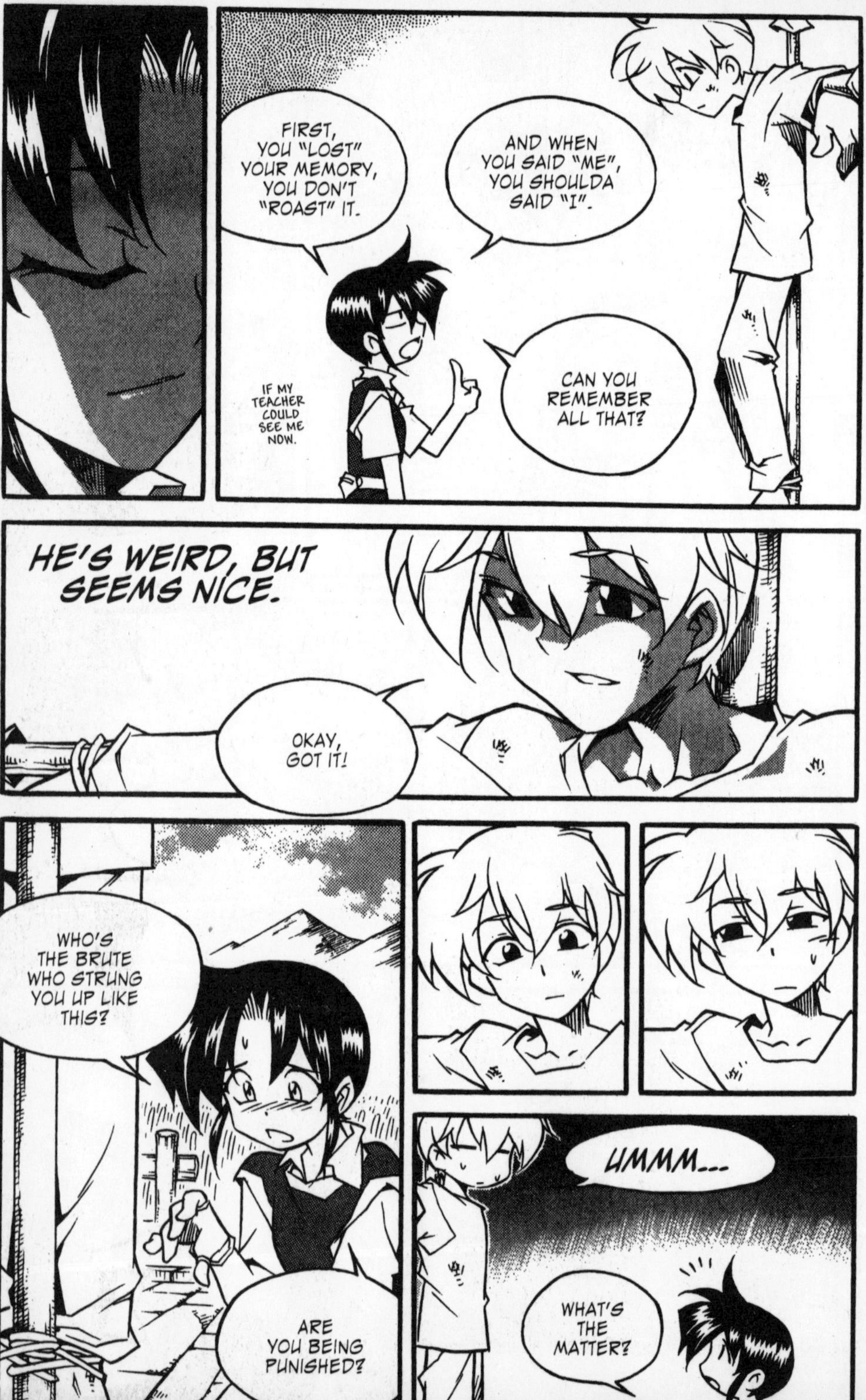
FIRST, YOU "LOST" YOUR MEMORY, YOU DON'T "ROAST" IT.
AND WHEN YOU SAID "ME", YOU SHOULDA SAID "I".
IF MY TEACHER COULD SEE ME NOW.
CAN YOU REMEMBER ALL THAT?
HE'S WEIRD, BUT SEEMS NICE.
OKAY, GOT IT!
WHO'S THE BRUTE WHO STRUNG YOU UP LIKE THIS?
ARE YOU BEING PUNISHED?
UMMM...
WHAT'S THE MATTER?

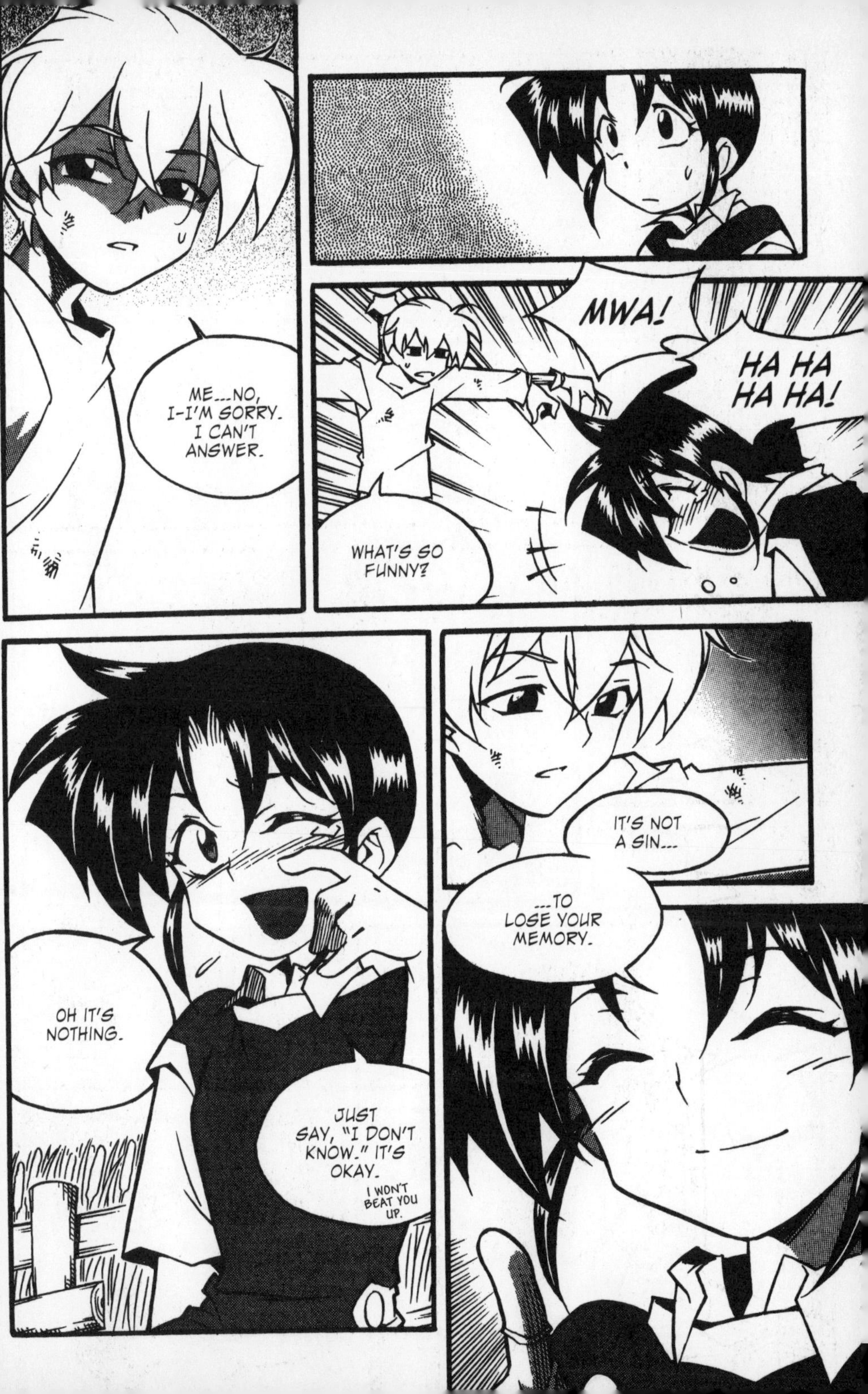
ME...NO, I-I'M SORRY. I CAN'T ANSWER.
MWA!
HA HA HA HA!
WHAT'S SO FUNNY?
OH IT'S NOTHING.
JUST SAY, "I DON'T KNOW." IT'S OKAY.
I WON'T BEAT YOU UP.
IT'S NOT A SIN...
...TO LOSE YOUR MEMORY.

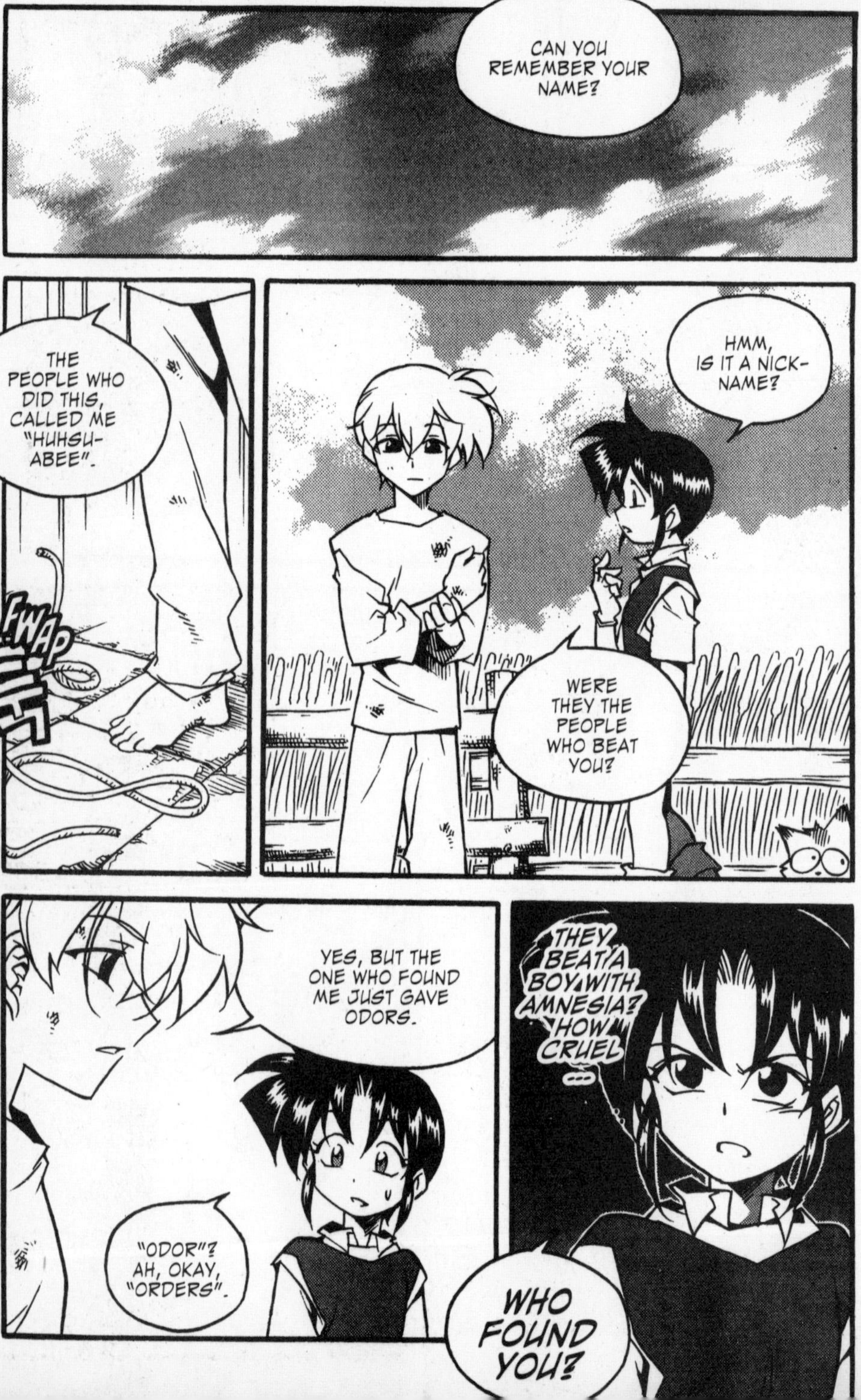

CAN YOU REMEMBER YOUR NAME?
THE PEOPLE WHO DID THIS, CALLED ME "HUHSU-ABEE".
FWAP
HMM, IS IT A NICK-NAME?
WERE THEY THE PEOPLE WHO BEAT YOU?
YES, BUT THE ONE WHO FOUND ME JUST GAVE ODORS.
"ODOR"? AH, OKAY, "ORDERS".
THEY BEAT A BOY WITH AMNESIA? HOW CRUEL ...
WHO FOUND YOU?

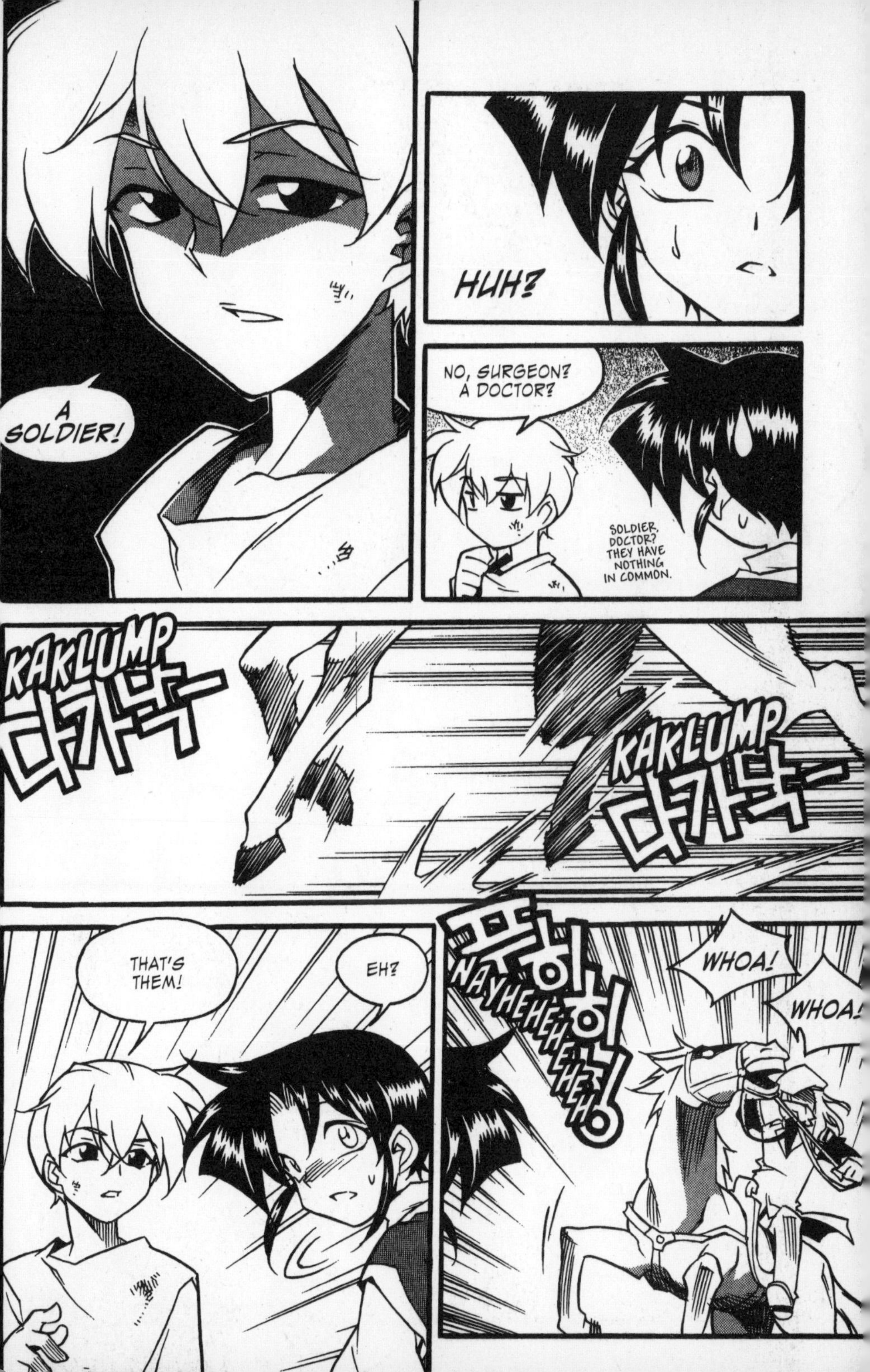

A SOLDIER!
HUH?
NO, SURGEON? A DOCTOR?
SOLDIER, DOCTOR? THEY HAVE NOTHING IN COMMON.
KAKLUMP
다가닥
KAKLUMP
다가닥
THAT'S THEM!
EH?
푸히힝!
NAYHEHEHEHEH!
WHOA!
WHOA!

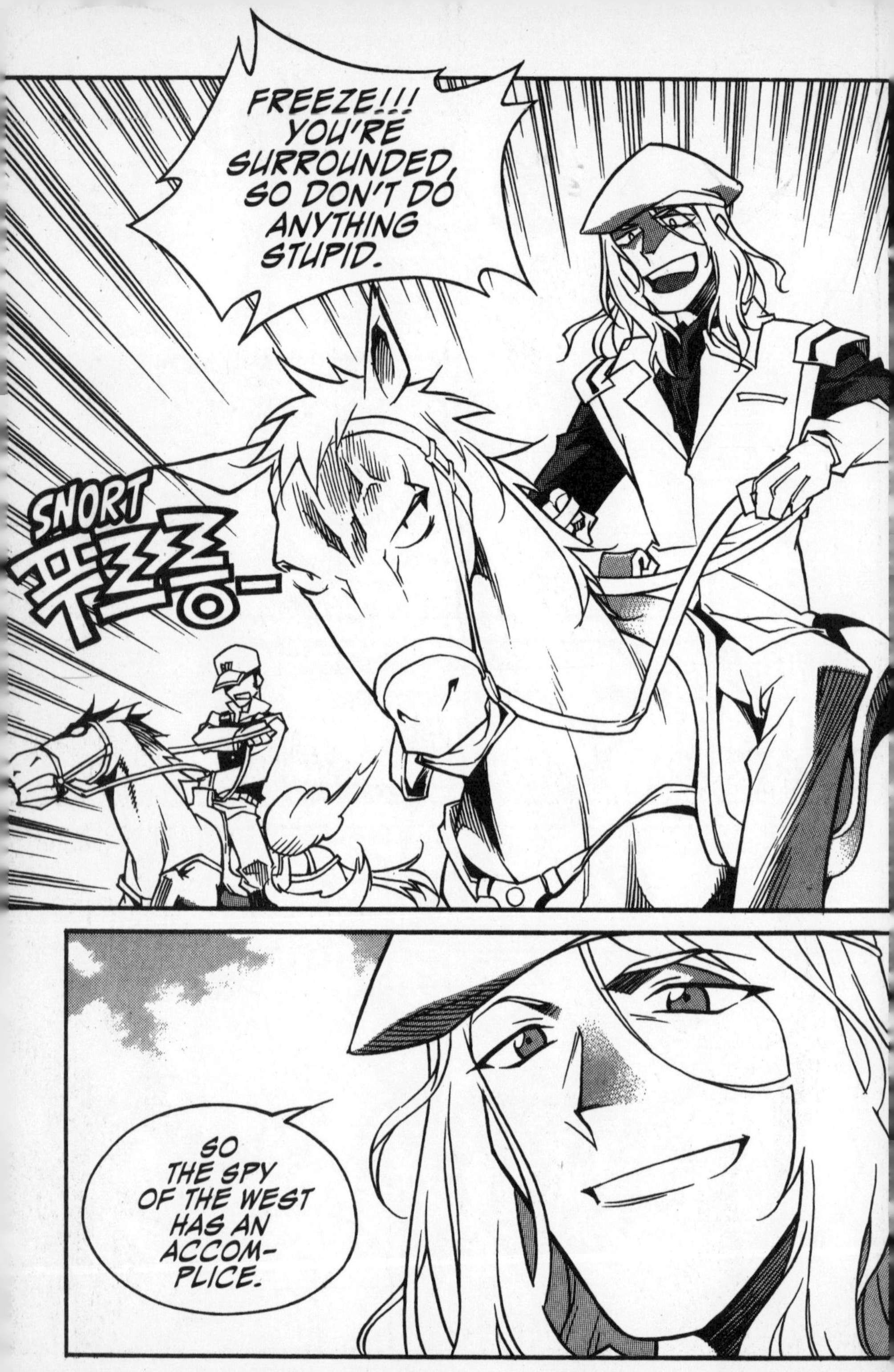
FREEZE!!! YOU'RE SURROUNDED, SO DON'T DO ANYTHING STUPID.
SNORT
SO THE SPY OF THE WEST HAS AN ACCOM-PLICE.

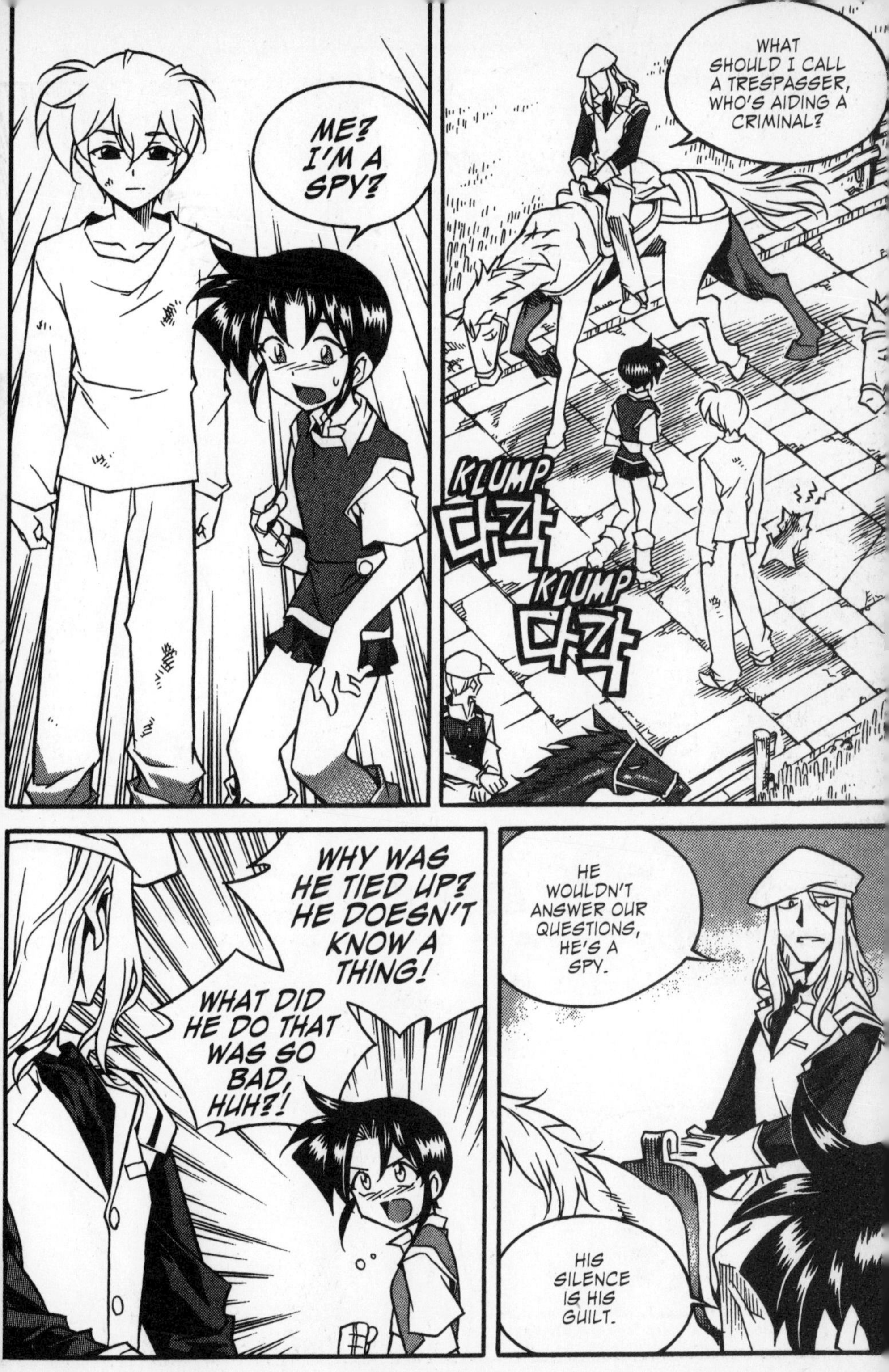

ME? I'M A SPY?
WHAT SHOULD I CALL A TRESPASSER, WHO'S AIDING A CRIMINAL?
KLUMP
다각
KLUMP
다각
WHY WAS HE TIED UP? HE DOESN'T KNOW A THING!
WHAT DID HE DO THAT WAS SO BAD, HUH?!
HE WOULDN'T ANSWER OUR QUESTIONS, HE'S A SPY.
HIS SILENCE IS HIS GUILT.

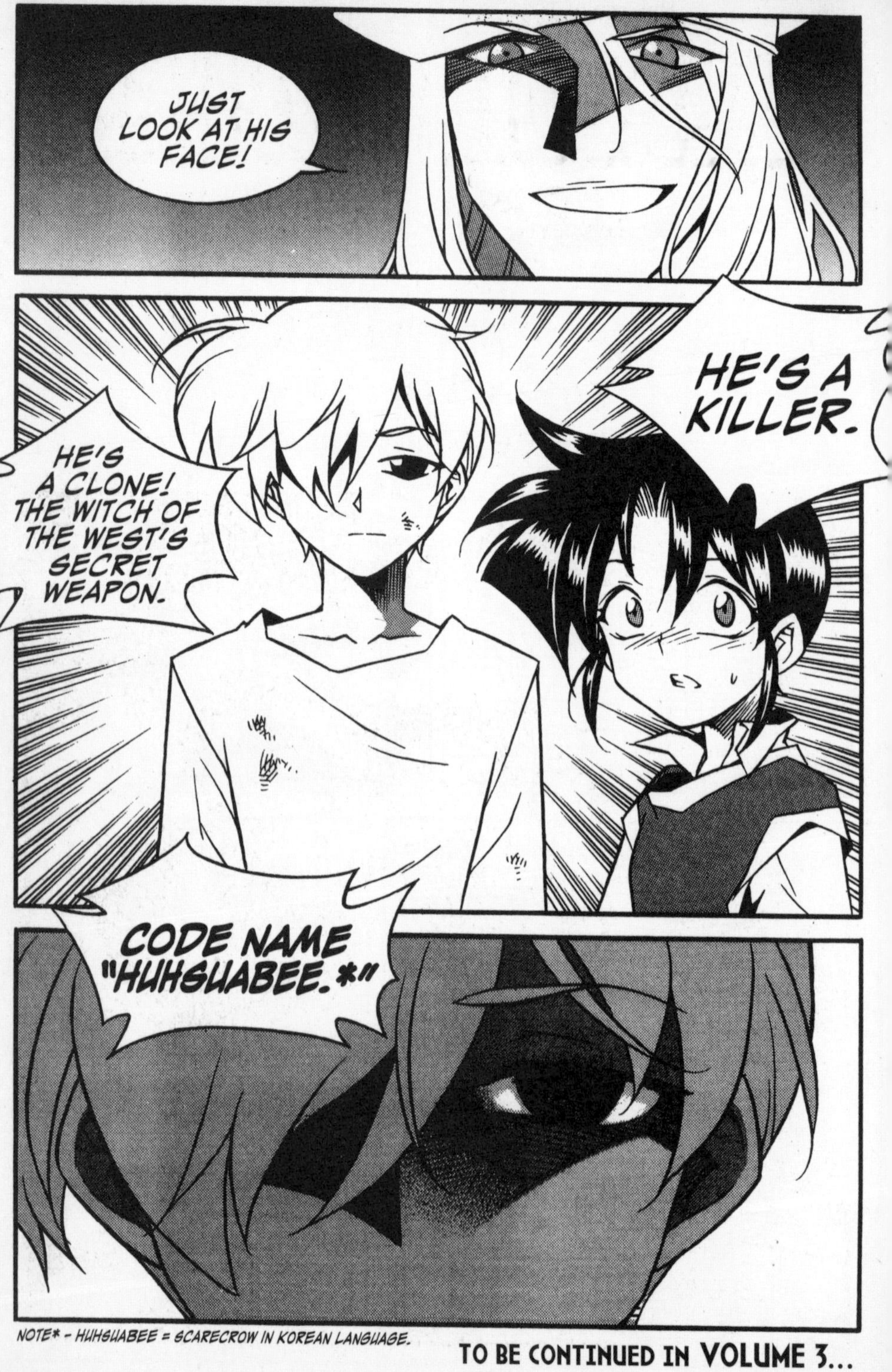
JUST LOOK AT HIS FACE!
HE'S A KILLER.
HE'S A CLONE! THE WITCH OF THE WEST'S SECRET WEAPON.
CODE NAME "HUHSUABEE.*"

NOTE* - HUHSUABEE = SCARECROW IN KOREAN LANGUAGE.

TO BE CONTINUED IN VOLUME 3...

DEADLINE BLUES

데드라인 블루스

BATTLER

REGRET

SAGA <DEAD SONG>

HYBRID GEUN-OH

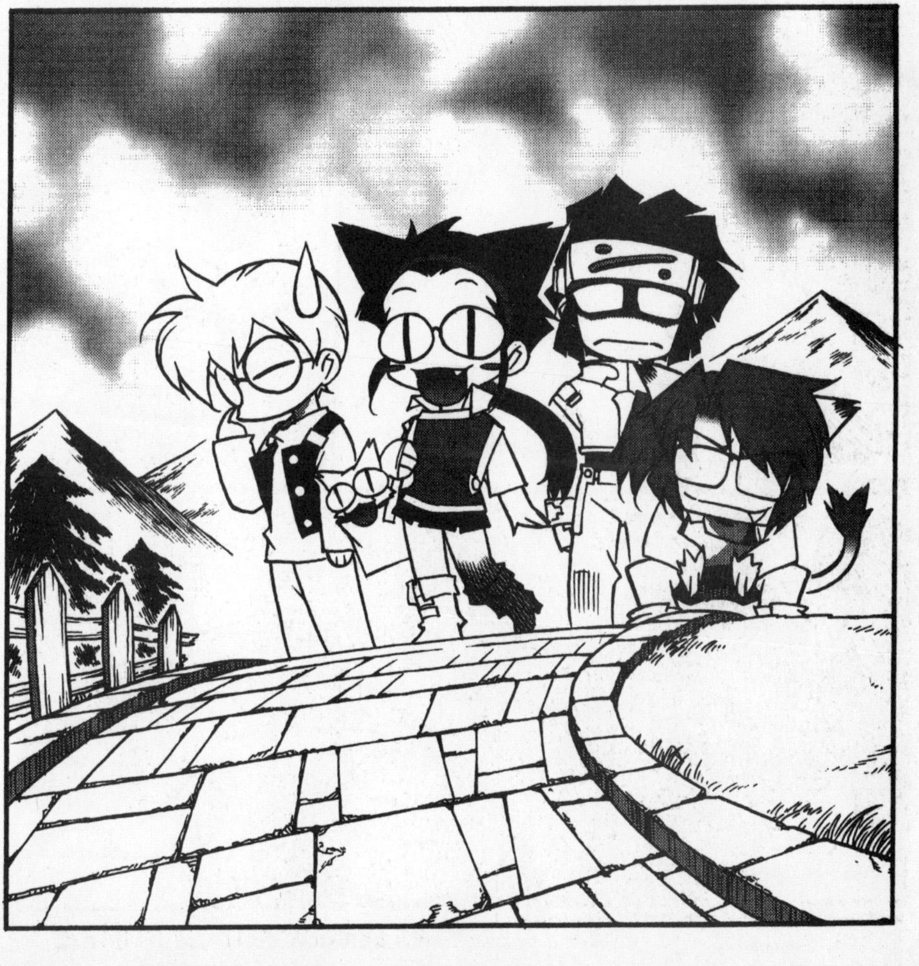

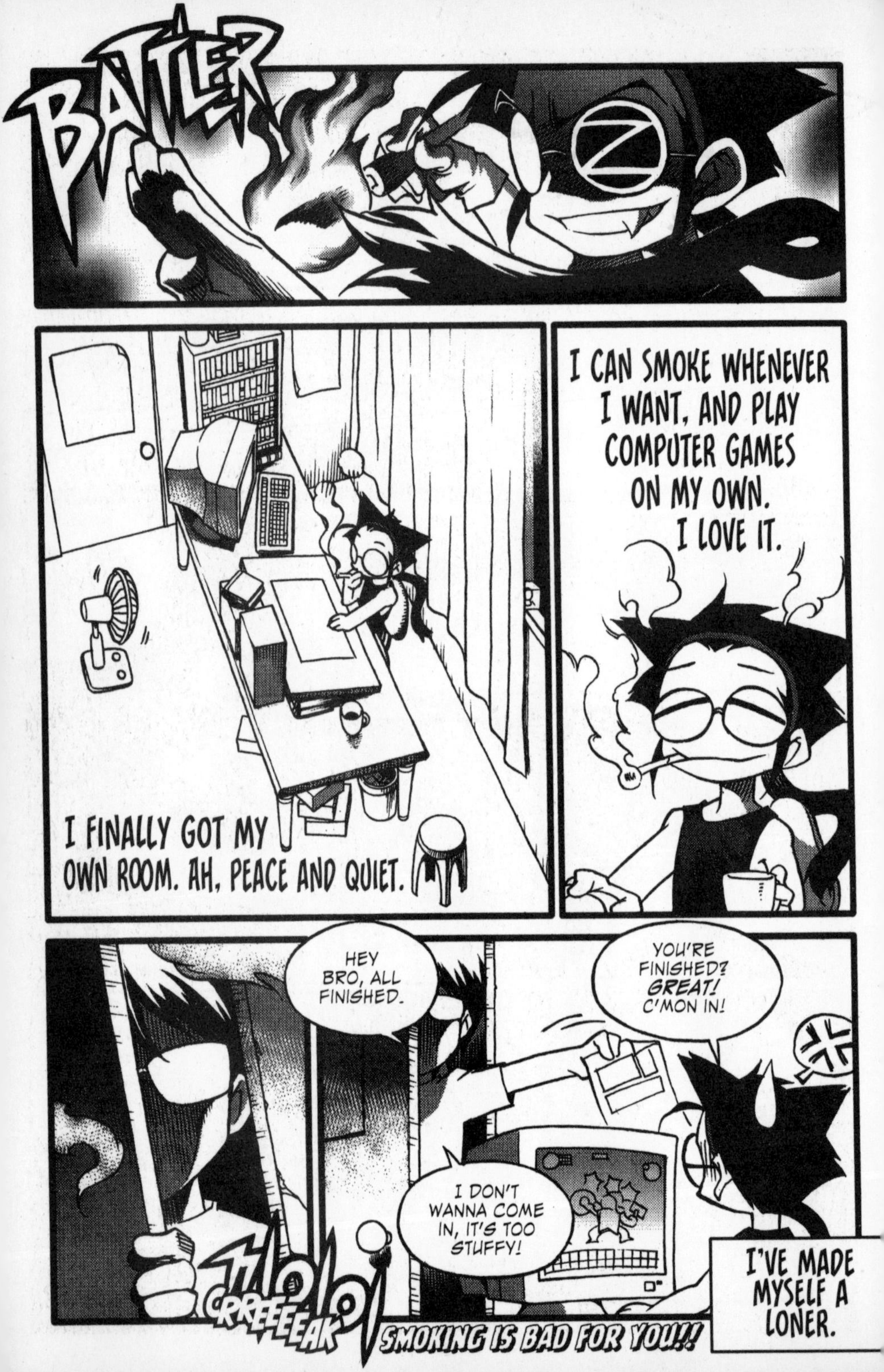
BATTLER
I FINALLY GOT MY OWN ROOM. AH, PEACE AND QUIET.
I CAN SMOKE WHENEVER I WANT, AND PLAY COMPUTER GAMES ON MY OWN. I LOVE IT.
HEY BRO, ALL FINISHED.
YOU'RE FINISHED? GREAT! C'MON IN!
I DON'T WANNA COME IN, IT'S TOO STUFFY!
CRREEEEEAK
SMOKING IS BAD FOR YOU!!
I'VE MADE MYSELF A LONER.

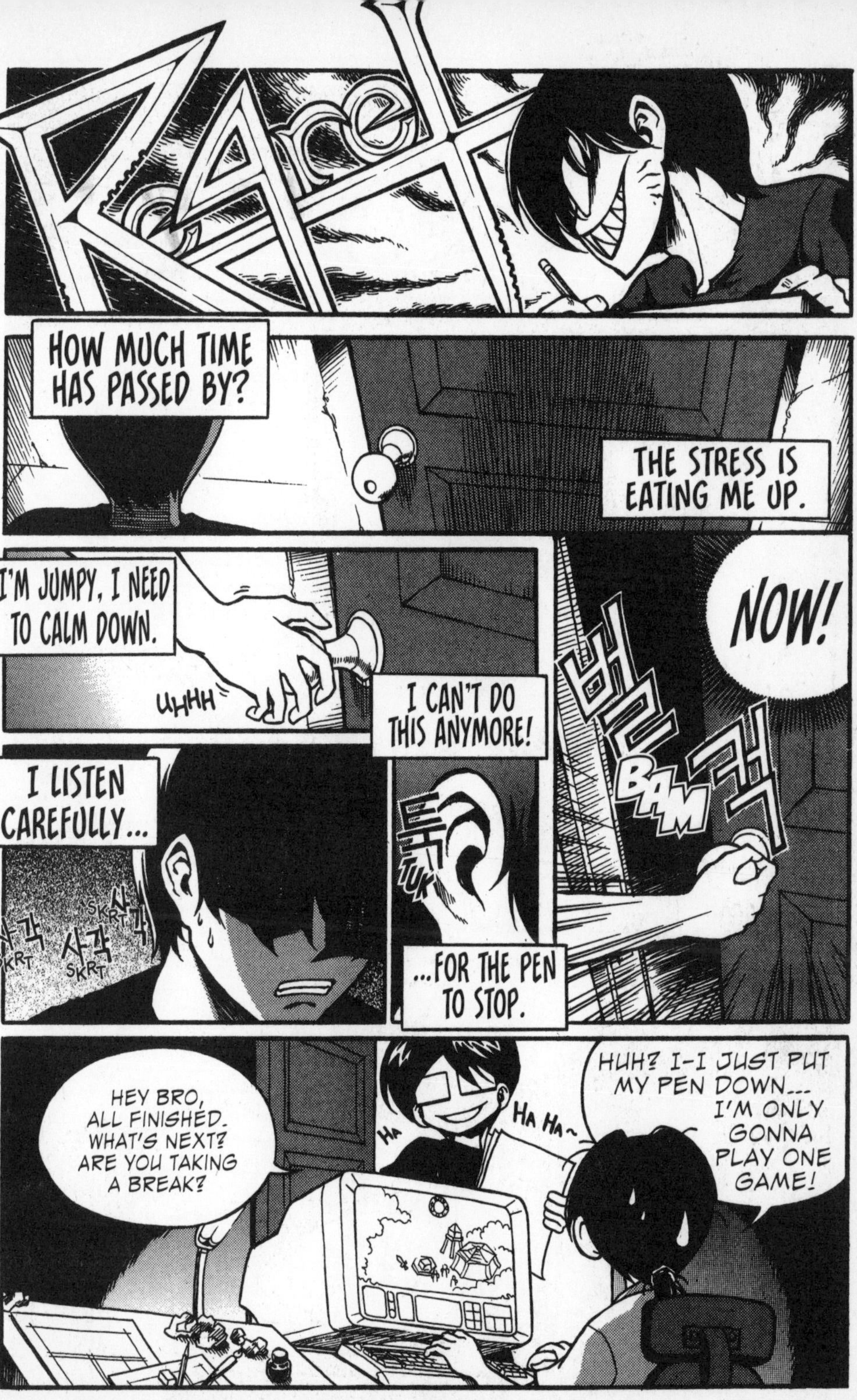
HOW MUCH TIME HAS PASSED BY?
THE STRESS IS EATING ME UP.
I'M JUMPY, I NEED TO CALM DOWN.
UHHH
I CAN'T DO THIS ANYMORE!
NOW!
BAM
I LISTEN CAREFULLY...
SKRT
SKRT
SKRT
TUK
...FOR THE PEN TO STOP.
HEY BRO, ALL FINISHED. WHAT'S NEXT? ARE YOU TAKING A BREAK?
HA
HA HA~
HUH? I-I JUST PUT MY PEN DOWN... I'M ONLY GONNA PLAY ONE GAME!

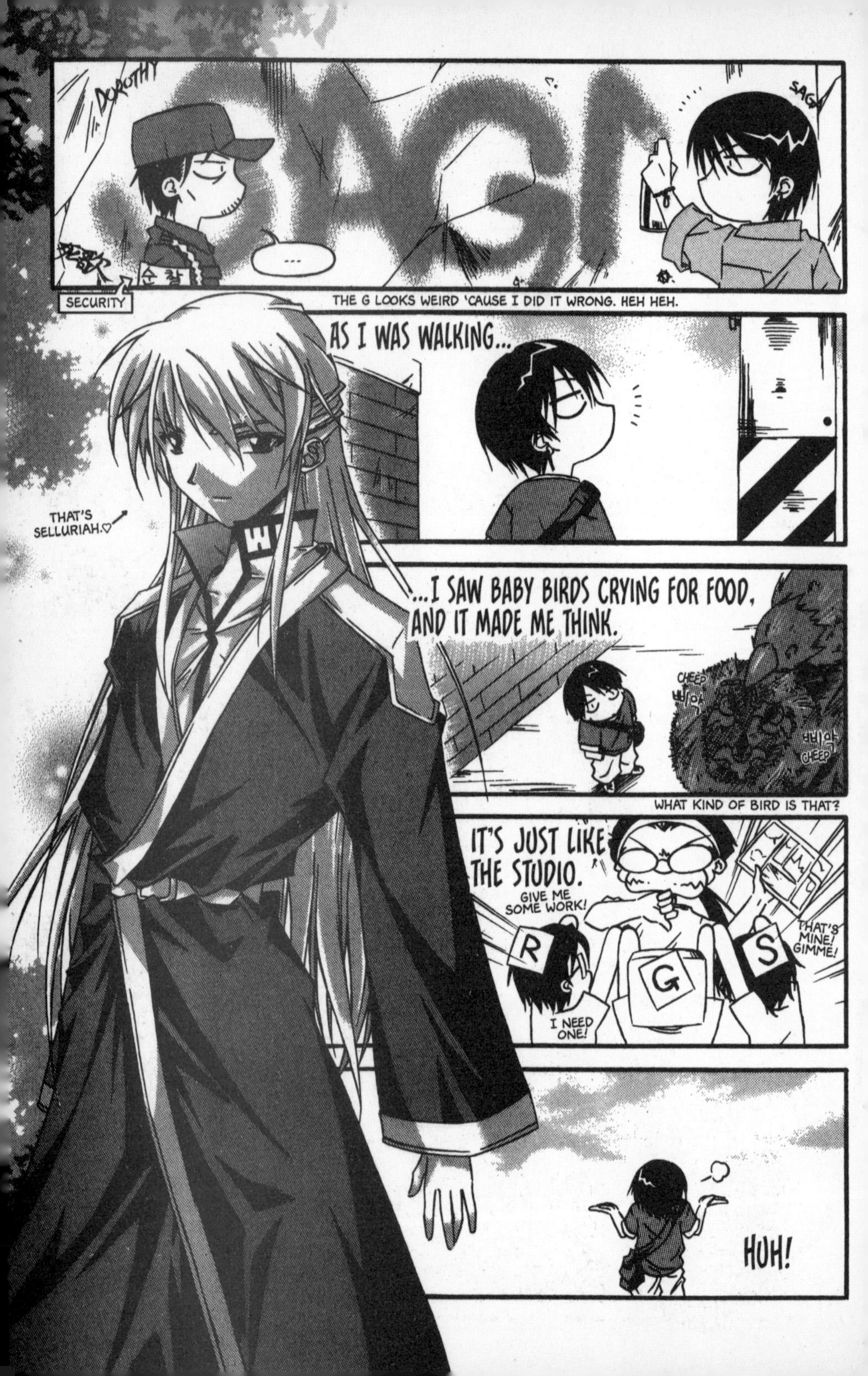

DOROTHY
SAGA
SAGA
...
순찰
SECURITY
THE G LOOKS WEIRD 'CAUSE I DID IT WRONG. HEH HEH.
AS I WAS WALKING...
THAT'S SELLURIAH.♡
...I SAW BABY BIRDS CRYING FOR FOOD, AND IT MADE ME THINK.
CHEEP
CHEEP
WHAT KIND OF BIRD IS THAT?
IT'S JUST LIKE THE STUDIO.
GIVE ME SOME WORK!
THAT'S MINE! GIMME!
R
G
S
I NEED ONE!
HUH!

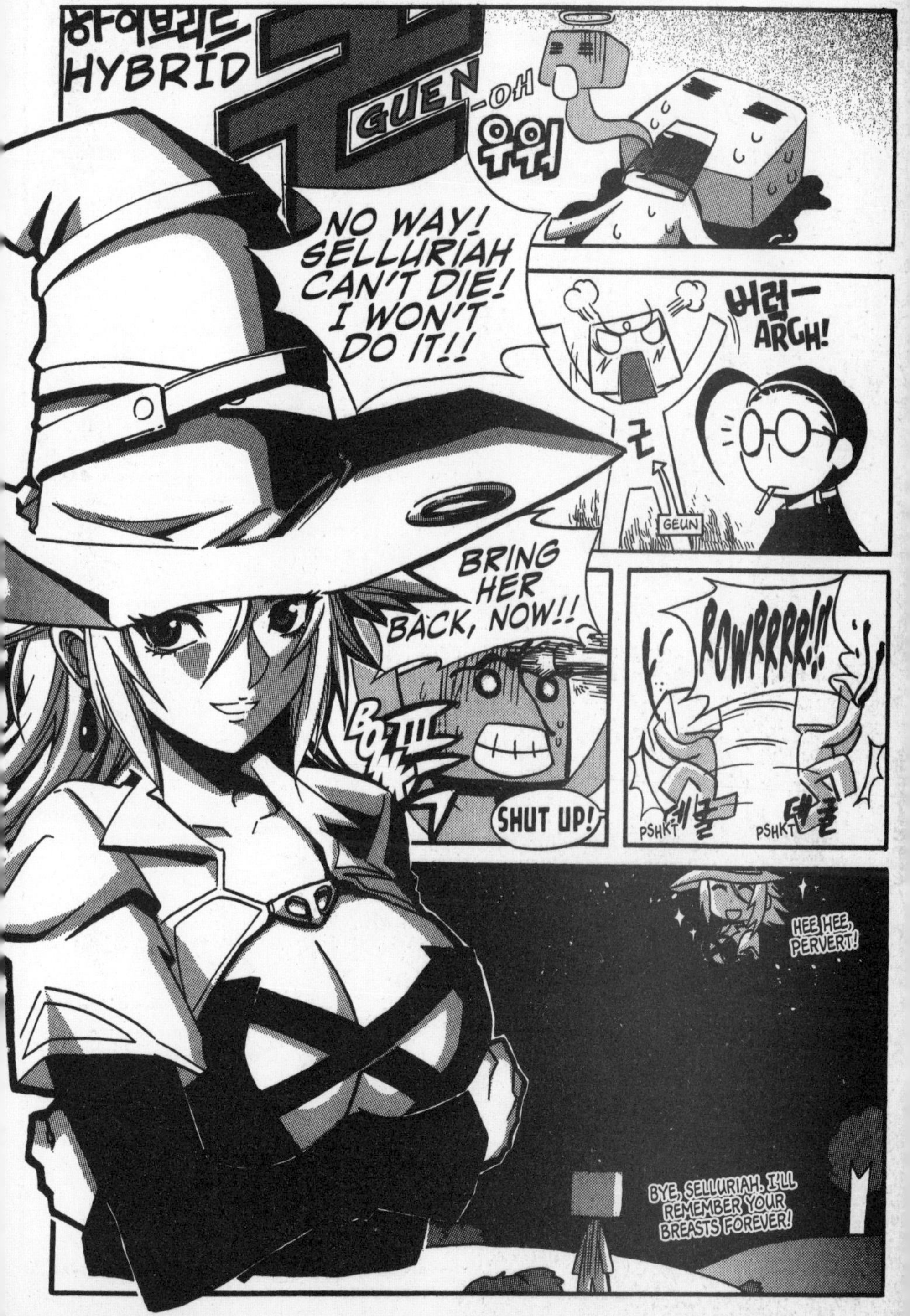

하이브리드
HYBRID
GUEN
-OH
우웍
NO WAY! SELLURIAH CAN'T DIE! I WON'T DO IT!!
버럭—
ARGH!
GEUN
BRING HER BACK, NOW!!
BONK!!!
SHUT UP!
ROWRRRR!!
PSHKT
PSHKT
HEE HEE, PERVERT!
BYE, SELLURIAH. I'LL REMEMBER YOUR BREASTS FOREVER!

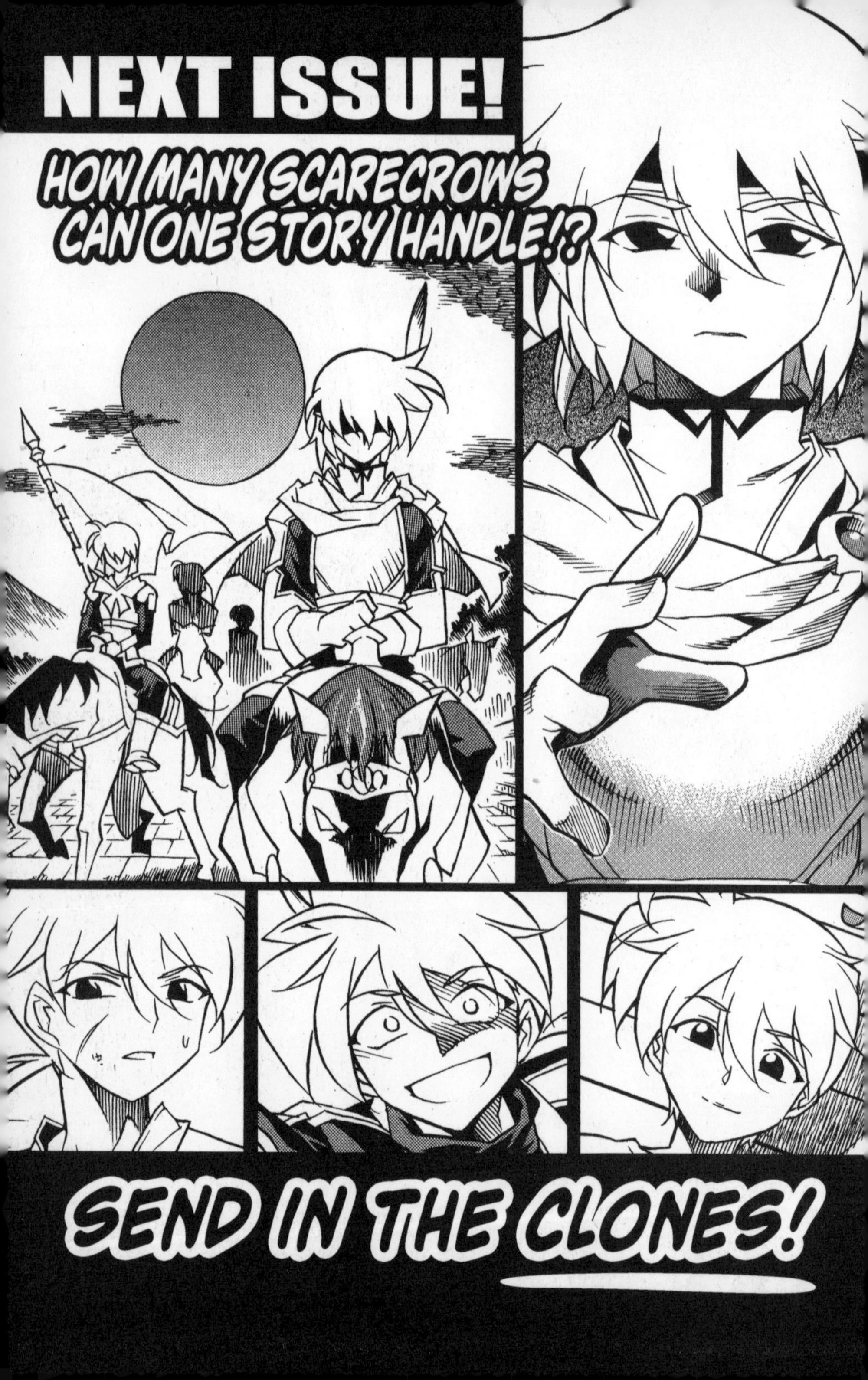
NEXT ISSUE!
HOW MANY SCARECROWS CAN ONE STORY HANDLE!?
SEND IN THE CLONES!

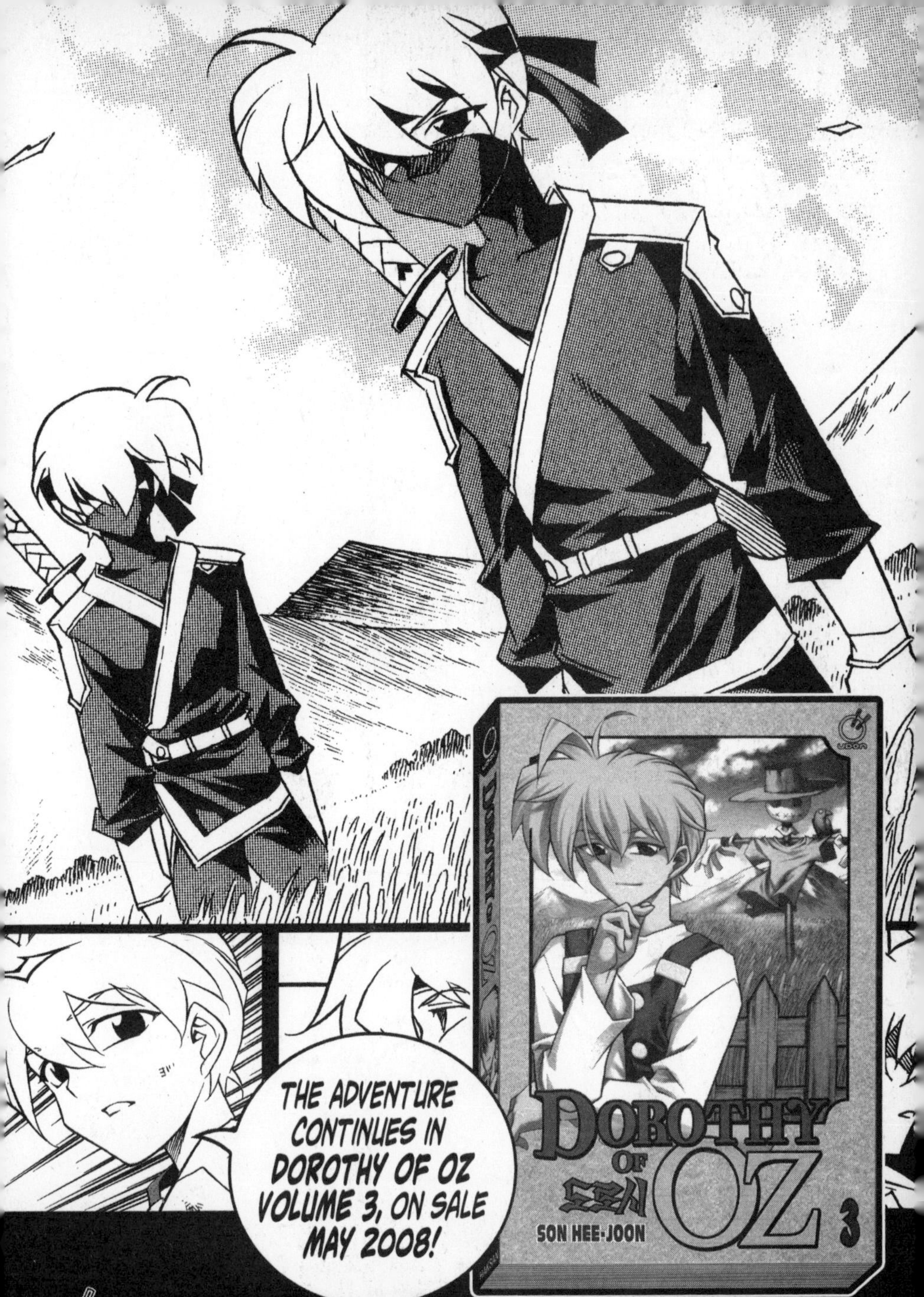
THE ADVENTURE CONTINUES IN DOROTHY OF OZ VOLUME 3, ON SALE MAY 2008!
DOROTHY OF OZ
SON HEE-JOON
3

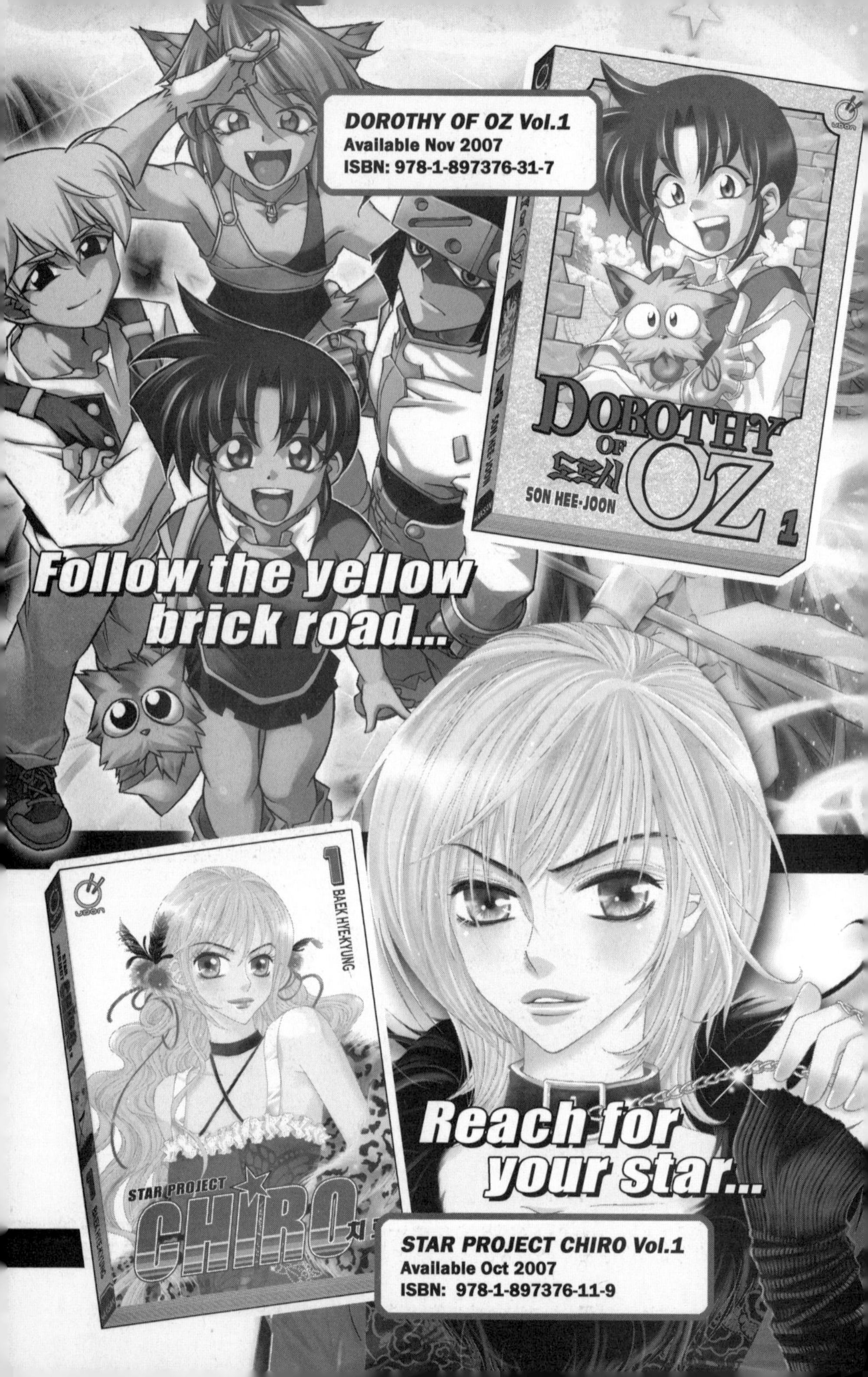
DOROTHY OF OZ Vol.1
Available Nov 2007
ISBN: 978-1-897376-31-7
DOROTHY OF OZ
SON HEE-JOON
1
Follow the yellow brick road...
1
BAEK HYE-KYUNG
STAR PROJECT
CHIRO
Reach for your star...
STAR PROJECT CHIRO Vol.1
Available Oct 2007
ISBN: 978-1-897376-11-9

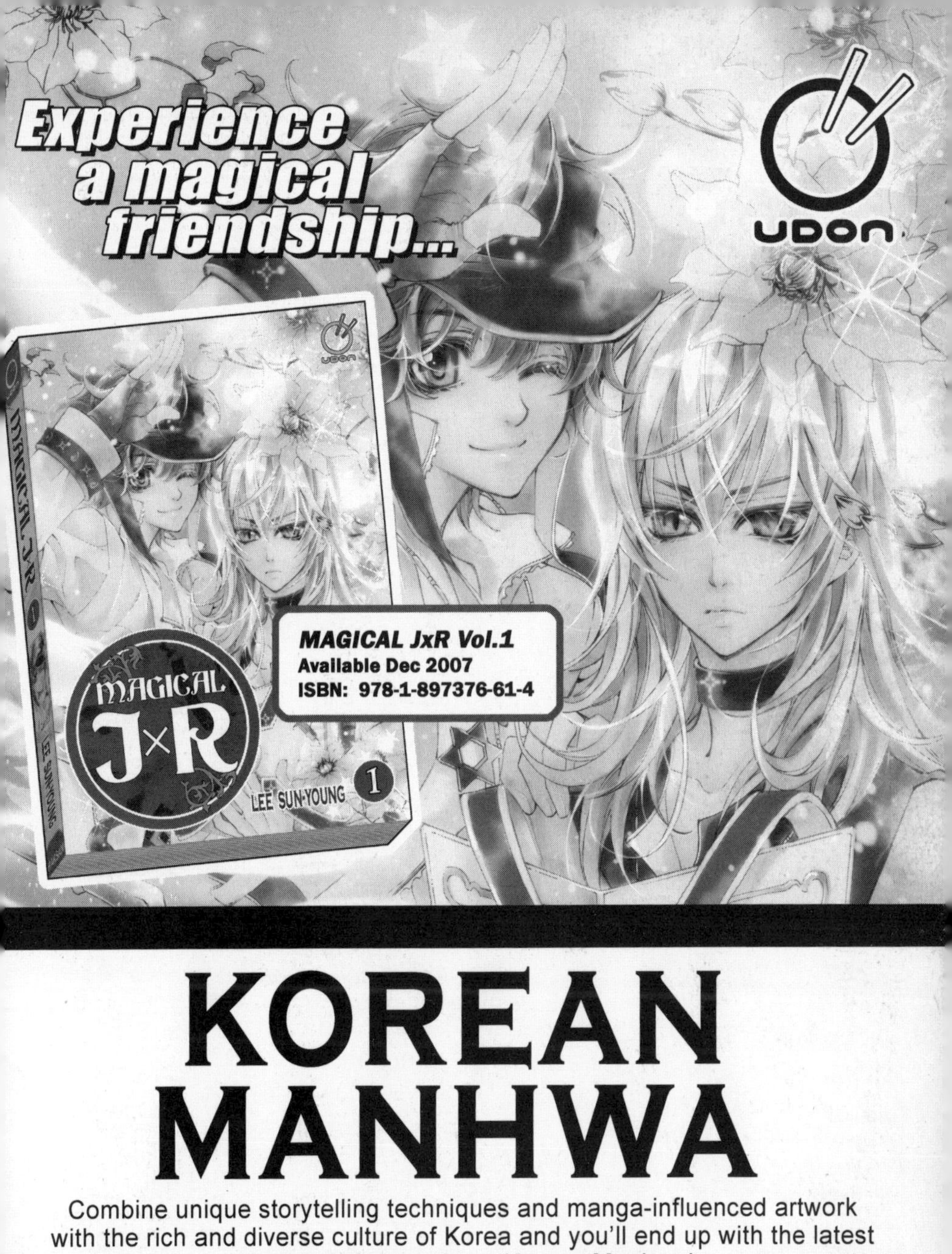
Experience a magical friendship...
UDON
MAGICAL JxR Vol.1
Available Dec 2007
ISBN: 978-1-897376-61-4
MAGICAL J×R
LEE SUN-YOUNG
1

KOREAN MANHWA

Combine unique storytelling techniques and manga-influenced artwork with the rich and diverse culture of Korea and you'll end up with the latest craze in Asian comics – Korean Manhwa!

Learn more at our web site:

WWW.KOREANMANHWA.COM

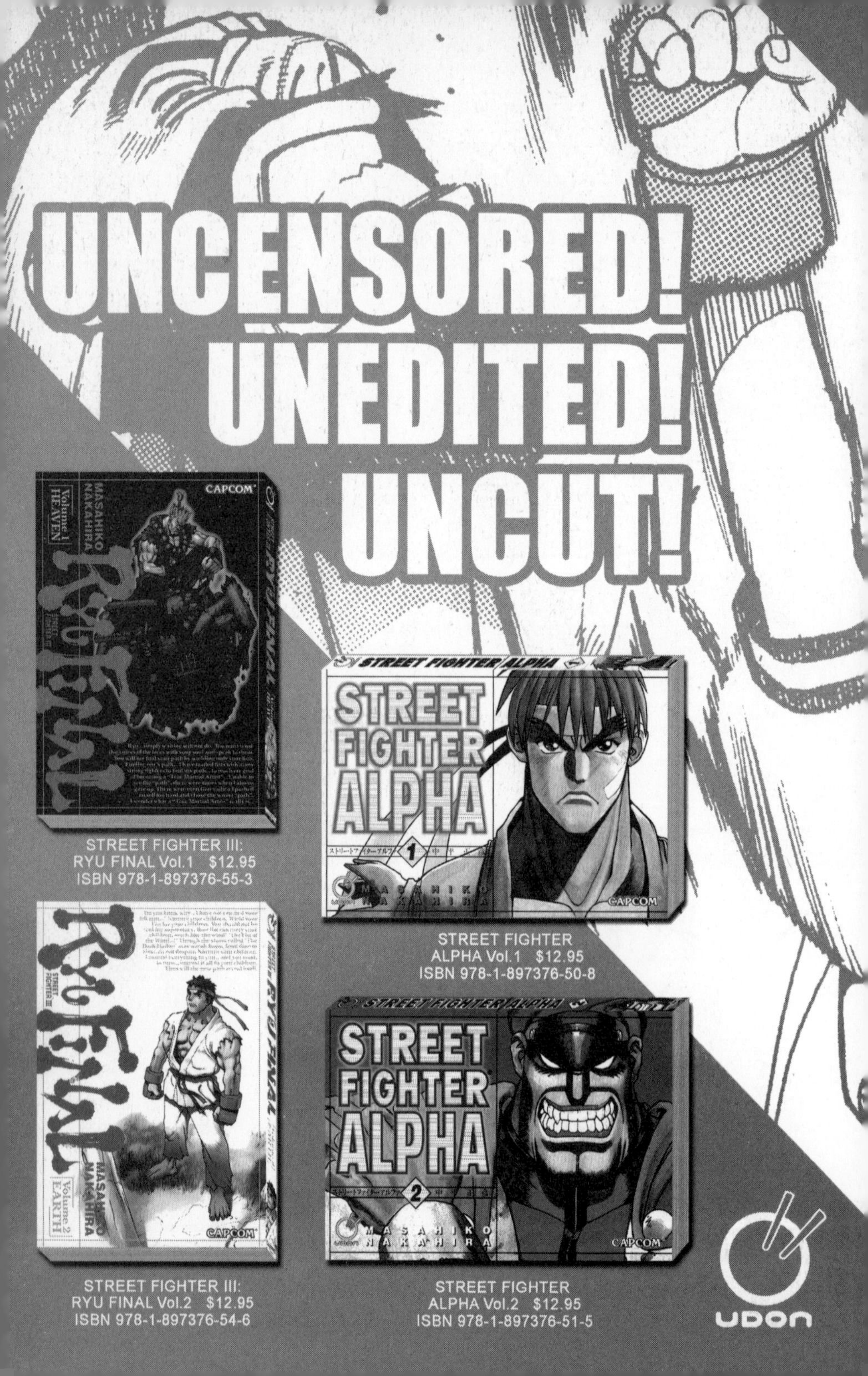
UNCENSORED!
UNEDITED!
UNCUT!
STREET FIGHTER III:
RYU FINAL Vol.1 $12.95
ISBN 978-1-897376-55-3
STREET FIGHTER
ALPHA Vol.1 $12.95
ISBN 978-1-897376-50-8
STREET FIGHTER III:
RYU FINAL Vol.2 $12.95
ISBN 978-1-897376-54-6
STREET FIGHTER
ALPHA Vol.2 $12.95
ISBN 978-1-897376-51-5
UDON

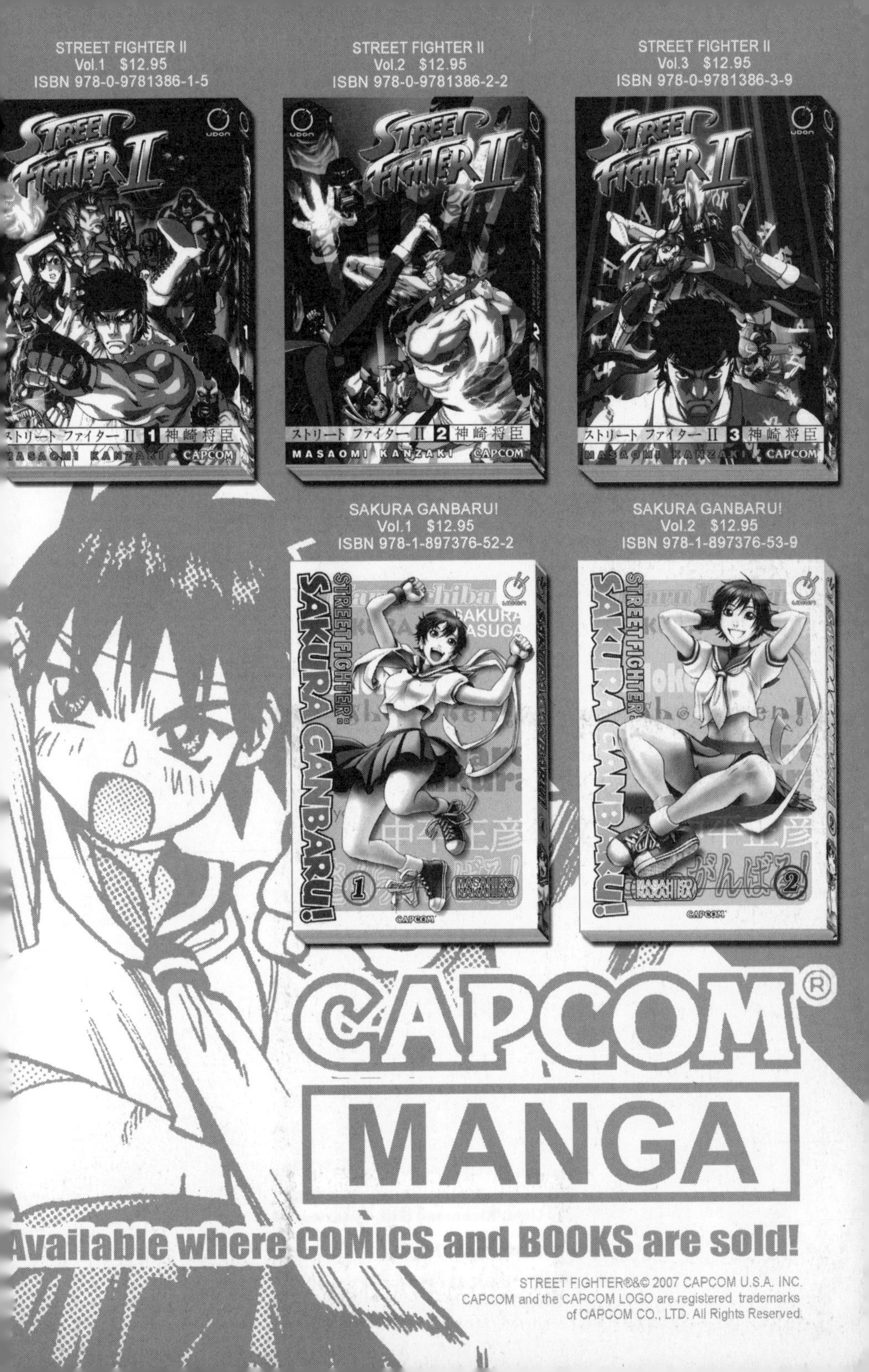
STREET FIGHTER II
Vol.1 $12.95
ISBN 978-0-9781386-1-5
STREET FIGHTER II
Vol.2 $12.95
ISBN 978-0-9781386-2-2
STREET FIGHTER II
Vol.3 $12.95
ISBN 978-0-9781386-3-9
SAKURA GANBARU!
Vol.1 $12.95
ISBN 978-1-897376-52-2
SAKURA GANBARU!
Vol.2 $12.95
ISBN 978-1-897376-53-9
CAPCOM®
MANGA
Available where COMICS and BOOKS are sold!
STREET FIGHTER®&© 2007 CAPCOM U.S.A. INC.
CAPCOM and the CAPCOM LOGO are registered trademarks
of CAPCOM CO., LTD. All Rights Reserved.

DOROTHY OF OZ   Volume 2

Story and Art : Son Hee-Joon

English Translations : Nahee Jung
English Adaptations : Kevin M. Kilgore

Editorial Consultant : J. Torres
Coordinating Editor : Hye-Young Im

Lettering : Marshall Dillon with Terri Delgado

Cover & Graphic Design :
Erik Ko with Matt Moylan

English Logo : Alex Chung

DOROTHY OF OZ #2
©2006 SON HEE-JOON.
All Rights Reserved. First published in Korea by Haksan Publishing Co., Ltd.
This translation rights arranged with Haksan Publishing Co., Ltd.
through Shinwon Agency Co. in Korea.

English launguage version ⸻⸻⸻⸻⸻ N Entertainment Corp.
P.O. Box 32662, P.O. Villag⸻⸻⸻⸻⸻ 4X 0A2, Canada.

www.udonenterta⸻

First Printing: February 2⸻   ISBN-10 : 1-897376-32-4
Printed in Canada